Dark Side of Fortune

Dark Side of Fortune

TRIUMPH AND SCANDAL
IN THE LIFE OF OIL TYCOON
EDWARD L. DOHENY

MARGARET LESLIE DAVIS

UNIVERSITY OF CALIFORNIA PRESS
Berkeley   Los Angeles   London

University of California Press
Berkeley and Los Angeles, California

University of California Press, Ltd.
London, England

First paperback printing 2001

The images of *La Calavera del Conquistador, La Calavera del Comerciante,* and *La Calavera del Final* on the title pages of parts 1, 2, AND 3, respectively, are by José Guadalupe Posada. The first and third are from Posada's *El gran panteón amoroso* and the second from *La calavera de cupido.* Courtesy of Dover Pictorial Archive Series.

Library of Congress Cataloging-in-Publication Data

Davis, Margaret L.
    Dark side of fortune : triumph and scandal in the life of oil tycoon
Edward L. Doheny / Margaret Leslie Davis.
        p.   cm.
    Includes bibliographical references and index.
    ISBN 0-520-22909-6 (pbk. : alk. paper)
    1. Doheny, Edward L. (Edward Laurence), 1856–1935.
2. Industrialists—United States—Biography.   3. Petroleum industry
and trade—United States—History.   4. Petroleum industry and
trade—California, Southern—History.   5. Petroleum industry
and trade—Mexico—History.   6. Teapot Dome Scandal, 1921–1924.
I. Title.
HD9570.D64D38   1998
338.7'6223382'092—dc21

[B]   98-7240
                                                              CIP

Printed in the United States of America

08   07   06   05
9 8 7 6 5 4 3 2

The paper used in this publication meets the minimum requirements of
ANSI/ NISO Z39.48-1992 (R 1997) (*Permanence of Paper*). ♾

For Roger Vincent

Contents

List of Illustrations ix

Preface: La Calavera xiii

Prologue: September 11, 1935 1

part one LA CALAVERA DEL CONQUISTADOR

1. The Young Prospector Doheny 7
2. Her Coldest Welcome 21
3. Rivers of Black Gold 34
4. Spoony Visits 51
5. The Golden Lane 61
6. Powered by Oil 80
7. Millions Made Knowing How 97

part two LA CALAVERA DEL COMERCIANTE

8. Perfectly Legal 125
9. The $100,000 Bagatelle 140
10. Gaps in the Record 168
11. Scared Rich Man 199
12. The Last Appeal 216

part three LA CALAVERA DEL FINAL

13. Night of Terror 229
14. A Broken and Changed Man 246
15. The Final Trial 255

Epilogue: La Calavera del Futuro 283

Notes 289

Bibliography 315

Index 325

Illustrations

Posada's image of *La Calavera del Conquistador*   5
Posada's image of *La Calavera del Comerciante*   123
Posada's image of *La Calavera del Final*   227

following page 110

Edward and Estelle Doheny's wedding day

Interior of the "Estelle," Doheny's private railcar

Edward Doheny, Estelle Doheny, and two women

Edward Doheny at the Ebano, Mexico, oil camp, ca. 1901–5

Estelle Doheny, August 1900

Edward and Estelle Doheny, Lucy Smith, Daysie Anderson,
and members of Estelle's family

Edward and Estelle Doheny and friends, ca. 1901

Ned Doheny, four years old, in 1897

Ned Doheny feeding a deer, ca. 1901–2

Doheny's Pierce Arrow, with Estelle and Ned Doheny, ca. 1901–2

Fourth of July gala celebration at Chester Place, ca. 1902–3

The Mexican Petroleum Company's steam tractor, ca. 1901–5

Posada's *Gran calavera eléctrica*

Map of major oil fields in Mexico

Panorama of Doheny oil camp in Mexico, ca. 1905–10
Doheny and eight of his American managers at drilling site
in Mexico, ca. 1905–10
Charles Adelbert Canfield, ca. 1900
Chloe Canfield, 1879
Cerro Azul No. 4 in February 1916
The men who brought Cerro Azul No. 4 under control
Ned Doheny at Venice Beach with Grace ("Dolly") Martin, ca. 1910
Ned Doheny in U.S. Navy uniform
Lucy Marceline Smith on her wedding day, 1914
Edward Doheny, 1923

following page 270

8 Chester Place, ca. 1910
The aviary
Inside the aviary
The Pompeian Room
The Doheny's Steinway piano
Estelle Doheny's bedroom suite
The library
The sitting room
The exterior and interior of Ned's New York City apartment
"Hogan's Alley"
Teapot Rock at Teapot Dome, Wyoming
Albert Bacon Fall
Albert Fall's IOU to Edward Doheny
Edward and Estelle Doheny at Chester Place, 1930
Greystone Mansion in Beverly Hills
Members of the Doheny family
The cornerstone-laying ceremony for the Edward L. Doheny Jr. Memorial
Library at the University of Southern California
The completed Edward L. Doheny Jr. Memorial Library
Harry Ford Sinclair, ca. 1927–28
Ned McLean, ca. 1930

Frank Hogan with Edward and Estelle Doheny, 1930

Edward L. Doheny Memorial Library at St. John's Seminary in Camarillo, California

The groundbreaking of the Edward L. Doheny Memorial Library

Estelle Doheny and her personal secretary, Miss Lucille Miller

Edward Doheny in 1932

Preface
La Calavera

Soon after I began work on this biography, I learned that Edward Doheny's widow had burned his personal papers on the evening of his funeral in September 1935, and that his descendants had refused to be interviewed. I was told that it would be next to impossible to unravel the historical details behind Doheny's complex and contradictory life.

In the industrial exuberance of the 1920s, Doheny was the "Emperor of Oil." His success began with his first commercial well in Los Angeles in 1892 and led to explorations of the rich Tampico fields, the home of his Mexican Petroleum Company. In the twists of history, however, his name is forever associated with the infamous Elk Hills and Teapot Dome oil lease scandals in which he and oilman Harry Sinclair were accused of bribing a U.S. cabinet official. His explanation of a $100,000 loan to his friend, Albert B. Fall, the secretary of the interior, was that to a rich man like himself, the cash was a bagatelle—no more than $25 or $50 would be to an ordinary person. His arrogance and self-assurance were severely tested during the ensuing trials when his only son, who had delivered the alleged bribe money, was murdered by a family confidant. The tabloids of the day reported the tragedy with salacious details, rumor, and innuendo, leaving much to be sorted out by later researchers. Doheny's story is one of enigmatic fate—poverty and wealth, renown and disgrace, fortune and tragedy—a tale of the skeleton, *la calavera* of Mexican lore, ever present at his banquet table, a reminder that fortune has a dark, hidden side.

In the years since the oil scandal and the murder, writers have presented Doheny in historical accounts and in fiction as the archetypal evil Yankee and a man of unconscionable greed. Yet Doheny had lifelong supporters, well-informed persons of importance who held him in high esteem. How was it possible for the same man and the same facts to be perceived so differently by equally diligent observers? And how could a man of global aspirations be undone by one of America's most notorious political scandals?

An important break came when I visited the Center for Southwest Research at the Zimmerman Library in Albuquerque, New Mexico. A staff member informed me that correspondence in Doheny's hand was contained in a collection that had been donated by Albert Fall's granddaughter to New Mexico State University in Las Cruces. To my astonishment, the collection contained 1,500 documents, including personal letters between Edward Doheny and Albert Fall spanning the years 1919 to 1935—the most tumultuous years of Doheny's life.

Emadair Chase Jones, the granddaughter of Secretary Fall, had kept the materials safely hidden until donating the historical items to the library. The full set of letters reveals Doheny's personal thoughts from the challenging days of his financial success in Mexico, operating a worldwide petroleum enterprise that enmeshed him in domestic and international politics, to a darker time when he found himself under suspicion, embroiled in a national scandal. Doheny's letters tell much about his feelings as he watched hundreds of witnesses called to the Senate investigating chambers, and he muses philosophically about the workings of the world and the source of his inner strength. Written during the blackest testimony and most startling moments of the Senate hearings and later during the multiple civil and criminal trials in Washington, D.C., and Los Angeles, the correspondence reflects a deeply thoughtful and tortured man. The taint of corruption would consume a decade of Doheny's life, cause three cabinet-level resignations, generate multiple Supreme Court decisions, and culminate in the imprisonment of one of his closest friends.

The letters are an indispensable record of the Doheny story. I am extremely grateful to Mrs. Jones for her gracious permission to allow me to quote extensively from the correspondence. I am also indebted to Austin Hoover, director of the Rio Grande Historical Collection, University Library, New Mexico State University, for his generous time and assistance.

Passionate opinions ran high in the 1920s in both Mexico and the United States. Economic optimism and the sanctity of progress clashed with the predictions of doomsayers, journalists, and conservationists. The name Doheny ignited fire in all camps. The nature of his zeal emerges from family correspondence.

I'm grateful to Monsignor Francis J. Weber for his permission to enter the Estelle Doheny Collection at the Archival Center, Archdiocese of Los Angeles, in Mission Hills, California. This collection of letters and memorabilia owned by the Catholic Church includes hundreds of intimate letters written by Doheny's second wife, Estelle, who was a confidante and central figure in Doheny's life. It also includes letters written by Doheny to his wife during the harrowing years spent developing an oil industry in Mexico. This previously unexamined correspondence illuminates the couple's personal goals, their thirty-five-year relationship, and the activities of this very private family. The letters of Estelle Doheny were written over a fifty-year period, from the early days after her marriage at age twenty-five aboard a railcar in Albuquerque, in New Mexico Territory, through her developing role as wife of one of the richest men in America, to her final years as an executive managing the remaining Doheny holdings.

Another important source of details about Edward Doheny, particularly his goals and fears, is to be found in the trial transcripts. As the oil lease scandal intensified, Doheny struggled to extricate himself from mounting accusations and increasing public hostility. He faced not only the rigors of a Senate investigation but two criminal trials, shareholder suits, and civil litigation. Doheny hired for his defense the finest legal talent, which included attorneys Frank Hogan and Henry O'Melveny. The defense case that Doheny's attorneys prepared was a marvel of legal craftsmanship. The voluminous trial record was a critical aspect of researching this book, and I am grateful to Dorothy Molsted and Roxanne Schenzel, West Publishing Company, for access to Westlaw and other online legal research tools.

Doheny's relationship with his attorneys turned into abiding friendships, and their memories of their famous client extend well past the trial years. I would like to thank Bob Glen Odle, managing partner of Hogan and Hartson L.L.P., of Washington, D.C., for his permission to review the scrapbooks, photographs, and memorabilia of attorney Frank J. Hogan. The personal collection of Doheny's lead defense lawyer is a rich resource for information on the behind-the-scenes trial strategy and a key to participants in the oil scandal trials. My thanks also extend to Austin Doherty, director of the Information Resource Center at Hogan and Hartson.

The personal diaries of attorney Henry W. O'Melveny, the director of Doheny's powerful defense team, provided additional insight into Doheny's character and the trial tactics, and I am thankful to Allen Jutzi, curator of rare books at the Huntington Library in San Marino, for the opportunity to read the O'Melveny journals.

In November 1996, I was invited by Edward Doheny's grandchildren and great-grandchildren to talk with them about the life and work of their famous relative. I am extremely grateful to the family for their assistance and for access to family records and letters. By sharing their point of view and providing family documents, they made an important contribution toward my understanding of Edward Doheny. It is an invaluable experience for a biographer to meet the descendants of her subject and hear firsthand recollections.

Doheny had the spirit of an earlier generation of bold adventurers in a time when risk taking was celebrated and daring often well-rewarded.

PREFACE xvii

The era is under considerable scrutiny now as the world evaluates industrialization and the role of oil, so it is all the more interesting to revisit the promise and optimism of the opening decades of the century and examine the unyielding drive of men like Doheny.

Los Angeles researcher Nicholas A. Curry, who has made an extensive study of the early days of the oil industry in the southland, has spent ten years cataloging documents about Doheny's life and his business holdings. I owe a great debt to him for sharing with me research that evoked an era of great challenges and competition for high stakes. His expertise and his generous assistance in fact-checking the manuscript are greatly appreciated.

I gratefully acknowledge Victoria Steele, head of Special Collections of the Edward L. Doheny Jr. Memorial Library at the University of Southern California in Los Angeles, and Rita S. Faulders, former curator of the Estelle Doheny Collection of Rare Books and Manuscripts at St. John's Seminary, Camarillo, for her generous assistance in educating me about Estelle Doheny's substantial art and book collection as well as her philanthropies.

Special thanks to Elliot Abemayor, M.D., Larry Ashmead, Catherine Campbell-Towell, Michael Cart, Karen Chappelle, Rudy Cole, Ed Cray, James H. Davis, Michael Dougherty, Donald N. Duke, Carol Easton, Robert Feinberg, Noel Riley Fitch, Jeffrey Forer, Ann Gray, Larry Haile, Charles Johnson, Burt Kennedy, Keith and Alena Lehrer, Charles Lockwood, John Luder, Kerri McKenzie Kemble, Amy Meo, Stephen Mitchell, Duke Moosekian, Loretta and Albert Morgenstern, Wallace Neff Jr., Frank Q. Newton Jr., Cheri Oteri, Tom Owen, Steve Paymer, Daniel Pucca, Joe Ryan, Leslie Siewierski, Dace Taub, Laura Tucker, Chris Turner, Amelia Vetrone, and Les Zoeller. Appreciation is due Susan Vaughn for her advice and careful reading. Heartfelt thanks to Roger Vincent, whose enthusiasm and support for this project included driving me to Las Cruces, New Mexico, in the middle of the summer. I must extend my deepest appreciation to my mother, Catherine Davis, for her editing and insights.

A very special thanks to Joe Kraus, T. Sumner Robinson, and Jim Bellows of Excite for their support and encouragement.

I am extremely indebted to my editor at the University of California Press, Naomi Schneider, and to Sue Heinemann and Alice Falk, who brought considerable talent and insight into the preparation of this manuscript. I also owe a great debt of gratitude to my literary agent, Richard Curtis.

Prologue
September 11, 1935

Aromatic wafts of incense blended with the fragrance of thousands of flowers filling the ornate sanctuary of St. Vincent's Church. Prominent figures in business, politics, and religion had come to Los Angeles to pay their last respects to Edward Laurence Doheny. More than 1,200 guests crowded the richly ornamented edifice and another 2,000 stood outside, assembled in tribute to the man "who had spent his youth in hardship, his middle years in a phenomenal rise to wealth, power and fame, and much of his old age in grief and humiliation."[1] Yet many in attendance had shunned Doheny for the last ten years of his life, fearful of appearing connected to the scandal that had tarnished his name.

Eight men bore the bronze casket the short distance from the Doheny mansion on Chester Place to the magnificent Roman Catholic church built with Doheny millions. Accompanied by chanting priests and leaning heavily on the arms of her two oldest grandsons, the widow, Carrie Estelle Betzold Doheny, walked behind the bier, which was covered in white carnations and lilies-of-the-valley.

Bishop John J. Cantwell of the Archdiocese of Los Angeles, dressed in formal black robes, intoned the solemn prayers of the requiem mass. In a moving tribute he lauded the oilman for his strength of purpose, wisdom, and religious faith. Doheny was eulogized not only as a giant among the giants of fortune but as a humane and generous man:

> He was one of those rare men who would give more than a tithe of their increase to God and God's children. He was a fount of generosity ever flowing. It poured itself out on every side. This very church . . . a large church in Tampico, other religious institutions . . . owe much if not all to his and Mrs. Doheny's generosity.
> An American steeped in the history of his country, he put himself and all he had at the disposal of his government in a world crisis, and his contribution was worthy of one who had an undying love of the land of his birth.[2]

Bishop Francis C. Kelley of the Oklahoma Diocese, in the manner of an accountant, told of an extraordinary business genius, a man who had achieved the rewards of worldly success:

> Yesterday these golden rewards were heavy in his hands, today the magician Death has breathed on them and lo! they are there no longer. Thus Death laughs at the world, for he makes failures of us all. With the grim tax-gatherer there is no question of percentage. He takes all. Even of genius he leaves only a memory. . . .
> The nation, the state, the city owe Edward Laurence Doheny much; but let nation or state, or city, now try to pay one penny of the debt, even by a kind thought or a word of long-delayed justice, and it will not in the slightest degree matter to him.

Bishop Kelley spoke of the dedication to patriotism and friendship that had enriched Edward Doheny's character but also cost him dearly. "All Edward Laurence Doheny got from his effort was sorrow. But he could smile and say: *I did it anyway. No one can take the reward of honest service away from me.*"[3] Those attending the service knew that the effusive references to friendship and generosity included Edward Doheny's controversial loan of $100,000 to Albert Fall, who was at the time secretary of the interior in President Harding's cabinet.

Some concealed a derisive grimace at the description of Doheny's munificence and patriotism, noting the cryptic references to the bribery charges in what came to be known as the Teapot Dome and Elk Hills oil scandals. But far more in the gathering shared grief at the passing of a man who they believed had been falsely charged, whose reputation was roughly handled, and whose name was unfairly connected to the Teapot Dome irregularities. They may have felt that Doheny's impulsive, perhaps rash, response to a friend's request for a loan had been incautious. But who could have anticipated the chain of events that followed? Pernicious fate, many felt, was responsible for such incongruous events being interpreted with such poisonous ill will. Many grieved for Doheny and saw in his troubles a warning for themselves.

The service was covered by the Los Angeles newspapers with reportorial restraint. The bribery scandal that had blazed in headlines for a decade now received scant mention, and Doheny was permitted to depart from the mortal world with dignity.

The magnificent funeral service was a comfort to Edward Doheny's widow. Estelle Doheny felt that her husband was receiving recognition he deserved. In the years after the congressional hearings, the trials, and the terrible murder of Edward's only son, Estelle Doheny had joined her husband in the quest for peace, redemption, and the restoration of the Doheny image. As custodian of that image, she took it upon herself to take whatever measures were necessary.

After the funeral, Estelle returned to the family home at 8 Chester Place; she quickly formed a resolution. During the night, in the hours that followed her husband's burial, she painstakingly gathered the records of the oil empire he had built. In secret, with the aid of her sister, Daysie May Anderson, she searched Edward's locked file drawers and cabinets, collecting hundreds of personal letters and business documents. Then, the women went down to the basement, where they opened the double doors of the walk-in steel vault that contained his remaining papers. Moments later, they lit a roaring fire in the mansion's huge incinerator and burned the written remnants of Edward Doheny's life.

It had to have been an engrossing story that she consigned to flames—a final act of devotion to ensure that the record of her husband's life and fortune would forever remain beyond subpoena and safe from further scrutiny. Many years later, Estelle Doheny would confess to her longtime personal secretary, Lucille V. Miller, that it was an act she deeply regretted.

part one La Calavera del Conquistador

One The Young Prospector Doheny

In later years, praising the rugged origins of Edward Doheny, by then a wealthy oilman far from his frontier days, publisher B. C. ("Bertie") Forbes claimed the young Doheny preferred outdoor life to indoor comforts: "Rarely did prospector Doheny sleep under other ceiling than the wide heavens. Each night he lay down with his faithful rifle at his side, his six-shooter ready for action and his hunter's knife at his belt."[1]

The romanticizing of Doheny's mining days was more than the usual workings of nostalgia; it was a rewriting done by expert publicists and lawyers to humanize a millionaire under suspicion of high-handed dealing and to shift the focus to his early years as a stalwart frontiersman. Although there was no lack of colorful adventures to attribute to the young Doheny, later versions of his life omitted important details and enlarged or fabricated exploits. Such rewriting was abetted by the tendency in the mining camps to prize a tall tale over accuracy. In the saloons, western etiquette was observed and men were rarely asked to reveal much about their past. Some had reached the territories ahead of the law, and others had abandoned stolid pursuits as draymen or dry goods salesmen to try their luck at mining. Some had left farms and some had kicked over the traces of married life for adventure in the West. Some were sons from established families who wanted to prove themselves; others had cut all family ties.

What is known of Doheny is that he arrived in the New Mexico Territory, barely twenty years old, hell-bent, like so many others, to make his fortune in mining. It was a tumultuous life in the 1880s, a long way from the seats of government and the niceties of society. Kingston, a mining town in New Mexico's Black Range mountains, was not the sylvan camp described by Forbes and the adventure magazines of the day. Prospectors lived a rough and vicious life among men of diverse, and often violent, backgrounds. The displaced and angry Apaches rode out of the hills and down through the canyons and streambeds in surprise attacks. Mining was a hazardous occupation.

Doheny arrived in Kingston driven to succeed. His vision was always "just over the passes," as he trekked into ever more rugged territory. Born on August 10, 1856, in Fond du Lac, Wisconsin, he was the son of an impoverished Irishman who had fled from Tipperary to escape the Great Famine. Passage across the Atlantic had been brutal, and of four brothers only Doheny's father, Patrick, and one uncle, William, survived the journey to reach Canada.

Patrick became a whaler, sailing the icy and treacherous waters of Labrador, where he eked a meager though adventurous livelihood. He gave up the seas when he met Eleanor Elizabeth Quigley. The two courted, married, and had five children.[2]

By all accounts, Edward was a bright, earnest child. He studied hard and graduated from high school in 1872, valedictorian at age fifteen. He had an early grasp of mathematics and an excellent memory—as noted by the local newspaper, he "excelled at mental arithmetic."[3] During the summer months he worked in the fields or at the town's sawmill. Times were hard and immigrant families were resented by the townspeople. The Irish newcomers were held in particular contempt by rural Protestants, who hired them as farm laborers but despaired for their Catholic souls and feared their "Popish" intentions.

Edward's mother had hoped that her son would study for the priesthood. She was a woman of strict principles, who prided herself on thrift and simplicity. His no-nonsense father, who worked as a laborer and gardener,[4] taught him from the start that anything worth having must be earned. Edward was forced to grow up quickly; just months after his graduation, his father died suddenly at age sixty-three.

Edward took a job with the U.S. Geological Survey Department; still a teenager, he traveled to the Southwest surveying boundaries. Much of the time he rode with government mule buyers, who were trading with the local tribes. In the rough outdoor life he depended more on his wits than on physical strength. He was of slight build, weighing only 125 pounds; at his full height, he would be five foot seven. With reddish-brown hair, light skin, and blue eyes, he possessed the course and unrefined manner of a farm youth. He was described at this time as pale and rosy, as if he were constantly blushing, but he was already ambitious and fiercely independent.[5]

The story is told that Edward soon embarked on his first entrepreneurial venture, purchasing ninety-two horses at a government auction for $5.35 each. After breaking and training the horses, he then sold them, pocketing a $2,000 profit. He continued to buy and sell horses and perfected his skill at driving a bargain.

In 1873 Edward was sent to Kansas to assist in subdividing the Kiowa-Comanche reservation lands. The following year, barely eighteen years old, he quit his job with the Geological Survey to take up prospecting in the isolated regions of the West. He joined a gold-mining expedition—led by Charlie Quidero, a famous seeker of fortune—into the Black Hills of South Dakota. This adventure ended when U.S. government troops drove the miners out of the region for trespassing on the Blackfoot Sioux reservation. But the teenage Doheny had listened to the campfire stories of his older companions, and with his touted facility for "mental arithmetic," he calculated the riches from one good strike in the mines. With the zest and confidence of early manhood, he set out to claim his fortune.

Doheny's travels took him to Arizona, which was then part of New Mexico Territory; but when the Arizona mines failed him, he collected his belongings and moved to Lake Valley, a site in the Black Range mountains rumored to be rich in silver. There his luck turned. He worked the "Iron King," a legendary mine that attracted droves of hopeful miners and gave the boomtown of Kingston its name.[6] Doheny remained in the region from 1880 until 1883, living in a small adobe house. "Fifty dollars a year saw [me] through, with game plentiful and salt cheap," Doheny recalled.[7]

The lands of the New Mexico Territory had been inhabited by indigenous people for hundreds of years, and the Navajos and Apaches believed a vitality emanated from the rugged peaks and deep canyons of the Black Range long before white men arrived to extract treasure from the mines. The tiny town of Kingston was scarcely a spot on the map—a half-day stagecoach ride from the nearest railroad. It was as remote as it could be from the financial centers of the East and the political life of the capital. Yet the town was to produce three men who would meld their youthful energy and friendship into common goals and strike out from Kingston to gain wealth and power that would shake eastern authority.

At the poker tables of Kingston, Doheny would encounter the colorful Albert B. Fall, who was to gain fame as a western political boss and would later become a controversial secretary of the interior in President Harding's cabinet. Charles Adelbert Canfield, with a reputation as a hard-working, devoted family man, would enter Doheny's life as a fellow prospector and would later be Doheny's partner in multimillion-dollar undertakings. Unlike the scions of prominent families in the East who were attending universities, these sons of the West were getting a far different education, schooled by the fierce frontier. Later, their shared philosophy would create a far-reaching debate over the nation's resources, and reminiscences of their Kingston days would be offered and hotly debated. In future years, people in Kingston would speak of Edward Doheny, Charles Canfield, and Albert Fall as though boasting of giants.

LURE OF THE BIG STRIKE

By May 1882, having made a firsthand study of mining operations, Doheny launched himself in the business. Mining required a constant infusion of capital—something young prospectors like Doheny lacked. Many times he had seen mining companions exhaust their resources in pursuit of the "big strike." Destitute and desperate, the unlucky miners were forced to sell their stakes at rock-bottom prices or walk away for want of a buyer with capital in hand. Putting his theory into action, Doheny and a prospecting partner developed claims on two mines in Lake Valley, the Phoenix and Old Reliable. When his partner faltered, Doheny scraped together cash to purchase his share for $150. It was not Doheny's plan, however, to work the mines. After retaining the claims about a year, Doheny sold them for a whopping $6,000.[8] In total, Doheny's trade in mining claims earned him nearly $12,000 between July 1882 and 1883.[9]

On the heels of that success, Doheny purchased the Mount Chief Mine. In 1885 he leased it to Charles Canfield. It was a fateful encounter, for the thirty-seven-year-old Canfield was to become Doheny's most trusted friend and would be involved in his rise to wealth.[10] Canfield contracted with Doheny to work the mine with him, and as the two men labored side by side, they developed a hearty regard for one another, despite their very different temperaments. Canfield was restrained in his voice and movements, often seeming exhausted from chronic insomnia, and was slow to make a decision. Doheny was an energetic risk taker who fostered a Spartan indifference to pain and fatigue.

Like Doheny, Canfield was a frustrated miner, desperate for a big strike. The former water pump salesman from Alma, Minnesota, had arrived in Kingston practically destitute after failing in mining expeditions to Chloride and other sites in the territory. Canfield was married, having wed former schoolteacher Chloe Phoebe Wescott, a striking dark-eyed brunette from Grand Island, Nebraska, in 1879. The couple began housekeeping in a small cabin near one of Canfield's mines at Ruby Hill, Nevada. Their first child, Florence, was born later that year. But after Canfield exhausted his financial resources, he was forced to send his wife and their infant daughter back to Grand Island to live with her parents. The distraught Canfield told one and all that he was determined to succeed for their sakes.

Charles Canfield was of English-Scottish ancestry, born near Springville, New York. He was one of eight children. He had friendly, dark brown eyes, a strong forehead, and a charming cleft in the middle of his chin. He sported a thick salt-and-pepper mustache. His Kingston companions described him as a serious man known for common sense and diligence and well regarded for honesty. Doheny's assertive nature was annoying to the more seasoned Canfield, eight years older, who attributed Doheny's self-importance to the zealousness of youth. While Canfield spent hours each evening writing long letters to his wife, Doheny remained uninterested in domestic affairs: his dreams were of the fortune he was sure destiny and hard work had in store for him.

By the time Doheny and Canfield became mining partners in 1885, Canfield's daughter Florence was six years old and his son, Charles Orville, had celebrated his third birthday. Canfield had spent ten grueling years in the frontier camps, seldom seeing his family, and throwing all his energy into searching for the elusive strike. For the next year, he toiled in Doheny's mine. Chloe Canfield begged him in plaintive letters to abandon his mining efforts and return to Grand Island, but he was inflexible: "I am confident I can make money in this camp," he gently explained. "Only hold your grip a little longer to see how I come out, is the wish of your ever loving husband."[11] But Canfield's assurances to his wife were not soon realized. Again and again he ran out of supplies and money. Nevertheless, his daily letters reflect not only the harsh conditions but also his firm resolution:

> It is snowing very hard tonight, about eight inches on the ground. The old tent is leaking like a sieve, our bedding is all wet and I am alone. . . . My chances to make some money here are first rate and I expect to be all right in the Spring.
> . . . I will make you and the children comfortable if I live. If you will keep up courage all will come right.[12]

Although Doheny admired Canfield's dedication, he did not envy Canfield's position as a cash-strapped family man.

Doheny had been a determined bachelor, believing he had little time and attention to devote to a woman. But in the spring of 1883, he was introduced to Carrie Louella Wilkins, an extroverted twenty-year-old who occasionally graced the stage in local musical productions. She was the daughter of Mariah Brophy, one of the first pioneers to have settled in the Kingston area, said to have come "when the brush on Main Street was so thick that no person could ride through it."[13] Mrs. Brophy, a widow, ran Kingston's boardinghouse, the Occidental Hotel, a two-story wood-frame structure along Main Street. Carrie Wilkins worked there with her mother.

No reliable photograph exists of Carrie Wilkins, but she was described as an attractive brown-haired woman with hazel eyes and sun-tanned skin; neighbors knew her as strong-willed, with a mind of her own. She and Doheny were very much alike, which may account for both their attraction and later discord. Intrigued by Carrie's outgoing nature, Edward began to spend many evenings at the Occidental Hotel after his long days in the mine. Their courtship was short, and they were married on August 7, 1883, in Silver City, three days before Edward's twenty-seventh birthday. Following the wedding, the Dohenys took up residence with Mrs. Brophy at the Occidental.[14] In December 1885, Carrie gave birth to a daughter, Eileen, who arrived safely but was very frail. A few months later, the Doheny family moved into a house of their own on the south side of Main Street.

Carrie Doheny volunteered for the Ladies Episcopal Guild and continued to sing in Kingston's church choir. The *Kingston Weekly Shaft* described a hospital benefit at which "Mrs. Doheny took the large audience by storm in her charming song, 'The Wanderer's Return.'"[15] Other news items of the time were less cheerful, revealing that she was struggling with increasingly serious health problems, forcing her to spend great amounts of time in isolation. Carrie Doheny's ailment remains a mystery, but its symptoms, as noted by others, were wild mood swings, bouts of depression, and paranoia.

Rumors circulated that Carrie had begun to drink heavily. Miners and their wives speculated that the new Doheny union could not endure. At one point, a visibly shaken Edward Doheny confided to Johnny Moffitt, a mining companion, that a physician had ordered Carrie to travel to El Paso, Texas, for medical treatment but that he could not afford to send her there. Moffitt gave Doheny all the money he had in his pocket, saying, "Carrie is a good woman, even if she is a bit excitable, and she deserves help."[16]

Kingston was a rough place to raise a family. Coarse prospectors and drifters gambled, drank, and fought on the streets. Fist fights and knifings were common occurrences. The few miners' wives had to adopt very restricted lives; they attended church, made infrequent forays to purchase dry goods, and found little opportunity to socialize. They remained largely housebound.

Carrie Doheny and Eileen often stayed with Carrie's mother at the Occidental Hotel; Edward continued to work at the mines and to spend his time with Charles Canfield and the other miners. His complexion had turned ruddy, brutalized by the wind and sun. He was usually seen in a hat, his blue-gray eyes bright in the shade of the brim. Though he was portly in later life, in these early years he hadn't much bulk to him and undoubtedly counted on quick thinking rather than strength to get him out of a scrape. He was a regular at the dance halls, variety shows, and saloons where workingmen would "lay their week's 'clean up' on the altar of chance" every Friday night.[17] At the Main Street Saloon, Doheny gained a reputation as a veteran cardshark. His quick mathematical mind (and lifelong abhorrence of alcohol) gave him an edge in poker over his slower-witted acquaintances, who were often inebriated when they played. His winnings were welcome income.

It was during this period that Edward Doheny met Albert Fall. Combative and boisterous, Fall also loved cards and was described as possessing the sort of piercing black eyes that indicated a "man who could take care of himself in almost any sort of company." He was tall and lean, with a bronze-toned complexion. He spoke with a soft drawl (more Kentuckian than Western), and he was rumored never to be without a gun—and to have been known to use it.[18]

One tale that Fall enjoyed telling about their Kingston years made Fall an eyewitness to a brawl when Doheny was purportedly threatened and chased wildly by an enraged drunk. Doheny hot-headedly retaliated with gunfire: he nearly missed his target entirely but did manage to wound his attacker in the leg. Fall boasted that he was the first person to step up and congratulate Doheny on his "coolness under fire" and his skill with firearms that enabled him to send a bullet only to the leg.[19] Such stories chronicled the beginnings of an interlocking friendship. Their paths would continue to cross during the rowdy and dangerous days in the mining camps around Kingston and, much later, in the nation's capital. Their friendship over fifty years would coincide with the economic expansion of the country, a vibrant time that would assign them both important roles; but when the fortunes of Albert Fall turned dark, the consequences for Edward Doheny would be dramatic.

Albert Bacon Fall was the son of William Ware Robertson Fall, a former captain in the Army of the Confederate States of America who became the editor and publisher of the *Independent Democrat Newspaper* in Las Cruces, New Mexico, during territorial days. As a child he had been ably home-schooled by his father; later he studied law in the office of Judge William Lindsley, who would become a U.S. senator. But young Fall did not take readily to the confining environment of a law office, and in the early 1880s, chronic illness forced him to find an occupation that would take him outdoors.[20] Fall's biographer, Gordon Owen, describes Fall's ailments as "flu-like," including bronchitis and pleurisy. Fall spent time in Arkansas, the Oklahoma Territory, and Texas working as a cowboy and chuck wagon cook. At the age of twenty, he worked as a miner in Zacatecas Province, Mexico, where he became fluent in Spanish.

His health improved, and Fall ventured north to Clarksville, Texas. There, he sold insurance and real estate, picked up law again, and in 1882 met Emma Garland Morgan. She was an orphan; her mother had died shortly after her birth, and her father, Simpson H. Morgan, president of the Memphis and El Paso Railroad, had recently died and left her a large estate (mostly in land and railroad stocks). Emma Morgan was a statuesque, handsome young woman and a ward of her uncle, Dr. Jack Morgan.

Owen notes that in courting Emma, Albert "had serious hurdles to overcome. She already was engaged to a young Texan, and probably, constituting a more serious barrier, her uncle did not look favorably upon Albert Fall as a suitor. Albert recalled . . . Uncle Jack calling him an 'upstart and whippersnapper' and accusing him of being a 'fortune hunter.'" When the two were married in Readyville, Texas, on May 8, 1883, it was agreed that Emma's funds would be placed in a special trust. With great fanfare, Fall signed a unique premarital contract pledging himself to match his wife's fortunes. He told his bride's family, "I'll have papers drawn up protecting her money form me[.] . . . [E]ven she [won't] have use of the money until I can equal it with what I earn."[21]

Fall thought silver mining would be the quickest means to his goal. So it was that he arrived in Kingston not long after Doheny, joining hundreds of other eager young men in the mining camps who were digging for riches. Emma Fall remained in Clarksville, Texas, to care for their two infant children, Jack and Alexina.

As times grew hard in Kingston, the steady drain on Edward Doheny's financial resources forced him to borrow money—not for investments or mining endeavors, but merely to buy food.[22] These money problems strained the Doheny's already fragile marriage.

Soon it was obvious that the Mount Chief Mine was not going to provide a bountiful haul of silver ore. Charles Canfield began to scour the countryside for other potentially lucrative sites, while continuing to toil at the maddeningly unproductive Mount Chief Mine. He feared that he faced another year of self-denial, labor without reward, and separation from his family. At the close of one more weary afternoon in late March 1886, Canfield discovered a steep trail that led high above a nearby mine, the Comstock (not to be confused with the famous Comstock Lode of Virginia City, Nevada), which was about a mile and a half west of Kingston. Alighting from his horse, Canfield surveyed the area, then rested briefly under a shade tree; he idly scratched the ground with a prospector's pick. Suddenly, he noticed what miners call "scattered float." His heart began to beat wildly, for he realized the shiny granules meant that he was sitting atop a very rich vein of silver ore. After returning to the site above the Comstock several times that week, Canfield concluded that the outcropping ore probably had its origins deep within the Comstock mine. He approached the Comstock's owners and requested a lease to the property. In exchange, Canfield told them he would give them a one-third interest in anything he discovered.[23]

After securing the potentially valuable lease, Canfield took Doheny to

visit the property. Their first few forays into the mine proved far from aus-
picious. For weeks they labored without discovering significant quantities
of ore. Eventually, Doheny became exasperated and stopped accompanying Canfield to the site, a decision he would later regret. Canfield continued to prospect at Comstock despite his dwindling finances and supplies. He was intent on finding a substantial vein. Within two months, he
had done so: he struck an incredibly rich silver ore chamber, eighty feet
long by twenty-five feet wide, larger than any that had been discovered
in the region. Surprised prospectors told Canfield that he stood to earn as
much as $1 million from his discovery.

Doheny was astounded by his friend's remarkable luck and he was
also greatly envious. He had prospected as long as Canfield had. But a
strike akin to the "Great Canfield Bonanza"—as the country now called
Canfield's discovery—had perversely eluded him.

By May 22, 1886, Canfield was reaping $1,000 daily as he worked day
and night in the mine, extracting silver ore. As the end of his six-month
lease drew near, Canfield doubled his efforts. Soon he was maintaining an
almost superhuman work pace. He grew so utterly exhausted that he
collapsed from what miners called "brain fever."

Chloe Canfield was summoned from Grand Island to Canfield's bedside, for she was told he was near death. His wife's arrival soothed the
desperately ill miner and somehow Charles rallied, although he never
fully recovered. For the rest of his life he would suffer frequently from debilitating headaches. The attractive young woman's calm and dignified
presence invigorated the camp, and Canfield's crew labored harder than
usual, undoubtedly for Chloe's benefit as well. A weakened Charles Canfield supervised dozens of workers in twelve-hour shifts as they extracted
$10,000 a day in silver ore from the Comstock mine. By the time his lease
expired, he had grossed nearly $390,000 from the sale of his silver ore.
Canfield promptly paid the mine owners their royalties in cash and gave
50 percent of his own share to his partners and crew. Then, bidding
farewell to Doheny and his acquaintances, he and his wife departed from
Kingston, bound for California. In his possession was more than $112,000
in cash.[24]

The absence of his close friend, the turbulent relationship with his wife, and the suffocating poverty that entrapped him plunged Doheny into gloom. The stampede of fortune hunters who had come to town had succeeded in depleting the mines' once-abundant resources. Additionally, a nationwide glut of silver in the marketplace had depressed the price. Kingston was no longer a thriving boomtown but a sorry, poor man's mining camp.

In July 1889, Doheny was forced to accept a job painting a pharmacy in nearby Hillsboro in order to feed his wife and daughter. This may have been the last straw. He packed his bags in disgust and moved his family to Silver City, New Mexico. The *Kingston Weekly Shaft* reported that "Mr. Doheny will study law under Mr. H. L. Pickett, a well-known lawyer for the district."[25] It appears, however, that Doheny's plans changed in Silver City. There is no evidence that he was granted a license to practice law, despite his later claims to the contrary. We only know that four months after settling in the town, Doheny received a commission as a notary public and began to process mining claims and patents in an office he set up.[26]

At first, Carrie Doheny tried to embrace her new home. She performed in a gala at the Silver City Opera House featuring local talent,[27] but that was her last appearance on stage. News of her declining health was reported in the local newspapers, and by the fall of 1890, she became so ill that her mother, Mariah Brophy, rushed to Silver City several times to take care of her.[28] That support was soon to become less available, for in early 1891 Carrie's mother married for the second time, wedding Martin Barber at a ceremony conducted at the Dohenys' Silver City home.[29] Finally, in February, Edward escorted his wife to El Paso for treatment.

THE GOLDEN STATE

Doheny continued to work in the mines, again to no avail. Local newspapers dutifully reported his many partnerships—none of which reaped noteworthy profits. He decided to head farther west. Undoubtedly, one decisive factor was Carrie Doheny's continuing health problems. On March 6, 1891, the *Silver City Enterprise* reported that her health had improved and hinted at the couple's imminent departure. The nature of

Carrie's illness, however, still remained unmentioned: "Mrs. Edward Doheny, who has been quite ill and was taken to El Paso last week by her husband, is improving rapidly. The lady's general health was seriously affected by the altitude here. She will probably visit San Diego as soon as the washouts are repaired."

Edward's decision to leave Silver City was also influenced by Charles Canfield's great success in California. Doheny had heard that Canfield had become a highly successful real estate speculator in Los Angeles and had purchased an enormous mansion in elite Westlake Park. The fever of land speculation was raging throughout the city; and thanks to the profits he had obtained from the Comstock mine, Canfield had been able to benefit from the excitement. His investments in real estate were substantial and widespread. To Charles, nothing was too good for Chloe and their children, and he spent his money quickly. His son-in-law later wrote of these years that "money went out with a more lavish hand than the little fortune warranted."[30] Canfield also indulged his love of horses. After purchasing the well-known O.K. Stables in Los Angeles, he had thoroughbreds shipped to him from as far away as Nebraska and Minnesota. A four-year-old trotter named Billy was his particular favorite of the horses he proudly raced at popular matinee racing events throughout Southern California.

But the land fever that had fed the great boom cooled and after a spectacular three years his fortune was swept clean away. The good life seemed over, as Canfield suddenly found himself worse off financially than ever before. This time he was not just flat broke, as he had been many times when he was working in the mines, but deeply in debt. Canfield was forced to liquidate nearly everything he owned—his stable and beloved horses were sold and his real estate holdings were "wiped out for a cruel loss." He was heartsick about the disaster now facing his family, and he vowed to win his fortune back. He took off to prospect in the Mojave Desert, and when that proved futile, he headed for San Diego, where he had leased a gold mine called the Ophir. "I am to blame for your coming to such a fix," Charles wrote Chloe. "I am doing all I possibly can to replace what justly belongs to you and the babies."[31] Again Charles promised Chloe that he would return as soon as his fortunes had been restored.

The news that the land boom had collapsed and that his friend was broke did not reach Doheny before his departure for California. On Doheny's arrival in Los Angeles in the winter of 1891, he was shocked to learn that Canfield had lost all of his extensive real estate holdings, except his residence, was deeply in debt and had left town to start anew. In an astonishing coincidence, while traveling through the district looking for work just weeks after arriving in California, Doheny spotted Canfield on a train platform in Victor (now called Victorville). He rushed from his railcar and clasped his surprised friend. Canfield told Doheny about the Ophir mine. Doheny hastily abandoned his plans to return to Carrie Doheny and Eileen, who were waiting for him in Los Angeles; instead, he joined Canfield and hopped aboard the railcar bound for San Diego.[32]

There the two men found lodging and formed the Pacific Gold and Silver Extracting Company. Despite their great efforts, the mythical big strike escaped them again. Months later, they admitted defeat and boarded a train for Los Angeles to return to their families, beaten and downcast, with only a handful of dollars in their pockets.

$\mathcal{Two}$ Her Coldest Welcome

Edward L. Doheny sat alone on the porch of the Bellevue Terrace Hotel, a low-rent boardinghouse at Sixth and Figueroa Streets in downtown Los Angeles. He was nearly forty years old, well past the age when he'd hoped to make his mark on the world.

He had been living in a small hotel room with his chronically ill wife, Carrie, and his frail seven-year-old daughter, Eileen. He was months behind on his hotel bill, with no prospects for earning the money he needed. He had little interest in his own future and even less in his ten-year marriage. Frequently, when he was near the breaking point, he'd leave his family at the hotel to wander the city, searching for work or at least inspiration. After twenty years of prospecting in the rugged, unsettled regions of South Dakota, Colorado, Nevada, Arizona, and New Mexico, he had absolutely nothing to show for his labors. The grueling work had taken its toll; his hair was now completely gray and his face deeply lined. His once-jovial grin was fixed in a scowl, and he walked with a stoop-shouldered gait, as though unable to shake a world of problems. But his blue-gray eyes were still warm; beneath his bluster and cynicism lay an agreeable, energetic man who simply was down on his luck.

Perhaps it was an unwavering belief in himself that carried him through his dark moments, when he admitted that his trip West had been a dismal failure in every sense. Los Angeles had given him her coldest welcome: she offered no employment, no income opportunities, and no business partners with cash. Each day in the city brought Doheny a new disappointment: his small daughter's worsening health, another emotional outburst from Carrie, an unexpected expense, another rejection. The city seemed to be challenging him to pack his bags, return to the Southwest, and admit defeat. But he refused.

His stubbornness and mental stamina were about to pay off. One spring day in 1892 he noticed a decrepit wagon lumbering past his hotel. The driver was hauling chunks of a greasy, brownish substance. What could that cargo be? Doheny wondered. For no good reason, he rose from his seat and ran after the dray, calling out, "What are you hauling?" "It's *brea*," the driver replied, using the Spanish word for "pitch." "Where does it come from?" "A hole out near Westlake Park." The driver slowed to a stop and allowed Doheny to scoop up a handful of the dark brown gunk and examine it. It felt viscous, slimy, and tarlike in his hands.

Intrigued, Doheny decided to hop aboard a streetcar and visit Westlake Park, where the material had been unearthed; he had nothing better to do. Once there, he easily located a great hole oozing with gobs of the brea. Doheny tentatively drew out a sample of the substance, held it under his nose, and sniffed. The material's odor was sickeningly sweet. When he asked a nearby worker what it was used for, he learned it was a tarry exude (or exudate) that, when mixed with soil, could be used as a velvety-black combustible oil.[1] Most of the stuff, the worker added, was being hauled to a nearby ice factory, where it would be used for fuel in place of coal. At the time, coal was the main energy source in the city. "My heart beat fast," Doheny later recalled. "I had found gold and I had found silver and I had found lead, but this ugly-looking substance . . . was the key to something more valuable than any or all of these metals."[2]

Domestic coal had been retailing in California at $20 a ton. A similar quantity of this new fuel, oil, could be processed and marketed for far less. Already, small local manufacturing plants were utilizing the brea in lieu of coal. Soon, Doheny reasoned, larger companies would consider the same conversion. Could he risk his pride and attempt another money-making scheme? What would Carrie think? Could he try his hand at yet another occupation? The answer came quickly: what did he have to lose?

Edward Doheny returned to his hotel and quietly began to formulate a new business plan that, if it worked, would change his life. He would summon Charles Canfield, tell him about the brea, then entice him with visions of wealth, fanfare, and excitement. He would suggest that they form a new oil-producing partnership. Doheny was unsure how Canfield would react to this proposition; following his terrible losses in the Los Angeles real estate bust, the older man had become excessively cautious about his financial dealings. It would take all of Doheny's effort to persuade him to invest even a tiny sum.

As expected, Canfield initially balked at Doheny's daring plan to drill for brea. They were miners, Canfield argued. What could they possibly do with the strange exude, and how could they gauge its potential worth as fuel? But Doheny persisted. After listening for days to Doheny's rapturous visions, the skeptical Canfield grudgingly relented. Although penniless, he was able to raise nearly $400 in loans for the venture from lenders who still considered him honest and a good risk.

With the newly gained $400 in hand, Doheny and Canfield leased a three-lot parcel of land at the corner of Patton and State Streets. Their acquisition was by no means prime real estate; the entire plot was swampland, bubbling with the tarry crude. Despite the lot's appearance, others soon sensed its worth. H. B. Ailman, a mining acquaintance of Charles Canfield's, and Sam Cannon, a local banker, became intrigued by the venture and asked to join even before Doheny and Canfield had broken ground. Ailman had just arrived broke from New Mexico and was desperate to generate cash. When he realized how difficult the excavations would be, he recruited two additional "workers" to help with labor: his father-in-law and thirteen-year-old son. As the group gathered at the bubbling, oozing site, Doheny could barely contain his excitement.

The first step in this onerous endeavor was to dig a well. Although they were unfamiliar with oil excavations, the former miners were well-versed in sinking shafts and shoveling dirt. First, they hitched a rope to a horse, and connected the rope to a pulley to raise and lower buckets into the muck. Then, with picks and shovels, the men began to dig. It was a slow, exhausting, and frustrating process. They would break ground, shovel the muddy dirt into the buckets, and then load the contents onto a cart, which would be transported by mule to a nearby lot. They continued this grueling routine for the next thirty-nine days, working from dawn to dusk, until they reached a depth of sixty feet—where they discovered literal pay dirt. Under their feet was oil-soaked shale, emitting considerable quantities of gas and crackling like heated popcorn. Doheny and Canfield could not believe their eyes. Choking from the fumes, eyes tearing in the noxious haze, they squinted at the ground below them, dripping with oil. They tied rags over their faces, and continued feverishly digging. Just a few more inches, they told one another, and they would reap huge rewards.

But good fortune failed to arrive as expected; sadness came instead. His small daughter, Eileen, died of heart disease on December 14, 1892, only days short of her eighth birthday. The frail child stopped breathing in her mother's arms in the family's small hotel room; Doheny had not been by his daughter's bedside during the last days of her life. Severe, chronic heart problems had weakened her; her lungs filled with fluid and she could not breathe.[3]

Doheny believed that he had failed his daughter and himself. He could not afford to pay her doctor bills when she was alive, nor send her to the hospital. Doheny began preparations for the funeral. Canfield helped him raise enough money to buy a small coffin and a headstone. On December 20, Doheny traveled to Evergreen Cemetery in the Boyle Heights district of East Los Angeles and, with Canfield by his side, delivered a simple farewell as Eileen's body was lowered into her grave. Carrie Doheny did not attend the funeral; she remained in the hotel, grief-stricken. After the services, Doheny made plans to return to the oil pit. He could not—and would not—stay any longer at the hotel with his inconsolable and now very disturbed wife.

Back at the work site, Doheny prayed for a flowing well. Stone-faced and speechless, he dug deeper until he reached a depth of 140 feet. Still no oil burst forth. Below his feet, the earth continued to taunt him: it tantalizingly seeped oil but refused to bless him with a gusher. Tired and bitter, Doheny turned to Canfield and cursed their luck. However, much later, Doheny would realize just how lucky they had been: "If we had found what we were looking for," Doheny pointed out, "it would have meant our certain death. If we had struck oil in commercial quantities we would have been instantly overcome by gas and asphyxiated before we could have scrambled out of the shaft."[4]

But in January 1893, Doheny and Canfield were still ignorant of the dangers of oil drilling. They continued to excavate until they had reached a depth of 155 feet. That in itself was an amazing achievement, since the men employed only crude techniques. At this depth, however, both Doheny and Canfield encountered the powerful gas fumes being released from the earth. Canfield quietly announced to Doheny that he could stand the suffocating excavations no longer; he was abandoning the partnership, relinquishing his shovel, and returning to mining. The two exited the shaft in silence. Doheny knew he could offer no enticement that would keep Canfield at the well. Now, he had to devise a new strategy—in a hurry—or lose both the lease and their $400 investment.

Doheny's remaining crew could not burrow any further with only pick and shovel, for they were becoming dangerously ill. Doheny needed to raise money to purchase a drill. Only Canfield's friend, Sam Cannon, had any funds to invest further in Doheny's oil venture. Fortunately for Doheny, Cannon willingly agreed to finance the new equipment. After bidding good-bye to Canfield, the weary crew erected a twenty-foot-tall oil derrick out of four-by-fours, modeled after the derricks they had seen in newspaper photographs. They fashioned their actual drill by attaching a cross-shaped bit to a three-inch iron rod. Then they assembled a pump, which would be driven by old-fashioned horsepower.

The entire rig was completed and installed by March 1893. Doheny volunteered to operate the drill; Ailman would serve as his assistant. By this

time, Canfield had regained enough of his health and composure to return to the work site and stand quietly observing their progress. Doheny
lowered the drill and breathed a sigh of relief when it operated perfectly
during its first run. But on the second attempt, the 300-pound apparatus
slipped from Doheny's grasp and plummeted 155 feet to the bottom of the
shaft, where it crashed and splintered apart. Doheny and his co-workers
were distraught, but he still refused to walk away from his investment.
He quickly devised ways to resurrect the equipment from its oily grave
and make repairs.[5]

First, Doheny rigged a grappling hook, fastened it to a cog-wheel
drum, and lowered it into the well. He hoped to scoop up the drill, but it
would not budge. Then Ailman volunteered to descend into the dark
hole himself to try to liberate the drill. Clad in a borrowed rubber rain
slicker, Ailman spent two and a half hours digging out the drill and fas-
tening it to a makeshift pulley device as Doheny coached loudly from
above. All the while, Canfield paced the lot, urging his associates to be
cautious. Several times he mentioned that Ailman's life was worth far
more than a few barrels of oil. But finally a cheer arose from the workers
beside Doheny as Ailman—and the valuable drill—appeared at the well's
opening, both relatively intact.

Once the drill was again operational, Doheny's crew began to "make
hole." During the next seven days, they drilled thirty additional feet
downward. On April 20, however, they were stunned when the drill
struck something solid. At first, they could not budge it, but after several
more attempts, they were able to force the drill to penetrate the hard material and again to plunge through soft strata.

"Let's pull her out!" Doheny yelled to the others. His knees and arms
ached from the harsh vibrations. The men began to pull the drill upward,
wondering what its bit would look like after pummeling the mysterious
hard layer. To their astonishment, the bit was soaked in oil. Rivulets of the
viscous substance trickled down the bit's metal casing and fell to the
ground. There was a moment of shocked silence, and then the men
shouted with joy. They began to leap into the air and dance. Two hundred
feet below them lay a new source of wealth. This hole, at State and Pat-
ton Streets, soon was transformed into the first free-flowing oil well ever
drilled in the city of Los Angeles.

Ailman's son ran to gather empty barrels for the oil being hauled to the surface. By the following morning, they had filled every available barrel, and still the drill's bailer was coming to the surface drenched in black, runny crude. For weeks, Doheny, Canfield, Ailman, Ailman's young son, and a hired man continued to fill barrels with oil. Their shoulders ached and their hands were covered with blisters, but they ignored such trifles.

On one occasion, Doheny and Canfield, at the end of a long day's work, narrowly escaped injury in the shaft. Piles of heavy rock suddenly dislodged from the timber supports above them. Neither man had time to move out of harm's way, but, miraculously, the avalanche rumbled only inches past them and crashed to the shaft's floor below.

After a long moment, Canfield said slowly, "Ed, if that had struck you on top of the head it would have put a dent in your hat."[6] Doheny was too shaken to reply.

Once the group had secured a large quantity of heavy crude from their first well, they began to sell the product to local businesses for $2 a barrel—$0.50 below market rate. As Doheny had predicted, they found many eager buyers. Doheny and his crew continued to labor at the site for several more months, finally selling their leasehold and well for $900. They could use the profits to purchase better equipment and exploit another site.[7]

These hardworking investors had been smitten by oil fever. Doheny, Canfield, Ailman, and Cannon drilled three more wells in the Los Angeles area and several more in nearby cities such as Puente and Newhall. By 1894 they had amassed enough capital to hire a crew of workers and lease more acreage. They then spent the next eighteen months overseeing several small wells and selling their oil yields to local buyers. Finally, it seemed, Doheny had managed to find a lucrative vocation. He had not yet become wealthy, though as he remembered years later, he "felt like a millionaire."[8] But his joy proved to be short-lived. Differing views on expansion divided the partners.

Ever optimistic, Doheny wanted to snap up every available Los Angeles land lease that could potentially yield oil. Ailman and Cannon, however, wanted to invest their newly earned wealth more conservatively. They shocked Doheny when they announced that they intended to transfer their moneys into "more secure" investments. Finally, after intense argument, Ailman and Cannon said they were pulling out in order to start their own production company. Doheny and Canfield were left as partners with the remaining holdings. It was decided that Canfield would supervise the financial transactions and business concerns, while Doheny would become the "field marshal" and devote his energies to solving problems and supervising workers.

As news of oil strikes spread, hundreds of money-hungry speculators and miners flocked to Los Angeles. Homeowners sacrificed their yards and palm trees, and, in some cases, tore down their houses in order to make way for drilling rigs and oil derricks. In the words of one historian, "Black derricks sprung up among the shrubs and flowers of elaborate gardens, steel-shod mules dragged loads of oil equipment across velvet lawns, finely graded roads were rutted by the wheels of the oil tanks that surged through the streets drawn by four, six and eight mules, sometimes four abreast."[9]

Within the next two years, dozens of start-up companies leased land near Doheny's first field, digging some 300 wells within a 160-acre area. Every Los Angeles citizen, newcomer and settler alike, seemed to harbor dreams of amassing a fortune by piercing an underground reservoir of black gold. Warfare over claims began as neighbor fought neighbor for possession of potentially oil-rich land. The landscape of Los Angeles was now dramatically altered. Black grimy drills ground noisily day and night, yielding for their owners thick muddy earth and black smoke . . . and ultimately thousands of gallons of oil.

FIRSTBORN SON

Doheny's improved prospects arrived at what seemed for him his darkest hour. His daughter had just died, and he believed himself partly responsible. He was growing more estranged from his wife, whose emotional health was declining every day. She remained in seclusion at the Bellevue Terrace Hotel, while Doheny worked and slept in the fields with Canfield and the oil workers. Doheny returned to the hotel on weekends in order to provide Carrie Doheny with whatever earnings he had managed to accrue. The increase in Doheny's income seemed to provide small solace to the couple in these tense months.

Edward and Carrie Doheny must have attempted to reconcile during this time, for on November 6, 1893, nearly one year after Eileen's death, Carrie gave birth to Doheny's first and only son, Edward L. Doheny Jr. Unlike little Eileen, who had been frail at birth, "Ned," as he was nicknamed by his father, had arrived in the world strong and healthy. Doheny was overjoyed, and he swore that he would achieve great wealth to provide a secure life for the boy.

Carrie Doheny nursed the child and coped alone as Doheny returned to his fledgling oil enterprises. Again, the couple's relationship deteriorated as Carrie, isolated and depressed, railed about her husband's perceived abandonment. Edward exacerbated matters during his infrequent visits to the hotel by devoting his attentions almost exclusively to Ned. Not being able to overcome her alienation and depression, Carrie began to drink heavily.

Doheny and Canfield now widened their search for potential oil fields. Doheny acquired a geological report by a state-employed geologist, W. A. Goodman, that showed the locations of all existing California oil exudes. Doheny spent months traveling the state, surveying the listed properties and staking claims for as many as he could afford. During the next five years, he drilled eighty-one wells in Southern California, which eventually yielded some 350,000 barrels of oil.

He had finally achieved the success he had hungered for throughout his life, but he remained unsatisfied. He craved larger stakes, more important sales, and bigger profits. Although small businesses were now eagerly purchasing Doheny's oil, he realized that only large corporations could generate the sales volume he needed to be in the same league as the day's great industrialists. The cash provided by large companies' orders would enable him to extend operations to other ports in North America. With this in mind, Doheny began soliciting executives at the Atchison,

Topeka, and Santa Fe Railway, the most important and largest passenger carrier in the West. He urged railroad officials to substitute oil for coal in their locomotive engines. But railroad executives were extremely leery. They questioned the new fuel's quality and wondered whether Doheny's supplies could truly meet their long-term needs.

Eventually, after much negotiating, A.T. & S.F. executives agreed to allow Doheny to furnish fuel for their locomotives in California's Orange and Kern Counties.[10] The land that the railway owned there was oil-rich; perhaps the company could save money using fuel from its own sites. During this time, Doheny became a significant stockholder of the A.T. & S.F., simultaneously becoming part of the railroad industrialists' social milieu.[11] While developing railway lands in Kern County, Doheny was able to acquire some nearby properties for himself, eventually purchasing 1,537 acres and sinking thirty wells.

Canfield meanwhile journeyed to Coalinga, California, a "blight[ed] stretch of no man's land,"[12] to form the Coalinga Oil Company with a new partner, Joseph A. ("Joe") Chanslor. It is not known why Doheny did not join Canfield in this activity, but the two men remained in close contact. In February 1896, Canfield and Chanslor drilled several wells in Coalinga's Section 17, which reaped a modest four barrels a day. Canfield decided to continue to exploit the wells; he was convinced they would yield far more oil once he'd dug deeper. He dutifully wrote his wife daily letters about his progress, alternately espousing optimism and expressing disappointment.

For ten more months Canfield toiled until, on December 5, 1896, he received a letter from his distraught wife, Chloe, informing him that his eldest son, Lee, nine, had died. Over the past few months, the boy, who bore an uncanny resemblance to Charles, had grown progressively weaker as the result of a serious illness. Canfield immediately left Coalinga for Los Angeles. Doheny, too, temporarily abandoned his own work in order to attend young Lee's funeral and console his distraught friend.

Canfield remained in Los Angeles for several months before returning to Coalinga in 1897 to sink five more wells. Finally, after solving equipment difficulties, Canfield had the wells yielding increasingly larger quantities of oil. By winter 1898, they were producing so much petroleum that Canfield and Chanslor were unable to store and transport their output. "Everything looks bright," Charles wrote to his beloved Chloe on March 6, 1899. "We have taken lately contracts for nearly 10,000 barrels monthly in addition to our other contracts."[13] He then promised to buy her the best diamond he could find once he received his soon-to-come windfall.

News of the bounty again spread, and fortune hunters throughout the region hurried to Coalinga. Seemingly overnight, shacks were erected and derricks positioned across the horizon. A *San Francisco Evening Post* reporter described the scene:

The ride from Coalinga to Oil City is across six or seven miles of desolate prairie and through three or four miles of tortuous fields amid barren hills. Not a blade of grass nor even a bunch of sage is to be seen on this journey in the uplands. And the desolateness of the landscape is only accentuated by the unpainted frame dwellings and gaunt derricks that represent Oil City.

The town—if it can be dignified with that title—occupies one of the turtle-back hummocks of which the typography of the region is largely composed and no attempt had been made to beautify it. Yet about half a hundred men, seven or eight sad-faced women and several little children call the place their home. By day sun scorches and at night the winds freeze. On all sides rise higher hummocks, brown and black, and from their sides protrude their unsightly derricks.[14]

By winter 1899, Canfield's Coalinga wells were the most prolific oil producers in all of California. At their peak, they yielded 70,000 barrels of crude per month. Now Canfield was beginning to reaccumulate his fortune—this time in excess of $1 million—and he swore that he would not squander his money a second time.

A.T. & S.F.'s executives were showing renewed interest in oil as a substitute for dirty, wasteful, expensive coal, which was bulky and costly to ship. Years before, railroad executives had attempted using oil, but had abandoned their plans when their oil-driven prototype locomotives did not run smoothly. Later, an oil-fueled prototype ship exploded in San Francisco's harbor. Doheny chipped away at the executives' objections by offering engineering and transport solutions that would prevent such crises. Eventually, albeit hesitantly, they conceded. A.T. & S.F. leaders would permit one of their executives, E. A. Edwards, to convert a loco-motive engine from burning coal to oil and test it on their tracks. Charles Canfield's partner, Joe Chanslor, poured Coalinga light oil into the en-gine's firebox, then hitched a ride in the locomotive's front car as "fire-man" during its smooth maiden run from Los Angeles to Riverside. The men were ecstatic. Sadly, however, a few weeks later, a worker carelessly dangled a lit lantern into the engine's oil tank, causing the converted en-gine to explode into flames.

Doheny and Canfield were taken aback. They immediately appealed to A.T. & S.F. officials to allow them to convert another locomotive's engine so they could start new trials. But the wary railway executives were afraid they might lose a second engine and declined. Finally, however, Doheny and Canfield were able to persuade the general manager of a division of the A.T. & S.F., Southern California Railway's K. H. Wade, to lend them an engine. "Old Switch Engine No. 10," a locomotive that had been sitting idle in a San Bernardino scrap heap for several years, was turned over to them. Doheny and Chanslor helped remodel its firebox, install an oil burner, and set up an oil tank in its tender. Then, they nervously prepared the oil-fueled locomotive for its first trial run.

To Doheny's dismay, the run was unsuccessful. Edwards, who had converted A.T. & S.F.'s first locomotive to oil, helped them improve the engine's performance by installing a force-fed burner and steam jet de-signed to facilitate oil uptake. For six months, Doheny and his partners sent the train on test runs, continuing to modify it as needed. Finally, af-ter several more weeks, Doheny was convinced that it was running smoothly; in fact, as he was quick to tell officials of A.T. & S.F., it was per-forming more trips than any other engine in Southern California Rail-way's possession.[15]

Doheny and Canfield realized that Old Switch Engine No. 10's suc-cessful conversion was the harbinger of a new era of petroleum-fueled transportation.[16] By 1899, both the A.T. & S.F. and Southern Pacific had converted all of their locomotive engines from coal- to oil-burning. Soon, A.T. & S.F. executives contracted with Doheny to provide over 100,000 barrels of oil to fuel its entire locomotive fleet. Doheny agreed to sell approximately 30,000 barrels per month to the company, at $0.96 per barrel. As Doheny had predicted, this one client's large contract alone could assure him over $1 million in future income.[17]

Doheny and Canfield now formed the privately held "Petroleum Development Company," which mostly comprised Doheny's valuable Kern County properties, as well as other Southern California holdings. Doheny served as president, Canfield acted as vice president, and the distinguished Los Angeles judge Olin Wellborn served as the company's secretary. The three men opened an office in downtown Los Angeles at 424 Douglas Street, where they hastily made plans for further expansion.

Although Edward Doheny's career was rapidly ascending, his personal life remained in shambles. In 1899 Carrie Doheny abruptly left him, taking their son, Ned, 500 miles north to San Francisco. She established residency at 805 Shrader Street, near Golden Gate Park. Within a few months, she hired a local lawyer to file a divorce action against her husband of sixteen years.

Following Carrie's departure, Edward moved to 1417 South Figueroa Street in downtown Los Angeles, near his new oil company's office. He did not fight Carrie's divorce petition. He was never to see her again.

Three Rivers of Black Gold

By 1900 black gold fever had infected most of the North American conti-
nent. Oil towns had sprung up in western Pennsylvania, West Virginia,
Ohio, and Indiana. Heads of railroad companies searched for reliable
suppliers and untapped reserves of this new fuel. Albert A. Robinson, formerly with the Atchison, Topeka, and Santa Fe Railway but now president of Mexican Central Railway Company, was one such executive.

He had noticed bubbling black oil pits along the route of his rail line
deep in the countryside of Mexico. Robinson asked Edward Doheny to
travel aboard his railcar to personally investigate the sites. Robinson
hoped that oil on company-owned land could fuel their locomotives and
increase Mexican Central Railway's profitability. A recently built spur, a
short railway system in Mexico's Tampico area, was proving unprof-
itable. Reductions in expenses were needed to offset the line's huge losses.

Doheny was eager to visit the Mexican sites. Like other oil merchants, he had heard rumors about vast untapped reserves, though no oil had yet been successfully produced by anyone inside Mexico's borders.[1] But Doheny hoped that if he made haste, he could be the first to reap riches from the tar-encrusted fields. And so, accompanied by Charles Canfield and A. P. Maginnis, he traveled to Tampico, in a plush Pullman car complete with trained chef and willing porter. The Mexican Central Railway Company had obtained enthusiastic approval for the trip from the Mexican government, currently under the control of President Porfirio Díaz, since any future oil strikes could stimulate Mexico's economy.

For six days, in stifling heat, Doheny and his entourage toured the Mexican countryside. Each day, they alighted from their Pullman and explored the jungle wilderness of Tampico, led by a local guide. The inhabitants were very familiar with the seepages; they used the tar as waterproofing for their buildings and caulking for their canoes. The men hacked their way through the dense jungle vegetation, coped with food spoilage in the oppressive heat, and fought nocturnal insects and harassing jungle pests—including the *pinolilla* and *garrapata*, the giant wood ticks of the jungle. Doheny realized that developing productive oil fields in this country would prove daunting. Not only did Mexico lack paved roads and commercial waterways, but it also suffered from a serious shortage of trained labor. Convincing investors to offer capital to build pipelines, purchase equipment, erect refineries, and hire a workforce would be an incredible challenge.[2]

In March 1900, Doheny's party reached the Gulf Coastal Plains, about thirty-five miles west of Tampico. This was the site of the oil springs that Robinson had spotted. Their guide directed them to an active exude— bubbling springs laced with oil—about three miles north of Chifol, the Mexican railway station. This area, too, was dense with vegetation and blanketed in heavy fog. As the team approached the site, they smelled the thick tarry vapors and saw great clouds of steam. Soon, they encountered what seemed to be a giant volcanic crater, percolating with molten black tar.

Surrounding the crater were *chapopotes*, ponds of brown pitch through which gas bubbled from deep underground crevices. These *chapopotes* were so dangerous that local inhabitants erected makeshift fences around them to prevent people and livestock from wandering into their quick-sand-like muck, to be trapped and suffocated. Doheny approached the edge of the bubbling cauldron, squatted, and tentatively placed a finger into the ooze, which was overflowing to form a steaming-hot ebony blanket across the nearby earth. Doheny examined the substance and put his finger to his mouth. It was oil, all right. He recognized the burning sweet taste. Taking a sleeping blanket from his guide, he soaked it in the oil until the black viscous ooze had penetrated the fabric. He held the cloth to his face and, sinking to his knees, inhaled the substance's vapors to study its properties.

For the next several weeks, Doheny and his team roamed the area, traveling southwest from Tampico and covering approximately one hundred square miles, in order to take a detailed inventory of the oil seeps. They were awestruck by the vast number of untapped and potentially lucrative sites. Doheny found that the richest exudes were located at Cerro de la Pez, thirty-five miles west of Tampico in San Luis Potosi, near the border of Vera Cruz.[3] That site would become extremely important to him in the coming years. Doheny warned Canfield that they needed to purchase the oil-rich lands right away—ahead of anyone else.

The business plan Doheny unveiled to Canfield would have seemed fanciful and even megalomaniacal to more pragmatic minds. He hoped to create a giant international concern that would produce, refine, market, and transport oil to buyers throughout the world. Such a behemoth would require millions of dollars in start-up capital. Wealthy financiers eager to risk their money for quick, and perhaps astronomical, profits would have to be found. But first, the Mexican fields had to be secured; they were "crying out for development," a favorite expression of Doheny's when encountering untouched terrain.

Doheny wanted to acquire select fields quickly and produce oil to create an immediate income stream. His nearest competition for oil refining and storage was nearly 3,000 miles away in Pittsburgh, Pennsylvania. To enter the world market, Doheny realized he would have to transport his oil by pipeline and rail to Tampico Harbor, at the Gulf of Mexico, for distribution to his buyers.[4] He needed to have oil flowing and money coming in to meet the cost of a transportation system, as well as of refinery and storage facilities. His sense of his own destiny had expanded dramatically: he saw himself no longer as a mere oil producer but as future owner of a fully integrated international oil company. Despite their sound personal finances, Doheny and Canfield could not consider carrying the colossal enterprise alone. The timing could not have been better; no other competitor had yet stepped foot into the area, and Doheny was convinced that he and Canfield could raise the necessary funds to get the great venture rolling.

With a completed map of the terrain in hand, Doheny and Canfield returned to Los Angeles to recruit investors for their mammoth project. They approached R. C. Kerens of St. Louis, former ambassador to Vienna; E. D. Kenna of Chicago, head of the A.T. & S.F.'s legal department; W. G. Nevins of Los Angeles, Santa Fe's general manager; and J. A. Chanslor, Canfield's early partner at the Coalinga fields. All were eager to be involved in the Mexican venture. Kenna offered Doheny letters of introduction to several lawyers in Mexico, among them Don Pablo Martinez del Rio, who was to become Doheny's Mexican legal advisor. He was a competent attorney who also spoke English. Once sufficient capital had been raised, Doheny and Canfield hastily returned to Tampico to acquire land, secure necessary mineral rights, and, most important, obtain the Mexican government's approval of their enterprise. Doheny asked General Powell Clayton, U.S. minister to Mexico, to introduce him to President Porfirio Díaz for this purpose.

José de la Cruz Porfirio Díaz, who rose to prominence as a general, had married into a wealthy family. He was himself from modest origins, a mestizo of Spanish and Mixtec blood, born in Oaxaca in 1830. Díaz was a pupil of Benito Juárez in law school, and later he served as an officer in the Mexican army. He fought in the war against the United States (1846–48) and was at the beginning active in support of Juárez's presidency. But following the withdrawal of the French in 1867, he opposed first Juárez's authority and then that of President Lerdo de Tejada. In 1876 his revolt against Lerdo succeeded and he established himself in the presidency. A charismatic leader with perfect facility in Spanish and English, he maintained power through an informal apparatus in which state and local leaders depended on him for their economic well-being. According to Thomas Weil, "Each district and city was ruled by a local boss, whose accountability to the national leader was even greater than it had been under the colonial system. The national congress and judiciary were staffed with obedient and loyal clients who did their benefactor's bidding."

General Díaz continued the services of the traditional elite in government posts, and as judges and heads of departments. In addition, among his supporters was a group known as the *Científicos*, interested in applying scientific methods to the operation of government and bringing Mexico into the modern age. Indeed, his time in power did manage to foster Mexico's economic growth. The long period from 1876 to 1911, the year Díaz was dislodged, came to be known as the *Porfiriato*. The country had experienced continual upheavals and rebellions after claiming independence from Spain in 1810, and the *Porfiriato* was a period of uncharacteristic stability.

In 1900 Mexico was not yet ready for free-market capitalism. Not only did it lack the infrastructure of roads, railways, and ports necessary for industrial growth, but the political and social structure was also ill-prepared. Mexico's preindustrial social order was hierarchical, with a small, powerful elite entrenched at the top, preserving their status from generation to generation; a middle class that struggled to maintain superior status above a working class with limited opportunity; and an unassimilated peasantry descended from various indigenous groups. Amid such social extremes, good order was maintained by authoritarian power and responsible paternalism.

Successive governments had in varying degrees preserved the state's national resources for the benefit of the people. Native communities held land not in private ownership but communally, for the use of the present generation and its descendants. The great landholders owned vast acres but were lax with trespassers and squatters who farmed underutilized parcels. Disputes were often brought to El Patrón, the head of a prominent family, whose rulings had as much to do with accommodation as with strict legal interpretation. Indeed, the local judiciary often operated by a similar code.[5]

Díaz was fully aware of the latent value of his country's oil resources, but his government lacked the funds and expertise to fully exploit the underground treasure. He realized foreign developers like Doheny and Canfield were needed to launch this promising industry and, in so doing, bring a much-needed boost to the economy. After meeting with Doheny and Canfield, Díaz offered them generous tax breaks as additional encouragement. He told Doheny that he hoped Doheny's visiting American laborers would teach his people "how to write, how to live, and how to progress."[6]

Another reason for Díaz's largesse to Doheny was inherent distrust of John D. Rockefeller and his monolithic Standard Oil Company.[7] Díaz's agreement with Doheny prohibited Doheny's selling to Standard Oil. He was to offer any future sale of his holdings to the Mexican government first. Although Doheny had taken pains to squelch rumors that he was an agent of Standard Oil, Díaz wanted to be sure that Standard Oil couldn't come in the back door.

The Mexican opportunities raised Edward Doheny's spirits. He welcomed the chance to immerse himself in a new, glorious adventure. Since his divorce, he had not sought out female companionship, but in the summer of 1900 this suddenly changed. While placing telephone calls to wealthy investors, Doheny initiated a conversation with the twenty-five-year-old Sunset Telephone and Telegraph Company operator who was assisting him, Carrie Estelle Betzold.[8]

Over the next few weeks, the two spoke several times as Estelle Betzold placed business calls for the oilman. While they would wait for Doheny's party to answer, Edward and Estelle would discuss a wide range of topics. Soon he found himself smitten with the mysterious faceless voice on his telephone who seemed to converse intelligently with a pert comment on any subject that came up. Later, Edward Doheny would explain that it was the "timbre in Estelle's voice" that first enticed him. Her sharp and sassy conversation seemed to have additionally piqued his interest.

Estelle Betzold was born in Philadelphia, Pennsylvania, on August 2,

1875. She was the older of two daughters; her father was a railroad employee. When Estelle was three years old, her family relocated to Marshalltown, Iowa, fifty miles northeast of Des Moines. In 1890, following Estelle's fifteenth birthday, her father moved the family to Los Angeles, where he took a job as a streetcar operator, or "motorman," for the city's streetcar system.[9] Between 1896 and 1898, Estelle worked as a clerk at the Broadway, a then-small retail store owned by Arthur Letts, a British-born merchant who subsequently developed a chain of highly successful Broadway department stores and later founded the Bullock's Department Store chain. In 1898 Estelle left the Broadway to work as a secretarial clerk for a "Mrs. J. Moffat." She left this job one year later to become a telephone operator at the Sunset Telephone and Telegraph Company.[10]

When finally Edward Doheny met this fetching, pale-skinned brunette, he was captivated by her assertiveness, wit, and charm. Although Estelle Betzold was nineteen years his junior, she had the sophistication and refinement of a woman more nearly Doheny's age. Unlike Carrie, who had lived among coarsened miners and pioneers, Estelle had been raised in an urban setting, in modest but genteel society. And much to Edward's relief, Estelle exhibited a very stable, easygoing personality—something very different from that of his former wife. Edward was additionally pleased (and surprised) to find that Estelle seemed equally smitten with him. Their courtship was fast-paced. The two lovers, although opposite in many ways, found that they nicely complemented one another. Edward Doheny had been criticized by partners and employees for being too blunt, impatient, and demanding. Estelle Betzold, however, was refined, cordial, and understanding. As Doheny's "other half," she would soon take on the role of an adept public liaison for both Doheny's commercial operations and his personal interactions.

On August 22, 1900, after a three months' acquaintance, Edward Doheny and Estelle Betzold were wed.[11] Because he was a divorced Catholic and she was a Methodist, a church wedding was deemed out of the question. Nonetheless, Edward saw to it that his wedding was nonpareil. The ceremony took place in his newly purchased private Pullman railcar parked beside the main transcontinental tracks in Albuquerque, in New Mexico Territory.[12] A justice of the peace read the service. The railcar-turned-wedding-chapel was a luxurious conveyance with expensive black walnut paneling, plush carpeting, chandeliers, French mirrors, even an early air-conditioning system, and a fully stocked kitchen for the postwedding feast. The couple exchanged their vows inside the car's "drawing room." Ned Doheny, now seven years old, and Charles Canfield looked on. Afterward, Doheny rechristened the private car "Estelle," in honor of his bride.

Because of Doheny's extensive travel plans, the railcar would serve as the couple's first home. They would keep the car for the next three decades, using the mansion on wheels to travel throughout the United States and Mexico. Private railroad cars were a familiar part of the western scene from the high passes of the Rockies to the fashionable resorts of California, even though they were a luxury available only to the very wealthy. To own and operate a private car was a particular distinction, and the young bride, twenty-five years old, was now the Pullman's mistress.

Edward Doheny was exuberant about the rapid, dynamic improvement in his life—just eight short years earlier he had been destitute, depressed, and suffocating in an unhealthy marriage. Now, everything had changed for him: first solvency, then a multimillion-dollar enterprise, a new Mexican oil frontier at his beckoning, and, most recently, the acquisition of an attractive, loving bride. However, within five weeks of the wedding ceremony Doheny received grievous news. His troubled ex-wife Carrie, who had been upset about this sudden new marriage, had consumed battery acid and was dead. Her body had been discovered by a neighbor inside her home at 622 Walsworth Avenue in Oakland, on September 27, 1900.[13] At the time of her death, she was only thirty-eight years old. Although many California newspapers politely labeled Carrie's death accidental—even quoting acquaintances who hypothesized that Carrie had mistaken the battery fluid container for a similar-sized medicine bottle—forensic evidence soon showed that Carrie's intentions had been very clear.[14]

Carrie's nurse and housekeeper told police that she had swallowed such a large dose of the fluid that despite the efforts of a doctor who had been called to the scene, Carrie died in great agony just hours later. Further investigation revealed that she had purchased the battery fluid from a local druggist only days earlier. She then placed the bottle on a closet shelf beside her medicine, a tonic in a bottle that was indeed similarly sized and colored.[15]

Perhaps Carrie Doheny had lost her will to live; perhaps her illness and the loss of her marriage had finally overwhelmed her. Three months prior to her death, she had received her final divorce decree.[16] She had moved from her San Francisco flat to Oakland, hoping to start a new life; instead, she remained haunted by her old one. Carrie's emotional health deteriorated further and she soon required round-the-clock nurses and medical supervision.

Edward Doheny remained stoic about Carrie's death. They had been emotionally estranged from one another for so long that he felt only great sadness at her demise. To the end of his life, he would refrain from mentioning her publicly again, even when offering autobiographical details about his early life; he always left the impression that he had been a bachelor until he met Estelle Betzold. Nonetheless, feeling he owed her one last duty, he had Carrie Doheny's body shipped by train to Los Angeles so that she could be buried beside their daughter Eileen at the Evergreen Cemetery.

As months passed, Carrie Doheny faded from memory. Even Ned soon was referring to his father's new wife as "mommie," and as the boy matured, he, too, would lead others to believe that Estelle Doheny had been his birth mother. Now, because of Carrie's suicide, Estelle was suddenly thrust into the role of mothering a seven-year-old boy. Her letters to Doheny during his frequent trips to Mexico reflected her determination to provide Ned with a safe and happy home. One of the earliest ones read: "You and I are so fortunate to escape some things. I wish I could tell you what I have faith in. But I will tell you only when I am fortunate enough to win Ned's love. He is so sweet and how I do love him. You'll promise not to be jealous, won't you love? But his little heart just craved for someone to go to, and know their arms were ready to clasp him to her heart, and not reprimand him for something."[17]

She realized that the pudgy, shy child was disoriented by his hasty relocation back to Los Angeles. She redoubled her efforts to make the boy comfortable in his new surroundings. She read Ned stories, ate meals with him, and proved herself a devoted playmate: "After dinner we played golf—and turned your umbrella upside down and knocked a rubber ball until bed time—why I wouldn't miss the fun of nursing that child for a fortune. . . . I only hope I can keep young, and cling to Ned's heart."[18]

Each year on Decoration Day, Estelle Doheny would go alone to Carrie's and Eileen's gravesides, place flowers by their headstones, and say a silent prayer in their memory.

TAMPICO, MEXICO

Edward Doheny chose to extend his stay in Tampico during October 1900. He publicized an offer to reward Mexican natives five pesos apiece for leading him to new oil exudes or tar pits. Doheny's quest for these sites was growing much easier now; he had recently learned that Mexico's early mapmakers had painstakingly named local regions after their geological attributes. The phrases "El Chapopote," "El Chapopotal," "Chapopotilla," "Cerro de la Pez," and "Ojo de Brea" all indicated tar or pitch. Such map appellations would lead Doheny and Canfield directly to oil-rich land.

Doheny's first major purchase in the Tampico area was 283,000 acres at Cerro de la Pez (Hill of Tar) on the Hacienda del Tulillo; for this expensive terrain he paid $325,000. Then he anted up another $600,000 for 160,000 acres of the adjoining Hacienda de Chapacao. Doheny was particularly pleased with his new tracts: not only were they rich in exudes, but they were also close to the Tamesi and Panuco Rivers as well as the area's sole rail line. On December 18, 1900, fully confident of his success, Doheny incorporated the Mexican Petroleum Company (MPC) of California, with $10 million capital from investors. The Mexican Central Railway became one of MPC's first customers; it requested an ongoing supply of oil for its Aguacalientes-to-Tampico run. Two months later, Doheny set up an "oil camp" at "Kilometer 613," which was given the name "Ebano Station."

Now Doheny's workers were ready to erect their first derrick. An appropriate spot for the undertaking was selected in March near Ebano. Two months later, it was fully operational. On May 14, an excited driller awakened Doheny and Canfield to inform them that when the drill reached a depth of 545 feet, it had struck oil—such quantities of oil that as it shot up into the air, it lifted the drill from the hole floor and temporarily halted drilling operations. Although initially overjoyed when he inspected the site, Doheny became crestfallen when the well did not produce at the anticipated volume. At its peak, it yielded only ten to fifty barrels a day of coarse oil, "thick as cold honey," which would be difficult to refine. Acting swiftly, Doheny decided to sell this oil as asphalt and as postrefinement heavy fuel oil, two unpopular—but salable—forms of the substance. At this time, however, few buyers were interested in thick crude. Irritated but undaunted, Doheny instructed his crew to dig deeper, for he remained convinced that a better grade of oil lay in large quantities deeper below the earth's crust. At his behest, Doheny's employees ordered special cable from Pennsylvania, which could increase bore speed to an impressive 100 feet per day. But, again, no black geyser rose.

Unflagging in his determination, Doheny brought in a new operations manager, Herbert G. Wylie, a loyal and tireless employee who had supervised Doheny's Bakersfield operations. Energetic and fair-minded, the 300-pound Wylie proved effective at supervising 3,000 Mexican laborers in the construction of a new refinery and at keeping close watch over Doheny's burgeoning Mexican oil empire. Wylie would ably serve Doheny for the next twenty-five years, becoming instrumental in every aspect of his business success. Under Wylie's vigilant gaze, Mexican workers cleared acres of jungle brush, built wide roads, and erected wood-frame houses, an electrical plant, a water distillery, sawmill, machine shop, cold-storage warehouse, and blacksmith shop.[19] Unlike most other American managers, Wylie was determined to learn the Spanish language, and these efforts, combined with his forthright personality, commanded the respect of his laborers.

As Wylie assumed more responsibilities and executed Doheny's plans with dispatch, Doheny found he could rely implicitly upon Wylie's business savvy and offered his employee additional perquisites. In later years, he would recall Wylie's many attributes: "untiring efforts, good judg-

ment, vast knowledge and ability to overcome the unforeseen and seemingly impossible difficulties of engineering, and of working untried men
whose language he did not then understand."[20]

Doheny and Canfield toiled on, praying for a miracle to come soon.
Their anxieties were well-founded; both their American stockholders and
the Mexican government were growing concerned that Doheny's venture
might fail. Then, to make matters worse, in June 1901 the Mexican Central Railway reneged on its guarantee to purchase oil from Doheny for its
Tampico line. Its executives claimed that Doheny's oil was too heavy to
refine. Thousands of miles away, frustrated stockholders began to withdraw their support. Ruin suddenly seemed dangerously near. While
Charles Canfield grew fearful about MPC's prospects, Doheny never faltered in his conviction that the company would succeed. MPC's financial
backers were putting pressure on Doheny to sell his Ebano well and abandon the new camp in order to cut losses. But Doheny, unwilling to make
those sacrifices, was determined instead to find a market for his heavy
crude. He had to, or the collapse of MPC was virtually inevitable. As
stockholders continued to sell their MPC shares, Doheny steadfastly re-
purchased whatever stock he could afford. When he ran out of ready
cash, he pawned Estelle Doheny's most expensive jewelry and sold off his
Kern County, California, oil interests for $1.8 million.[21]

Originally, Doheny had held only 8 percent of the Mexican Petroleum
Company's stock; now he owned nearly 40 percent of the seemingly
worthless company. Doheny's challenge was to profitably unload his
growing inventory of heavy crude. He approached government officials
in the cities of Mexico City, Guadalajara, Moelia, Tampico, Durango,
Puebla, and Chihuahua and offered to sell them asphalt to pave their
primitive roads inexpensively. Many of the town authorities responded
positively, but some Mexican nationals remained steadfastly opposed to
doing business with the "gringo oilman." Finally, after a melee of domestic politics, Doheny was permitted to build a small refinery at Ebano
to produce asphalt from the heavy crude.[22]

Doheny invited Fairchild and Gilmore, America's premier asphalt
and paving concern, to join him in the asphalt venture. The New York
City firm promptly notified Doheny that his product was superior to

nearly all the brands of asphalt produced in the United States and expressed "utmost confidence in its quality." Doheny was elated; he knew this endorsement would help him win contracts.[23]

Although Doheny's paving profits were not substantial, they kept his beleaguered Mexican Petroleum Company afloat. Within a few months, Doheny was able to recover Estelle Doheny's jewels from the pawnbroker. He returned to Los Angeles via his private railcar and presented the baubles to his much-relieved wife. The sale of his Kern County oil properties and the contracts to sell the Ebano asphalt permitted Doheny, for now, to proceed apace in his campaign to become the dominant oil interest in Mexico.

CHESTER PLACE

In the autumn of 1901, Doheny began negotiations to purchase a 10,500-square-foot mansion in the West Adams District in Los Angeles, for the then-astounding price of $125,000. The fourteen houses in this exclusive residential neighborhood had first been developed by Judge Charles Silent in 1896. Doheny paid the sum in cash. The estate at 8 Chester Place had been built by famed architects Theodore Eisen and Sumner Hunt in the Gothic revival style, with turreted towers and a foreboding exterior. It had over twenty rooms and extensive grounds for the future addition of an enormous indoor swimming pool and tennis courts. The three-story house had been constructed in 1899 for Oliver P. Posey, the general manager of seven mining corporations based in the western United States and Mexico, and his wife, Sara, who had achieved her own celebrity and fortune as a canny Los Angeles real estate agent.

Edward was entranced with the impressive edifice. But as the purchase was being completed, he realized that Estelle was far less enamored of the home. She pointed out that the interiors were extremely dark, the halls narrow, and the windows few. She begged Doheny to consider other sites: "I know dear love, that you want to please me, but I was heartsick when I saw the inside of that house. I know I am not a very important factor in this matter and really darling, I am ashamed to tell you how I really do feel about the house . . . but I thought if you only knew how I despised cloudy days, whether caused by atmosphere or mental trouble, you wouldn't purchase the place, but only rent until we better ourselves."[24]

Despite Estelle's pleas, Edward remained enthusiastic about the large estate. He gently attempted to persuade her to accept his decision; ever the peacemaker, Estelle reluctantly agreed. Two months later, Edward, Estelle, eight-year-old Ned, Louise the cook, and a nanny known as "Miss M." moved in. For the next few months, while Edward returned to business in Mexico, Estelle oversaw the construction and maintenance on the estate. He instructed her to hire work crews and build a private bowling alley, music room, and wildlife menagerie, which would house deer, parrots, rare birds, an anteater, and a frisky monkey named Mike. The latter animal had been shipped from Mexico by A. P. Maginnis as a gift to Ned. Mike soon became the favorite Doheny pet and was permitted to wander freely about the premises.

Among Estelle Doheny's most time-consuming tasks was worker supervision. She oversaw the painting of the mansion's exterior (pale green with dark trim), the removal of several large, overly shady trees from the mansion's front lawn, and the day-to-day domestic responsibilities of the Doheny household staff. Of course, taking care of Ned was one of her major concerns. She enrolled him in the best nearby private school and hired a special tutor to coach him in his studies and a music teacher to teach him to play the cornet. Each afternoon, she would supervise Ned and his school playmates in the bowling alley or yard, and in the evenings she would help her stepson with his schoolwork and then read him stories.

Over the years Estelle would succeed in making the dreary mansion a comfortable home. She entertained guests and assisted Edward with his heavy schedule and myriad business ventures when he was in town. She conducted her social planning and handled most of her husband's personal affairs from a large flat-topped desk in her office, which was an unusual six-sided room festooned with garlands of paper wisteria.[25]

As the refurbishing at 8 Chester Place neared completion in 1902, it drew large numbers of appreciative passersby. When it was featured in

House Beautiful, the steady flow became a flood. Almost daily, Estelle Doheny would find tourists standing on her lawn snapping pictures of her home with their Kodak cameras. Occasionally, journalists and tourists would grow so bold as to knock on her front door. "I have had people from magazines come and want to take pictures inside and out," she complained to her husband. "But I can't tell if they are really representatives of the magazines or impostors so I don't let them in."[26] As years went by, Doheny purchased the surrounding thirteen homes to ensure his privacy. Gradually, the Dohenys' new home became a sprawling, garden-encircled compound, an oasis of tranquillity and grandeur.

However, the first year at Chester Place was a difficult one. Edward's growing obligations in Mexico forced him to spend protracted amounts of time away from his new bride and son. As Thanksgiving 1901 drew near, Estelle became lonesome and anxious. She would spend her first Thanksgiving holiday as a married woman alone inside a dark, drafty mansion that she loathed. "Do you think the time will ever come when you will give me less money and stay home more?" she wrote plaintively. When it became obvious that Edward would not curtail his Mexican trip to return to her, Estelle began a blitz of daily letters that reflect her increasing frustration and anger:

Nov. 28, 7:00 P.M.

I think you are real mean, not once telegraphing me and letting me know how you are or if you arrived safe or what is the matter. After you get away from us you don't care what happens or how much worry you may cause us.

You ought to have arrived in Tampico Tuesday evening, and not one word have we heard—

Here was our Thanksgiving dinner, and don't you skip this—bouillon, celery, baked chestnuts, stuffed olives, escalloped oysters in shell, turkey, cranberry sauce, new peas, mashed potatoes and good gravy, mince pie, fruit cake, frosted walnuts, demitasse, and finger bowls. Wouldn't you liked to have carved that turkey? If I don't hear from you by tomorrow I will wire Mr. Maginnis [a trusted Doheny associate].[27]

The following evening, when no missive from Edward arrived, Estelle wrote again, even more infuriated and concerned:

Nov. 29, 6:30 P.M.

I haven't heard from you, you must have received my telegrams by this time. Although I have allowed you all sorts of time to go out hunting and prospecting. . . .

Ed now see here, wouldn't you feel bad if I didn't write, or wire, and let you hear anything from us? When you came in from a hard ride, and no letter, or message was waiting for you, wouldn't you feel a little anxious about Ned?

You said in your last letter "don't worry about anything," and you turn right around and give me all the cause to worry by not letting any of us hear from you. . . .

Ned said to me at the dinner table "Mama we could be awfully happy if we were poor, couldn't we?" I asked him, "Dear, dear little tot, why?" He said "because Papa wouldn't go away so often."

I guess he knows that I am worried. Oh well, good bye.

Estelle[28]

Three days later, Doheny finally responded by wire to his wife's unhappy pleas. He told her that he had been "up to his neck" in business troubles and had been unable to reply sooner. Although relieved to hear from him, Estelle retorted, "If you make me worry again like that I will punish you in fine style. Now don't be stingy with the telegrams and letters as I never was so home sick in my life as I am for you this trip."[29]

Perhaps hoping to keep his wife's mind more fully occupied, Edward sent Estelle further instructions for renovating 8 Chester Place. He asked her to redecorate the mansion's "Great Hall" in a hunting lodge motif to commemorate his early frontier days. Obediently, Estelle ordered a large bear rug for the room and placed moose and elk heads above the fireplace. Over the mantel, she hung a plaque with the inscription "Come friends and join in hearty Saxon cheer, / Our deeds and words will give you welcome here." It was not drunken cheer that was offered, as Doheny was a confirmed teetotaler and forbade the drinking of alcohol at Chester Place. Edward also asked Estelle to refurbish the "Wigwam Room," a game room in a separate structure on the back of the grounds. Again, he requested a frontier motif. To comply with his request, Estelle ordered animal skins and exotic hunting trophies. Edward later said that he considered the room his favorite; when home, he would spend hours in it, chatting with friends near an enormous roaring fire.

But despite Estelle's increased duties, she still spent her evenings penning bitter chastisements to her husband. She realized that because Edward was still mired in business problems, he probably would not be coming home for Christmas. Making matters worse, he again was not responding to her missives. On December 6, 1901, she anxiously wrote:

> The letter you said you would write after your trip to the wells never came. You can imagine the frame of mind I am in, when you don't let me hear from you any oftener.
>
> We are having a dreadful Santa Ana [windstorm]. I can almost hear the house crack, and as for being nervous, I never was so nervous in my life.
>
> Good-bye, CARRIE.

Doheny chose not to inform his wife that he was quite alarmed about the sluggish production of the Ebano wells. The family had already weathered one financial setback; he did not want to upset Estelle by forecasting another. In addition, by keeping her in ignorance, Edward was practicing rumor control, not writing of any prediction or event that might frighten stockholders and bankers. Such a slip could cost him millions. The display of opulence at Chester Place was a key component of this strategy. Only to his closest business confidants, such as Canfield and Wylie, did Doheny mention his uncertainty about keeping his operations afloat long enough to reap the rewards he hoped awaited him.

Four Spoony Visits

New Year's Day 1902 found Estelle Doheny alone in the Chester Place compound and markedly depressed. She now knew it would be months until Edward returned. Throughout the cool, rainy winter, Estelle continued to pack her husband's Tampico, Mexico, mailbox with letters, each one posing the same lonely question: how much longer?

Ned Doheny, too, was beginning to show signs of being greatly disturbed about his father's protracted absence; he was sullen and morose. Estelle, with compassionate attention, attempted to fill the boy's time with uplifting diversions. She purchased one of the first manufactured "talking machines" for the music room, so that Ned could listen to records. He would lie on the floor, stare up at the ceiling, and sing with the recording as Estelle sat in a French baroque–style chair, humming quietly with her eyes closed. Then, after dinner, in an evening ritual, she would accompany Ned to the writing desk where the two would write short notes to Edward. These would be picked up by the postman the following morning.

Ned's composition skills improved markedly under Estelle's stewardship. Soon the seven-year-old's notes to his father were entirely his own:

> Dear Papa,
>   I am having a good time with the monkey Mr. Maginnis gave me. Please thank him for me. I am not going to school this week because I am sick. I hope I can be promoted just the same. I will try and study at home.
>   The monkey climbs all over me and mommie. The monkey looks like a spider when he climbs. Every time we sit down to dinner we wish you were here to enjoy Louise's good dinner.
>   Good-by from your loving son,
>   Edward L. Doheny[1]

Because Estelle had never reared children before, she had to learn all elements of Ned's upbringing on the fly. Sometimes, her lack of experience made her worry more than was necessary. She became overprotective of Ned and hypervigilant about his health. Once, for example, she grew frantic when Ned complained loudly of stomach cramps. She summoned a doctor, who laughingly diagnosed simple indigestion. Within a few hours, Ned was dashing about the Chester Place grounds, playing with Mike the monkey once again. "Goodness how I wish you were here, Toots," Estelle wrote to Edward, after recounting the details of this false alarm. "You won't have to go so often now, after this trip will you? After you get Herbert Wylie initiated can't you stay longer? There is an article in this week's *Capital* saying you had gone to Mexico for another month. All the papers seem to know more about your plans than I do."[2] The greater cause for family alarm was in Mexico, where Edward was nursing the ailing Mexican Petroleum Company.

Finally, in August, Edward invited Estelle to meet him in Albuquerque; they could have a cozy rendezvous aboard the "Estelle." The young woman excitedly traveled to the New Mexico rail station where she passionately embraced her husband. The couple shared a report-

edly "spoony" visit in the luxurious quarters. The visit was brief, however. Within two weeks, Doheny was summoned back to Ebano, just a
few days prior to his second wedding anniversary. Once again separated, husband and wife wired messages of love to one another when
that anniversary arrived on August 22, 1902: "Your telegram made me
happy to think that you remembered the day. You just bet your boots I
will go with you next time. Plenty of love and kisses for you—my ribs are
good and strong so try your best at breaking them—good-bye sweetheart. Your devoted little wife, Phyllis" ("Phyllis" was Doheny's pet name
for Estelle).[3]

When the following school term began, Estelle proudly informed Edward that Ned was now the youngest pupil in his class and was excelling
in his course work. She also wrote of Ned's growing musical talents. Already, he could accompany her in a duet: as he would play his child-sized
cornet, she would play the piano. Soon, Estelle and Ned began to perform
for Louise, Miss M., and the household staff, who would gather in the lavish music room and clap enthusiastically after each lively number. One
day, Ned surprised Estelle by telling her that he wanted to learn the
drums. She immediately contacted the Orpheum Theater management so
that he might be taught by a professional drummer.

In Doheny's continued absence, Estelle tried to keep her mind focused
on day-to-day tasks, but she found it difficult. She was growing intolerably weary of her cloistered existence and monotonous routines. "I am getting mightily tired of it all," she confided to her mother and sister. "It is
such stupid work trying to be interested in something like housekeeping—
when one's heart and thoughts are somewhere else."[4]

In October 1902 Estelle's doldrums turned to anxiety when she learned
that a prowler had broken into the compound and burgled a neighbor. Estelle ordered Ned and Louise to sleep in the green-and-lavender room beside her own bedchamber, and she instructed Janice, another servant, to
sleep in a room down the hall. She also hired a special night watchman
to patrol the compound grounds, as she wrote to Edward: "I have engaged Mr. Churchill to come every night, I will pay him $4 a night. I
would sooner lose the money than my nerves. I don't want to make this
trip hard for you, but I am afraid."[5]

Fortunately, no trespassing was reported at 8 Chester Place. Shortly thereafter, Edward wired Estelle that he would be home soon. Overjoyed, Estelle responded:

> You bet I'll be ready, waiting at the depot. You can thank your lucky stars because this is the *very last* trip without *ME*. See that word *ME*.
>
> When I received your letter I was just as pleased as if it were a diamond. I'll tell you all about that when I get you in my clutches. I pity you. Don't plan on anything for Sunday. You can't keep any engagements, because we will hold *DEVOTIONAL* all day.[6]

The couple shared another affectionate reunion in the dusty rail station at Las Vegas, but within days, Doheny returned to Tampico. Estelle continued to make improvements to the Chester Place compound and fret about her life without her husband. Each night, after putting Ned to bed, Estelle would retire to the home's drawing room and play solitaire in company with Louise. They would discuss the day's events and wonder aloud about the lord of the estate's return.

The profitability of Edward Doheny's Mexican ventures increased only slowly. He had exhausted most of his available cash in development costs.[7] Because his oil yield was not sufficient to attract investors, he would have to take drastic actions to raise funds: he decided to sell his remaining oil holdings in Kern County, California, for the desperately needed cash. Currently, the Mexican wells were producing 500,000 barrels of oil per year; but most of the heavy crude produced was being sold as lower-priced asphalt. Still, Doheny was convinced that his growing Mexican empire would eventually yield great rewards, something his investors and the Mexican government now seriously doubted. Despite his reassurances, they remained skeptical of his claims of "hidden black rivers" below the Mexican earth.

Doheny was necessarily involved with Mexico's politics as well as the country's economic goals. General Porfirio Díaz's power was maintained by a political apparatus that spread itself throughout the country: local leaders, judges, and even elected officials were accountable to the president. With a well-maintained army, centralized police force, and the infamous mounted rural police, the *rurales*, Díaz was able to enforce his authority, maintain order, and contain the banditry that had been rampant during the years of rebellion. But this peace came at a price of unceasing authoritarian control.

Díaz and his advisors were anxious to increase employment in order to smooth the road toward social tranquillity. Future uprisings could not be avoided unless all elements of society, from the peasantry to the elite, found themselves participating in the coming good times and believed that life was better and safer in Díaz's Mexico. Foreign ownership of factories and other enterprises was a particularly sensitive issue. Mexicans who had overthrown colonial rule were wary of finding themselves economically subjugated by foreign entities, especially U.S. companies. Doheny was aware that his welcome in Mexico was dependent on successful oil production that would boost the Mexican economy. If he faltered, Díaz would smile on other entrepreneurs.

In 1903 more luck than he first realized came Doheny's way when he was introduced to Ezequiel Ordóñez, a thirty-six-year-old Mexican geologist who was considered one of the foremost experts on oil sites in the Gulf Coast of Mexico. A native of the region, he knew its potential firsthand; he was known for bragging about its untapped resources.

Ordóñez and Juan Virreyes, a geology professor at the University of Mexico, had been chosen by José Yves Limantour, the Mexican finance minister, to conduct a feasibility study along the Gulf Coast to locate potential sites for government-owned oil production. Limantour also hoped that the study would yield information about the finances of foreign-based concerns in the area such as Doheny's Mexican Petroleum Company (MPC) and the Waters-Pierce Company owned by Henry Clay Pierce.

At Limantour's request, Ordóñez and Virreyes traveled to Doheny's Ebano site and filed their reports. Ordóñez was convinced that Ebano's potential yield was great; however, Virreyes believed the contrary. For both political and financial reasons, the Instituto Geologico, which had sponsored the reports, supported Virreyes's claims; and it was his opinion that was sent to Limantour. Ordóñez protested profusely, prompting the president of the Instituto Geologico to hold up a small vial of heavy tar and say sarcastically, "That is the whole of the production of Ebano."[8] When Ordóñez then tried to argue about this, he was summarily fired.

Angry and eager to be vindicated, Ordóñez joined forces with Doheny and Canfield. He knew this move would further upset his former colleagues at the Instituto. Ordóñez soon proved to be one of MPC's greatest assets. An exacting man, completely fluent in English, he was obsessed with his work and totally loyal to Doheny. Doheny came to trust Ordóñez's opinions, and eventually the two became friends. Edward Doheny was frequently invited to the Ordóñez home in Mexico City; in exchange, Estelle Doheny began to ship homemade American jellies and jams and store-bought gifts to the Ordóñez family on birthdays and holidays.

In 1903 Doheny wrote to Ordóñez: "I hope that you will always remember and bear in mind that my interest in the successful carrying out of all details of our great plan is unabated, and that my determination is just as great as it ever has been to make a financial as well as an historical success of the Mexican Petroleum enterprise."[9] But by early 1904, Doheny himself was losing confidence, as Canfield's financial projections grew dire; without markedly increased oil production, the Mexican Petroleum Company might soon collapse. A miracle was needed, Doheny stressed. And then he asked if Ordóñez could produce one. Still hoping to outshine his former Instituto colleagues, Ordóñez told Doheny that he believed he could meet the challenge.

In March, Doheny and Ordóñez traveled to MPC's most recent drill site at Cerro de la Dicha. After inspecting the area, Ordóñez realized that Doheny's operations needed to be moved from their present flatlands location to the foot of the Cerro de la Pez (Hill of Tar). This area contained two of the largest *chapopoteras* (the local term for *chapopotes*) west of Tampico. Ordóñez reported to Doheny that the "bituminous oil" seeping to the surface in the *chapopoteras* was most likely caused from a weakened nexus of basalt and shale, which had been created millions of years ago when molten lava scorched the underground shale as it surged to the earth's surface.[10] The geologist assumed that Doheny would be excited by this information. But instead, Doheny bristled as he heard Ordóñez's report. If Ordóñez was right, then Doheny had grossly miscalculated and had wasted his company's time and money. He began to bicker with Ordóñez, out of embarrassment and stubbornness.

Ordóñez continued to patiently reason with Doheny. "He could spend entire hours speaking about only one negotiation, trying always to dominate the listener," Ordóñez said later about his boss. "If someone dared contradict him, he would start to shout, pound his fists, his eyes irritated and face-reddened."[11] Ordóñez also noted Doheny's "superior airs," an irritation to others.

Finally, Doheny uncharacteristically swallowed his pride and asked Ordóñez to select new drill sites. With Wylie, Canfield, and Doheny in tow, Ordóñez traveled first by rail, then by canoe to the La Pez area. Visible *chapopoteras* were only a few meters from steep lava outcroppings at the foot of a ridge. Doheny expressed mild pessimism, but Ordóñez argued to proceed. Wearily, Doheny ordered his crew to begin drilling. Several days passed without any success, and Doheny left the camp in disgust. He did not halt operations, though, and this forbearance enabled him to receive his miracle.

On Easter Sunday, April 3, 1904, three months after Doheny's men began laboring at the site, they struck oil at 1,450 feet below the surface. La Pez No. 1 gushed black liquid sky-high. Doheny's rejoicing was heard by all. The well soon was producing more than 1,000 barrels per day, gradually increasing its daily output to a startling 1,700 barrels. The oil was the best Doheny had produced in such quantities.[12] He lavished praise and gratitude on Ordóñez.

Doheny's celebration was tempered, however, by frightening logistical worries. The task of erecting a commercial oil plant in the remote jungle terrain of La Pez would be daunting. "Doheny was the first oilman equal to the challenge," notes historian Jonathan C. Brown.[13] Lands needed to be cleared, a water supply had to be created, and a narrow gauge railroad had to be built to transport the oil, because heavy crude could not be funneled through a pipeline. Although that method would have been faster and cheaper, heating the oil to increase its liquidity for such transport would have rendered it unfit for use as fuel.

With the La Pez well producing handsomely, Doheny once again encountered marketing difficulties. To whom could he sell the heavy crude? And at what price? While struggling with these questions, Doheny acquired two additional properties at Cerro Viejo and Cuchillo del Pulque, near Tuxpan, obtaining for them in the process concessionary exemptions from both state and municipal pipeline tax. At these sites, he hoped to produce enough kerosene to sell to millions of Mexicans nationwide. He also hoped to export oil to Great Britain and cut into Standard Oil's market.[14]

President Díaz was remaining extremely tolerant of MPC's presence in his country. During his lengthy regime from 1876 to 1911, Díaz was to allow more U.S. and European companies to exploit more sites, and market more Mexican oil, than any other national leader in the country's tumultuous history. Díaz's leniency increased competition for valuable terrain, and Doheny constantly worried that rival companies might suddenly discover untapped sites or, even worse, wrest control of the Mexican marketplace from him. He took some comfort in noting that his most lucrative locations did not draw attention since they were difficult to reach and were rarely mentioned in newspapers outside Mexico.

In June 1905, Doheny negotiated a fifteen-year contract to sell oil to the Mexican Central Railway, even though oil merchant Henry Clay Pierce, an avowed rival, was its board's chairman. The Mexican Central executives realized that they could save a considerable amount of money each year by using Doheny's domestically produced oil, especially since his price had recently dropped 50 percent because of increased supply. The previously rejected Doheny oil was now in good favor. The rail carrier was already purchasing some 6,000 barrels per day from Doheny, in effect keeping his company afloat. Now it would purchase additional petroleum to supply fifteen of its locomotives and would build large earthen reservoirs along its rail lines to store the "heavy molasses" oil.

Mexican Central looked forward to Doheny's promised 20 percent savings over the cost of coal. Press reports about Doheny's contract with the Mexican Central eventually reached the United States and influenced reluctant industry leaders to convert coal boilers to oil burners, a step they had resisted thus far.[15]

Following a four-month absence, Edward Doheny returned home. For her thirtieth birthday his gift to Estelle was a stunning gilt-wood Steinway grand piano, custom-made in the Louis XIV style. Under the lid was painted Estelle in a white lace dress at the entrance to Chester Place. Flanking the keyboard were two small, gilded wooden busts of Ned.

As usual, Estelle was overjoyed to see her husband. But she could not contain her frustration at his continued long absences. Sadly, her upset turned to badgering, and, after a particularly distressing confrontation, Edward abruptly left again for Mexico, berating her for her ill-humor. Immediately, Estelle penned an apology, sweetly but firmly pleading her cause: "I hope you are successful dearie in every way—I am awfully fond of my sweetheart and want him to realize his ambition. You'll forgive my unkind remarks I made last Friday—I am very sorry I made you unhappy. I love you too dearly for that but I want to be with you more. You don't really know how sweet I can be—you see so little of me."[16]

For the next several months, Estelle and Ned were alone again. They settled into their former routine, spending afternoons together and listening to Caruso on the gramophone. Occasionally Estelle, Ned, and Louise the cook would sip Welch's grape juice in Tiffany cocktail glasses, toast Doheny's health, and wish for his speedy return. Estelle Doheny began to attend social functions and even hosted several dinner parties of her own. But her melancholy as an abandoned spouse did not abate; her appetite deserted her and she lost weight during Doheny's long absence.

Ned, too, grew sullen when he learned that his father would not be returning to Los Angeles for his twelfth birthday. Estelle attempted to cheer him up by throwing a lavish party, inviting not only his school pals but all the Chester Place neighbors. At the party, she presented Ned with a custom-made billiard cue and told him that the gift was sent from Edward. But she confided to her mother: "I picked one out that suited him. I had six inches cut off and bored out so it weighs only 15 ounces. I intend to have a little cap put on the end with an engraving that reads 'ELD Jr. from Papa, Nov. 6 '05.'"[17]

Ned's growth spurt followed his birthday. Suddenly he was taller, more slender, muscular and handsome. He developed a funny, easygoing temperament that made him seem mature beyond his years. But he would show his immaturity when presented with an unpleasant or boring task; he would grow impatient and distant and, like most teenagers, concoct ways to escape his responsibilities.

During this time, six years after they had first moved in, Estelle was still making improvements to the compound at Edward's request. She had just completed a private shooting gallery and had workers renovating the front porch. All the projects were dutifully reported to Edward by Estelle and Ned. Finally, in December, they received great news from Edward: he agreed to return home for Christmas.

Estelle and Ned rejoiced, and Estelle hastily wrote, "I will be so glad to see you, just to get you in my arms and hug you good and tight. I can't hardly wait until I hear the engine come whistling around the pickle factory." Then, on a serious note, she cautioned her husband about Ned's fervent wish to spend private time with him: "He has expressed a desire to have his papa stay home the day or afternoon of his arrival so he can spend a little while with him—I told him you most certainly would, so please plan accordingly."[18]

Five The Golden Lane

After the joyous 1905 holiday season in Los Angeles with their wives and children, Edward Doheny and Charles Canfield returned to Mexico to direct their energies to the Mexican Petroleum Company. Doheny remained the enthusiastic and driving force behind the company, with Canfield working quietly at his side.

Emboldened by their success at Cerro de La Pez, and by their multi-year contract with the Mexican Central Railway, Doheny and Canfield were determined to acquire more oil sites. Doheny had become interested in the Huasteca, a coastal plain about seventy miles south of Tampico and several miles west of an undeveloped swampland known as Laguna de Tamiahua. The oil-rich lands of the Huasteca were said to be the most promising in Mexico, and they had recently been abandoned by a series of leaseholders who lacked the funds to exploit them.

The men had hoped to start their exploration of the Huasteca after the winter rains had ceased. But on January 27, 1906, tragedy changed their plans. While they were in the field away from base, frantic telegrams were being sent every few hours to the Doheny camp to tell them that Charles's wife, Chloe, had been murdered at their home in Los Angeles. On hearing the awful news, Canfield collapsed in Doheny's arms. Doheny made travel arrangements for a hasty return to Los Angeles. A locomotive from the Mexican Central Railway was summoned to meet Doheny's railcar at Sileo, Mexico, and carry the grief-stricken Canfield to El Paso, where a Southern Pacific engine hooked up Doheny's private car and whisked him home.[1]

When he reached Los Angeles, Charles learned the details of his wife's murder. She had been slain on the porch of their home by a discharged family coachman. Described in news accounts as a "dope fiend and half crazy," Morris Buck, twenty-eight, had approached Chloe Canfield for a $2,600 loan, but she had refused him. He had returned several days later, on January 27, 1906, and made a second enraged demand. When Chloe again said that she would not loan him any money, he drew his revolver and fired. Although wounded, Chloe grappled with the man, but he shot her again; this time the bullet pierced her chest. The sound of the shots attracted the attention of the Canfields' daughter, Daisy, who ran to the kitchen window, screaming, "He's killing mama!"

Buck then fired a third shot and Chloe Canfield slumped to the ground. Horrified witnesses reported that he remained on the porch "wandering coolly around, stepping over the wounded woman" and that he then finally seated himself in a chair on the verandah, gazing indifferently at the body slumped at his feet. Courageous neighbors carried the fatally injured woman past the gunman, into the mansion's master bedroom. Attempts were made to revive her, but Chloe could only murmur, "Oh give me air, I can't get air," before dying.

Special Officer Charles Foster of the Los Angeles Police Department, who arrived by bicycle, rushed toward the house with his pistol drawn. Morris Buck ran to the end of the porch, jumped onto the lawn, and ran down the street. A dozen or more men chased after him, as Foster fired his revolver twice. Buck continued down Eighth Street toward Westlake Park and the lake. Once inside the park, he pleaded with the boatman to lock him inside a small boathouse to protect him from the pursuing mob. "They will lynch me!" he cried.

Officer Foster found Buck crouched behind the boathouse counter. Without uttering a word, the gunman meekly surrendered his pistol.[2]

Distraught and enraged, Charles Canfield demanded that Morris Buck be executed for the murder of his wife. Thousands of citizens who read of Chloe Canfield's murder in local newspapers shared Canfield's grief. Soon, Canfield announced to reporters that he would spend millions if necessary to make sure the man hanged. News of the tragedy was splashed across the front pages of the newspapers for weeks. Charles remained in seclusion inside the family's stately home. Edward could do little more than offer his partner moral support.

Edward and Estelle Doheny were deeply stricken by the loss of their good friend; Chloe, with her eldest daughter, Florence, had spent many companionable days together with Estelle while Edward and Charles were in Mexico. Estelle, grieving and frightened, took to her bedchamber in mourning and remained there for days.

The murder trial commenced several months later. Morris Buck's defense attorneys sought to have him adjudged insane, while the prosecution attempted to convince the jury that he was a cold-blooded killer. The defense introduced Morris's brother William, newly arrived from Arizona, as a witness: William testified that years before, Morris had been hit in the skull with a cleaver by a drunken man at a mining camp. A nephew further testified that Morris had been kicked in the head by a horse, and other defense witnesses recalled various head injuries suffered by Morris. At the end of this testimony the defense dramatically ordered Morris Buck to bow his head so the jury could see his scars.[3]

During cross-examination of Morris's brother, the prosecution exposed William himself as a convicted murderer who had been serving a life sentence in the Arizona Territorial Prison at Yuma. He had been pardoned and released after he killed a fellow prisoner during an uprising, purportedly saving the warden's life. In the end, despite substantial testimony by defense witnesses about alleged mental deficiencies, the jury found Morris Buck guilty of murder. He would be executed by hanging at San Quentin Prison on December 6, 1907.[4]

Edward and Estelle Doheny attended Chloe Canfield's funeral and subsequent burial in the Canfield family mausoleum at Los Angeles' Evergreen Cemetery. They continued their support for Canfield by attending sessions of the highly publicized trial. As Edward prepared to return to Mexico, he was forced to admit that his grief-stricken friend might not be able to resume his responsibilities as a partner of MPC. Since learning of his wife's death, Charles had become lethargic and depressed. He showed no interest in business dealings—or life in general. Doheny later commented that Canfield was forever changed by the tragedy and was certain that had it not been for his surviving children, Charles would have preferred to join Chloe in death.

When Canfield declined to return to Mexico, Doheny did not insist that he do so. Instead, Doheny boarded the "Estelle" alone and assumed sole responsibility for the burgeoning Mexican Petroleum Company.

Doheny now turned to Herbert Wylie for support and asked him to assume many of Canfield's responsibilities. When Wylie showed great competence at his new duties, Doheny promoted him from superintendent to general manager. He began to rely heavily on the large, amiable Wylie, who was able to handle the myriad complexities involved in producing, storing, transporting, and marketing the company's oil.

Herbert Wylie was well suited to his new position in experience and temperament. Born in Dublin in 1867, he was the eldest son of a prominent preacher. Wylie had been educated at the Royal Belfast Institute of Ireland, and he came to the United States at the age of nineteen. In 1893 he went to Los Angeles where he had a brief partnership with J. S. Maltman in contract drilling in the Los Angeles oil fields, not long after Doheny and Canfield had brought in their first well. He had accepted employment with Doheny as superintendent of Doheny's Petroleum Development Company, where he had managed Doheny's wells superbly. Now in Mexico, Wylie proved himself a "master of men and master of nature," and soon was nothing short of Doheny's "Industrial General."[5]

Soon the men became close friends as well as business associates. Doheny invited Wylie to Chester Place and sold him one of the homes inside the compound, where Wylie would reside with his wife during his infrequent visits to Los Angeles when he attended to Doheny's U.S.-based business.

In the fall of 1906, following the Mexican Central Railroad's commitment to purchase his Ebano oil, Doheny felt emboldened to renew his aborted exploration of other potentially oil-rich lands. He asked Wylie and Dr. Norman Bridge to travel with him to the Huasteca region to survey properties. Bridge, a close family friend, was a prominent Chicago physician who had moved to Los Angeles in 1891. He had invested $5,000 in Mexican Petroleum Company stock in its early days when Doheny most needed capital; Doheny had never forgotten the gesture. Now, three years after Doheny had formed the company, Bridge had become an active and conscientious member of its board of directors.

Doheny, Wylie, and Bridge traveled south by water from Tampico to the mouth of the Carbajal River and through a canal a few miles long into the shallow Lake Tamiahua, before mounting horses to ride into the interior. The first leg of their trip was by gasoline launch, operated by local guides who could skillfully pilot across the shallow lake, which was filled with sandbars and vast fields of water plants. More than once, the expedition's propellers became tangled in debris, and the men would spend hours idly waiting for the guides to set the boat free. On one occasion, this took an entire night of effort. Writing later about the expedition, Bridge described the camp that night. They decided to build a small campfire; Doheny made a "perfection of a shortcake" and baked it in a pan leaned up toward the fire. The men ate every bite, calling the meal a "banquet." Later, they bathed in the lake, and slept soundly under the stars.

From Tamiahua, the expedition proceeded south along the Canal Angosta through a tortuously narrow channel in the dense forest. Here they went by a canoe poled by two men, one at each end. The explorers now chose to travel at night, in order to avoid the incessant heat and the harassment of jungle insects. They slept in the canoe. Bridge recalled that the polers sang softly until daylight, in a strange and precious lullaby.[6]

Once ashore, the men battled *pinolillas* (wood ticks), dense foliage, and torrential rain. Some jungle areas were so thickly overgrown that they were nearly impassable. The guides were forced to cut *brechas* (clearings) with their machetes. Deeper into the Huasteca, the expedition came upon farmhouses belonging to the local indigenous people, the Tuxpan. The buildings were of crude construction—mostly adobe or mud plastered on "loose bamboo wattle-work," topped by thatched roofs.[7]

The Tuxpan were extremely cordial to the visiting white men. They saluted the Americans and shouted *"adíos"* (go with God) when they parted company. The friendly Tuxpan offered the oilmen a meal that in the jungle was a sumptuous repast: eggs, chicken, tortillas, frijoles, and coffee with brown coarse sugar and milk. The eggs and frijoles (dark beans) were cooked in hot lard. Doheny later remarked to Estelle Doheny that the frijoles were better than anything he had ever tasted.[8] Although the Tuxpan showed Doheny, Bridge, and Wylie how to eat using their tortillas folded like little scoops to bring food to their mouths, the adventurers insisted on using the forks and spoons they had carried in their pockets.

The men then traveled farther inland, to the remote spot where Doheny hoped to drill for oil. Doheny inspected several visible oil exudes. The oil was of lighter weight (and therefore more valuable) than that produced at Ebano. Seeing this, he became extremely excited. Doheny quickly surveyed the land with Wylie and concluded that he had to buy the property right away—before someone else beat him to it. It took two months of heated negotiations with landowner Manuel Saldivar before he could acquire the properties.[9] During the Christmas season in 1906, Doheny entertained all the Huasteca landowners lavishly, bringing them to his oil camp at Ebano by boat and horseback. Edward wrote to Estelle four days after Christmas about his experiences:

My Dear Mommie,
   During a lull at lunch I am writing this. I received today a Christmas card marked or addressed "My Sweetheart." I wish I could have been within reach of *my sweetheart* when I received it.
   I was at Ebano at Christmas, when a large aggregation of Huastecans had congregated to do business with us.
   I succeeded, after a hot time in getting the owner of the La Pitahaya, Manuel Saldivar to live up to his arrangement made in Tuxpan in October. I paid him $49,000 and we are now owners of 5000 acres of surface and all subsoil rights of said Hacienda.
   I can't give any opinion as to when I can get away. Everything is progressing favorably. Inform Canfield. Hug little Ned for me and tell

him that on Christmas I wished he could be at Ebano to see the games, although I was in the office and did not see them. I know from hearsay that they had a fine time. The men were jumping, running races, throwing heavy weights from the shoulder etc. At the latter game, Wylie beat everybody in camp, even Kirkham, the heavyweight acrobat.

I hope you all had a good time and will not suffer any bad effects. I will return the day the business reaches a stopping point. Kiss each other for me. I showed your pictures and the case that Ned gave me for Christmas to Wylie and many others. They all thought it was beautiful and I was mightily proud of both mugs. Lots of love to you from "fadder."

Affectionately,

Edward Doheny[10]

Later, he traveled by train to Mexico City, where he met with his lawyers and bankers, then lunched at the American Club. Following his successful efforts to acquire the Casiano Hacienda in the Huasteca region, Doheny created the Huasteca Petroleum Company (organized under the laws of Maine on February 12, 1907) with capital of $15 million. He also created two subsidiaries, the Tuxpan Petroleum and Tamiahua Petroleum Companies. By now his Mexican holdings were so extensive that he was instructed by his lawyers to designate the Mexican Petroleum Company as a presiding holding entity for both his northern fields near Tampico and his southern fields. Looking ahead, Doheny secured additional concessionary contracts with the Mexican government. These enabled him in 1908 to expand his opportunities in the Tamaulipas and San Luis Potosi regions, close to the Ebano site in his northern fields.

The government also approved Doheny's plans to build a refinery at Mata Redonda, across the river from Tampico, and to construct a pipeline from the refinery to Huasteca. Furthermore, it permitted Doheny to import equipment duty-free and export oil "free of all taxes and duties." In return, Doheny agreed to invest $250,000 (500,000 pesos) in the project over the next five years and to submit all plans for construction to Mexico's Ministry of Development. In 1910, however, the Mexican government instituted an unexpected oil tax hike, raising its per-ton rate to fifty dollars. Doheny's oil shipments, previously exempt, now were ordered taxed. This upset Doheny terribly, because under the new mandate, his oil would be taxed twice: once as a petroleum product and then again as it was transported from Tuxpan, in its crude form. Even worse, if the crude were shipped to yet another Mexican port, it could be taxed a third time.[11]

Despite these constantly changing and perpetually daunting government rules and regulations, President Díaz still favored Doheny and his enterprises. Doheny affirmed this, but added that some of Díaz's supporters "considered our interests . . . inimical to theirs."[12] There was a faction concerned that the oil companies would reap profits that should stay within the country. Opposition to foreign business interests existed in the highest political circles, and conflicts and unpredictable entanglements were an inescapable part of Mexican business dealings. It was well established that a foreign businessman's political savoir faire could determine his success or failure in Mexico. Doheny attempted to exploit his relationship with Díaz in order to further his corporate concerns. He also initiated friendships with the governors of the states in which he operated: San Luis Potosi, Tamaulipas, and Veracruz, in particular. Although Doheny never obtained land grants from these men, he was able to secure spectacular financial concessions in the form of tax and import/export duty exemptions and other accommodations.

Some historians would later criticize Doheny for politicizing the economic environment; one went so far as to assert that Doheny regularly resorted to bribery to further his goals. Dan La Botz writes, "He understood that in Mexico, as in the United States, bribery and corruption were intrinsic to the political structure. Doheny was prepared to pay the right man for the right policy." Gene Z. Hanrahan, author of *The Bad Yankee*, reports that Doheny reputedly told a member of the American Tampico Club, "You first try to win a man over, and failing this, you buy him."[13] Hanrahan also insists that Doheny used one of his Mexican attorneys, Joaquin D. Casasus, to deliver bribes to key members of the Díaz administration: "Still Doheny may have carried [bribery] to new heights for there were hints that it was his *mordida* [bribe] which convinced the Instituto Geologico and Díaz officials not to nationalize the fledgling oil industry in the early years."[14]

Doheny, however, denied such allegations, which circulated widely even during his stay in Mexico. He claimed that his visits with various Mexican leaders and officials were merely friendly tête-à-têtes: "I can testify that the treatment was uniformly courteous [and] considerate. [No] other means were necessary to obtain the rights and privileges which we were requesting, [beyond a] statement of a good reason." But according to Jonathan C. Brown, who quotes Doheny's denial, the oilman took perverse pride in overcoming the open hostility and obstructionism he encountered from some of the lower-level Mexican politicians. He believed that his friendship with Porfirio Díaz would enable him to overcome any political obstacles in his path: "It made his ultimate success in Mexico that much sweeter," notes Brown. "It confirmed he was a man of destiny, and they were among the unbelievers."[15]

It was particularly galling to Doheny to have to renegotiate concessions he thought he had already achieved. In an industry known for financial peril, these sudden policy changes were no small matter. But he had coolly faced the terrors of oil production before. He raised the immense amounts of capital needed, knowing that the result could be dry holes and a total loss. Success also had its risk—oil flowing in abundance, but no way to transport it or store it, or lack of market or falling prices. Failure at any point could mean disaster.

Doheny had known that exploration in Mexico would take him to a part of the world stranded in an earlier era—he knew that building roads, rail facilities, and pipelines would be an additional capital drain. What he had not anticipated were the problems associated with land acquisition, labor, and the vagaries of government edicts. He thought he had arrived early enough in the Huasteca to beat the competition and have a fairly free hand. To his surprise, and to that of other oil company agents later, there were strange traditions in Mexico regarding matters of title. Surveys were often inaccurate or lacking, and boundaries were often determined by informal agreements. Title issues submitted to legal procedures meandered through a system in which the judiciary frequently resorted to delay when justice was felt to be at variance with the facts. Landowners were sometimes hostile and suspicious of the oilmen, sometimes canny or naive—one widow sold the same valuable leasehold to two different oil companies. Tribal elders were reluctant to sell or lease the lands of indigenous peoples, irrespective of price, and often refused to have pipelines traverse ancestral parcels.

Doheny had thought his operations would be welcomed as a long-awaited blessing in a backward economy, and he couldn't understand why he was so little appreciated. He was later to describe himself as having paid fair wages and as having operated in strict accord with accepted business practices. Doheny could not understand why the local inhabitants failed to meet his expectations as workers, forcing him to bring additional U.S. and other foreign laborers to his drill sites. The work habits of the Tuxpan may have been well suited to the steamy, stultifying climate, but their pace was not conducive to the schedule needed for oil production. They also had an inexplicable habit of walking away from the job after a period of time and returning to their villages—turning their backs on more pay than they could otherwise see in a lifetime.

The foreigners coped with the heat, the lack of sanitation, and the frequent outbreaks of yellow fever. The mud, filth, and insect infestation would grow so bad at times that the oil camp's housing had to be demolished and burned. The foreign workers treated the Mexicans with disdain and there was little transfer of knowledge between them—nothing like the training Díaz had hoped for. Among the local inhabitants, superstition continued to prevail. If a well was out of control and shooting oil into a 600-foot-high column, Doheny saw it as money going into the air. The Tuxpan gave it more ominous meaning. When a well was struck by lightning and set ablaze, they took note. The disastrous Los Bocas blowout, which left a crater several miles wide and deforested and poisoned the surrounding area, making it uninhabitable for generations, made a fearful impression on the indigenous people.

The sudden surge of money into the region upset traditional relationships. Laborers left old employers stranded as they took to the oil fields and refineries. Landholders sold or leased land out from under longtime occupants. Politicians all wanted a piece of the lucrative industry, and plans to tax and exploit the sudden marvel swirled ominously about. Paying bribes, making gifts, and trading favors were accepted practices. Doheny found himself trying to operate a business in a bewildering world, one he never came to understand—though in it he risked everything he had.

Gambling that his friendship with Díaz would remain stable, and believing that he would soon be able to produce a lighter grade of Mexican petroleum in sufficient quantities to justify his expenditures, Doheny boldly expanded his operations in the "Faja de Oro" (Golden Lane), the location of his potential Casiano well sites. Still confident about the fields he had acquired in 1906, Doheny ordered his crew to begin constructing a tremendous new pipeline from the jungles of Casiano to the port of Tampico, 125 miles north, to transport the "oceans of oil" that he anticipated from the Casiano wells. In addition, Doheny ordered the construction of ten pumping stations and twelve 55,000-barrel steel tanks. When one landowner refused to permit the pipe to be laid across his land, Doheny became enraged; to Wylie's amazement, he ordered Wylie to keep building despite the seven-mile gap.

This massive undertaking was begun before one barrel of oil had been pumped from Casiano. Doheny was absolutely certain about the potential of the wells. Relying on the principles that Ordóñez taught him at Cerro de la Pez in Ebano, he had undertaken no geological surveys prior to the drilling at Casiano. To his shock and dismay, the first five holes his workers drilled were completely dry. Nevertheless, Doheny plunged ahead with his plans, getting further in debt. He needed to produce at least 3,000 barrels of oil per day to cover the costs of the huge oil pipeline. Doheny's confidence that he would strike oil may have been based on a report of oil seepages obtained from an English engineer and contractor, Sir Weetman Pearson (made Lord Cowdray by the Crown in 1917), who also had large oil holdings in Mexico.

Pearson had built Mexico's Tehuantepec National Railroad and salvaged Mexico City's Grand Canal under Díaz-supported government contracts. After the Doheny-Canfield discoveries, Pearson had organized a British company to conduct oil explorations on Tampico's southern coast. It was his well, Los Bocas, which should have produced an impressive quantity of oil for the British businessman, that had spectacularly exploded: catching fire, it burned out of control for forty days. The great conflagration was seen as a mysterious beacon by ships many miles out in the Gulf of Mexico.

The firestorm completely destroyed Pearson's well. No one could estimate how many millions of barrels of oil had been lost.[16] Pearson abandoned the well but realized, as did Doheny, that tremendous quantities of oil remained hidden in the region. The Casiano property, from which Doheny was optimistically building his pipeline, was only a few miles south of Pearson's abandoned crater.

THE GREAT CASIANO NO. 7

Early in 1910, Charles Canfield was emotionally prepared to return to Mexico and resume his corporate responsibilities. To Doheny's great relief, Canfield still possessed his keen instinct and zest for the oil business. Within weeks of Canfield's arrival in Mexico, they selected a drill spot in the Casiano District that would ultimately unleash a great gusher for the oilmen.

On Sunday, May 1, 1910, thirteen weeks before the gusher blew, Doheny wrote to Estelle about his hopes for an anticipated windfall:

> My dear Mommie,
>   The work is progressing well—in fact I was astonished and pleased at the manner in which Wylie had succeeded in handling the construction on most of the pipeline.
>   The route selected is very much easier than I thought it would be. . . . The right of way, or "brecha," is cut the entire distance and is a *very fine* natural automobile road. The pumping stations are exceedingly well located and the machinery and manner of installation are of the best workmanship—The pipeline will probably be in operation before July 1 next. The two weeks at Juan Casiano are very good ones and will soon be supplemented by others of the same character.
>   I expect to meet General Díaz on Wednesday by appointment and will probably start home on Thursday. We have had a very pleasant party of men. They are without exception jolly good travelers.
>   I returned about an hour ago from an auto trip to the Tanusics Water Station and to the Chifol wells and had a 35 mile spin. Pretty warm, my face [is] badly burned.
>   I received two letters from you, one typewritten the other with pen. I received one from Ned last night enclosing his examination papers. I am glad he is doing well. He asked me to wire Gill what I thought about his

not letting Ned run the car alone. I won't let Ned run it until I return. I am going to write Ned now—so good bye for today and lots of love to you both.

Yours affectionately,

El Eduardo[17]

While Doheny sought financing for the construction of pump stations, boilers, and receiving tanks, the men continued to drill. At last, a gusher, Casiano No. 6, was sending oil into a holding tank. The volume gradually increased; by the end of ten days, oil was pouring out at a rate of 15,000 barrels per day. Satisfied with the well's prolific output, which exceeded his ability to store it, Doheny temporarily halted production in order to wait for the pipeline to be completed.

Through a lucky bit of timing an important investor was at the site when Casiano No. 6 boisterously erupted July 26. Joseph C. Trees and Mike Benedum were highly individualistic and successful Pittsburgh wildcatters who formerly had worked for the profitable South Penn Oil Company of Pennsylvania (a Standard Oil Company producing subsidiary).[18] Hoping to entice them to invest, Doheny invited the men to tour his camp at Casiano and inspect the Mexican properties. Trees, without Benedum, arrived and was caught up in the excitement of the anticipated gusher.

Doheny explained that after his crew drilled deep enough, they would lay piping in the hole to stay the flow of oil until additional storage tanks became available or the oil pipeline was finished. But as Doheny was finishing his sentence, there came a familiar ominous rumble, followed by a volcanic explosion of oil from the well.

A few months later, on September 11, Casiano No. 7 arrived, an even more tremendous gusher, flowing at the unbelievable rate of 60,000 to 70,000 barrels per day. The well's yield was so great that it soon turned sections of jungle glistening black. The roar of oil thundering from the derrick was deafening; the output was such that Doheny's crew was forced to burn several hundred thousand barrels of oil to keep the well's concrete reservoir from overflowing and contaminating a nearby river. When the derrick's valve finally closed and the oil was directed into the pipeline, hydraulic force burst the pipe's casing, causing yet another river of oil to shoot forth 300 feet away from the derrick. On September 20, Doheny was able to have the valve adjusted so that the pressure was reduced to 295 pounds, and the well decreased its yield to 23,000 barrels per day with no oil escaping.[19] Describing Doheny's wells to Benedum, Trees exclaimed, "Those [wells] we drilled in Illinois and Caddo were just little creeks of oil. I tell you those Mexican wells are oceans."[20]

To Doheny's delight, Trees and Benedum invested $500,000 for 5,000 shares of preferred stock and 2,500 shares of common stock in the Mexican Petroleum Company. Two other Pittsburgh financiers also invested lesser amounts, after hearing their optimistic reports.[21] Doheny and Canfield were exhilarated at their long-overdue good luck. Wylie directed his crew to work feverishly to build a 750,000-barrel earthen reservoir and 105 storage tanks of 55,000-barrel capacity. At Doheny's behest, Wylie ordered more pipeline, terminal storage, derricks, and drilling machinery, and he began construction on additional pumping stations to accommodate the oil. The pipeline was installed by Wylie's crew in record time. The amounts of oil now produced at Casiano were so overwhelming that Doheny was able to obtain an emergency order from President Díaz to construct his oil pipeline over the recalcitrant landowner's acreage. Doheny agreed to pay for any resulting damage. The missing seven miles of pipe were quickly laid in place.

With the jumbo pipeline completed, millions of barrels of oil flowed to Doheny's shipping facilities at Tampico. The production from the Casiano gusher was the envy of oilmen throughout the world. At its peak the well yielded an extraordinary 70,000 barrels a day, and for the next nine years it produced all the oil that Canfield and Doheny could market. (By the time it ceased flowing in 1919 the well had produced 85,000,000 barrels of oil, which is among the greatest oil yields of all time.) To Doheny's delight the oil from the Casiano region measured 20 degrees Baume, sufficiently light to be used for kerosene, fuel oil, lubricating oil, and gasoline.

The amazing well at Casiano No. 7 exceeded even Doheny's grandiose predictions. Hearing the solid sound of pipeline machinery smoothly working filled the oilman's heart with pride and gratitude. Doheny and

Canfield stood side by side watching the Casiano produce liquid gold. Laughing, Doheny said to Canfield that prospecting for oil was much like heaven: "Many were called and few were chosen."

The year 1910 saw the arrival of Casiano No. 7 followed by yet another gusher, two extraordinary wells for Doheny and Canfield, forecasting riches equal to Doheny's dream; but Mexico itself was unraveling at the seams. The economic leap into the modern age that President Díaz longed for was not to occur.

Strikes were breaking out across the country as disenchanted workers joined forces with ambitious rebels and former Díaz supporters. The peasantry, dislocated and set adrift in the course of legal decisions about private property, roamed into the cities and became part of one protesting faction or another. Díaz's network of police became more oppressive as opposition to his modernization policies grew. In these troubled years prior to the revolution, the booming oil industry in which Doheny played a central role was the healthiest sector of the economy. Political writers and cartoonists found abundant material for satire amid the political turmoil, and the wealthy foreign oil barons were a frequent target.

José Guadalupe Posada, a popular illustrator and poster artist of the day, created vicious attacks on Díaz, accusing him of giving Mexico's vast natural wealth to rich foreigners who in return supported Díaz and had kept him entrenched in power for thirty-four years. Posada depicted the plight of the workers and peasantry and the arrogant disinterest of the government and the elite. His blackly humorous portraits presented human figures as skeletons, *calaveras*, mimicking important events and everyday life.[22]

The skeleton was a familiar figure in Mexican folk art. Skulls were part of the iconography of pre-Hispanic indigenous art as well as a religious symbol of Catholicism. *Calaveras* came to express Mexicans' stoic, but not humorless, acceptance of death and the random workings of fate. Posada used *calaveras* in his trenchant criticism of Díaz, protesting the imposition of foreign philosophies of progress, private property, and rampant free enterprise on traditional Mexican ways. In "Collision between a Streetcar and a Hearse," the skeleton-filled streetcar represents electricity, machinery, and modern inventions; the horse-drawn carriage, the broken coffin, and the hapless corpse depict tradition run down by *progress*.

Las Calaveras in Mexican lore were a reminder of omniscient, malevolent fate, a warning of the possibility of disaster, even in the midst of good fortune—the skeleton at the feast. The image was a part of the Mexican psyche that Edward Doheny never understood. During his long years in Mexico, Doheny watched the street festivals with cavorting skeletons and the annual Day of the Dead celebrations with their ubiquitous skulls. But the Mexican ease with a quizzical and mocking fate did not comport with his self-confident belief that with energy, diligence, and right-mindedness he could control his destiny.

As news of Doheny and Canfield's great gusher spread around the world, oilmen, drillers, lease takers, and fortune seekers swarmed into Mexico.[23] They arrived at Tampico by boat and train. The "Great Mexican Oil Boom" had now begun, and hundreds of would-be oil producers were searching the *monte,* the tropical rain forests of the Veracruz lowlands, for potential drill sites and available oil leases.

Doheny had to move oceans of oil into the marketplace, and he had to do it quickly. He asked his new investor, Mike Benedum, to approach Standard Oil for a substantial sales contract, as Standard was one of only a handful of concerns that could afford to buy oil in such quantities. Next to finding oil, Benedum's greatest pleasure was just such a trading contest. In New York, Benedum talked Standard Oil's executives into buying 12,000 barrels daily at $0.52 a barrel; pleased, he even threw in a free shipload of oil for their engines to test. Triumphant, Benedum returned to Tampico, but to his shock Doheny opposed the transaction. Doheny said that he was in negotiations with the Mellons and believed he could forge a better deal with Gulf Oil. Benedum was so annoyed that he and Trees decided to sell their Mexican Petroleum Company stock and return to Pennsylvania; the association abruptly ended.[24]

In hindsight, it should have been apparent that the strong personalities of Benedum and Doheny would mean a short-lived relationship. Both men were fiercely independent, stubborn, and aggressive. The two were shrewd bargainers, though Benedum had more experience in dealing with U.S. oil purchasers. Following their breakup, Benedum advised Standard Oil against the Mexican Petroleum Company deal. Benedum's timing could not have been worse for Doheny; he was unable to conclude his negotiations with Gulf Oil, and now the deal with Standard was no longer available. To Doheny's dismay, the Standard Oil executives now offered him only $0.39 cents a barrel.

As the Mexican Petroleum Company stood on the brink of drowning in its vaunted ocean of oil, rescue came from an unexpected direction. A controversial decision by the U.S. Supreme Court shook the Rockefeller boardroom at 26 Broadway in New York but saved the fortunes of Doheny's Mexican empire. In May 1911 the Court's historic and sweeping order broke the giant Standard Oil Company Trust into thirty-four separate companies.[25] Before the restructuring, the enormous company transported more than four-fifths of all oil produced in Pennsylvania, Ohio, and Indiana. It refined more than three-fourths of the nation's crude oil, marketed the majority of domestic kerosene, and controlled its own virtual navy with over seventy-eight steamers and nineteen sailing vessels.[26] Cartoons of the day depicted Standard Oil as an octopus with a stranglehold on the industry.

After the Court-ordered breakup, the largest remaining entity was Standard Oil of New Jersey, which eventually became Exxon; it retained almost half of the former company's total net value. Next in size, with 9 percent of the net value, was Standard Oil of New York, which later became Mobil; others were Standard Oil (California), which eventually became Chevron; Standard Oil of Ohio, which later became Sohio and subsequently the American arm of British Petroleum (BP); Standard Oil of Indiana, which became Amoco; Continental Oil, which became Conoco; and Atlantic, later part of ARCO.[27]

Pursuant to the breakup, the linchpin of the old organization, Standard Oil of New Jersey (a.k.a. Jersey Standard), inherited refineries, oil tankers, and marketing apparatus—but no oil-producing subsidiaries. As a result, Jersey Standard was now receptive to Doheny's sales pitch for his Mexican crude. Jersey purchased 2 million barrels a year for a period of five years, at a handsome rate per barrel. In addition, it paid much of its fees in advance, to Doheny's great relief.[28] Other customers appeared. Soon Doheny was able to procure contracts to sell his oil to the National Railways, Waters-Pierce Oil Company, Mexican Natural Gas Company, Gulf Refining Company, and the Atchison, Topeka, and Santa Fe Railway.

With his Mexican properties finally proving lucrative, Doheny concentrated his efforts on increasing his visibility in the New England and North Atlantic market. He succeeded spectacularly. Over the next few years, his oil sales in that marketplace would increase from zero to millions of barrels per year. He was the beneficiary of a "new era" that "had quickly come into existence," as Daniel Yergin notes in his history of the oil industry. "It was born of several coincidences: the rapid rise of the automobile; the discovery of new oil provinces in Texas, Oklahoma, California, and Kansas; new competitors; and technological advances in refining. Added to these, of course, were the far-reaching implications of the break-up of Standard Oil and the resulting restructuring of the industry."[29]

Doheny was supplying demand in the new petroleum market with fuel oil for steamships and industry and with gasoline for automobiles. He continued to maintain a strong presence in the traditional market for kerosene and lubricating oils. It was his good fortune to have extraordinary wells producing abundant product, for which he luckily had outlets. He attributed his achievement to hard work and shrewdness—and failed to notice *las calaveras* in the shadows.

Mexican officials were looking hungrily at the foreign oil holdings. Mexican workers were pressuring the government for social services they thought they had been promised and felt they deserved. Unemployed and disoriented peasants were turning to banditry or joining militias. The foreign-owned oil businesses were booming, and there was a general feeling that the industry was not giving back to Mexico a fair share of the profits. Nor was fear of government encroachment Doheny's only worry. Sir Weetman Pearson struck paydirt when his newest well, Potrero del Llano No. 4, began to produce nearly 110,000 barrels of oil per day. From that moment, Doheny's exclusive reign in Mexico was over.

Doheny unhappily watched Pearson create the Eagle Oil Company (El Aguila) and appoint President Díaz's son as a member of his board. Pearson then organized the Eagle Oil Transport Company and Anglo-

Mexican Petroleum Company. The British engineer and former member of the House of Commons (where he was known as "the member for Mexico") solidified his political friendships in Mexico through favors, loans, and gifts. He considered it expedient to "lean over backwards" to favor the Mexicans in all his business dealings.[30] His wife, Lady Annie Cass Pearson, presided over a well-appointed colonial mansion in Mexico City and threw lavish parties for Mexican society.

Doheny realized that he needed to increase oil sales north of the border in order to absorb the production from the Golden Lane. To sell his oil to the north, he had to get it there—transportation was his weak link. He thus shuttled more funds into his pipeline, tank, refinery, and shipping projects, purchasing six oceangoing tankers so he would not have to rely on third-party transporters. To accomplish this he needed additional investors. A New York investment bank, William Salomon and Company, agreed to finance $5 million worth of MPC's securities, backed by mortgages on Doheny's Mexican properties. The transportation problems grew dire when his tankers were slow in being delivered. The first, which arrived in 1912, was joyously received and named the *Herbert G. Wylie*, after Doheny's general manager. To Doheny's great relief, the remaining five tankers were delivered within the next year. He named each tanker after important men in his company: *C. A. Canfield, Norman Bridge, Charles E. Harwood, Edward L. Doheny Jr.,* and *J. Oswald Boyd.*

Doheny continued to keep an active watch on Pearson's activities. He feared that this British competitor would threaten his burgeoning Mexican enterprise or steal his place as the favorite foreign son of Porfirio Díaz. Doheny knew the importance of political connections and knew his secured place in Mexico was dependent on Díaz's support. Unfortunately, Díaz's protection was soon to evaporate, leaving Doheny's great empire at risk.

Six Powered by Oil

Doheny's ambition for great wealth had been realized. One aghast writer has estimated that after the fantastic oil strikes in the Golden Lane, Doheny reaped nearly $10 million a year from his Mexican ventures. His personal fortune was estimated to be as much as $75 million.[1]

If the Mexican political climate had not darkened at this time, Doheny would have continued to amass great wealth. But as President Díaz celebrated his thirty-fourth year in power, Francisco I. Madero, a wealthy industrialist and landowner from northern Mexico, decided to run against the president. Although Díaz attempted to crush this opposition, the ranks of Madero's supporters continued to swell. Internal strife grew, and rebellion took seed—the Revolution in Mexico had begun. The Mexican Liberal Party, led by Ricardo Florés Majón, attempted to overthrow Díaz by instigating a series of strikes at large industrial centers.

On May 11, 1911, as Doheny's first shipment of Mexican crude left the port of Tampico bound for Sabine, Texas, President Porfirio Díaz was ousted from power. As he fled to Europe, Madero assumed office as the new president of Mexico. Doheny had lost his protector; the revolution threatened his entire oil empire as Madero's soldiers shut down mining and drilling operations, commandeered rail tracks, and destroyed trains. Many foreign investors feared that their businesses would be seized and their workers harmed. Once again, as had happened many times before in his life, Doheny, flush with victory, stood to lose everything. Madero's unstable regime could appropriate his holdings at any time and he would be powerless to stop it.

The first sign of trouble for Doheny's company occurred when Mexican demand for petroleum products fell dramatically. The Mexican Central Railways (now known as the National Railways) accepted only half the oil it had contracted to buy from Doheny, and it could not produce the cash even for this lesser purchase.[2] Doheny consulted legal experts and political strategists to determine what, if any, precautionary steps he could take to secure his Mexican holdings. Because the new regime looked tenuous, the recommended course was to wait it out; but sitting back was hard for Doheny, with hundreds of thousands of barrels of oil at risk in his Mexican tanks.

Hoping to raise additional capital during this anxious time, Edward Doheny visited Salomon Company's Paris office, traveling to France with Estelle and Ned, who had just graduated from Los Angeles High School. By taking his family on a first-class tour of Europe's great cities, Doheny would keep his mind off his pressing Mexican concerns. It was a rare holiday for Doheny, though it was also punctuated with business calls.

Ned was eager to see this part of the world; over the previous few years, he had grown into a handsome, slim teenager, who showed great curiosity about everything and already had a steady girlfriend. He was a far cry from the melancholy, pudgy child who had complained about his father's long absences seven years earlier. On his return from Europe, Ned would matriculate at Stanford University in Palo Alto, California, perhaps study law or business, and then join his father's company. Like his father, Ned had great facility at mathematics.

Edward surprised and excited Ned by permitting him to take along his girlfriend, Lucy Marceline Smith, on the extended European trip. Seventeen-year-old Lucy was the youngest daughter of William Henry Smith, vice president of the Pasadena Rapid Transit District Company. Attractive and intelligent, she had recently graduated with honors from South Pasadena High School. The Smiths were enthusiastic about their daughter's blossoming relationship with Ned, and readily consented to Lucy's joining the Dohenys for the long holiday.

In the spring of 1912, Edward, Estelle, Ned, Lucy, and the family chauffeur, "Old George," left Los Angeles for New York City. After a short stay at the Plaza Hotel, the group boarded the RMS *Olympic* and set sail for London on the morning of April 14. The Dohenys' first-class cabin was filled with flowers, fruit baskets, and wires that had been sent by business colleagues and well-wishers. Publishing baron William Randolph Hearst had sent Doheny a set of European maps and a guidebook that he had penned himself. He also had one of his employees contact the Dohenys once they were aboard ship to determine if they needed any other services.

Estelle found Hearst's guidebook both informative and entertaining; throughout the trip, she would refer to it religiously in order not to waste "unnecessary time seeing what we don't want to." And when Estelle wrote to her mother about Hearst's generosity in composing an itinerary for the couple, she commented, "He spent a great deal of time on it—more than Edward would do for anyone."[3]

When the great ship departed, the family remained at the rails to watch the shoreline disappear. At the beginning they encountered rough seas, but in deeper ocean the ship coursed smoothly. At their first meal in the ship's great dining hall, Estelle discovered their table to be the loveliest in the room. Later, the family wandered the ship's deck, marveling at the luxurious staterooms and at the enormous ship's swimming pools, game courts, gymnasium, and Turkish steam baths.

For the first time in many months, Edward and Estelle were able to spend time alone together. Estelle wrote her mother that following their first night aboard ship, they slept comfortably until noon, then enjoyed a fabulous three-course lunch served in the formal dining room at 2:00 P.M. The ocean air had a soothing effect. "I don't understand how we can possibly sleep so much," Estelle commented to her husband.[4]

The family's delight at their exciting voyage was marred, however, when on the day after setting sail they learned from the captain of the *Olympic* of the colossal tragedy occurring farther north in the dark Atlantic. The magnificent RMS *Titanic*, considered the world's first unsinkable ship, had struck an iceberg, and, by 2:26 A.M. on Monday, April 15, had begun to slip beneath the icy waters. Hundreds of passengers were feared dead. On hearing the news, Doheny sent a wireless message to Hearst and the editors of the *Los Angeles Herald*,[5] alerting them to the sinking of the luxury liner. That evening, the front-page headline of the late edition of the *Herald* read: "1342 on Titanic Missing, 868 Safe on Carpathia Is Official Report: 675 Saved, E. L. Doheny Sends Wireless Message to the Evening Herald." Alerted by Doheny's wire, Hearst had the first complete story of the tragedy to be printed in any U.S. newspaper.[6]

The Dohenys were distressed by the unfolding tragedy. Estelle worried that the sinking of the *Titanic* could have been due to the incompetence of the crew. She wrote to her mother, "When one stops to think how many lives were placed in the care of those . . . men, one wonders—we live so long and so comfortable—engineers, chauffeurs, Marconi operators—not any of them have more than a grammar school education, and to use their own judgment when it comes to the trusted care of hundreds of lives, when they are only boys after all. . . . It is heartsickening."[7]

At last, on April 24, the Dohenys arrived safely in London. After only a two-day stay, the family traveled by boat to Paris. One of Estelle's and Lucy's first acts on arrival was to have their hair curled in the Hotel Majestic's elegant beauty parlor. "You ought to hear Lucy speak French to the hairdressers," Estelle gushed later to Edward. "In fact everybody says she is a perfect wonder."[8]

Edward and Ned, meanwhile, spent their first day wandering the streets of Paris. By day's end, the two men had purchased a Renault automobile. The car had been custom built for Joseph Pulitzer, the publishing mogul and former owner of the *New York World*, who had recently passed away. Doheny and Ned were ecstatic about their new purchase, an "awfully good looking car,"[9] and Old George was encouraged to get behind the wheel and take them on a short tour of the City of Lights.

That night, Edward Doheny dined with Harold Walker, a key MPC executive and political lobbyist, as well as with other businessmen from the Salomon Company. After concluding business, he escorted his family to the famous Folies-Bergère, where Estelle was shocked by the skimpy outfits worn by the dancers. "Believe me much!" Estelle exclaimed to Edward. "I never knew a woman would dress with such a deep 'C' front and no back—I looked too—I was afraid I would miss something." Edward confessed that he took a glance, and "risked one eye."[10]

Estelle's letters home to her mother and sister show the travelers to be unintimidated by cosmopolitan Europe. An anecdote the group enjoyed telling concerned Estelle's being approached by a stranger in the Hotel Majestic's grand lobby.

"Do you speak English?" the woman asked Estelle.

"Well, I should say so," Estelle answered coldly. "I'm an American."

Estelle related the incident to Edward at breakfast. "I bet she won't forget me," Estelle said, laughing.

Lucy's four years of high school French served the Dohenys well during their peregrinations about Paris. Edward grew to admire Lucy, whom he began to address affectionately as "Sweetheart." "Just think," Estelle told Edward when Lucy was out of earshot, "I once was as dear, unselfish, and without temper, and with as many other charms as she is now . . . she is so dear and sweet."[11]

At one point during their trip to Paris, Edward Doheny was visited by General Porfirio Díaz, his former benefactor and Mexico's exiled leader. A quiet hush fell on the hotel's lobby as the two men warmly shook hands. They spoke privately and were later joined by their wives for a sumptuous French dinner, far from the violence and political entanglements of Mexico.

By the third day of their stay in Paris, the Dohenys, particularly Estelle, had been charmed by the city. "Paris is lovely beyond words," she wrote to her sister. "[It] is lovely beyond our expectations."[12] Eager to share details of her first trip to Europe with her mother, Susan Betzold, Estelle sent daily letters to Chester Place, where her mother was staying. A light-hearted, almost giddy, note on May 13, 1912, reveals Estelle as a vibrant young matron. She was now thirty-six, enthusiastic about her first experience abroad but preoccupied with her family and domestic concerns.

> My but it is exciting. I feel as if I were going on my honeymoon. I must tell you about my new typewriter it is a tiny little thing and folds up in a little case and weighs less than six pounds. I am going to call it "Susan" because it weighs so little.
> Don't laugh mama, I am almost dying laughing myself but I am going to call it Susan because it is so charming, and I am going to be of some help to Edward in doing something for him, which will make me happy. You have made me happy many many times, so it will be named Susan after you.
> Goodnight mama, I must close. I hear Edward is making himself a soda cocktail and maybe he will ask me to join the sour stomach brigade. Have a good time and keep well—don't care what it costs—have a good time, heaps of love to you all and everybody who asks about me.
> Lovingly,
> Estelle[13]

But over the next few weeks, Estelle began to tire from the relentless pace that Edward set for their travels. "If you ever lived with your husband from morning until night for several months, you would be glad to have the responsibility shifted," Estelle confided to her sister Daysie.[14]

By June 1 the family was on the train to Rome, where they had reserved suites at Le Grand Hotel. On the first morning of their visit, Edward escorted Estelle to the ruins at Pompeii. Estelle was ailing that day because of the heat, so Edward had her carried by two stout Italians on a sedan chair "like Cleopatra," Estelle wrote to her mother. During their tour, it began to rain and Edward quickly instructed the two men to set his "lovely Cleopatra" beneath a colonnade until the Italians could return with umbrellas and blankets.[15] Once the rains had ceased, Edward and Ned led the way as the group completed its tour. Pompeii inspired decorating ideas that the Dohenys would later incorporate at 8 Chester Place.

With Old George at the wheel of the Renault, and a local guide beside him, the Dohenys and Lucy traveled to Bertolini's Palace in Naples, a world-famous hotel situated atop a mountain and accessible from the road only by funicular. The Dohenys insisted on the most lavish accommodations available, which offered panoramic ocean views from each room. The next day, however, they had a scare: Ned wandered off to run an errand for Estelle, but did not return for several hours. Estelle became extremely worried and reported to Edward that Ned was missing.

"Ned's hurt!" his father exclaimed. He grabbed his hat and ran out of the master suite. In fact, Ned had gotten lost when he left the hotel's elevator at the wrong floor. Doheny found him nearly an hour later, and hugged him tightly, laughing mostly out of relief. Before leaving Italy, the party visited Venice, where they took a nocturnal ride through the canals in a gondola. Estelle wrote to her sister: "Well I am going to bring a gondola home, and row it around the fountain. Such a grand good rest, no one ever wants to get out. It is such an even stroke you glide along heavenly."[16]

The Dohenys stopped briefly in Carlsbad, Germany, where Edward was to meet an MPC lawyer and executive, Frank B. Kellogg, to discuss various legal matters. Estelle seemed unimpressed by the manners of the Teutonic guests at the spa: "You ought to have seen the big fat Jews and Germans. Ugh! Everybody carried their own cup on a strap around their shoulders like a Kodak or a set of field glasses and all they do is eat and eat and eat!" she complained.[17]

In July, as they neared the end of their travels, the Dohenys visited Glasgow and Edinburgh, then drove to Belfast, where they were to rendezvous with Herbert Wylie and attend the wedding of a member of Wylie's family. Along the way they became desperately lost and weren't able to understand the directions villagers gave them. The misadventure gave them a tale they would repeat often after they returned home, as in frustration, Ned finally called out—seemingly to no one—"Is this the road to Ballymahon? Why, I thank you, sir."

Perplexed, Edward Doheny said, "Why I didn't see anything but a donkey."

And Ned responded, "I know it, but he gave me just as good an answer as any of the other jackasses along the road."[18]

Edward Doheny was captivated by the home of his ancestors, and this visit influenced him to support the call for an Irish republic; he became a regular and generous contributor of money to support independence. According to Walter W. Jennings, in the years to come the American Association for the Recognition of the Irish Republic would elect him president of their organization.[19] Doheny would underwrite a $4 million fund for Irish relief. His generosity to Ireland would be held against him later when he sought British support for intervention in Mexico.

In Ireland, Estelle was taken aback by the wretched living conditions: "I never saw so much poverty in my life. . . . Ireland almost ruined our trip it was so pitiful. . . . There is nothing at Galway, and Mr. Wylie was much disgusted when he heard we were there, as he said it was the poorest part of Ireland, and the only good looking part was the lovely domains owned by titled people in England."[20]

When at last they reached Belfast, the Dohenys found Herbert Wylie. Doheny enthusiastically greeted Wylie and immediately inquired about his Mexican holdings. Wylie gave his boss a detailed report. Production was going forward in spite of labor problems and disrupted transportation. However, the current political climate in Mexico didn't look good. Doheny thought Wylie a capable man in a crisis and was glad to have him looking after the Mexico operations.

Wylie proudly introduced the entire extended Wylie family to his prominent employer, and Edward Doheny was treated as the special guest of honor at the festive wedding. Ned, Lucy, and Estelle enjoyed themselves and danced all night with the Wylie clan. "They are a big family of daughters and sons and grandchildren," Estelle wrote home. "But the loveliest thing is they are a healthy family, all intelligent and all working. It really was a wonderful sight. Both families danced and dined the night away, as Wylie's young niece is married to an important European family."[21]

The Dohenys' great European holiday was nearing its end. Estelle had become homesick; indeed, she spent her last few vacation days pondering the state of affairs at Chester Place. She composed detailed and elaborate letters to her staff about the tasks that needed to be completed prior to her return to the compound:

Have Mr. Banister draw me a design of a glass sitting room off the wisteria room, and over the oriental, with French doors from the bed room to the sitting room.

Don't move anything back into our room but the double bed so I can see if I like your way of fixing my room. Have him think of some nice place to utilize all the space in back of the secret closet off Edward's bathroom. I want a double wash basin, and the bathtub to be placed north to south.

For each of the servants, Estelle had purchased sterling silver spoons from each city she visited. She notified her property manager to give each employee "a week off at my expense";[22] she wanted them all refreshed and chipper for Mr. Doheny's return.

In August, the family arrived home. "I was never so thankful to be anywhere in my life," Estelle remarked.

Ned remained home for only a few weeks before traveling by car with Old George to Stanford University (after bidding an emotional good-bye to Lucy). But to Edward's great dismay, Ned proved to be a half-hearted student. Before semester's end, he dropped out. Doheny, however, was determined to have his son graduate from college; he ordered the boy to transfer to the University of Southern California in Los Angeles, in January 1913.

Estelle threw herself into the challenge of refurbishing Chester Place. Her European trip had filled her with ideas she wanted carried out. She commissioned Louis Comfort Tiffany, the son of the famous New York jeweler, to design a Favrile glass dome to enclose a space that was to be used as a ballroom. The room was known as the "Pompeian Room" because of its striking multicolored marble floor and columns. Estelle used the room for lavish formal dinner parties that were attended by as many as 110 guests. To Estelle's delight, one visitor likened her soirees to those at the White House.

In March 1913, Edward hired architect Alfred F. Rosenheim to build a $150,000 steel-and-glass plant conservatory, which would be used as a "palm house." When the room was completed, he filled it with over 10,000 orchids, cycads, palms, and tropical trees imported from Mexico that would grow to reach the upper regions of the ninety-foot-high conservatory.[23] Edward must have felt a special need to create in Los Angeles the exotic flora of the Mexican jungle where he had expended so much energy.

Remembering their European tour, Edward and Estelle petitioned the Italian government to permit a Russian-born artist, Eugene Murmann, to copy the Pompeian furniture found in the Museum of Rome. Once permission was granted, they took Murmann's sketches to the California Furniture Company, which manufactured the pieces and covered them with French fabrics.

Despite her time-consuming interior design projects and the attention she was receiving from her husband, Estelle felt bereft of companionship. She enjoyed her mother's infrequent company but was saddened that her younger sister, Daysie, with whom she had always had a close bond, was now estranged from her over a conflict with Edward. Daysie had married a man who was critical of Doheny and his wealth. Although he was on the payroll of Doheny's company, J. Crampton Anderson continued to speak poorly about Doheny and his financial dealings. Finally, when Edward could take no more of Crampton's hypocrisy, he told Estelle he intended to fire her brother-in-law and to leave him and Daysie to their own devices. He had been dismayed at their purchase of an automobile and at changes in their housing arrangements that he felt they could ill afford.

But Estelle pleaded for Doheny to reconsider:

My Dearest:
    Eddie you and I have lived together over ten years. You know me well by this time.
    Believe me, I try very hard to be considerate, thoughtful, amiable and not argue. Sometimes I fall from grace only to realize I ought to be stronger.
    I don't want my ills or my family to burden you, but don't think Peggy a "dirty little brat" we are sisters and if she is, what am I . . . ?
    . . . My only pleasure is my home and my family—but dearie, please, please, I beg of you don't take their future from them.
    Crampton's stock—I think is mortgaged so he could lend the company money and every month he had tried to help you in his poor way.
    And being able to get a machine on deferred payments, especially when the payments were easy and not in the near future and coming to live near us was so alluring dearie. I am certain dearie, he made one of the greatest and most foolish of blunders.
    Eddie we are all dependent on you and you must believe we appreciate all you do for us. Really, believe me, it is impossible for words to

express my gratitude, all I can do is devote my life to you . . . but being pinched for a lifetime and being closely associated with such an abundance of wealth as yours makes older ones than Peg and Crampton go off the straight and narrow path. . . .

Your burden is great my love—I know how many silver hairs it adds to your noble head and my life—my jewelry, my interest in the house and business are yours.

Dearie I would steal for you, I would do the most terrible things you could imagine just to help you lift this present burden and they don't want to be an extra burden. Dearie dear, Daysie isn't a dirty little brat, she is such a dear but being poor such a long time and prospects of such great wealth as you were giving them just helped her want something awfully nice—you have never wanted as we have believe me—or you would realize how hard it is, *not* to get something absolutely unreasonable when you think your heart craves it. . . .

. . . They injured my truest and best friend—besides my dearest love, forgive me, forgive me as I too am human: We all love you, you have been our idol, our genius, we all worship you as a god and here we fell—forgive us sweetheart—we didn't mean to.

Lovingly,
Estelle[24]

Eventually, Doheny yielded to Estelle's pleas, and Crampton remained on the Doheny payroll. Edward continued to have little regard for him.

OIL AND REVOLUTION

Meanwhile, as Edward Doheny endured irritating family squabbles on the home front, he was contemplating far more wearisome troubles south of the border. Felipe Díaz, the nephew of the overthrown president, was attempting a coup against the Madero government. Aided by General Victoriano Huerta, Felipe Díaz succeeded in ousting Madero and appointing Huerta president. Doheny was particularly pleased to have Madero dislodged since he was thought to favor Standard Oil. Indeed, there were rumors that Standard Oil money was behind Madero.

Now the balance of power was shifting. Relieved industrialists—such as Edward Brown, president of the Mexican National Railways; James Speyer, chairman of the board of Speyer and Company, a New York banking firm with large Mexican bond investments; and Edward Doheny—urged President Woodrow Wilson to formally recognize Huerta. In May 1913, Edward Doheny, Julius Kruttschnitt (chairman of the Southern Pacific Company), and leaders of the Phelps-Dodge Company and the Greene Cananea Copper Company signed a letter to President Wilson calling for him to take action in support of Huerta. They pointed out:

> The British government has already recognized Huerta in a most marked manner by autographed letter from the King due to the efforts of [Sir Weetman Pearson] . . . who has the largest interests outside of American interests in the Mexican republic. He is using his efforts to obtain a large loan in England, and we are informed that he has succeeded on condition that the English government would recognize Huerta, which has been done.
>
> If Mexico is helped out of her trouble by British and German influence, the American prestige will be destroyed in that country and Americans and the commerce of the United States will suffer untold loss and damage. On the other hand, if the Huerta government falls as the result of the hostility of the American government or its inactivity in the present crisis, it will make us morally responsible for consequences too frightful to contemplate.[25]

Doheny remained very concerned that Pearson (later Lord Cowdray) and his El Aguila operations would soon dwarf Doheny's Mexican empire. Under the acceptable guise of patriotism, Doheny argued that it was important for U.S. interests to maintain a strong hold on Mexico's oil industry. President Wilson was said to have regarded the letter's pleadings with ambivalence; he wished to support the interests of the industrialists but was sickened by the bloody tactics used by Huerta to gain power. Wilson was in the process of drafting a compromise proposal when he learned Huerta was barring free elections; he didn't want to be in the position of supporting a Mexican dictatorship. Acting swiftly, the president fired his current ambassador to Mexico and appointed a friend—John Lind, former governor of Minnesota—as his replacement. Wilson then sent Lind to Mexico with instructions to call for an immediate armistice, free elections, and the removal of Huerta as a presidential candidate. This was opposite the action that Doheny wanted from Wilson.

Ambassador Lind initiated negotiations with Frederico Carriboa, Huerta's foreign minister. He was reaching an agreement for Huerta to step down when Pearson interceded with support from the British government for Huerta. The United Kingdom was desperately in need of inexpensive oil, as demand for the fuel had skyrocketed. The Royal Navy, in the process of converting from coal to oil, was depending on Pearson's shipments. Were there to be a war in the European theater, the fleet could be crippled by lack of oil. Therefore, it was imperative that Pearson's Mexican production not be interrupted.

British efforts to keep Huerta in power were welcomed by Doheny, though he felt that the lack of U.S. support for Huerta gave the political edge to Pearson and his British oil operations. The feared conflict would erupt in one year's time into the Great War, and it would be fought with both men and machines. The machines, however, were now powered by oil. During the course of the war, oil and the internal combustion engine changed the common understanding of strategic mobility. Earlier, warfare had depended on railway travel, and the movement of troops was limited by "physical endurance, muscular capabilities, and the legs of man and beast." But "how much could be carried, how far and how fast—all that would change with the introduction of the internal combustion engine," writes Daniel Yergin in his history of the oil business.[26]

First Lord of the Admiralty Winston Churchill vowed to do everything possible to prepare Britain for war. His charge was to ensure that the Royal Navy was ready to meet the German challenge. The strategic benefits of oil rather than coal—making possible both greater speed and more efficient use of manpower—were obvious, and Churchill determined that Britain would base its "naval supremacy upon oil." As he stated simply, "Mastery itself was the prize of the venture."[27]

Yergin confirms the wisdom of the observation: "Churchill[,] on the eve of World War I, had captured a fundamental truth, and one applicable not only to the conflagration that followed, but to the many decades ahead. For oil has meant mastery throughout the twentieth century."[28] Doheny's control in Mexico of vast supplies of oil would make him a pivotal figure in the war years ahead and would ensure dramatic escalation of his oil production and profits.

Before Edward Doheny could travel south to meet with members of the newly installed Huerta regime, he received sorrowful news: his closest friend and trusted business partner, Charles Canfield, had died unexpectedly on August 15, 1913. Canfield had been sitting in his living room, entertaining his father-in-law and daughter, when he developed shooting pains in his chest. He clutched his hand to his breast, shut his eyes, and lost consciousness.[29] He was dead within minutes.

"I followed Charlie Canfield on many, many a trip behind an old burro," Doheny told reporters later. "I always found him a man who never gave up and who believed that some time, some where, things would break right for us two."[30]

Out of respect for the great businessman, the Los Angeles City Council adjourned its session early for his funeral, which was held at the Canfield home. Floral arrangements lined the drawing room and the entire first floor. Los Angeles' most prominent business and social figures were present, and over one hundred mourners stood outside the mansion straining to hear the service. The rites, read by the Rev. Joseph H. Johnson, were short and moving. Following the ceremony, Charles Canfield's body was transported to the Evergreen Cemetery for a private burial. He would be laid to rest beside his beloved wife, Chloe, and their son Lee.[31] The pallbearers, all longtime friends and associates of Canfield, included Edward Doheny, J. A. Chanslor, Dr. Norman Bridge, and Herbert G. Wylie. Among the many beautiful floral tributes that were placed at his grave site was an oil derrick made completely of flowers, which stood eleven feet high.

Doheny, the man who knew Charles Canfield best, gave an interview to the *Los Angeles Daily Tribune* the evening after his friend's death, praising Canfield as a man whose ambition and hard work produced wealth for the country in the course of creating a fortune for himself:

Mr. Canfield was a magnificent example of the very best type of American pioneer. He became a miner in 1868 and went into the desert to do what no other man has done quite so well in the southwest—built his fortune and the fortunes of the exploited country.

I knew him for twenty-nine years. I knew him as a young man, in middle age and in his later years. Together we attended nearly every great mining rush for twenty years in the days when we were prospectors, and in the rough life of the camps I found him neither a brawler, a wastrel nor an unclean man. He was of the very finest type of American citizen.

He married young, and he labored always for the betterment of his own condition and that of his family. He sought to become rich, but he worked honestly and hard for everything he got. He was loving and kind, strictly honest and the very soul of probity. . . .

If the development of the oil industry has meant anything to California and the nation at large, then to Mr. Canfield much of the praise for the tremendous work belongs. On that industry our state's prosperity has to a great extent been founded, and in Mr. Canfield's life is to be found the big chapters of the story of that industry's growth.[32]

The *Los Angeles Times* set Canfield's worth at the time of his death somewhere between $9 and $15 million, but the newspaper grossly underestimated his wealth. Canfield not only had extensive holdings in oil companies and financial institutions but also owned thousands of acres of land throughout California.[33]

In the memorial tribute issued by the Mexican Petroleum Company, Doheny said of him: "He was more than a partner, more than an associate in business, more than a fellow worker; he was a friend—kindly, serene, warm hearted and unfailingly dependable."[34] The death of Canfield deprived Doheny of a bulwark of strength and caution that otherwise would have helped him in facing the difficult years ahead.

Were it not for the unrest in Mexico, Doheny would probably have spent additional time with his wife and son in Los Angeles mourning his lost friend. But in October 1913, Doheny learned that Sir Lionel Carden, an aggressively anti-U.S. politician from the United Kingdom, had been appointed ambassador to Mexico. Carden had scarcely arrived in Mexico City before Huerta staged a brutal raid on the Chamber of Deputies, arresting 110 pro-Madero members. Now, without doubt, Mexico was a military dictatorship, and Woodrow Wilson would not support the regime. Just twenty-four hours after the raid, Carden arrived at the presidential palace to offer his credentials. The British government was definitely showing its support for Huerta. It was no surprise, then, that Huerta soon granted substantial new concessions to Lord Cowdray.

Doheny and his business associates agonized over the worsening state of affairs. In November 1913 the U.S. Navy notified the State Department that "the large oil wells of the American Huasteca Petroleum Co. [a subsidiary of Doheny's Mexican Petroleum Co.], at Juan Casiano [sic], are threatened with destruction by the revolutionists."[35] To their dismay, Wilson not only did not act on the navy's warning but soon announced American neutrality in the Mexican struggles and placed an embargo on the sale of arms to all factions in Mexico. But the neutrality was a ruse: unbeknownst to the U.S. public, Wilson had decided to oppose Huerta and surreptitiously to support Venustiano Carranza, a Constitutionalist. He sent word of this to Carranza via his friend William Bayard Hale, a former Episcopalian minister and journalist, who was willing to travel to the beleaguered city of Nogales where Carranza was entrenched. Although Carranza refused to promise free elections, as Wilson had desired, he agreed in January 1914 to respect American property rights and concessions in Mexico. After receiving this message, Wilson approved the sale of arms to Carranza's Constitutionalists.

It was Wilson's aid that enabled Carranza to defeat Huerta's federal forces in the early spring of 1914. Francisco ("Pancho") Villa, one of Carranza's supporters, captured Torreon and San Pedro; another faction leader, Pablo Gonzalez, amassed victories in Coahuila, Nuevo Leon, Tamaulipas, and Monterrey, Mexico's largest northern city. In late March 1914, Carranza's Constitutionalist forces began a march toward Tampico, headed toward the site of Doheny's prolific oil fields and his most productive wells at Casiano. Their goal was simple: to capture the strategically important port city and gain control of the oil fields and refineries.

Doheny was wild with anxiety over the possible seizure of his property. The U.S. government now shared Doheny's concern, since the United States was becoming increasingly dependent on oil from Mexico to meet its domestic fuel needs. Soon, anxiety turned to fear. In April

1914, as the Constitutionalist forces swarmed into the state of Tamaulipas, American oil companies telegraphed the U.S. State Department that their Tampico oil fields, refineries, storage tanks, and shipping docks were being destroyed. With other oil executives, Doheny dashed off furious letters to the State Department demanding immediate U.S. intercession. Doheny, in particular, had reason to be nervous.

U.S. intercession at this point would be tricky: industrialists favored Huerta, who supported their interests, but Wilson favored Carranza, who represented Mexican democracy. The only thing that both parties could agree on was that the strategic port city of Veracruz needed to be occupied by U.S. Marines so that the Constitutionalist forces, fighting in what was now Mexico's Revolutionary War, could not destroy or control the oil area. Thus, at Wilson's request, on April 21, 1914, a fleet of U.S. warships sailed to Veracruz and blocked its port. The fleet landed several hundred sailors and marines who engaged in a battle with Mexican cadets and civilians, killing 200. Doheny lent the U.S. government his company yacht anchored off Tampico, *The Wakiva*, for use as a central command center during the blockade.

In Veracruz, U.S. General Funston (whose exploits in the Spanish-American War were famous) and Admiral Fletcher appointed a civilian government composed of U.S. lawyers and businessmen, among them William F. Buckley Sr., to run the city. Senator Henry Cabot Lodge of Massachusetts proposed a resolution that would empower the president to send the armed forces anywhere in Mexico in order to protect U.S. lives and property. The controversial resolution was defeated in the Senate, however. Secretary of War Lindley Miller Garrison then called for a march on Mexico City, but Wilson rejected the suggestion. Doheny now worried that by the summer of 1914, General Victoriano Huerta's government would fall, and Doheny's Mexican oil interests would be up for grabs.

Seven Millions Made Knowing How

In Los Angeles the Doheny household was focused on plans for Ned Doheny's and Lucy Smith's upcoming wedding. Now that Edward Doheny had amassed the fortune he had always dreamed about, he was determined that his family live a life of consummate luxury and privilege. He spared no expense in providing for the young couple and looked forward to the wedding planned for June 1914. Handsome, athletic, and wealthy, Ned was one of Southern California's most desirable bachelors, but at twenty-one, he only had eyes for his first love. Both families had encouraged the union; when Lucy returned home from her European vacation with the Dohenys, even more smitten with her beau, all concerned were delighted that a wedding was imminent.

The young couple had first grown fond of each other when Ned and Lucy had accompanied "Ma and Pa D" (Edward and Estelle) on a trip to

Mexico in February 1912. "We were together every day for several months," Lucy wrote in her wedding journal, "so it was either kill or cure—in other words fall in love or fight all the time. In about two weeks love won out and ha[d] the upper hand for good."

The journal, chronicling events that led up to the couple's engagement, described a weekend in 1912:

> I went up to the "big game" with Ma and Pa D in November, 1912 [and] arrived Saturday morning and left Ned in Oakland Sunday night. Pa and Ma D received word Monday night that Ned was taken with appendicitis . . . so they rushed back that night in a special car with Doctor Howard. They brought Ned down Tuesday and took him direct to the Angelus Hospital and operated on him Wednesday.
>
> The shock of having Ned operated on was so great that as soon as Ned got home and popped the question I was forced to say yes instead of teasing him along awhile. He still insists I forced him into an engagement when he was too weak to refuse but I'll get him for that after we are married.[1]

Estelle Doheny and Lucy's mother, Laura Smith, spent six months meticulously planning the wedding. Estelle made sure that the matrimonial plans were reported in the society pages of Los Angeles newspapers.

The nuptials took place on the afternoon of June 10, 1914, at the home of Lucy's parents in South Pasadena. Lucy's father, William Henry Smith, escorted Lucy to the drawing room. Six pedestals had been arranged to form an aisle; each was topped with a basket filled with trailing vines and white rosebuds. An altar of flowers, ferns, and white gauze ribbons had been set up at the far end of the drawing room. Above it hung a luminous wedding bell filled with white roses.[2]

Lucy wore a "Lucille" gown of fluffy white satin and chiffon, with tiny clusters of orange blossoms attached to the skirt and bodice. The dress had been hand-sewn in Paris, modeled on a design that Lucy and Estelle had spotted during their European tour two summers earlier. As she walked toward the altar, Lucy carried an extraordinary "arm shower" of white orchids and lilies of the valley. Never the modest wallflower, Estelle chose a Lucille dress as well; hers, cut from expensive white satin, was embroidered with tiny silver flowers. Mrs. Smith wore a blue satin gown. Lucy's older sister, Mrs. Anson Lisk, served as the matron of honor and Lucy's little niece, Laura Ann Lisk, was the flower girl.

As the bridal party entered the room, a male quartet sang "This Is the Moon of Roses" while an orchestra, hidden behind a screen of ferns and foliage, accompanied them. Ned took his place beside the Rev. John C. Conger and watched anxiously as his bride, escorted by her father, descended the home's grand staircase and entered the drawing room.

Among the well-wishers were relatives and intimate friends of both families, as well as several of Doheny's most important business associates and employees, including former partner Judge Olin Wellborn Sr.; wealthy beer baron Edward Maier Sr.; prominent lawyer and civic leader Isidore Dockweiler; banker James Slauson; pioneer capitalist J. Ross Clark, dean of the University of California Medical College; Dr. W. Jarvis Barlow; and MPC's general manager, Herbert G. Wylie. Many of Ned's fraternity brothers at the University of Southern California were in attendance. Beta Theta Pi and Phi Nu Delta houses had hosted a lively bachelor party for Ned earlier that week, and, just prior to the ceremony, young members jostled and joked with the nervous groom. Warren Smith, Lucy's brother, served as Ned's best man and Warren's twin, J. Clark Smith joined Lucy's brother-in-law, Anson Lisk, as an usher.

Also in attendance at the society wedding was Theodore Hugh Plunkett, a machinist who had worked at Lucy's father's service station in downtown Los Angeles. Some months before, Lucy had introduced Hugh to Ned, and the two men, who were about the same age, hit it off despite their markedly different backgrounds. Hugh, at the time, was making a few dollars a week changing tires and servicing cars; Ned was a university student expected to join his father's oil business.[3]

The ceremony was followed by a formal dinner and reception in the garden under a huge white tent. Edward Doheny delivered an emotional formal toast to the young couple, promising them a bright future. Ned embraced his father in a tearful hug. The orchestra began to play, and the bride and groom stepped to the improvised dance floor. Soon Edward and Estelle and the parents of the bride stepped in as well, dancing alongside Lucy and Ned before the rest of the wedding party joined in.

The following day, the couple traveled by train to New York City, where they stayed at the Plaza Hotel during an extended honeymoon. On their return to Los Angeles, Ned and Lucy Doheny took up residence with Edward and Estelle in the mansion at 8 Chester Place.

On July 15, 1914, just one month after Ned's wedding, Doheny received word that General Victoriano Huerta had been defeated in Mexico. President Wilson's ploy to control the Veracruz port had greatly figured in Huerta's fall. Each week, more U.S. troops had landed in Mexico, engaging Huerta's guard in skirmishes and eventually overcoming them. Although Venustiano Carranza was able to gain control of the government, he remained furious at Wilson for what he considered a strongman intervention in his country's civil war. And the country was still far from peace. When revolutionary forces met in Aguacalientes between October 12 and November 14, 1914, Pancho Villa and Emiliano Zapata adopted a radical program of agrarian reform. Carranza repudiated the convention, and in retaliation, Villa declared war on Carranza, prompting a new set of skirmishes between the "Constitutionalists" of Carranza and the "Conventionists" of Villa and Zapata.

Although angry at the U.S. government, Carranza remained close to the officials at Standard Oil who had steadfastly backed his efforts. For the next three years he would enable the giant oil concern to quietly acquire lucrative new Mexican properties. Nevertheless, in January 1915, because of the grumblings by his beleaguered Constitutionalists, Carranza attempted to regulate the foreign-owned oil industry. On January 7, 1915, he issued a decree that required individuals and companies to secure drilling permits, a move that infuriated U.S. and British oil executives. Some feared it was the first step toward appropriation and nationalization of their oil operations. They attempted to rally opposition to Carranza, and it was rumored that financial backing was available to anyone willing to unseat him.

In February 1915, at Doheny's behest, U.S. Consul William Canada complained to Jésus Ureta, Mexico's minister of foreign affairs, that Doheny's business activities in the Huasteca had been illegally disrupted. On March 9, Ureta responded, claiming that the charge was false: Doheny was free to export fuel; Carranza's forces would not interrupt his operations. But despite Ureta's calm assurance of business as usual, there were indications that Mexico's unrest would continue to threaten Doheny's and other foreign oil concerns' holdings. Industrialists were placing pressure on the State Department to act against Carranza. On March 30, 1915, U.S. Secretary of State William Jennings Bryan sent a strongly worded communiqué to Mexico's vice consul about the issue: "If an engagement is threatened near Tampico, you will please confer immediately with the respective leaders and caution them against the destruction of the oil properties, point out the danger of conflagration and the possibility of great damage being done to both life and property."[4]

Whether the vice counsel relayed Bryan's admonition is not known, but in April, the oil fields at Ebano became targets of Carranza's ire. Doheny's Huasteca Petroleum Company plant, containing 5,000 barrels of distillates, was destroyed; two petroleum tanks, each containing 40,000 barrels, were demolished; and one tank containing 55,000 barrels of crude was set afire by the Constitutionalist forces. Doheny now feared that his Tampico fields would be the next target of the soldiers. Again, in response to Doheny's pleas, Secretary of State Bryan urgently wired officials in Mexico: "Urge [Carranza] to issue definite orders at once to his military commanders to prevent further damage to [U.S.] oil tanks and plants."[5] It was clear that Doheny's incredibly valuable oil holdings in Mexico had become expensive bargaining chips for the U.S. and Mexican governments.

Far across the Atlantic Ocean, a world war was under way. By 1915, the Great War had cost millions of lives and destroyed inestimable property. A German submarine blockade was effectively obstructing British ports. Although the United States had not yet joined the conflict, each day made this seem more likely.

Despite warnings of the danger, Doheny needed to go to London to confer with prospective investors. Edward and Estelle left New York City for Liverpool aboard the *Adriatic*, a large first-class British passenger ship, on March 20, 1915. Though the ship carried very few passengers, it was heavily loaded with valuable contraband freight. Because of the weight of the undeclared shipment, the vessel rode three feet deeper in the water than normal, and the trip across the Atlantic was unusually long—taking nine days instead of five.

During the first two days of the journey, the weather was bad, but thereafter, the skies were clear and the seas, according to Estelle, resembled "corrugated glass."[6] Edward and Estelle played shuffleboard on several afternoons and took advantage of the shipboard entertainment. On Sunday, March 28, after dark, the ship's captain gave the order to proceed at full speed, cruising at double the ship's normal rate. The Dohenys had just retired to their large stateroom. Alarmed, Edward insisted that they try on their life preservers and keep them nearby. Fortunately, however, they had no need for them; the following morning they awoke to find the ship docked at Liverpool.

Shortly after disembarking, Doheny received word that two ships had been sunk on the very path taken by the *Adriatic* the past night. More than half of the passengers on the *Falaba* had been drowned and 100 others had been rescued by an Irish fishing schooner, the *Eileen Emma*, which was 200 yards from the *Falaba* when a U-28 German submarine torpedoed her. The schooner's crew immediately set to work rescuing people from the icy black waters. Shaken, and enraged at the Germans for their callous indifference to human life, Edward wrote of the frightening incident to Ned in Los Angeles on April 2:

> It was a very cold blooded, not to say murderous, procedure, and was, in my opinion, undoubtedly intended for the *"Adriatic,"* as the boat which was destroyed, the *"Falaba,"* was sailing from England to South Africa, and was not nearly as important a capture as would have been the *Adriatic*, for the reason that we had on board several thousand tons of copper, several thousand cases of rifles and ammunition, and one hundred and thirty Peerless trucks, destined for war uses.
>
> If we had realized, before sailing, what the risks were, we certainly would not have taken passage in a boat carrying the English flag. (p. 3)

After their dangerous journey, grateful to be alive, Edward and Estelle Doheny retired into their suite at London's Ritz Hotel, which overlooked Picadilly Square. Because of the war, the English government required all

guests to draw their curtains tightly. The streets of London outside Doheny's window remained dimly lit as search lights, positioned throughout the area, scanned the night sky for enemy zeppelins. Nearly all the
adult men who passed below the Dohenys' window wore khaki or blue
British military uniforms. The reminders of war were everywhere.

Doheny described his experiences to Ned:

> While the trenches are across the channel and some distance from
> London, the Belgium ports are now the enemy's frontier, beyond which
> the submarines and Zeppelins carry the war to the very shores and
> cover the soil of England itself; there is a firm conviction in the minds
> of everyone you meet here that the ultimate result of the war will be the
> defeat and humiliation of Germany—it is very difficult to listen to them
> without becoming as firm of the same opinion.
>
> There are times when I have talked with our acquaintances about the
> war and its effects and results, that it is difficult to get a person's mind
> back to as trifling a subject, from the general stand point, as that of our
> particular business, nevertheless, we find those whom we came to see
> immeasurably interested in the prospects of an advantageous affiliation
> with us, and we really expect that when we leave here that we will have
> concluded a bargain with these people that will mean very much more
> for our company in many ways, in fact more than double its present
> importance. (p. 4)

Doheny negotiated a lucrative alliance with investors tied to Britain's
major shipbuilding and engineering firms; and even though his Mexican
Petroleum Company would benefit because of the war, he was proud to
be providing much needed fuel to an ally. But he hadn't counted on a life-
endangering passage aboard the *Adriatic*.

Despite the dark atmosphere of the war, Doheny was able to engage in
various business and social encounters in London. Doheny spent an evening with Lord Grey, the former governor-general of Canada, which was of
special significance to Doheny since Lord Grey was one of England's most
distinguished statesmen. Grey held great political and social power in
London, and this prompted Doheny, the former down-and-out miner, to
reflect on the radical changes in his life. "So you understand," Doheny

remarked with amusement to his family, "our business has developed to be of such importance that it enables people of our *obscure origin* to be feted and dined by the *noblest* in the land" (p. 5). Certainly, this was no exaggeration. For on April 3, Doheny dined privately with Winston Churchill, First Lord of the Admiralty.

As the English weather turned chilly, Estelle became less enthusiastic about extending their stay. Even more cold and oppressive was the atmosphere of the war. "We are both having a fairly good time," Edward wrote his son, "although I am inclined to think that Mommie is more in love with Chester Place than ever, she is so anxious to get back" (p. 6).

Estelle had reason to hasten back to Los Angeles; she was anxious to be reunited with Ned and Lucy to await the birth of the first Doheny grandchild. On June 21, 1915, just days after their safe return, Lucy gave birth to a healthy baby girl named Lucy Estelle, who would later be affectionately nicknamed "Dickie Dell."

The summer of 1915 remained a tense time for Edward Doheny, particularly when he learned that President Wilson had granted de facto recognition of the Carranza regime. Doheny changed his plans for expanding his business in Mexico, turning instead back to the United States. He formed a new corporation called the Mexican Petroleum Company of Louisiana, and it soon acquired 1,112 acres of oil lands on the Mississippi River in Destrehan, twenty miles north of New Orleans. There he built a tremendous oil storage tank with a capacity of over 1.4 million barrels.

About this time, Doheny received a handwritten note from Mexico's exiled president, Porfirio Díaz, sent from Paris; it expressed Díaz's anxiety about his exile and about his financial status, which had forced him to sell his stock in Doheny's company:

> My Dear Friend,
>   Sometime ago I wrote to our friend Mr. Norman Bridge telling him that owing to the difficult circumstances in which I find myself, on account of the dreadful condition of my poor country, I am now obliged to sell my shares of the Mexican Petroleum Preferred.

The little I had in Mexico has been either stolen, dreadfully damaged or ruined by the bandits. Of what is left, nothing produces, and for my living I am compelled to sell the only thing that has been left, that is my shares.

I am sending for that purpose to Los Angeles to the First Savings Bank my 508 shares of preferred stock of Mexican Petroleum Company of Delaware thinking that perhaps I could sell them at a better price than here where there is practically no market for them on account of the war.

I always remember your kind deeds and friendship towards me, so I come to you today asking you should this be possible to please sell for me in that market my shares. If you can do this for me, please let me know by cable saying only "accepted" and I will cable at once asking the bank to put the shares at your disposal. . . .

Please excuse the trouble I give you and with my intense thanks, believe me yours truly,
    Porfirio Díaz[7]

The exiled leader now believed that Mexico's greatest days had ended, and that nothing could be done to reverse the revolution. The foreign-owned oil companies could no longer rely on the stability of the Mexican government to protect their interests, and to Doheny Díaz's request to cash in his shares of the Mexican Petroleum Company undoubtedly forecast more trouble to come.

THE MIGHTY CERRO AZUL NO. 4

As Doheny struggled to find ways to protect his producing wells, he learned through Wylie that one of his most promising sites was predicted to unleash what could be a record-setting quantity of oil. Cerro Azul was situated in a 10,000-acre area of rolling plains and hills. Before Doheny's Mexican Petroleum Company had acquired the land, the acreage consisted of vast *potreros*, or lands for grazing cattle. Hundreds of live asphalt springs dotted the area with bones of cattle mired in the seepages.

Fifty kilometers of road had to be carved through the heart of the jungle, and forty-seven kilometers of railroad run across the valley and over the hills to service the oil derrick known as Cerro Azul No. 4. "To the drillers," wrote Doheny, "Cerro Azul No. 4 was a record of geological strata encountered and penetrated; to the Company's accountants a page of figures; to the managers an expectation; and to the other companies in the Southern Fields a source of lively curiosity."[8]

Doheny instructed Wylie to make preparations for the expected gusher. Wylie had his men set up empty holding tanks and bring two eight-inch pipelines to within fifty feet of the well, ready to connect it to the jumbo pipe to Tampico. At Doheny's request, Wylie also had a photographer set up his equipment in readiness at a safe distance from the well to record the event in still photographs and moving pictures.

On February 9, drillers reached a pocket of gas that forced water out of the drill hole. Later that night, a cold rain began, accompanied by heavy winds, and a true "norther" began blowing. Despite the weather conditions, the men resumed work the following morning. They were nervous about the anticipated explosion of oil, knowing the danger to them all. After a half dozen drill strokes, the drill's cable went slack. Wylie immediately ordered the men to extinguish the flame of the boiler and shut off its gas supply. Momentarily, an ominous rumbling far beneath the surface was heard, deepening in volume as the workers fled the derrick. Suddenly, the terrific explosion occurred. Before the drillers could get fifty feet from the shuddering well, the huge drilling tools shot into the air as if fired from a cannon, soaring through the crown block of the derrick while reducing the upper parts to kindling; when they crashed to earth 120 feet away, they embedded themselves 16 feet deep in the ground.

Barely twenty feet from where the equipment—two tons in weight— had landed, the courageous, if not foolish, moving picture operator continued to grind his camera and, "true to the traditions of this youngest of industries, stuck to his post and kept on cranking."[9] His steadfastness preserved for Doheny a unique and valuable record of the birth pangs of Cerro Azul No. 4.

The oil itself did not come for seven more hours. But when it did, it came with such outrageous, awe-inspiring force that no photographic recording—then or now—could have done it justice. Oil was shooting hundreds of feet into the air unconstrained. Cerro Azul No. 4's torrential production could not be checked for several days. As the oil gusher raged skyward, workers tried desperately to bring it under control. One worker almost lost his hands when he accidentally held a rope over the top of the well. Instantly, the rope was grabbed by the black column of oil, jerked from the man's hands, and pulled directly up. Workers watched stunned as two hundred yards of stout hemp uncoiled as rapidly as a striking rattlesnake and rose up the column of oil toward the clouds.

As the volume of oil increased, its column rose higher and higher until, on the morning of the 11th, it attained a height of 598 feet. The well's total output was so great it was nearly impossible to measure; however, on February 19, workers estimated that it had produced 260,858 barrels in twenty-four hours.[10] To calculate Cerro Azul No. 4's production, MPC engineers constructed several spillways, each about five meters in length, in order to time and measure the oil's flow per second across a measured expanse. The deluge from Cerro Azul No. 4 would never be forgotten by the drillers who witnessed it, nor by the indigenous residents; the land within a two-mile radius literally was saturated with Cerro Azul No. 4's petroleum and made uninhabitable for years to come.

To the surprise of all, the well continued to increase its daily output. More than half a million barrels of oil were saved in temporary reservoirs, which had been hastily converted from an arroyo. MPC's master mechanic, George W. Barnes, and his staff worked feverishly in Tampico with draftsmen, foundrymen, machinists, and blacksmiths to create a device that could bring the well under control. A heavy-tongued machine part with grooved clamps for the rig's casing was completed and rushed by launch to San Geronimo, placed on a train, and transported to Cerro Azul. At the well site, it was placed on the well's casing and fastened against the valve with thick screws. Because workers could not work close to the well, they were forced to manipulate the device via a thirty-foot-long pipe that had been attached to the valve stem. Few expected the humble invention to subdue nature's power, but, as ordered, the workers began to turn the screw to advance the valve slowly over the casing. Some of the men fully expected to see the heavy ironwork bent, twisted, and cast aside like a rejected tin toy.

But the valve met the casing and remained stubbornly in place, causing the oil column to divert slightly. Gradually and evenly, the men continued to turn the screw, further pushing the valve over the casing and deflecting the column of oil. Miraculously, the clamps still held. The column of oil was deflected at an acute angle to the casing, then suddenly it split into two columns—one rushing straight up through the valve where they wanted it, the other bending away at a 90-degree angle. Gradually, the vertical stream became much thicker, and the diverted stream much thinner, until the entire column of oil was rushing through the valve straight into the air—no longer uncontrolled, but carefully harnessed.

Fittings were secured, and in a short time oil from Cerro Azul No. 4 was flowing, as Doheny described it, "completely under control and as accurately regulated as the water from the hydrant with which the housewife sprinkles her little flower garden." Within weeks, the geyser was producing 260,000 barrels of crude daily and was being described as one of the most prolific gushers in the history of oil production. Over the next fourteen years it would produce an astounding 57,082,755 barrels of crude.[11] Overnight, Doheny had became one of the world's wealthiest men.

He later wrote of bringing in Cerro Azul No. 4:

> The comparative quiet of the jungle with only the creak of the walking-beam, the muffled clang of iron on iron, the hiss of steam, was first broken by a growling mutter, swelling at length into a menacing roar that shook the earth and was heard like the sound of distant thunder in Casiano, 16 miles distant.
>
> A little later, every leaf, every flower, every blade of grass now vivid with the green and brilliant colors of the tropical jungle, was converted as if by magic into the fantastic dream of some futuristic painter, all glistening black as if fashioned of highly burnished metal.
>
> In the center of this strange picture, amid ruins of what had been a short while before a sturdy derrick of bolted timber, a column of oil many hundreds of feet high ran straight into the air thick as a barrel, black as night, and in appearance as smooth as ebony. Cerro Azul had come in![12]

The bounty of Cerro Azul seriously taxed Doheny's distribution facilities. The extraordinary well committed Doheny to Mexico, but he also realized that to be even moderately efficient he would have to construct facilities to refine, transport, and market the oil at numerous ports elsewhere. From 1916 until 1921, he would use much of his profits to this end.

Doheny created a holding firm, the Pan American Petroleum and

Transport Company, incorporated in Delaware, to control his new facilities on the Gulf and Atlantic Coasts of the United States, his Mexican subsidiaries (Huasteca and Mexican Petroleum), and his remaining California interests. Rumors spread that Doheny's corporations were producing nearly $1 million of oil each week. Cerro Azul No. 4's miraculous yield made it possible to finance projects Doheny had only dreamed about in the past. Not only did he establish marketing facilities and distribution centers in ten cities along the Eastern seaboard, he also constructed a new 25,000-barrel-per-day refinery at Destrehan, Louisiana. Doheny also began to construct South American depots for oil shipments in the Canal Zone, Para, Pernambuco, Bahia, Rio de Janeiro, Santos, Montevideo, and Buenos Aires, where Mexican oil had recently been approved for importation after the opening of the Panama Canal. And in Europe, he established distribution centers in Southampton, Liverpool, Avonmouth, South Shields, and Glasgow.

Doheny's main concern at this time was Mexico's continuing political instability. Revolutionary leader Pancho Villa had raided the city of Columbus, New Mexico, in retaliation for Wilson's recognition of Carranza as Mexico's president. As Wilson contemplated the United States' next move in the matter, Doheny was restless with anxiety. In March 1916, President Wilson ordered General John J. ("Black Jack") Pershing to lead an expeditionary force of 5,800 men—later increased to 10,000—to attack Chihuahua and defeat Pancho Villa. It was Wilson's second invasion of Mexico in two years, but this time the act was a complete failure. Not only did Villa evade Pershing for over a year, but Wilson's aggressiveness convinced Mexican nationals to support Villa's further actions against the "Yankee invaders."[13]

Doheny was appalled by Wilson's clumsy tactics and decided to join other industrialists in stirring up anti-Carranza sentiments. These corporate leaders wanted U.S. troops to protect vital oil interests through a well-planned occupation of Mexico; they did not want Wilson to wage war in such a way as to provoke Mexican nationals to destroy their properties. Doheny's friend William Randolph Hearst supported this approach. He used his newspapers to stir up anti-Mexican feeling, employing such headlines as "MEXICANS PREPARE FOR WAR WITH U.S." On June 19, 1916, Hearst's *New York Journal* carried this editorial comment: "Is it

not time for the soldiers of the United States to do something PERMA-
NENT? . . . Nothing worthwhile will be accomplished by occasional 'puni-
tive expeditions.' . . . The way to IMPRESS the Mexicans is to REPRESS the
Mexicans. The way to begin is to say to them: ' . . . We are no longer planning to catch this bandit or that. We are GOING INTO MEXICO. And as far
as we GO, we'll stay.'"[14]

When Carranza led a second raid on U.S. soil at Glen Springs, Texas,
Wilson ordered a detachment of troops under General Pershing to enter
Mexico. Carranza responded by calling for their immediate withdrawal,
threatening war if his demand was not heeded. U.S. Chief of Staff Hugh
L. Scott instructed the War College to plan a Mexican invasion using the
major rail lines. President Wilson called upon the entire National Guard,
totaling 100,000 men, to patrol the border. By the end of 1916, it appeared
that Doheny's pleas were finally being heard.

Fearing that the Mexican revolutionaries would either destroy or con-
fiscate the oil fields, some members of the Wilson administration wanted
to invade and occupy them. In his autobiography, *Baruch: My Own Story*,
Bernard Baruch records a meeting in the White House on this subject: "It
was shortly after we entered World War One. President Wilson had invited me to a White House discussion of an oil shortage which threatened
to disrupt our military plans. One official proposed that we seize the
Mexican oil fields in Tampico. Squadrons of marines had already been
alerted. The President had only to give the word for them to push off."[15]

But soon afterward, Wilson began to waffle about the extent of a
planned U.S. invasion. He came to endorse "limited military intervention," which infuriated Doheny. Doheny now fumed that the U.S. government was unable to protect his vital business interests. He began to
contemplate various means of using his newly acquired great wealth to
secure his Mexican holdings. Alarmed by what he perceived as weakness
on Wilson's part, angered that his lobbying efforts were ignored, and
deeply frustrated with the federal bureaucracy, Doheny began to hire
publicists and journalists to make his agenda known. Doheny believed
that if he could convince government officials and their constituents that
America's fuel supplies were dangerously jeopardized, he could coax
Wilson into more aggressive action.

One publicist who proved instrumental in Doheny's cause was the

Edward and Estelle Doheny's wedding day, August 22, 1900. A justice of the peace in New Mexico Territory presided over the ceremony inside Doheny's private Pullman railcar, later christened the "Estelle." *Left to right:* Carrie Estelle Betzold, Edward L. Doheny, Albert Canfield, and Edward ("Ned") Doheny Jr. Courtesy of the Estelle Doheny Collection, Archive of the Archdiocese of Los Angeles, Mission Hills, California (AALA).

Interior of the "Estelle." Doheny's private railcar transported the oilman in comfort from Los Angeles to the jungles of Mexico. The rolling mansion boasted expensive black walnut paneling, plush carpeting, chandeliers, French mirrors, air-conditioning, and a fully stocked kitchen. Courtesy of the AALA.

Left to right: Edward and Estelle Doheny and friends in front of the "Estelle." Courtesy of the AALA.

An early photograph of Edward Doheny ca. 1901–5, at the Ebano, Mexico, oil camp, the site of the Mexican Petroleum Company's first producing well. Courtesy of the AALA.

Estelle Doheny, August 1900. It was her voice that entranced him,
Doheny claimed. She was the unseen telephone operator connecting
his calls to investors for his Mexico venture. They married after a
short courtship. Courtesy of the AALA.

Edward Doheny enjoying the company of the ladies in the Doheny circle. Doheny is seated between Estelle *(left)* and her sister Daysie Anderson. Lucy Smith (who wed Ned Doheny in 1914) is sitting in front. Courtesy of the AALA.

Edward and Estelle Doheny and friends on the lawn at 8
Chester Place, ca. 1901. Courtesy of the AALA.

Ned Doheny, four years old, in 1897. He was
Edward Doheny's only son. Courtesy of the
AALA.

Ned Doheny feeding a deer in the zoo at Chester Place, ca. 1901–2. Edward Doheny brought the deer to Los Angeles aboard the "Estelle" after it wandered into the oil camp at Ebano, Mexico. Courtesy of the AALA.

Doheny was one of the few owners of a Pierce Arrow. Photographed at Chester Place, with Estelle hatted for a ride in the open touring car and with Ned posing at the wheel, ca. 1901–2. Courtesy of the AALA.

Fourth of July gala celebration at Chester Place. Estelle and
Edward Doheny are seated at the center table *(top)*, ca. 1902–3.
Courtesy of the AALA.

The Mexican Petroleum Company's steam-driven tractor hauling a complete drilling rig from one site to another, ca. 1901-5. Courtesy of the AALA.

José Guadalupe Posada's print *Gran calavera eléctrica* (1907) used his famous *calaveras* to picture victims of modern invention, here run down by the new electric trolley. Posada asserted a view in marked contrast to Doheny's faith in industrial progress. Courtesy of Dover Pictorial Archive Series.

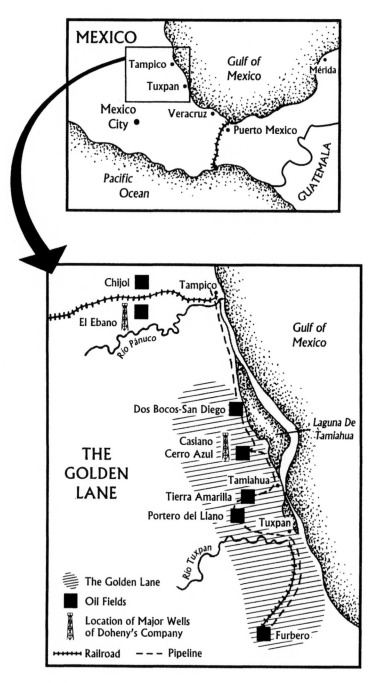

Map of major oil fields in Mexico.

Panorama of a Doheny oil camp in Mexico, ca. 1905–10. Courtesy of the AALA.

Doheny and eight of his American managers at a Pan American Petroleum drilling site in the jungles of Mexico, ca. 1905–10. Doheny is third from the left. Courtesy of the AALA.

Charles Adelbert Canfield, Doheny's partner
in the New Mexico mining days and later
while developing an oil industry in Mexico,
ca. 1900. Courtesy of the Doheny family.

Chloe Canfield, Charles Canfield's wife and
the mainstay of his life, in a possible wedding
photo, 1879. She was murdered by a servant
in 1906. Courtesy of the AALA.

Cerro Azul No. 4 before it was brought under control. On February 9, 1916, it erupted into a gusher that exceeded the output of all other wells in the Mexican fields. Overnight, Doheny became one of the world's wealthiest men. Courtesy of the AALA.

The men who brought Cerro Azul No. 4 under control. The deluge from the oil saturated the land and everything on it within a two-mile radius. Courtesy of the AALA.

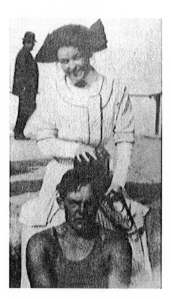

Ned Doheny at Venice Beach with Los Angeles High School classmate Grace ("Dolly") Martin, ca. 1910. Photo courtesy of John Martin Luder, Esq.

Ned Doheny in uniform during his World War I service in the U.S. Navy. Photo courtesy of the Doheny Family.

Lucy Marceline Smith, the bride of Ned Doheny, on her wedding day, June 10, 1914, inside the Smith family home on Columbia Street in South Pasadena, California. Courtesy of the AALA.

Edward Doheny in 1923 at the peak of his power and prestige, before the oil scandals broke. Courtesy of the AALA.

journalist and author Caspar Whitney (who later married Charles Canfield's daughter). In 1916 he published *What's the Matter with Mexico?* Whitney's book praised Edward Doheny, Charles Canfield, and several other American businessmen for bolstering the Mexican economy with oil production. Whitney depicted the Mexican revolutionaries as thugs and called for the American government to use force to bring about "the return of law and order" in Mexico.[16] Whitney's book became popular in the United States and did influence public opinion.

Doheny also fanned numerous press attacks against U.S. policy makers by commissioning journalists to write "pro-Doheny" editorials in large-circulation newspapers. His "pen-for-hire" tactics became so brazen that press insiders joked about his "secretly owning" some of the leading journalists. Malcolm E. Nicholas, head of the Hearst newspapers, loudly complained to acquaintances that he had wanted to hire an editor from the *Boston Telegram Newspaper*, "but [couldn't] get him until after Doheny stops paying him $125 a week to write editorials in defense of Doheny."[17]

Frustrated by the failure of his government to protect his interests in Mexico, Doheny decided that he was now forced to buy his own protection. He needed a reliable army for this task, and, if his government would not send one, he would build his own. Doheny, along with other concerned businessmen, hired a local landowner named Manuel ("General") Pelaez to oversee a private army. A significant sum of money was collected for this purpose.

Doheny's relationship with Pelaez seems to have developed as early as 1916, if not sooner. On August 11, 1916, Claude Dawson, the U.S. consul at Tampico, had sent a confidential communication to U.S. Secretary of State Lansing discussing Pelaez's dangerous role in helping U.S. industrialists maintain private troops in Mexico. It included the following warning:

> I have of late received information from two sources that Manuel Pelaez, leader of the independent faction in the Huasteca, or southern country, against whom the de facto forces have proved impotent, would like to have an understanding with the American authorities under which he would afford guarantees for the protection of foreign oil properties in return for assistance in the shape of supplies and ammunition to maintain his present stand and be prepared to prevent the threatened destruction of property when intervention becomes an actuality. . . .

. . . If the de facto troops should unexpectedly defeat and disperse
Pelaez's forces and regain full control of the Huasteca oil fields, the risk
of huge damage and loss from willful destruction would be tremendously increased in case of war or intervention.[18]

There is no record of a reply in the secretary's correspondence, but
clearly the U.S. government representative in Tampico was sympathetic
to the arrangement made between Pelaez and various U.S. businessmen.
As Friedrich Katz writes in *The Secret War in Mexico*, "American authorities either actively supported Carranza's opponents or quietly tolerated
the activities of groups in the United States which supported them. Thus
the State Department endorsed the oil companies' financial support for
Pelaez."[19]

It has been suggested that William Greene, vice president and general
superintendent of Doheny's Huasteca Petroleum Company, carried money
and "instructions" to Pelaez at Doheny's behest. Doheny complained
loudly and publicly that Pelaez was extorting money from his firm. Certainly, Doheny's protestations were believable: Pelaez was in an excellent
position to demand large sums of "protection money" from terrified foreign oil executives who feared that without Pelaez's vigilantism, they
could lose their entire Mexican holdings. Rumors circulated that Doheny
and Lord Cowdray had hired Pelaez and were each paying nearly $10,000
per month to his forces for "peace of mind" even while accusing Pelaez of
extortion. Indeed, these actions are hardly mutually exclusive.

On February 5, 1917, Carranza's government introduced a new Mexican Constitution, radically different in character from its predecessor. Of
most concern to Doheny was the new Constitution's Article 27, which
proclaimed that Mexico had "direct dominion" over all minerals and
other substances in her soils, including but not limited to "petroleum
and all solid, liquid, or gaseous hydrocarbons." Although countless court
battles and political editorials would analyze the implications of this article, there was little doubt of the authors' intentions: they sought to reserve Mexico's natural resources for the state and possibly to pave the
way for the nationalization of Mexico's oil industry.

The adoption of this new "confiscatory Constitution," as Doheny publicly called it, increased his anger at the Carranza government even fur-

ther. He reputedly strengthened his support and encouragement of Pelaez, who, some months later, announced the birth of a new counter-revolutionary movement, the "Huasteco [sic] Home Defense Movement." In a manifesto issued on May 5, 1917, Pelaez denounced the Carranza government and its new Constitution. He intended his "Constitution of 1857 Revolutionary Army" to serve as a provisional government to displace Carranza and to give notice of a return to an earlier era. But despite these grandiose declarations, Pelaez's actual firepower was limited. According to U.S. Naval Intelligence at the time, "Pelaez's army was principally . . . employees of the oil fields with only a small body of reserves." Doheny's continued financial support helped Pelaez gain more clout, however, and by late 1918 he had assembled 6,000 troops—in the opinion of the U.S. State Department, "an ample sufficiency of arms and ammunition to conduct a very large campaign."[20]

A "petroleum state" quickly took shape in the fields of the Huasteca, and, while Pelaez was its chief guardian, "it was Doheny who . . . ruled it from afar."[21] But, unfortunately for Doheny, Pelaez held sway only in the oil fields, and not in the cities of Tampico or Veracruz, which were controlled by the Constitutionalist armies. This meant that Pelaez controlled the oil wells, but the refineries, storage facilities, and shipping docks remained under the control of Carranza's revolutionary government.

Doheny fervently hoped that Pelaez's forces would swell in strength and numbers sufficient to overthrow Carranza's regime. But he knew full well that this had to occur without U.S. government support. Since the United States was now committed in World War I, U.S. forces overseas were heavily dependent on Mexican oil, and President Wilson would not risk taking any action that might cause Mexico to withhold it.

As war fever spread across the country, Ned Doheny graduated from the University of Southern California in June 1916 with a bachelor of arts in mathematics; five months later, he joined the navy as an apprentice seaman and was promoted to lieutenant in a matter of weeks. Lucy remained at Chester Place, pregnant with their second child.

Ned was first assigned to the USS *Huntington* (named for railroad financier Collis P. Huntington), and during his tour he introduced his father to his commanding officer, Captain John Keeler Robison. The meeting would prove to be a fateful encounter, as Captain Robison in 1920 would be made chief of the navy's Bureau of Engineering and thus in charge of the naval petroleum reserves.

Edward Doheny boarded the *Huntington* in 1917, at the Pensacola, Florida, harbor. The well-known oilman was warmly greeted by the tall and sharp-featured career navy man who had graduated with honors from Annapolis. After the two men exchanged greetings, Robison invited Doheny to his personal quarters. The men discussed the current status of the war and the possibility of a Japanese offensive measure in the Pacific.

During their conversation, Captain Robison raised the subject of the navy's administration of its oil reserves and asked Doheny what he thought. "Well, it is being handled very well [as an unintended benefit] for the people you have for neighbors," Doheny told him, explaining that the reserves were an invitation for neighboring oil drillers to put in offset slant-drilled wells, "but," he added ominously, "you are not going to have any [oil] property there in a very few years." Robison was "astounded" by Doheny's statement, for he had been previously unaware of any danger to the reserves from drainage. "It opened my eyes to a situation I never dreamed existed," Robison later said. Because the information came to him not from a "mere $2500 clerk" but from a man "who had made millions knowing how," Robison stated that what he heard from Doheny was the "kind of information [he] believe[d]."[22]

Doheny was proud that his only son was contributing to the war effort, but he was also extremely concerned about Ned's safety and obtained assurances from his commanding officer that he would be protected from danger. Frank Simpson Jr., an officer who also served aboard the USS *Huntington*, wrote to his parents in May 1917 that First Lieutenant and Executive Officer Alonzo H. Woodbine saw Ned as causing trouble. "Woodbine had had enough troublemakers at home [in the Los Angeles recruiting office] and didn't care for another aboard his ship."[23] Simpson also criticized the preferential treatment that young Doheny received following the visit of his famous father.

While still in the service, Ned bought 10 Chester Place from Dr. Norman Bridge, an MPC board member and close family friend. Lucy moved into the neighboring mansion while Ned remained aboard the *Hunting-ton*. He was, however, granted an extended leave to be present at the birth of his first son, Edward Laurence III or "Larry," on February 8, 1917. After Ned returned to duty, Edward and Estelle spent extra time with Lucy and their two grandchildren, Dickie Dell and Larry.

On June 16, 1917, Ned was transferred to shore duty; he was assigned to the Judge Advocate General's Office in Washington, D.C., where he would remain for the rest of the war. In September 1918, he was ordered to Wales, but illness forced him to remain stateside. He was then sent to a submarine base in San Pedro, at the Los Angeles Harbor, until his discharge from active duty on January 24, 1919.[24] Many of Ned's university classmates and fraternity brothers were also in service, as was his friend the family mechanic Hugh Plunkett, who served as a chief machinist mate on a submarine chaser. Hugh returned home from his wartime service without injury.

While Doheny was financing clandestine military operations in Mexico, he was also putting money into various patriotic fund-raising causes. The Pan American Petroleum and Transport Company and the Mexican Petroleum Company bought $2 million in Liberty Bonds, and Doheny personally purchased another $1.5 million; even more bonds were bought by Doheny and his businesses in subsequent Liberty Loan drives. His companies contributed $100,000 to the Young Men's Christian Association's war effort, and Doheny personally matched the contribution.[25] Doheny also lent the U.S. government five of his tankers—the *Edward L. Doheny Jr., Herbert G. Wylie, Norman Bridge, Charles E. Harwood*, and *Cantania*—to transport oil. However, as the business press wryly noted, "The vessels taken over are the smallest of Doheny's company."[26]

Meanwhile, in Mexico work in the oil fields accelerated with the growing requirements of the war. The *Gulf Coast Oil News* reported in May 1917 that "Tampico's tugs, launches and barges are working as they never worked before. Everything that can carry freight or tow a barge is working almost day and night. The freight to the Panuco, Topila and southern fields is increasing daily. Every vessel arriving from the states brings freight for the oil fields."[27]

The heightened demand for transportation during World War I hastened the world's conversion from coal-burning to petroleum-burning engines; two of the first oil-burning ships, the *Nevada* and the *Queen Elizabeth*, were built in 1914 in the United States and Great Britain, respectively. The allies were relying more heavily on gasoline-burning vehicles for their war efforts, in sharp contrast to the nineteenth century's heavy employment of animal power. The superpowers' munitions factories, too, were now switching from coal to petroleum. The forces' need for fuel greatly influenced military strategies; whoever controlled the world's petroleum-producing areas was in position to win the war. Realizing this, Doheny grew somewhat megalomaniacal about his role. Oil was turning the wheels of civilization and shaping the destinies of nations: Doheny considered himself a major player in the global drama.

The demand for Doheny's oil products skyrocketed as the war continued. He increased his Tampico production by adding pipeline pumps, tanks, and loading sites. During July 1917, his Huasteca Petroleum Company shipped 1,301,590 barrels of crude to buyers throughout the world. At this point, Doheny could move nearly 100,000 barrels a day to points across the globe via his fleet of thirty-one tankers. By year's end, his companies had shipped 35 million barrels from Mexico to United States ports alone. In his company magazine, Doheny proudly reported in November:

> Our ships have been moving gasoline from the Pacific Coast to New York, the West cooperating with the East in furnishing supplies to the Allied Armies. . . .
>   The Allies need gasoline, and the consumers of our oil, producing materials to be used in the war, must also be supplied. We are able, with difficulty, to fill our contracts, and the new ships in process of construction should enable us not only to meet our obligations but also to supply our share of the ever-increasing demand for fuel oil.[28]

Doheny's "share" was one of the largest in the world, and the rewards were correspondingly great. Profits from the Pan American Petroleum and Transport Company enabled the company to pay out dividends totaling $1.1 million in 1917; the following year, the company paid $3.1 million worth of dividends on its common stock. Pan American's revenues now totaled $17 million, and its net profits reached nearly $7 million.

Doheny was relieved to learn that President Wilson had agreed to establish a Joint High Commission with Carranza in order to attempt to resolve all U.S.-Mexican discord. Wilson was forced to the table, because his war fleet in the European theater needed assurance of an uninterrupted supply of oil. U.S. corporations supported Wilson's negotiations with the Mexican leader. They hoped that Carranza would agree to the terms of a proposal submitted by Wilson's secretary of the interior, Franklin Lane (who was later hired by Doheny), that mirrored the Cuban Platt Amendment of 1901: "The Government of Mexico solemnly agrees to afford full and adequate protection to the lives and property of citizens of the United States, or other foreigners, and this protection shall be adequate to enable such citizens of the United States . . . [to operate] industries in which they might be interested. The United States reserves the right to re-enter Mexico and to afford such protection by its military forces, in the event of the Mexican Government failing to do so."[29] But the final sentence in the proposal was extremely controversial, and not likely to garner Carranza's approval. It specifically permitted the United States to invade Mexico with military force should the Mexican government level "confiscatory" taxes on American oil concerns in the region. As expected, Carranza balked at such a request, and the proposal was set aside.

During this difficult period, Wilson appointed Mark L. Requa as U.S. fuel administrator, in charge of protecting and preserving the nation's wartime petroleum supplies. Requa has been described as the "virtual dictator of the oil resources to the United States during the war."[30] He was a strong defender of the oilmen's interests and continued to goad Wilson's administration toward employing military force in Mexico to seize control of the oil fields, and even topple the Mexican government if necessary. But Wilson remained the cautious strategist and refrained from deepening U.S. military presence in Mexico.

Throughout this difficult time, Estelle Doheny remained her husband's greatest source of support and encouragement. Usually, she asked very little of him in return—his presence and comfort were all that she needed. During Doheny's extended absences, she had been studying Roman Catholicism and had taken great solace from its teachings. She confided to her husband of eighteen years that she felt the need to convert. Thus on October 25, 1918, she reached the "high noon hour of her long life" when she was instructed by Bishop Joseph Glass of Salt Lake City into the Catholic Church. The formal conversion took place in New York City at the imposing Saint Patrick's Cathedral.

Despite his great wealth, Doheny's modest family background as well as his religion made it difficult for him to join the power elite of business and society. Even though railroad and mining executives, judges and university presidents were now his neighbors at Chester Place, the oilman was still an immigrant's son who could not easily join society's highest ranks, even in the progressive state of California. More generally, Doheny faced ostracism as both a westerner and a Catholic. As one analyst of American social stratification notes, "There was a more or less closed caste line drawn at the elite level which excluded those hyphenated Americans of the Catholic and Jewish communities."[31]

One arena in which Doheny could rise to prominence, however, was within the Catholic Church itself; and following Estelle Doheny's conversion, the couple began to cultivate relationships with prominent church officials. The couple befriended and socialized often with Bishops Francis Clement Kelley and John Joseph Cantwell and began to take a serious philanthropic interest in church endeavors. Bishop Kelley of the Diocese of Oklahoma City–Tulsa had met Doheny in London, after World War I, when the two had found themselves in agreement over the injustices of the Venustiano Carranza regime.[32] Bishop Cantwell shared Doheny's Irish heritage. Cantwell, after pursuing his theological studies at St. Patrick's College in Thurles, was ordained a priest in 1899. He was made bishop of Monterey–Los Angeles in 1917, when he met Edward and Estelle. He became an intimate member of the Doheny inner circle, guiding and directing much of the Dohenys' significant largesse to the Catholic Church.

The need to influence public opinion continued to concern Edward Doheny. In November 1918, he launched the Doheny Research Foundation, one of the first think tanks in the United States. The oilman provided an initial $100,000 grant for twenty university professors to study the sociological, political, and financial aspects of the Mexican Revolution and to propose new strategies, based on their findings, for the United States to adopt in order to safely intervene in the crisis. Although University of California at Berkeley's president, Benjamin Ide Wheeler, praised Doheny's altruistic efforts, Doheny's critics blasted him for hiring intelligentsia to blindly defend his business activities.

In the same year Doheny also created the National Association for the Protection of American Rights in Mexico and invited influential businessmen who possessed Mexican holdings to join. Among NAPAR's members were C. F. Kelly, vice president of the Greene Cananea Copper Company; George H. Carnahan, president of the Intercontinental Rubber Company; Walter Douglas, president of the Moctezuma Copper Company; Chester O. Swain, general counsel of Standard Oil Company of New Jersey; and Thomas W. Lamont of J. P. Morgan and Company. The executives initiated an extensive public relations campaign against Mexico. It produced pamphlets such as "Bread-Bolshevism-Binder Twine," which alleged that Mexico's Revolution had increased the price of American farmers' twine from Yucatán plantations; "Plow with Petroleum," a pro-industry flyer; "What Popular Writers Are Saying about Mexico," which was filled with anti-Carranza sentiment; and "Behind the Smoke Screen," a brochure that attempted to legitimize U.S. military intervention in Mexico.[33]

Although Doheny spared no expense in the attempt to protect his Mexican holdings, he could neither trigger an American invasion of Mexico nor even enable a counterrevolutionary government sympathetic to his interests to unseat Carranza. When World War I ended in November 1918, Doheny urged Wilson one last time to approve a confrontation with Mexican forces south of the border. Doheny's lobbyists (Harold Walker, Frederick Watriss, Frederick R. Kellogg, Guy Stevens, and Hillary Branch) simultaneously attempted to generate congressional support for such an invasion; but they, too, were unsuccessful. Doheny could not admit defeat; he would continue for another ten years to influence U.S. presidents and congressmen against Mexico's government, and he would not cease his efforts until the much-loathed Article 27 of the new Mexican Constitution was finally repealed.

It was at this time that Doheny was reunited with Albert Bacon Fall, his friend from the Kingston mining days. The former prospector was now a Republican senator from New Mexico, a key member of the Foreign Relations Committee and a vocal critic of Wilson's Mexican policies.

With proceeds from his mine holdings in Mexico and New Mexico, and income from his law practice, Albert Fall had begun to build a small fortune of his own, separate from that of his wife, Emma. His appointment as general counsel to Colonel William C. Greene, the owner of rich holdings in mining, timber, and railroads in northern Mexico, had provided Fall with ample opportunity to test his talents in investment. The Fall family now resided at Three Rivers (*Tres Rios*), a sprawling ranch near Las Cruces, New Mexico, where he had invested much time and money.[34] He thrived as a great southwestern rancher and was widely known as the "Political Boss of Southern New Mexico."[35]

Senator Fall was the Republican party's chief critic of Wilson's noninterventionist policy in Mexico. Both Fall and Secretary of State Robert Lansing urged Wilson to approve a preemptive military strike against Mexico's revolutionary forces or, more radically, to declare outright war.[36] Fall had called for Senate hearings about Mexico in order to discredit Wilson for his passivity and pressure him to approve armed intervention. The senator asked Edward Doheny, his wealthiest and most ardent supporter, to appear several times as a Senate witness, and Doheny willingly obliged. During this time, the Senate was simultaneously conducting an investigation of rumors alleging atrocities by Mexicans against U.S. nationals. The widely publicized hearings offered Doheny further opportunity to urge intervention.

Many were severely critical of the hearings, calling them an inquisition against the Wilson administration. In his memoirs, journalist Carleton Beals wrote that "Ill-feeling between the United States and Mexico had been fanned to bitterness by the oil companies and by the underhanded

Fall Senate Investigating Committee, a Doheny inquisition. . . . [Fall] and Doheny were doing all possible to foment difficulties between the two countries."[37] As Doheny, Fall, and their sympathizers had intended, the hearings cast a pall over Wilson's final months as president. Yet they did not effect the change in U.S. policy that Doheny so desperately wanted. More bad news for Doheny arrived when an urgent wire reached Washington on November 12, 1919, reporting that Mexican soldiers had forced Doheny's companies to cease drilling operations because they lacked oil permits. In response, Secretary of State Lansing fired off an official protest to the Carranza government. One week later, he called a conference with the heads of all major oil companies that might be affected by this new development (including officials from Panuco-Boston Oil Co., Standard Oil, Mexican Gulf Oil Co., and Doheny's Mexican Petroleum Co.). Lansing cautiously informed the executives that while Wilson would not declare war or break off diplomatic relations with Mexico, he would permit the State Department to intercede on a limited basis to protect U.S. interests.

Meanwhile, flare-ups continued between Mexico's government and U.S. nationals south of the border. In the spring of 1920, Carranza lost his former ally, General Alvaro Obregon, over ideological conflicts. Obregon garnered the support of most of the military forces, and early in May he was able to force Carranza to flee from Mexico City.

Carranza would be assassinated almost exactly a year later; a week after his death, Albert Fall's Senate committee would release a report that strongly supported recognition for Obregon's new government in Mexico. Although Doheny had hoped that Obregon would act swiftly to repeal Article 27, the new leader was not so rash. But Obregon was a shrewd politician who understood the benefits of an alliance; he let it be known that he would be sensitive to the needs of U.S. businesses on his soil. To Doheny's relief, in 1921 Obregon declared that his interpretation of Article 27 would not be confiscatory and would not be retroactive.

During this time, Warren G. Harding assumed office as the nation's twenty-ninth president. He had been staunchly supported by the oil companies, which had made large contributions to his political campaign. In preparation for the new administrations, both in Mexico City and Washington, D.C., the Association of Producers of Petroleum in Mexico convened on March 16 and 17, 1921. Roughly fifty top oil executives from forty companies, including Edward Doheny and his son Ned, assembled to strategize about lobbying tactics. The group received a tremendous boost when it learned that the Mexican Supreme Court had confirmed Obregon's view that Article 27 was not retroactive. In a case involving the Texas Oil Company, the court held that Article 27 did not apply to persons or companies that had carried out some "positive act" to indicate an intention to exercise subsoil rights (such as oil exploration or drilling) prior to the promulgation of the 1917 Constitution. The decision was applauded by Doheny. In effect, the substance of Article 27 was repudiated, as the decision rendered it nearly powerless against U.S. oil concerns. The U.S. oilmen and, above all, Doheny had succeeded in rolling back a major tenet of the revolution. After years of turmoil and chaos, it seemed Doheny's Mexican oil empire would be reasonably secure.

But now the spotlight was shifting back to Doheny's U.S. operations, and soon it would cast a harsh and ominous beam on his practices.

part two La Calavera del Comerciante

Eight Perfectly Legal

The 1920 Republican National Convention nominated a candidate who reflected the nation's war-weary mood—Warren Gamaliel Harding. Although his term as an Ohio senator had been undistinguished, he was liked for his straightforward manner and amiable disposition. More important, he was deemed a dependable conservative, a man "with his feet on the ground, a veritable Babbitt from Main Street, U.S.A." It also didn't hurt that Harding was extremely photogenic and said to have "the face of a Washington."[1]

Doheny and the other petroleum producers were determined to vote a business-friendly administration into office and get businessmen in the administration, men who could understand broad economic issues and could make decisions. There was general exasperation with Woodrow Wilson's delays and half-hearted actions. Business groups across the country debated election strategy. Doheny's name was submitted as a vice-presidential candidate at the Democratic Convention, but his inflexible demand for a plank backing Irish independence lost him support. After 1920 Doheny switched his allegiance to the Republicans, though he continued to cultivate important persons in both parties.

One of Harding's first campaign speeches seemed to summarize the nation's zeitgeist: "America's present need is not heroics, but healing; not nostrums, but normalcy; not revolution, but restoration; not surgery, but serenity."[2] His slogan, "Back to Normalcy with Harding and Coolidge," became the banner phrase during the campaign. Harding's election victory was impressive; he trounced his Democratic opponent, James Cox, whose vice presidential running mate was Franklin D. Roosevelt, by over 7 million votes. Harding had garnered the most popular votes of any presidential candidate to that time.

Ironically, Senator Harding had not been interested in the presidency; he wanted to run again for the Senate, but his campaign manager, Harry Micajah Daugherty, convinced him to seek the presidential nomination as a favorite son of Ohio.

Daugherty, a small-time but canny political operative in Ohio, was a colorful, hard-drinking, poker-playing figure about whom stories abounded. He was tall and balding with one blue eye and one brown— he did not go unnoticed. By the time of the 1920 Republican National Convention he had managed to offend sufficient people with his braggadocio and with statements to the press that *he* would control the nomination that he was denied delegate status. Working from backstage, he handled his candidate and moved Harding into the favored spot. In the famous smoke-filled room that was to forever characterize the 1920 convention, the front-runners deadlocked and only the compromise candidate, Harding, remained.

Businessmen everywhere threw themselves into the campaign, marshaling wide support for the candidate. When articles appeared disparaging Harding's qualifications, the response from the Republican camp was immediate. When rumors spread in the closing days of the campaign that Harding had *Negro* blood, Doheny laid out $25,000 for photo spreads of Harding's parents to contradict the claim.

On February 4, 1921, newly elected President Harding announced his cabinet. He appointed his longtime poker partner and former Senate colleague, Albert B. Fall, as secretary of the interior. Fall was disappointed not to have been selected secretary of state, but Harding had wisely chosen the well-known jurist and politician Charles Evans Hughes instead.[3] Fall told his wife, Emma, that the president had promised him an appointment to the Supreme Court should a vacancy occur.[4] Doheny, delayed in Tampico, Mexico, wired his personal congratulations to Fall: "We greet and congratulate you and through you the President upon the culmination of the event which marks the beginning of a new epoch in Americanism and we believe a period of progress and prosperity for our country."[5] The appointment was unanimously confirmed by Republicans and Democrats alike, following a motion by Senate Majority Leader Henry Cabot Lodge.

However, Harding's appointment of his friend and political mentor, Harry M. Daugherty, as attorney general was met with deep consternation by both parties. The *New York Times* sternly commented, "If a best mind is needed anywhere, it is in the Department of Justice. Instead, Mr. Harding has been content to choose merely a best friend."[6] Indeed, political analysts were beginning to scrutinize Harding's appointments as whispers of partisan favors filled the air. It was no secret that powerful oilmen, such as Standard Oil Chairman Robert W. Stewart, Harry F. Sinclair of Sinclair Oil, and Edward Doheny, had been extremely active on Harding's behalf. Many had helped secure his nomination, and their campaign contributions had helped finance his campaign.[7] Now Harding's key cabinet appointments were beginning to reflect his allegiance to his wealthy campaign financiers. He appointed industrialist and banker Andrew W. Mellon of Gulf Oil as secretary of the treasury; Sinclair Oil director Theodore Roosevelt Jr., as assistant secretary of the navy; Will Hays, Sinclair Oil attorney and Republican national chairman, as postmaster general; and, of course, Doheny's ally Albert Fall as secretary of the interior. So tight now was the alliance between the oil interests and the White House that Democrats openly dubbed Harding's administration the "Oil Cabinet."

Not long after Harding took up residence at the White House, Secretary Fall arranged a meeting between the president and Edward Doheny. Doheny, after returning from the White House, penned his friend a cheerful note about his high opinion of the new president:

> My Dear Secretary,
>   I cannot refrain from writing and thanking you for the interview which we had with the President. It was most satisfactory, and demonstrated to my friends that we have a real President, one who meets the people and recognizes that their interest in public affairs is worthy of consideration.
>   [I] left the White House more than ever convinced that the seven millions majority made no mistake in their selection of a President, and that insofar as his power can be exercised, he will endeavor to bring the country back to its condition of normal prosperity.
>   I want to say to you that we all feel under the greatest obligation to you for having arranged this interview. As Dr. Bridge [a longtime Doheny associate] said, "we have not only a great President, who is the President of all the people, but he has some great secretaries to advise with him." One of these I am proud to say he said [was you,] "Your friend Fall is one of the greatest, I now understand your statement that he is Lincolnesque in stature." There are several other Americans who believe as the Doctor does.[8]

When Harding assumed office in March 1921, the price of oil was at a twenty-year high. The large oil companies, small independents, and wildcatters were competing vigorously for additional sources of the valuable fuel. Doheny's Pan American Petroleum and Transport Company, Harry F. Sinclair's Sinclair Oil Company, and the Standard Oil Company of Indiana, controlled by board chairman Colonel Robert W. Stewart, held the largest shares of the marketplace. Next largest were the other Standard Oil companies—such as Standard Oil of California, Standard Oil of New Jersey, and Standard Oil of New York—whose financial clout was growing, and treasury secretary Andrew Mellon's Gulf Oil Company. In the Southwest, the Texas Company and other rapidly expanding firms were quickly building new complexes for producing, refining, transporting, and selling their petroleum products.

Across America the gasoline engine had eclipsed all other fuel-burning technologies in popularity. With peacetime prosperity, automobiles were rolling off assembly lines in staggering numbers, and the transformation occurred with amazing speed. In *Only Yesterday*, Frederick Lewis Allen painted a vivid portrait of the emerging automobile culture:

> Villages which had once prospered because they were on "the railroad" languished with economic anemia; villages on Route 61 bloomed with garages, filling stations, hot-dog stands, chicken diner restaurants, tearooms, tourists' rests, camping sites and affluence. The interurban trolley perished. . . . Railroad after railroad gave up its branch lines. . . . [T]he age of steam was yielding to the gasoline age.[9]

Not to be outdone, Doheny laid plans to develop a chain of gasoline stations across the country selling Panamco gas and Panolene motor oil and displaying his shamrock logo.

THE OIL RESERVES

According to Daniel Yergin, the change in the basic orientation of the oil industry was no less dramatic. In 1919 the total U.S. oil demand was 1.03 million barrels a day; by 1929 it would more than double to 2.58 million barrels. By the end of the decade, gasoline and fuel oil together would account for fully 85 percent of total oil sales; the consumption of kerosene became negligible in comparison. "The new light," notes Yergin, "had given way to the new fuel."[10]

As Doheny had feared, oil producers were now scrambling to buy up every potential drill site to meet this demand amid predictions that supplies of the "new fuel" were about to give out. The years 1917 to 1920 had been slow in terms of new oil discoveries, and some geologists claimed that limits on U.S. production were near. Some refineries could run at only half their capacity because crude oil was in short supply, and local retailers kept running out of kerosene and gasoline.[11] One group of undeveloped sites, in particular, was attracting attention: the Naval Petroleum Reserves, fields that had been set aside by the federal government for the navy in case of war. Oil executives were now heatedly vying for the right to begin drilling these rich fields located in the western United States. Soon the names of their locations would become ominously familiar to the general public.

Naval Petroleum Reserve No. 1, consisting of 38,969 acres, was situated at Elk Hills, in Kern County, California; Reserve No. 2, totaling 29,341 acres, was at Buena Vista Hills, also in Kern County; and the Reserve No. 3, consisting of 9,841 acres, was at Teapot Dome, in Natrona County, Wyoming.[12] (The Teapot Dome Reserve was named for an odd-shaped rock formation in the middle of the vast expanse that resembled a teapot; ironically, its "spout" was blown away during a severe windstorm in 1928.) These fields had been wisely set aside by the government to safe-guard against wartime oil shortages, enabling the navy to use its own fuel resources rather than pay possibly sky-high prices to outside vendors.

The oil under the federal reserve lands was extremely valuable. Geol-ogists estimated more than 135 million barrels of oil beneath Teapot Dome alone. And under the Elk Hills, there was an untapped reserve of be-tween 75 and 250 million barrels of oil, worth at least $100 million.

During Woodrow Wilson's administration, conservationists had urged his cabinet to continue withholding these fields instead of leasing portions to private concerns. In particular, conservation watchdog and Washing-ton lawyer Harry A. Slattery lobbied to maintain the fields "as an insur-ance policy for national defense."[13] Navy officials stalwartly rejected pe-titions by private oil companies to develop the fields. Wilson's navy secretary, Josephus Daniels, later wrote, "I remember one night toward the end of a session. . . . I remained at the Capitol all night long, watching the legislation of closing hours, fearing that some act might be passed that would turn over these invaluable oil reserves to parties who laid claim to them without even decent shadow of title."[14]

Toward the end of Wilson's second term, several private oil companies had leased lands *adjacent* to the Elk Hills and Teapot Dome reserves. Daniels then became alarmed that these companies might tap the naval reserves through "drainage." It was not necessary to drill wells directly above the reserves in order to tap their underground oil; a shrewd oil crew could simply set up a drill site nearby and then drain the oil away.

One investigation revealed that such a procedure could rob the Elk Hills Reserves of more than 20 million barrels.[15]

Daniels considered working with a reliable private oil producer, who would agree to safeguard the federal supply in exchange for limited leasing rights. One year before Harding's election, Daniels asked Congress for authority to lease portions of the lands for this purpose. On June 4, 1920, Congress consented, granting the secretary of the navy broad powers to use discretion in developing, operating, and leasing parts of the naval reserves.[16] Slattery and other dedicated conservationists, including former Pennsylvania governor Gifford Pinchot and Senator Robert M. La Follette of Wisconsin, believed that Daniels, also a stubborn conservationist, would now control the reserves.

When President Harding was elected, and Edwin Denby, a lawyer and former member of Congress who had risen from Marine Corps private to major during the Great War, replaced Daniels as secretary of the navy, these conservationists became alarmed. They believed Denby and the pro-oil cabinet would overturn Daniels's conservation policies. The naval "oil lease debate" became a hotly disputed matter during the early days of the Harding administration. In May 1921, with Harding's cabinet assembled in the White House Executive Office, Secretary of the Navy Denby asked that newly confirmed secretary of the interior, Albert Fall, assist him in resolving the naval reserve issue: "There is the man," Denby said pointing to Fall, "and his is the department to help the Navy with the handling of the troublesome problem of the oil reserves."[17] This brief interaction was to have fateful consequences before the year was out.

The matter was readdressed at a subsequent cabinet meeting. Interior Secretary Fall asked Attorney General Daugherty whether transfer of authority for the reserve fields from the Department of the Navy to the Department of the Interior could be made by Executive Order. Daugherty replied, "Certainly." And none of the other cabinet members objected. President Harding then arranged for a conference with Secretaries Fall and Denby. After meeting with the two men, he ordered the preparation of an executive order to fulfill Denby's request. The order was drafted and approved under the supervision of Edward C. Finney, assistant secretary of the interior. Finney also prepared a legal opinion, in which he averred the order was proper and legal. He then sent this opinion to Fall and Denby.

On receiving a copy of Finney's draft and legal opinion, Denby became furious. He had not intended to renounce his authority over the oil reserves; he had merely wished to include Fall in the handling of lease transactions. Denby communicated to Finney that he wished to be explicitly designated as having "approval authority" over all lease transactions, and Fall hastily modified the proposal accordingly. Now all transactions would take place under "consultation and cooperation with the Secretary of the Navy." Appeased, Denby then submitted the proposal to the assistant secretary of the navy, Theodore Roosevelt Jr., and to chief of the Bureau of Engineering, Admiral Griffin, who suggested additional changes in the order's language. After Fall and Denby approved this new draft, Roosevelt personally delivered the order to President Harding for his signature on May 31, 1921. In effect, the Executive Order transferred power over the naval oil reserves from the navy to the Department of the Interior. The genesis of this order was to be an important part of future investigations, with the series of events recalled by some and hotly contested by others.

Once this paperwork had been completed, Denby then announced that he would begin accepting bids from private companies for leasing rights to the naval reserves. Several weeks later, Fall notified Doheny that the Interior Department was fully involved in the endeavor: "There will be no possibility of any further conflict with Navy officials and this Dept., as I have notified Sec. Denby that I should conduct the matter of naval leases under the direction of the President, without calling any of his force in consultation unless I conferred with himself personally upon matter of policy."[18]

When pro-conservation lawyer Slattery heard the "unbelievable rumor" that Secretary Fall had managed to secure control of the naval oil reserves, he became outraged. He considered Fall's participation a direct threat both to national security and to natural resource conservation. "This was so bold a move," said Slattery, "that at first it did not sound true."[19] Slattery became even more distressed when he learned through news accounts that Denby was soliciting lease proposals from private oil companies.

Slattery wrote a letter to Gifford Pinchot, requesting an introduction to Theodore Roosevelt Jr. With Pinchot's letter in hand, Slattery met with the assistant secretary of the navy; detailing past hardships from wartime fuel shortages, he cautioned him about the need to preserve the navy's underground supply. But when Slattery mentioned Fall's poor conservation record, Roosevelt hit the ceiling. He told Slattery that Fall had been supportive of his father's Rough Riders' campaign in the Spanish-American War, adding that Slattery must not "say anything derogatory of this great, good friend."[20] It was after this outburst that Roosevelt informed Slattery that he himself had carried the Executive Order to President Harding, who signed it.

As he was exiting, Slattery told Roosevelt to consider the reserves lost, predicting that Fall would soon "turn over the naval reserves to private interests in the oil industry." Silently, angrily, Roosevelt showed Slattery to the door.[21]

During the fervent naval reserve debate, Doheny and Fall communicated frequently. Already good friends, they became more closely allied as a result of the political imbroglio. The two men visited one another often, and their wives and children began to associate as well. On June 12, 1921, Estelle Doheny penned a letter to Fall thanking him for a gift:

My Dear Mr. Secretary,

I have received the photographs of President Harding with his autograph which you so kindly secured for me.

I am indeed grateful to you for your kindness and appreciate you doing it.

We are more proud and pleased than we can ever tell to have the autographs.

It is a great comfort to Edward and me to tell you that he is our President too.

I am bringing with me on Wednesday night an autographed photograph of Mr. Doheny. It is the very first time he had autographed one of his photographs and never personally gave one away before. I have given them, but he hasn't and seldom consented.

I am looking forward to receiving yours when we come down. We have canceled our trip abroad owing to the illness of our older grandson who is on the road to recovery. Edward joins me in hoping you are feeling better than when we were down last week.

With love to Mrs. Fall and cordial greetings to yourself from Edward and me.[22]

The following month, Estelle wrote again, urging Albert Fall to take a short vacation at the Chester Place compound:

We are resting midst the flowers beneath the fig tree and we are wishing that you could be here. There is a hammock in the Aguacalientes shade and a rocker and lounge is there too. There is a pool within the Palm House waiting. There is rest and recreation. Won't you take a real vacation and come spend it here with your friends? Do come.

The Dohenys[23]

Fall responded soon thereafter by inviting Doheny to accompany him on an official tour of various federal lands, including Yosemite National Park. Although Doheny had to bow out of the trip because of a bout of influenza, he remained in close communication with Fall. He hosted Fall's wife, Emma, their eldest daughter, Alexina, and granddaughter Emmadair at the Chester Place compound for the remaining weeks of the summer while Fall concluded his federal lands tour.

On October 8, 1921, Secretary Denby announced to his naval councilmen that he was assigning the navy's responsibility for the oil reserves to the Bureau of Engineering to coordinate plans with the Department of the Interior. No objection was made to his decision, and on the following day he appointed Admiral John K. Robison as his liaison to the Engineering Bureau. From that moment forward, Robison would carry out Denby's directives and deliver his orders to the Engineering Bureau for execution.

Coincidentally, Admiral Robison had served as Ned Doheny's commanding officer during his short tour aboard the USS *Huntington* and Edward Doheny had met Robison in 1917 when he boarded the cruiser to pay his respects. At the time, the two men had spoken at length about their concern for national security and about the looming threat of drainage at the naval reserves. Now, in late October 1921, Robison and Fall were discussing the same issues, as well as exploring how the navy could maintain a proper store of fuel oil. At Denby's direction, Fall consulted the Pacific Oil Company in San Francisco to determine whether the company could consider a mutually beneficial arrangement: the navy would provide Pacific Oil with a fixed amount of *crude oil* if Pacific Oil would store an equal amount of *fuel oil* for the navy in its tanks. Fuel oil storage was most needed at Pearl Harbor, Hawaii, which was considered to be a strategic military location; Admiral Robison asked Fall to secure cost estimates for oil storage there. Try first, he urged, for a deal that would permit the navy to pay in crude oil rather than cash.

Two weeks later, Fall consulted Doheny about his onerous task. "Mr. Fall said the difficulty which confronted the Navy," Doheny said later, "was that it had no money with which to buy fuel oil for reserve to provide adequate storage for that oil even if it had the oil; that under a law passed by the Congress during the previous administration, there was [now] authority to exchange crude oil for fuel oil and storage facilities, provided any one could be found who was willing to take crude oil in payment for fuel oil and tanks."[24] Fall told Doheny that in his opinion, no tank manufacturer would accept such a deal, for they had no use for the navy's crude. He then asked Doheny if Doheny's own company, Pan American, could consider such an exchange and, if so, whether Doheny could submit a cost estimate for storing 1.5 million barrels of navy fuel at Pearl Harbor and further detail how much crude oil Pan American would require as payment from the navy. The deal was to be made much sweeter by being tied to the naval reserve lands; the company that was chosen by the navy to store its fuel was also to receive a lease option to drill wells on the reserve property.

Doheny promptly ordered his employees to secure the needed estimates. He also asked his accountants to calculate a fair exchange rate for swapping fuel storage for the navy's crude oil. Doheny learned from his advisors that storing the navy's oil supply would require approximately 27 commercial tanks at Pearl Harbor. His company, Pan American, would have to purchase the tanks, ship them to Hawaii, fill them with fuel oil, and then turn title over to the navy. In turn, the navy would reimburse Pan American by granting it the leases to valuable Elks Hills naval reserve fields.

Historians debate whether Fall's friendship with Doheny began to be tainted with political favors. It is certainly clear that while the navy was considering bids to solve their storage problems, Fall found ways to win Doheny's appreciation. On November 10, Fall sent a confidential note to James W. Weeks, the secretary of war, asking for tickets to permit Edward Doheny and Estelle Doheny to attend the ceremony honoring the Unknown Soldier at Arlington Cemetery on Armistice Day, November 11: "I am writing this note to you without consultation with [Mr.] Doheny, who has made no request, or hint of a request on the subject. . . . If this is possible, I will appreciate the courtesy as a personal favor to myself."[25]

Doheny was so moved by the gesture, and so enjoyed attending the historic event, that he typed a two-page letter to Fall expressing his thanks:

> Mrs. Doheny and I are deeply indebted to you for the opportunity which we had of being present at the memorial ceremonies. . . . Our seats were especially delightful and enabled us to hold a reception with all of our friends who gained ingress to the amphitheater at the west end entrance passing right by our seats.
>
> It was indeed a very impressive ceremony—one which inspired us with feelings of reverence, of gratitude, and of sweet memories for those who were represented by the burial of the "Unknown Soldier." . . .
>
> Mrs. Doheny joins me in very best regards, and hopes that you and Mrs. Fall have enjoyed good health, and that we may soon be able to see you again either in Washington or New York.
>
> When you intend to come to New York, please notify us, and make our apartment at the Plaza your headquarters. We will be delighted if you do so.[26]

Then, on November 23, Fall had a small envelope delivered to Doheny at his suite of rooms at the Plaza Hotel in New York City. It contained two tickets for the Army-Navy football game scheduled to be played on the

25th. "Of course I do not know just how these seats are situated," Fall wrote in his note accompanying the tickets, "but they are the tickets furnished to the cabinet officers."[27] The Dohenys attended the game with great delight.

Three days later, on November 28, 1921, Doheny sent Fall the Pan American bid for storing the navy's fuel at Pearl Harbor. After receiving the bid, Fall cautioned Doheny that the details they had been discussing were part of the "Navy's War Plan" and, hence, were "highly confidential"; Fall asked Doheny and his representatives not to discuss the information with anyone. The following day, at Denby's direction, Admiral Robison requested an official opinion from the navy's judge advocate general as to whether the proposed exchange of naval reserve crude oil for fuel oil and tanks at Pearl Harbor would pass muster. The judge advocate replied, yes, such an exchange was "perfectly legal."[28]

Conservationists continued to rally forces against Secretary Fall. Scrutinizing his every action in securing bids for the naval reserve fields, they publicly accused him of attacking the government's entire conservation program. When Fall proposed that his Department of the Interior take control of the Forest Service, Pinchot and Slattery enlisted the aid of the press to stop him. Pinchot believed that Fall and his allies were after "billions of dollars worth of . . . natural resources held by the government." He further feared that Fall intended to dismantle the Forest Service because of an alleged long-term dislike for the agency.[29] Fall's ranching operations in New Mexico had brought him into earlier, personal confrontations with the Forest Service.

David H. Stratton, Fall's biographer, has described the secretary's view of conservation as reflecting a frontier attitude, heavily imbued with the traits of western tradition: "He was by no means a conservationist in the popular conception of the term, as many of his speeches and actions while in the Senate and Interior Department revealed. By this time he had been utilizing the natural resources in the Southwest and in Mexico as a prospector, miner, mining investor, farmer and rancher for almost forty years. His belief in the unrestrained disposition of the public lands was as typically Western as his black Stetson and his love of good horse flesh."[30] The fundamental belief in unlimited natural resources open to unrestricted exploitation was shared by Albert Fall and Edward Doheny. Both men epitomized the spirit of the westerner: they were men who had matured in the great outdoors and who lived by the code of the frontier. Doheny and Fall both believed that the land, timber, and minerals of the western states should be used for development, just as such resources had been used earlier in the eastern states.

Once when an official of the National Park Service challenged Fall on his "wide-open attitude" toward the public lands, asking what sort of future this would leave the next generation, Fall replied: "Every generation from Adam and Eve down has lived better than the generation before. I don't know how . . . [the next generation will] do it—maybe they'll use the energy of the sun or the sea waves—but . . . [they] will live better than we do. I stand for the opening up of every resource."[31] This debate was part of a continuing public policy battle between those championing the development of resources on public lands by private interests and those who advocated conservation through governmental protection. The battle would in short order ignite a political inferno, with profound personal consequences for both Doheny and Fall.

As part of his publicity campaign against Fall, Slattery convinced reporters at the *Christian Science Monitor* to run a series of stories that harshly criticized Fall's conservation activities. Ten days later, Slattery contentedly reported to Pinchot: "In addition to . . . the *Monitor* . . . have got to NEA, *Chicago Tribune*, *New York Tribune*, Federated Press, and Consolidated folks to use a part or all of it. It is good stuff."[32] Pinchot's opening salvos had been successfully launched against Fall and had "pierce[d] Fall's crusty but sensitive armor."

Fall complained to Harding about Pinchot's "impropriety" and "vicious and unwarranted attack." He branded the conservationist's actions a "vicious propaganda campaign" and stalwartly defended his policies.[33] Vehemently, he cited his patriotic concern for national security and the benefit to the nation of private development. Secretly sympathetic to Fall, but unwilling to further alienate the conservationists, President Harding retreated into silence about Fall's proposal to incorporate the Forest Service into the Department of the Interior. Soon Harding began to lose patience with Fall as he publicly lashed out at the conservationists. Newspapers reported hints of "a widening gulf" between the president and his secretary of the interior, noting "surface indications" that Fall was so angry he might resign.[34]

There are conflicting reports about what happened next, but Fall's actions during the last weeks of November 1921 created intense outrage and suspicion. Two days after Thanksgiving, Fall purportedly contacted Edward L. Doheny and instructed the oilman to go ahead with the loan that the two men had discussed. Doheny agreed to Fall's request and asked his son Ned to carry the cash to Albert Fall in Washington, D.C.

Ned Doheny departed Los Angeles by train for his New York City apartment, accompanied by his longtime friend and employee, Hugh Plunkett. In the past nine years, Hugh had become a key confidant of young Doheny. He often accompanied Ned on his business trips and vacation jaunts. Because Hugh's five-year marriage to Harriet Marion Hall was in shambles, he spent most of his time in Ned's easygoing company.

Hugh had become increasingly important to Ned. He now worked for Ned full-time, catering to the young businessman's professional and personal needs. Ned trusted Hugh with many of the family's confidential dealings, and he had no reservations about asking Hugh to accompany him on this most unusual and fateful trip to Washington made at his father's behest.

Nine The $100,000 Bagatelle

Following his father's instructions, twenty-eight-year-old Edward L. Doheny Jr. walked into the offices of the New York City investment banking house of Blair and Company on November 30, 1921, and asked to withdraw $100,000 in cash from his personal bank account, which he held jointly with his wife. Blair's treasurer, Graham Youngs, immediately recognized young Doheny and escorted him into a private conference room that adjoined the bank's main office. Youngs asked assistant teller Charles Little to retrieve the requested cash from the bank's vault. The currency was presented in five $20,000 bundles, bound with rubber bands.

Youngs later recalled that he wrapped the bundles in plain brown paper and handed the five-inch-thick package to Ned, who examined it momentarily, then stuffed it inside a small dark-colored leather satchel.

The bag appeared to be an ordinary overnight traveling bag. Ned shook Youngs's hand, thanked him, and left the bank.

Ned Doheny returned to his apartment. Soon thereafter, he and Hugh Plunkett went to New York City's Grand Central Station, where they boarded a train for Washington, D.C. During the train ride, Ned kept the satchel either on his lap or tucked beneath his seat. On arriving in Washington, Ned and Hugh immediately went to the Wardman Park Hotel, located on fashionable Connecticut Avenue. The hotel's doorman saluted them smartly as they entered. Ned and Hugh took the building's elevator to the seventh floor, walked down the hallway, and knocked on a door that was immediately opened by Secretary Fall. Fall welcomed the two men and they exchanged handshakes. After making small talk, Ned reached inside the satchel, retrieved the five bundles of cash, and handed them to Fall. The secretary counted the money in plain view on the kitchen table and handed a promissory note to Ned.

For the rest of the afternoon, the three men remained together chatting. Late that night, Ned and Hugh took a train to New York City and returned to Ned's suite at the Plaza Hotel. The following morning, Fall traveled to his ranch in New Mexico. He stowed the money in his luggage.[1]

The size of the loan Doheny had made to Fall was enormous, even by today's standards, but it was a sum that Doheny could easily afford. He was at the peak of his earning power in 1921, with his Mexican operations finally showing impressive profits. The Mexican Petroleum Company, which Doheny liked to call jokingly "Mexican Pete," was now the largest and most lucrative concern in Mexico—which had become the most important oil-producing nation in the world. Doheny's greatest single well, the Cerro Azul No. 4, had already produced over 60 million barrels of oil, and was still producing 1 million barrels per month.[2] During the 1920s, Doheny's Mexican Petroleum Company would reap over $100 million in profits. Sitting on MPC's board of directors were fifteen individuals, including three Dohenys: Edward Sr., Estelle, and Edward Jr. In addition, several Doheny key staffers were directors, including general manager

Herbert G. Wylie and attorney Harold Walker. Other board members, staunch Doheny allies, were Dr. Norman Bridge and Frank R. Seaver. The remainder was made up of representatives of the banks, steel, and railroad companies with which Doheny did business.

Of all the foreign concerns in Mexico, the Doheny companies were the largest. The Pan American Petroleum and Transport Company had a fleet of oceangoing oil tankers and steamships that carried Doheny's oil to storage and distribution stations on the Gulf Coast and Eastern seaboard of the United States, the coasts of Central and South America, and across the Atlantic to Great Britain.[3] As he had dreamed, Doheny now controlled an international empire. His fantastic oil discoveries made him one of the richest men in the world.

As Edward Doheny's wealth and importance grew, he insisted upon sharing his good fortune—and concomitant responsibilities—with Ned Doheny. He appointed the young man to several directorial boards and included him in nearly all important corporate discussions; he was actively grooming his only son to inherit his oil empire.

THE NATION'S DEFENSE THREATENED

In mid-December, Admiral Robison visited Edward Doheny at Ned's New York City apartment. The two men held a wide-ranging conversation seated on the comfortable, cushioned sofas drawn up before the living room fireplace. Robison spoke earnestly as he explained to the oilman that grave military vulnerabilities had been revealed by confidential navy reports. Although Secretary Fall had briefed Doheny about Pearl Harbor's strategic location, it was Robison who explained to him in detail the navy's pressing need for the defense base.

"He told me," Doheny said,

> and this was the *first time* I heard of any such plan, that what the Navy wanted was the establishment of a complete and comprehensive fuel-oil station in Hawaii, and that this would necessitate . . . the providing of tanks in which to hold oil [and] the dredging of the Pearl Harbor channel in order that the deep-draft war vessels of the U.S. Navy could come into that harbor and get oil; the building of a concrete dock at which

these vessels could tie up; the erection not of ordinary commercial oil tanks to hold oil, but of specially constructed tanks for the peculiar purposes of the Navy; the providing of a complete pumping system and pipeline so that oil could be taken from the tankers that brought oil to Pearl Harbor for storage in the permanent reserve tanks, and when the hour of need came, could be pumped into the naval war vessels.

"In a word," Doheny said, "the plan was one that would require the expenditure of millions of dollars, and would result in the providing of [a] fuel station of a character which I had not the slightest idea was in contemplation when Secretary Fall . . . had first asked the assistance of our company in getting preliminary estimates."[4]

Robison told Doheny that military authorities believed the next theater of war would be the Pacific Ocean; extensive, confidential navy files contained sweeping intelligence about the danger. Every superior officer in the navy, added Robison, had received urgent confidential bulletins warning them "a great naval power" in the Pacific had amassed huge oil reserves in preparation for war, and at strategic Pacific ports held storage facilities that could be quickly used in a war against the United States. "He even startled me," Doheny recalled, "with information regarding orders which had been given to foreign war vessels and even to merchant steamships in the Pacific for their mobilization for war upon incredibly short notice; he pointed out that modern warfare had reduced the efficiency of coast defenses so greatly that they were no longer to be relied upon; he told me that experiments made at the Naval War College showed that in an attack upon this country of ours by a navy in the Pacific, defeat was sure to come to our fleet unless there was an adequate oil reserve in Hawaii and that victory of our navy and defeat of the foe would result from the establishment and maintenance of such an action." Doheny later admitted being hypnotized by Robison's eloquence, something Doheny "did not guess he possessed," based upon their previous conversations.

Robison disclosed that naval experts had in the strongest terms cautioned the president to fortify the Hawaiian ports, particularly Pearl Harbor, as they were the key to the entire defense of the nation. If the navy could successfully withstand an attack at Pearl Harbor, 2,100 miles from the mainland, no fleet would be able to launch a successful assault against the continental United States. Robison's superiors had warned that a surprise Japanese invasion of the Pacific Coast could have worse repercussions than the German invasion of Belgium and northern France.

Robison likened the weakness of Pearl Harbor to a systemic weakness of the entire U.S. defense system. This very subject was being quietly discussed at the Limitation of Arms Conference in Washington, D.C., Robison added. And finally, he revealed the message that his superiors had asked him to deliver to Doheny: "The Navy did not feel that it should go forward with its Pearl Harbor oil station plans until it had in advance some adequate assurance of the fulfillment of those plans," Robison said. And then he appealed to Doheny "not as a man in the oil business, but as a citizen of the United States to give to our Navy Department that assurance."

"And I gave it!" Doheny proclaimed. The next morning, Doheny informed one of his company's top executives, Joseph J. Cotter, to do "whatever was necessary to assist the goals" of the U.S. Navy in its "confidential project" at Pearl Harbor.

Robison may well have had naval intelligence about Japanese military intent, but in addition to secret military reports, he would also have been familiar with the then-current theories that the United States and Western Europe were imperiled by the surging population of Asia. The 1920s saw publication of a number of racist books and "scientific" theories on the danger. One widely read book was *The Rising Tide of Color*, by Lothrop Stoddard (with an introduction by Madison Grant), which urged vigilance in protecting the achievements of the white race from the fast-breeding nonwhites.[5] Among the safeguards Stoddard and Grant recommended were restricting immigration and reining in the activities of philanthropists and idealists, who they felt would ill-advisedly export traditions of democracy and free enterprise to races of color.

Frightening population figures, which showed whites losing ground rapidly, were frequently discussed at dinner gatherings of the privileged.[6] In the course of the long afternoon that Admiral Robison and Edward Doheny talked, they would have urged on one another the responsibility of men like themselves to be alert to the danger from Asia. They would have agreed that they had to take timely measures, acting for the protection of the country. As powerful men of high status they could speak freely to one another; and unlike the unnerved guests at dinner parties, they were men who could do something about the perceived peril. Doheny would, of course, agree to supply oil to the navy in the strategically placed Hawaiian Islands. And later, when he was asked to commit more to the project than obligated by the original terms, he would agree, duty bound.

While Admiral Robison was discussing critical matters of national security with Doheny, Albert Fall was sharing his own confidential concerns with Harry F. Sinclair about the naval reserves located at Teapot Dome, Wyoming.

At Christmas 1921, Fall met Sinclair, president of the successful Sinclair Oil Company, then the fifth-largest American oil producer, at Fall's sprawling ranch in Three Rivers, New Mexico. The vast ranch was in excess of 700,000 acres. Sinclair was noted for his shrewd business acumen, as well as his relentless energy and drive. The oilman traveled to Fall's New Mexico ranch on December 20, via his private railroad car, the *Sinco*, and spent the holidays with Albert and Emma Fall. During this visit, Fall and Sinclair explored ways for Sinclair to obtain rights to drill at the Naval Petroleum Reserve fields at Teapot Dome.[7] Fall saw to it that Sinclair was lavishly entertained during his visit. The men hunted deer, quail, and wild turkeys with Fall's cowpunchers, then attended a cowboy dance on New Year's Eve. Every evening, when all was quiet, Fall and Sinclair would sit by the ranch house's fireplace and hammer out details for giving Sinclair oil leasing rights at Teapot Dome in exchange for his storing fuel oil for the navy. The arrangement was similar to the proposition Admiral Robison had made to Edward Doheny.

Sinclair must have been pleased with the trip, because he sent Fall six heifers, a yearling bull, two six-month-old boars, and four sows from his New Jersey farm, "Rancocas," as tokens of his appreciation. One month later, Fall sent his son-in-law, Mahlon T. Everhart (a partner in Fall's Tres Rios Cattle and Land Company), to visit Sinclair in Washington, D.C. As a gift, Sinclair presented Everhart with $198,000 worth of 3.5 percent Liberty Bonds. In May, Everhart traveled to Sinclair's New York office, where he received an additional $35,000 in Liberty Bonds after presenting Sinclair with a $1,100 check as compensation for the livestock Sinclair had sent Fall. (Fall had begun to worry that his acceptance of the animals could be construed as an improper gift to a government official.)

Fall desperately needed money. The outbreak of the Mexican Revolution and the death of his old friend and former partner, Colonel William C. Greene, had deprived the interior secretary of his previous income from Mexican copper mines. He had been forced to sell much of his business interests and was in arrears on his property taxes. His debts totaled far more than $100,000. Doheny's loan and the additional gifts from Sinclair had enabled him to pay his back taxes as well as a $140,000 debt owed to the M. D. Thatcher Estates Company at Pueblo, Colorado. He even purchased the adjoining ranch owned by N. W. Harris. Fall now began to plan extensive improvements for both properties, including the construction of a hydroelectric plant, irrigation systems, and new roads.

In January 1922, H. Foster Bain, director of the Bureau of Mines, began at the behest of the secretary of the navy to visit officials of the leading California oil companies to seek bids for the Pearl Harbor project. Bain had promised his superiors that he would discuss the details of the government's plan with each oil executive personally, in order to ensure that the information remained confidential. With the navy's intelligence plans in his possession, Bain conferred with officers of Pan American, the Standard Oil Company of California, Associated Oil Company, Union Oil Company of California, and the General Petroleum Company (now known as Mobil Corporation) one by one. He also interviewed the engineers at Ford, Bacon, and Davis, the Foundation Company, the J. G. White Engineering Company, and the Pittsburgh and Des Moines Steel Company.

In total, Bain visited nine different companies: five of them oil producers and the remaining four highly regarded construction companies. All were given the same information and afforded an opportunity to submit proposals to the government for providing naval fuel at Pearl Harbor in exchange for an agreed-on amount of crude oil. From January until March, the navy made several modifications in its Pearl Harbor projections and altered its bidding requirements after reappraising its needs. Finally, Bain, Admiral Robison, and Assistant Secretary of the Interior Finney set the date of April 15, 1922, as the date for bidding to begin.

In April, Fall was informed by Bain of the difficulties he was encountering in securing bids from some of the companies solicited. On April 12, Fall drafted a letter to Navy Secretary Denby (three days before the bids were opened) suggesting that the entire matter be submitted to Congress for further legislation so that the navy could sell oil from its reserves and pay engineering companies directly for construction work without any potential legal obstructions. (Without Congress's authorization, the navy would have to direct all of its sales proceeds to the general fund of the U.S. Treasury, according to federal law.) Had Secretary Denby followed Fall's suggestion and approached Congress, most historians believe that the entire plan to exchange fuel storage for crude oil would have come under attack and been abandoned. Instead, he chose to go ahead with the scheme.

Denby opened the bids on April 15, 1922, in Finney's office. On hand were Bureau of Mines Director Bain and Arthur W. Ambrose, chief petroleum technologist for the U.S. Navy. Also present were representatives from the Standard Oil Company of California, the Associated Oil Company, the J. G. White Engineering Company, the Foundation Company, the Pittsburgh and Des Moines Steel Company, and Doheny's own Pan American Petroleum and Transport Company.

Doheny's bid was lower than that of any other company; thus Pan American appeared entitled to the contract. Assistant Secretary Finney made this announcement before the assembled group and then stated that the bids would be more closely analyzed so that all persons interested could be advised of the results. Finney turned them over to Bain and Ambrose, instructing them to present the bids to the Department of the Navy. At the time of this important event, Secretary Fall was at his New

Mexico ranch; Doheny was en route to Mexico City and was informed via telegram from Pan American executive J. J. Cotter that his bid had won.

On April 17, 1922, in a paper titled "Memorandum to Secretary Finney," Bain and Ambrose recommended that the proposal of the Pan American Petroleum and Transport Company be accepted as it was the lowest bid."[8]

Finney then sent a telegram dated April 17 to Fall at Three Rivers, New Mexico. (At a crucial time in the future this telegram and the one in reply would disappear, only to surface later in a peculiar fashion.)

> California reserve bids received and opened Saturday, Standard bid was for exchange only. Associated bid for oil in No. 2 reserve only 6,201,900 barrels. Pan American bid oil from both reserves. 6,092,700 barrels, with an alternate Pan American bid, 5,878,900 barrels, if given preference for drilling required by government in future Reserve No. 1. Pan American bid also advantageous in that it provides for reduction in cost in case storage facilities erected for less money than estimated. In opinion of Ambrose, Robison and myself, Pan American alternative bid best offered and should be accepted.

Finney concluded the telegram: "Suggest you authorize closing contract with Pan American. Details will require approximately three or four days to arrange. On conclusion of this contract, suggest you publish complete information concerning opening of all reserves. In any event, suggest you telegraph your desires to Denby at once."

On April 18, 1922, Fall promptly wired back his concurrence: "Telegram reference California bids, if Admiral Robison and Secretary think best, close immediately on basis Pan American deal and if authorized by Denby proceed immediately award and close contract and make public entire policy in fullest and complete manner."[9] Fall's telegram to Finney was turned over to the Department of the Navy. Secretary Denby agreed that Doheny should receive the contract; and this decision was conveyed to the Department of the Interior by Admiral Robison. Finney then addressed a letter to Doheny at the Pan American Company, confirming its award of the contract based upon "Alternate Bid B, found to be the lowest and best bid received." On April 18, 1922, the award was made, and the navy announced the news in press releases.

The formal contract between Pan American and the U.S. government was executed on April 23, 1922.[10] This contract granted to Pan American the right to drill and extract gas and oil from California Naval Reserve No. 1 (Elk Hills) and certain described lands in California Naval Reserve No. 2 (Buena Vista) for "twenty years or so long thereafter as oil or gas is produced in paying quantities." In return for the lease, the United States was to receive as royalty quantities of fuel oil ranging from 12.5 to 35 percent of the value of the crude oil extracted. Pan American agreed to construct storage facilities, some of which were to be paid by using the United States' share of the oil designated as royalty oil. Pan American agreed to advance all money necessary to build and transport the naval fuel to the Pearl Harbor plant.

Unknown to Doheny, Fall had just signed a similar contract with Harry F. Sinclair for leases to the Wyoming naval reserves. One week before Pan American's bid for Elk Hills had been opened and read, on April 7, Fall and Denby had granted Mammoth Oil the exclusive right to extract oil and gas from 9,321 acres of federal land at the Naval Reserve No. 3 in Natrona County, Wyoming, also known as "Teapot Dome," "as long as they could be produced in paying quantities." In consideration, the U.S. government would receive a percentage of oil as royalties from the exploited field. In a separate agreement (dated December 20, 1922, and February 9, 1923), Sinclair's Mammoth Oil agreed to construct government facilities for storing the "royalty oil," finance all necessary drill sites, and install a $20 million pipeline. The government would then reimburse Sinclair for its construction costs, using the royalty oil.[11]

In April 1922, a small-time oil operator from Wyoming became outraged when he learned that Sinclair had received an exclusive lease to Teapot Dome. The oil producer wrote an angry letter to his senator, John B. Kendrick, alleging that Sinclair was allotted the contract in a secret deal; according to this constituent, oil companies had not been invited to submit competitive bids for the Teapot Dome lease. The letter posed formidable questions: Why was the navy's land being leased at all? And why was the secretary of the interior permitted to independently dispose of naval reserve lands?[12]

Appropriately concerned, Senator Kendrick wrote Secretary Fall a formal letter asking for a statement of facts concerning the Teapot Dome transaction. He received no reply. On April 12, 1922, Kendrick introduced a resolution before the Senate, demanding that Fall and Denby fully advise the Senate about the details of this transaction.[13]

Several days later, the Department of the Interior issued a public statement, signed by one of Fall's subordinates, announcing two contracts: a lease of government lands in Wyoming granted to the Mammoth Oil Company and a contract for oil storage facilities given to the Pan American Petroleum and Transport Company, enabling it to drill wells at Elk Hills, California. The announcement stated that these two transactions were necessary because "oil was being drained from these reserves in very large quantities, amounting to millions of dollars of loss up to the present time, by wells on adjoining lands, and that in a few years the government well would be depleted."[14] On April 21, Fall finally responded to Kendrick, explaining that "secrecy" had been necessary during the leasehold negotiations because of reasons involving "the national defense."

As news of Secretary Fall's revelations spread through the Senate chambers, Senator Robert M. La Follette, Democrat from Wisconsin, who had been in contact with conservationists Harry A. Slattery and Gifford Pinchot, introduced his own formal resolution directing the Senate Committee on Public Lands and Surveys to investigate the "entire subject of leases of naval oil reserves" and to "compel the representation before it of all documents and official data connected therewith." A concerned President Harding took official notice of the Senate resolution and addressed a letter to the Senate defending Fall's actions and affirming that he had personally approved of the transactions conducted by Fall and Denby. Harding's June 7 letter to the Senate committee stressed: "I think it is only fair to say in this connection, that the policy which has been adopted, by the Interior, in dealing with these matters, was submitted to me prior to the adoption thereof and the policy decided upon and the subsequent acts have at all times had my entire approval."[15]

But the president's missive did nothing to stave off the tide of hostility toward Fall and his covert actions that was swelling through the Senate. Although Kendrick originally was spurred by a constituent to investigate the naval leases, growing numbers of anti-Fall conservationists were now joining forces to insist upon a full-fledged investigation. "This is going to be a national scandal before all is over," Slattery wrote in his diary, as he gloated over reports that a formal Senate investigation of Fall was about to be launched.[16]

THE SECRETARY RESIGNS

As the heat and pressure of the unfriendly, protracted government inquiry concentrated more intensely on Albert Fall, he could find no relief. On March 4, 1923, eight months after the Senate had approved La Follette's request for an investigation, Fall resigned.

According to journalist William Allen White, Fall's action was primarily triggered by his growing alienation from President Harding, who was now cautiously distancing himself from his secretary of the interior. In the winter of 1922, White visited with Harding at the White House, and left "with a feeling that it was the scene of a terrible struggle. Fall was the symbol of one of the forces . . . that was grappling [for] supremacy with the confused mind of the President." The old camaraderie between the president and the secretary was no more. To White, Washington seemed abuzz with a "thousand little stories, rumors and suspicions of irregularity," and he was convinced that Harding was suffering under the pressure of having to quickly break with longtime friends and associates such as Albert Fall and Harry Daugherty (now attorney general) and cut his link to a "sordid past."[17]

Amazingly, soon after his resignation, Fall engaged in even more activities with the very oilman who was also being investigated by the Senate. In July, Fall traveled with Harry F. Sinclair to the Soviet Union on a business trip to secure the right to lease oil lands on the Soviet island of Sakhalin. In exchange for his services, Sinclair paid Fall $25,000 in Liberty Bonds and gave him $10,000 for expenses.

Wearied from the Washington infighting, and also hoping to bolster his image with the American public, President Harding decided to take a part-business, part-barnstorming trip to Alaska in June 1923. He left Washington by train on June 20, stopping to deliver speeches in major cities across the United States. As Harding crossed through Kansas, Emporia newspaper owner White boarded the train for another chat with the president, who was resting in his private car. "I have no trouble with my enemies," the president sighed, "I can take care of them. It is my . . . friends that are giving me my trouble."[18]

Harding reached Alaska in early July. But on his return trip home at the end of the month he became severely ill as his train passed through Seattle, Washington. When they reached San Francisco his aides rushed the ailing president to a hospital, where Harding was diagnosed with extreme fatigue and ptomaine poisoning. He died on August 2, 1923, at age fifty-seven. At first, the president's sudden death was attributed to food poisoning from crab meat. But it was later established that Harding had been misdiagnosed; he died not from poisoning but a fatal stroke. The president's body was conveyed to Washington; after a state funeral in the Capitol, it was removed to his hometown of Marion, Ohio, for interment.

As speculation circulated throughout the nation over the real cause of Harding's untimely death, White asked sadly, "How could the doctors diagnose an illness that was part terror, part shame, and part utter confusion!"[19] One day, America would realize "how wickedly unfair the Republic was to pick up that man—weak, unprepared, with no executive talent . . . and pinnacle him in the most powerful place on earth. He was as a child in heart and head, set down to fight the dragon, and in the end his terror conquered him." And White quoted Harding's secretary of commerce, Herbert Hoover: "People do not die from a broken heart, but people with bad hearts may reach the end sooner from great worries."[20]

Vice President Calvin Coolidge was sworn in as the thirtieth president of the United States on August 3, 1923, and the fortunes of Doheny and Sinclair would take a bitter turn as a result. Intense pressure resumed from the Senate to continue its investigation of former secretary Fall's role in the naval oil lease debacle. Hearings were scheduled to begin in October.

Thomas J. Walsh, a respected Democratic senator from Montana, was named chairman of the subcommittee of the Senate Committee on Public Lands that would conduct the investigation into any "irregularities"

committed by Fall in relation to the naval reserve leases. Walsh was "a personally incorruptible man, who set high standards for public service. He was known as an unapproachable, austere, and relentless prosecutor." At the time he assumed chairmanship of the investigating committee, he was sixty-two years old, but still vigorous and "at the peak of his exceptional mental powers."[21]

Senator Walsh was the eldest son of Irish Catholic immigrants from Wisconsin and not one to shy from a task at hand. He intended to pursue Fall, Sinclair, and Doheny with a vengeance to determine if they had acted improperly. Contemporary accounts likened Walsh's single-minded investigation of the three to the work of a bloodhound. He proceeded slowly and methodically, and eighteen months passed before he was ready to submit his evidence to the committee. By this time, Sinclair's leases of the Teapot Dome Reserve and Doheny's contract and leases for the Elk Hills Reserves had already been executed. Sinclair and Doheny had taken possession of the lands, drilled wells, extracted oil, and built storage facilities as specified in their respective agreements.

Walsh received very damaging information about Albert Fall from a journalist, Carl C. Magee, who was the editor of the *Albuquerque Morning Journal*. Magee, a longtime political opponent of Fall, had been closely monitoring the secretary's public and private activities. He traveled to Washington to alert Walsh of his discoveries. Magee told Walsh that after Harry Sinclair's visit to Three Rivers, there was a "remarkable change" in Fall's financial status. Before his appointment to the Harding cabinet, Fall was "dead broke," his ranch at Three Rivers was in disrepair, and he was ten years in arrears on his property taxes. Yet shortly after Sinclair's Christmas visit, Fall had been able to pay off his back taxes, make over $40,000 in improvements on his ranch, and purchase an adjoining piece of property. Magee also noticed that Fall had purchased a number of "blooded stock" cattle and hogs. On learning this, Walsh asked Magee if he would be willing to testify before the Senate committee; Magee enthusiastically agreed.

Then, almost immediately after meeting with Magee, Walsh was contacted by another potential witness, Archibald Roosevelt, son of Theodore Roosevelt and brother of Theodore Roosevelt Jr., who was still assistant secretary of the navy. Archibald Roosevelt informed Walsh that he had just resigned as a vice president of one of Sinclair's oil companies. Roosevelt claimed he did so because Sinclair's confidential secretary, a man named G. D. Wahlberg, had told him that "somebody" might have sent Fall as much as $68,000; Roosevelt wanted no part of this.

Conservation watchdog Slattery, meanwhile, had learned that before resigning, Fall had planned private exploitation of resources in Alaska, after bringing the Forest Service under the control of the Department of the Interior. He contacted Pinchot with this knowledge, and the two agreed to continue their own investigations into Fall's potentially illicit actions while he was interior secretary.[22] Calling the oil lease transfers an "outrageous abuse of power," Slattery submitted all of his own damning discoveries about Fall to Senator Walsh and the members of the Senate committee.

As was to be expected, oil company rivals of Pan American and Mammoth Oil now became thoroughly caught up in the news of the ongoing investigations. Their executives realized that any findings that harmed Doheny and Sinclair could be a boon to their own businesses. Gleeful competitors began leaking rumors about the beleaguered oilmen to the press and they labeled the naval leases unfair and based on collusion involving the secretary of the interior.

THE HEARINGS

On Monday, October 23, 1923, at exactly 10:00 A.M., the Senate Committee on Public Lands and Surveys assembled in Room 210 of the Senate Office Building to begin their historic proceedings. Those present included Senators Walsh, Smoot, Lenroot, Ladd, and Jones, as well as a jostling crowd of reporters and spectators.[23]

The following morning Walsh summoned Albert Fall to the witness stand. As Walsh launched a steady stream of probing questions, Fall became arrogant and antagonistic. He argued that he had granted the navy leases to Sinclair out of patriotic duty and to prevent drainage of the oil fields. He reminded Walsh that large fuel oil reserves were needed to maintain American security. In response to a question, Fall testified emphatically that he had *not* overstepped his authority—he acted in his full capacity as interior secretary, using the powers that the president vested in him. He had "no apologies," he added. Although Walsh attempted to show that Fall had kept the negotiations secret and had discouraged competitive bidding, Fall again strenuously denied the charges. Yes, he had been secretive in his discussion about the leases, but only at the president's bidding: issues of national security were being discussed. When Walsh asked whether Sinclair had financed Fall's trip to the Soviet Union, Fall responded that he had not received "one cent in payment for it." Tense exchanges would continue between the chairman and the former secretary for two full days.

Walsh next summoned Secretary of the Navy Edwin Denby to the stand. Spectators later reported that he appeared ignorant and naive, and made a "pathetic witness." To Walsh's opening questions, Denby replied that although he, too, had been quickly convinced that drainage was a problem, he had known nothing about the leases' disposition; this was because custody of the reserves had been transferred by presidential Executive Order to the Interior Department. Since that time, he had been relieved of his responsibility for handling the reserves and had merely received periodic updates from his subordinates who were working with Interior. Denby said that he could not even remember whether he had signed any contracts and leases in regard to this matter. As Walsh questioned him further, Denby admitted that he knew pitifully little about U.S. government regulations covering the navy's responsibility for conserving oil. He said he could not remember ever reading the relevant congressional act that had committed the reserves to his custody.

The next witness, Harry F. Sinclair, testified with what seemed far more candor. He admitted meeting with Fall on his private railroad car, the *Sinco,* at the secretary's ranch in New Mexico at Christmas 1921. But Sinclair emphatically denied that he gave Fall a gift of any kind in return for the Teapot Dome lease. When Walsh asked Sinclair about snug political associations, Sinclair acknowledged that he had lately entertained and socialized with other members of the Harding cabinet.

The Senate hearings continued into November, and public interest began to wane. Die-hard attendees sat through endless tedious expert testimony from geologists who debated whether the reserve lands had been threatened by drainage. But in December, the nation's attention turned to the hearing room once again when Senator Walsh called Edward Doheny to the stand.

Doheny told the committee that he had accepted the naval reserve leases at Elk Hills largely out of "patriotic concern" and to prevent drainage. Unbelieving, Walsh kept hammering at Doheny with myriad follow-up questions. But he gained only an angry retort: "I do not want you to ask me to assume anything that is against my interest, and your questions are not going to make me do it. I claim my lease was made in the interests of the United States government, of which you are a Senator and I am a citizen. You cannot get me to admit that it is a bad lease, because I certainly do not think it is."

"I only want the facts," Walsh said angrily. And Doheny responded, "Well you cannot get the facts out of me by citing this as bad policy or that as good policy. Policy is not a fact. Don't ask me about conclusions, but ask me for the facts and we can go right along."

Walsh then asked Doheny why, when the U.S. Bureau of Mines estimated that drainage had cost the government 11.1 million barrels of oil, Doheny had claimed it would cost tens of millions. Doheny answered, "No man on earth has access to the same information I have, because my information comes from twenty-nine years of close study of the proposition, such as no other living man has given to the business. That sounds egotistical, I grant you, but that is absolutely the truth, since you have asked the question."

And, when Walsh's associates asked Doheny if Secretary Fall had profited from the transaction, Doheny replied, "Not yet. I want to say right here, though, that I would be very glad to take Mr. Fall in my employ if he ever wanted to come to us."

Again, Harry Sinclair was called to the stand. He reiterated Doheny's argument that his leases were made in the interests of United States security and again swore that Fall had "never received any benefits or profits, directly or indirectly, in any matter whatsoever."

By now the press was giving the investigations daily coverage. Fall's numerous enemies took great delight in this; some testified against him as character witnesses. One such witness was Carl Magee, who told the Senate panel about the unusual and sudden improvements at Fall's Three Rivers Ranch following Sinclair's visit. Other witnesses confirmed that in 1922, Fall purchased the adjoining Harris Ranch for $91,500 and then spent another $100,000 on land purchases, back taxes, and property improvements. Archibald Roosevelt testified that he resigned because of allegations made by Sinclair's secretary, G. D. Wahlberg.

The following day, Wahlberg followed his former co-worker to the stand and gave an almost farcical performance. Although he admitted conversing with Roosevelt about Fall's ranch, he said he believed Roosevelt had misunderstood him. He had not mentioned the sum of $68,000; perhaps he had said that Mr. Sinclair had sent "six or eight cows" to Fall's ranch at Three Rivers. He believed that Roosevelt had misheard "sixty-eight thous" for "six or eight cows."[24]

It was now clear to the Senate investigators that Fall had suddenly come into possession of a large sum of cash. The committee recalled Fall, who had already gone back to New Mexico, to determine how he had been able to pay for all the sudden improvements at his ranch. After a two-week delay, he returned to Washington, D.C., but notified the committee on December 26, 1923, that he was too ill to attend the hearings; instead he was submitting a statement of his finances that was intended to clear up their confusion.

Fall's unsworn—long and rambling—statement protested the relevance of the committee's inquiry into his private financial affairs. It contained a declaration from him that he had been able to make improvements to his ranch because he had obtained $100,000 cash from Edward B. ("Ned") McLean, of Washington, D.C. These words would haunt Fall until the day he died. His statement read in part:

> It should be needless for me to say that in the purchase of the Harris
> Ranch or any purchase or expenditure, I have never approached
> E. L. Doheny or anyone connected with him or any one of his corpora-
> tions, or Mr. H. F. Sinclair or anyone connected with him or any of
> his corporations; nor have I ever received from either of said parties
> one cent on account of any oil lease, or upon any other account
> whatsoever.

Now the spotlight turned instantly on the Honorable Edward B. McLean. McLean had inherited the *Cincinnati Enquirer* and the *Washington Post* from his father, John R. McLean, a man who had built a fortune in newspapers, utility companies, and banks after the Civil War. Ned's wife, Evalyn Walsh—who at that time owned the Hope Diamond—was an heiress whose fortune was as great as his own. The celebrated couple owned a mansion in Washington, D.C., and an estate in the suburbs called "Friendship," where they hosted sumptuous parties for Harding administration insiders. McLean was a close friend of Fall, and incredibly, he agreed to say that he had loaned Fall $100,000.

Not surprisingly, the investigating committee decided to call McLean to the floor to corroborate Fall's testimony. McLean wrote a letter to the committee in which he declared that it was true that in 1921 he had lent Fall $100,000 on a personal note. McLean stated that he was currently in Florida, and ill, and hoped that it would not be necessary for him to travel to Washington to appear before the committee. Walsh then visited the ailing McLean in his sickbed in Florida. Under Walsh's relentless questioning, McLean came up with a "new and startling story": he said he had drawn three checks totaling $100,000 on his personal account and had given them all to Fall. They were never presented to the bank for payment, however, and several weeks later, Fall returned them, stating that he had collected the money from another source. That, said McLean was the "whole truth": Fall had never received a dollar in cash from McLean.

The testimony, one reporter commented, clearly made Fall out to be a liar and McLean a fool. And it infuriated Doheny, who believed that Fall had "botched everything up" with his lie. "Why," Doheny demanded of Fall, "didn't you do as I told you in the beginning when this thing started—and tell all about this thing?"[25] Privately he said that Fall's story that McLean had loaned him the $100,000 was the "lie he could never forgive." In a moment of chilling resolution, Doheny informed Fall he now intended to tell the Senate committee everything.

Doheny returned to sit before the committee three times. His third day of testimony, January 28, marked the climax of the investigation. The facts furnished by Doheny in this exchange with Walsh would be the basis for much of the litigation that was to ensue.

The hearing room was packed to capacity with spectators who had heard rumors that Doheny was about to make revelations about the mysterious loan to Albert Fall. Senator Walsh opened the hearing: "I asked the committee to meet this afternoon because I was informed that Mr. Doheny desired to come before this committee and make a statement."

Doheny then rose to his feet and said that he had a prepared statement that he desired to read. Permission was granted, and the oil magnate proceeded:

> I wish to state to the committee and the public the following facts. . . . I regret that when I was before your committee I did not tell you what I am now telling you. When asked by your chairman whether Mr. Fall had profited by the contract, directly or indirectly, I answered in the negative. That answer I now reiterate.
>
> I wish to inform the committee that on the thirtieth of November, 1921, I loaned to Mr. Fall $100,000 upon his promissory note, to enable him to purchase a ranch in New Mexico. This sum was loaned to Mr. Fall by me personally.
>
> It was my own money and did not belong in whole or in part to any oil company with which I am connected. In connection with this loan there was no discussion between Mr. Fall and myself as to any contract whatever. It was a personal loan to a lifelong friend. We have been friends for over thirty years. Mr. Fall has invested his savings for those years in his home ranch in New Mexico, which I understand was all that remained to him, after the failure of his mining investments in Mexico, and nine years of public service in Washington, during which he could not properly attend to the management of his ranch.
>
> His troubles had been increased in 1918 by the death of his daughter and his son, who, up to then, had taken his place in management of his ranch. In our frequent talks it was clear that the acquisition of a neighborhood property controlling the water that flows through his home ranch was a hope of his, amounting to an obsession. His failure to raise the necessary funds by realizing on his extensive and once valuable mine holdings had made him feel that he was a victim of an untoward fate.
>
> In one of these talks, I indicated to him that I would be willing to make him the loan and this seemed to relieve his mind greatly. In the autumn of 1921, he told me that the purchase had become possible, that the time had arrived when he was ready to take advantage of my offer to make the loan.

Doheny then stated in response to questioning that he had long ago promised Fall, "Whenever you need some money to pay for the ranch, I will lend it to you." Fall had offered to put up the ranch as security for the loan, but Doheny said he would simply give Fall the money in return for a mere promissory note. Later, said Doheny, Fall telephoned him that he was ready for the money, and Doheny had his son deliver Fall $100,000 in cash.

Senator Walsh then asked an obvious question: "You are a man of large affairs and of great business transactions, so that it was not unusual for you to have large money transactions, perhaps, but was this not an extraordinary way of transmitting money?"

"I do not know about that," Doheny replied. "I realized that the amount of money I was loaning him was a bagatelle to me, that it was no more than $25 or $50 perhaps, to the ordinary individual. Certainly a loan of $25 or $50 from one individual to another would not be considered at all extraordinary, and a loan of $100,000 from me to Mr. Fall is no more extraordinary."

The room fell quiet for a long moment. Then a burst of heated questioning began, and Doheny again said that he regretted not having told the whole truth in his previous testimony. He admitted that he had loaned Fall the $100,000, although he denied that this loan had anything to do with the naval reserve leases. He continued to maintain that his interest in the reserve was exclusively patriotic, though when questioned he conceded that he thought his company would make as much as $100 million in profits from the leaseholds over the next thirty years.

The Senate subpoenaed Fall again on January 29; once more, he claimed he was too ill to appear. This time, however, the Senate sent its own doctors to examine Fall; they pronounced him "nervous," but not sick. Fall finally appeared before the Senate on February 2. He read a statement asserting that the committee did not have the authority to question him, and, since he might be criminally prosecuted, he was now invoking the Fifth Amendment, which protected him against self-incrimination. Fall's assuming his Fifth Amendment privilege may have pushed the already-shocked Senate committee to its next decisive action.

They called Doheny to appear again late in the afternoon on February 2. This time, Doheny told them he had brought with him for the committee's perusal Fall's promissory note for the $100,000 loan. However, to the surprise of all, Fall's signature was missing from the note. Doheny said he had ripped off the signature and had given it to his wife for safekeeping. When Walsh asked the reason for that action, Doheny explained that he did so to protect Fall; should Doheny and his wife both be killed in a train wreck, he didn't want his executors to foreclose against Fall for the unpaid loan. Under questioning, he also revealed that the $100,000 cash loan had been withdrawn from his son's bank account, and he admitted that there was no record of Fall's indebtedness in his own financial accounts.

The eyes of the public were now fixed on the prospector-become-oil-millionaire who revealed that he had been Albert Fall's mysterious moneylender. William Hard, reporting for the *Nation*, described Doheny in detail for readers who were becoming more and more curious about this star witness:

> Mr. Doheny is small, his shoulders are not too narrow, but they are not broad. They are not commanding. . . . At no point does Mr. Doheny seem commanding. He seems too gently inclined and too humorously inclined to be commanding.
>
> His eyes have a twinkling humor and also perhaps only at this moment a competing film over them of dull sadness. He is dressed very neatly and even dapperly. On his wrist he wears a watch. On the little finger of his left hand he wears a large ring. His hair is parted in the middle. It is wavy hair, browning, but beginning in streaks to be whitish. He has a mustache. It is gleaming and total white. His complexion is desert red. He wears spectacles with fine and almost invisible bows over his ears.
>
> He seems largely to consist of smiling pathetic eyes with a gleam of glass in front of them. He does not look dangerous. On the contrary, he looks extremely inoffensive.[26]

After his surprising disclosure, Doheny had presented a forthright presence on the stand, but Walsh was intent on pressing the wealthy oilman further for more information about the loan. Doheny explained that he had sent Ned (and Ned's friend and secretary Hugh Plunkett) to deliver the "little black bag" containing $100,000 in cash to Fall. Walsh then made Doheny concede that though the amount was small to him, it was a very large amount to Fall. "It was indeed," Doheny conceded. "There is no question about that. . . . And I am perfectly willing to admit that it probably caused him to favor me, but under the circumstances he did not have a chance to favor me. He did not carry on these negotiations. That is the point I would like for you to understand; that Senator Fall, in my opinion, was not influenced in any way by this loan, because the negotiations were carried on by men who were not under his control."

The committee members now began to perceive Doheny as a "slippery" witness. Several declared that they questioned Doheny's honesty and integrity. Senator Lenroot reminded Doheny that he had "greatly misled" the committee with his previous testimony. Doheny simply reiterated that he was sorry.

Senator Lenroot then asked Doheny if he had given Fall or any other cabinet members loans or gifts. Doheny replied negatively. "Have you employed any other cabinet officer subsequent to his retiring from the cabinet?" Lenroot continued.

"Yes sir," came the reply. When asked to give names, Doheny stated that he had hired Franklin K. Lane, former secretary of the interior; former attorney general Thomas W. Gregory; former secretary of war Lindley M. Garrison; George Creel, former chairman of Wilson's Wartime Committee on Public Information; and former secretary of the treasury William G. McAdoo. Doheny then reeled off a list of other prominent Democrats who were on his payroll—"like an ostentatious king giving an inventory of his possessions, like a parvenu art collector calling the roll of his Rembrandts and Van Dykes," in the words of one journalist.[27]

The revelation regarding McAdoo sent reporters rushing out of the Senate hearing room to call in their stories: until that moment, McAdoo had been the front-runner for the Democratic presidential nomination in 1924. Doheny explained that McAdoo had represented Doheny's oil company in Washington soon after he resigned from the Wilson cabinet. McAdoo, he asserted, was still his employee.

Frantic to keep his presidential bid intact, McAdoo rushed to Washington and demanded to be allowed to testify before the Senate committee. McAdoo swore that he had nothing to do with the naval leases. Nevertheless, the impression was created that he had been hired more for his influence as a former secretary of the treasury than for his skill as a lawyer, and his dreams of a presidential bid evaporated.

On March 24, 1924, Sinclair was called yet again before the committee. This time, to the shock of the assembled senators, Sinclair refused to testify or take the Fifth Amendment. Walsh asked the Senate to cite Sinclair for contempt because of his refusal to answer. The Senate voted 72 to 1 to cite Sinclair, and, on April 1, Sinclair appeared in the District Supreme Court (not to be confused with the U.S. Supreme Court), pleaded not guilty, and, with the aid of his lawyers, posted $5,000 in bail.

Democrats were ecstatic about the developments in this so-called Teapot Dome case, and they demanded that Fall, Sinclair, and Doheny be brought to trial. President Coolidge, preparing for reelection, was under increasing pressure from the Senate committee to appoint an independent prosecutor. The House and the Senate continued to debate the ramifications of the scandal. Walsh demanded that Secretary of the Navy Edwin Denby resign. "Unless the resignation of the Secretary of the Navy is in the hands of the President before the sun goes down," Walsh announced, "I shall ask action by this body appropriate to the occasion."

When the Senate passed a resolution that Coolidge should fire Secretary of the Navy Denby, the president responded that the Senate should stay out of the business of the executive branch. But not long thereafter, on February 18, Denby did resign under intense pressure; one month later, Attorney General Daugherty also resigned. Daugherty claimed he was driven from office by radicals in the Senate like La Follette and Walsh, whom he called "howlers." The administration was now in shambles, thanks to the eruption of this attention-grabbing scandal named for a piece of rock in the Wyoming flatlands.

In the middle of this uproar, shortly after New Year's 1924, Doheny released the Pan American Petroleum and Transport Company annual report for the previous year. The consolidated balance sheet as of December 31, 1923, showed an astonishing net worth of $173,464,242.24.[28] As large as the numbers were, Pan American's net earnings of $20,352,387.46

actually decreased 33 1/3 percent from the previous year. In a special statement to his stockholders, Doheny explained why: "To quote an expression used by our President, Mr. Wylie[,] . . . instead of having a large proportion of our current assets in the form of cash in banks, where it earns 3% per annum, we have it in the form of oil in tanks where its value is increasing this year at a very much higher rate." Doheny's report proudly asserted that the consolidated net profit for 1923 to his stockholders was $8.00 per share, and total dividends paid to stockholders in 1923 totaled $20,457,509; both figures reflected the corporation's strong financial condition.[29]

The most intriguing aspect of Doheny's 1923 *Annual Report* was his revealing discussion of the ongoing Senate hearings in Washington:

> In an attempt to provide some accurate and authoritative information with respect to your company's connection with the Government Naval Reserves in California, we provide the following information.
>
> Incorporated herewith is a copy of a statement made to the U.S. Senate Committee on Public Lands and Surveys by H. Foster Bain, Director of Bureau of Mines, Rear Admiral John K. Robison, Chief of Engineering, U.S. Navy, Edwin Denby, Secretary of Navy, and Edward L. Doheny to allow stockholders the best opportunity to inform yourselves as to the real merits of the controversy.
>
> *From Bain:*
>   Having had, as I have related, an active part in the making of the Pan American contract, I have no hesitation in expressing my entire approval of them as sound bargaining made on behalf of the government of the United States.
>
> *From Denby:*
>   If I could undo what I have done and were told that if I did not undo it I would be shot, I would say, "Bring on your firing squad and shoot me."
>   I belong in heart and soul to the Navy and nothing untoward that can happen to me or that has happened can cause me the slightest remorse over any action of mine on behalf of the Navy.
>   I must tell you face to face you have no need to be ashamed of me. There is not one man in the hearing of my voice, who if he entered the Navy under the circumstances I did and found the conditions that I

did in the oil reserve, would have done other than I did, if he were loyal to his country.

No man can see oil being drained away and lost to the Navy. I was charged with the duty to consume, exchange or sell oil, using my own judgment as to what best be done and nowhere will you find any requirement that the oil must be kept in the ground.

Attached to the report, following these excerpts, were over fifteen pages of Senate testimony from Bain, Robison, Denby, and Doheny. It was an accurate word-for-word transcript—a forthright presentation of the Senate testimony offered by Doheny to his stockholders. Following the transcription, Doheny concluded the report:

[The testimony reflects] the beneficial effects of your company's contract and leases, not only as a protection against depletion of naval reserve petroleum production by outside drilling but also of the Pacific Coast and our island possessions against hostile attack.

Respectfully submitted, Edward L. Doheny, Chairman of the Board

Doheny's testimony before the Senate committee had made him the object of widespread interest. His new role as a controversial Senate witness earned him a full-page spread in the *New York Times* Sunday edition. Doheny's six-inch portrait was featured with photographs of Doheny's Mexican tanker fleet. The headline read: "Doheny's Napoleonic Career in Oil, How the Miner and Vigilante Rose to Dominance in Petroleum and Politics."

"D" stands for Doheny in the social register of petroleum, and back of the name is a personality that dominates a large part of the world's oil. In ten years Edward L. Doheny has become a capitalist of the first magnitude although a very different sort from the conventional magnate. He is not cold and reserved; sometimes he is fired, at other times he can be chummy. His intimate friendship with men in high political position, as revealed in the Senate oil investigation at Washington this winter, has made him an object of national interest.

Doheny's figure is slight, with just a suggestion of a stoop about the shoulders. He never wears a hat, he avoids long-tailed coats, he ties his cravat with a careless gesture. He moves with a quick, impulsive action and talks the same way. He has blue-gray eyes, a stubby gray mustache, and the reputation of liking nothing better than a fight—fist or financial. At 67 he is one of the richest and most aggressive men in oil production.

The story of Doheny's activities in Mexico has two sides. Whichever is the nearest the truth, no one can doubt that he has been an empire builder. He followed the way of all empire builders—he came, he saw, he conquered . . . [30]

When Doheny read the feature, he must have been flattered, and perhaps reassured that the oil scandal was soon to pass.

THE SPECIAL PROSECUTORS

In February 1924, President Coolidge appointed Philadelphia lawyer Owen Roberts, a Republican, and Atlee Pomerene of Ohio, a Democrat, as special prosecutors for the oil cases. The Senate confirmed their appointments in mid-February. Roberts was in his late forties and deeply rooted in the Eastern establishment: a graduate of the University of Pennsylvania, a member of the Union League Club, and a trustee of the Episcopal Church. Pomerene was a former U.S. senator from Ohio, a confirmed Democrat, and a graduate of Princeton College.

Roberts and Pomerene began an intensive study of the Senate committee record and concurrently instigated their own investigations. The team faced a difficult job. The Department of Justice, the Department of the Interior, the navy, and U.S. military intelligence did everything they could to block the investigation—or at least make the job more difficult. As a result, Roberts was forced to use four Secret Service agents to act as his investigators.

Slowly, the special counsel unearthed facts to build cases against Doheny's Pan American Petroleum and Transport Company and Sinclair's Mammoth Oil Company that would enable the government to cancel both the Elk Hills and Teapot Dome leases. Roberts and Pomerene also believed they had ample grounds for seeking criminal indictments against Fall, Doheny, and Sinclair for conspiracy to defraud the United States and for bribery of a public officer.

Roberts and Pomerene worked at a furious pace. They were able to secure court-ordered receivers to control the Wyoming and California naval
reserve properties. The two able lawyers then quietly began to draft the
criminal indictments that could send a former cabinet officer and two of
America's most prominent and wealthy men to prison.

While the special prosecutors were at work, Doheny was faced with a
colossal stockholder lawsuit as a result of the Senate committee's investigation. The suit was brought in March 1924, on the basis that corporate
assets had been abused. Doheny openly admitted that completion of the
Pearl Harbor project was now in question. The construction work alone
required approximately $2 million in additional capital expenditures.

Owing a fiduciary duty to his thousands of stockholders, Doheny believed he could not authorize these additional moneys, unless their return
was guaranteed. "But I felt even more strongly," Doheny later told the
New York Times, "the necessity for completing the Pearl Harbor Station, as
I considered it within my pledge to Admiral Robison. Therefore when [the
stockholder suit] was brought against our company on March 8, I wrote
to President Coolidge and told him that the work would go on unless he
stopped it." At the same time, Doheny gave his personal guarantee to the
stockholders of Pan American to reimburse them to "the extent of every
dollar" that was necessary to "complete the work in the event the government did not recognize its obligation to do so."

"That letter [to President Coolidge] was never answered," Doheny
said, "but the Government of the United States allowed the work to go on
and the officers of the Navy continued to direct that work until its completion."[31] Doheny clearly felt he had acted to protect the security of the
nation, at great financial risk to himself. With the nobility of his motives
set in his mind, he would come to see himself as the bewildered victim of
prosecutors relentlessly pursuing him in coming years. Doheny was not
the first, nor was he to be the last, to decry the inordinate power and
funds afforded government prosecutors driven by fanatical zeal.

Ten Gaps in the Record

On June 5, 1924, Edward Doheny was formally indicted by the U.S. government on multiple charges of bribery and conspiracy. Oilman Harry F. Sinclair was also indicted in Washington, D.C., on separate federal charges of conspiracy and bribery; in both criminal actions, former U.S. secretary of the interior Albert B. Fall was named as codefendant. To Doheny's additional horror, his son Ned, now almost thirty-one, was named in the indictment for bribery, a federal offense that could result in a prison term of fifteen years to life.

But these charges were not the only legal threats Doheny was to encounter. In September, the government filed a separate civil lawsuit in Los Angeles Federal District Court against Doheny's Pan American Petroleum and Transport Company seeking to cancel the lucrative Elk Hills oil leases on the grounds that the contracts were obtained by Doheny through conspiracy, fraud, and bribery. A similar civil suit was filed in district court in Wyoming against Sinclair's Mammoth Oil Company in connection with the Teapot Dome field. The strident reporting of the nation's press—which christened Doheny a "Crooked Oil Millionaire" and Sinclair the "Mogul behind the Teapot"—convinced most Americans that the two oilmen were guilty as sin. Doheny would spend most of the next decade in court, fighting multiple civil suits brought by the government and by stockholders, three criminal trials, and a flurry of appeals.

The gossip in Washington focused on cabinet-level corruption, graft, and political favoritism. In Los Angeles rumors about Doheny's high-handed dealings flew. Predictably, a somber mood prevailed in the Doheny households at 8 and 10 Chester Place.

One anti-Dohenian was quoted in the *Literary Digest:*

> All you get out of his testimony before the Senate Committee and his known acts are some jigsaw scraps of a personality. A poor prospector who struck it rich, very rich indeed; a man who lends $25,000,000 to the President of Mexico; a man who gives $100,000 to a cabinet member from whom he expects a valuable lease, who sends money about in suit cases, who tears signatures from notes, who almost boasts that he will make $100,000,000 from naval oil-lands, who has an inordinate passion for collecting ex-Cabinet members as others collect old masters, who breaks before the Senate inquiry like some poor devil under the third degree.
>
> He's an old man; why does he go on, especially in such a fashion as this? What is it that drives him?
>
> "Almost a mania for power," [one insider] tells me. "He hires ex-Cabinet officers for the sense of power that it gives him to have ex-Secretaries of the Treasury, ex-Secretaries of the Interior and ex-Attorneys-General working for him. He tosses about the Government of Mexico, setting up one President and pulling down another. He blocks the recognition of Mexico and has it recognized when he chooses, or at least he flatters himself that he does. He loans money to a foreign government like one of those medieval banker-princes. . . . If you cross him in the slightest matter, he becomes apoplectic with rage."[1]

As public sentiment turned against him, Doheny realized that he needed to secure excellent legal counsel. For eight weeks, he considered who should take his case. He needed someone who was keenly intelligent, as well as influential, and who had expertise in a range of legal sub-specialties. Eventually, Doheny chose Henry W. O'Melveny of Los Angeles, founder of one of California's most esteemed law firms.

On Wednesday, August 6, 1924, Doheny was driven in his Pierce Arrow sedan to O'Melveny's downtown Los Angeles law offices at Fifth and Spring Streets. There, he was introduced to O'Melveny and Frank Hogan, a noted Washington, D.C., lawyer.[2] Hogan, forty-eight, was already on his way to being one of America's finest trial lawyers. A graduate of Georgetown University's law school, he practiced corporate and criminal law with partner William H. ("Wild Bill") Donovan. He had already won a string of sensational trials.

As Doheny entered the finely appointed office, O'Melveny rose to his feet and warmly shook the oilman's hand. The sixty-four-year-old O'Melveny had not participated in a courtroom trial for over twenty years,[3] but he was robust and more than able; and he was still considered the most prominent and powerful attorney in Los Angeles. O'Melveny was nearly bald, with a large, walrus mustache. His vigorous manner made him appear much younger when one encountered him in person. Hogan was slight in stature, less than five feet five inches tall, but possessed the bearing of a larger man. His ruddy face contrasted with silver-gray hair, and his eyes sparkled behind pince-nez spectacles.

Doheny wasted no time in explaining the situation as he saw it and detailing the way he wanted to proceed. He thought Hogan should prepare his case and try it, and he wanted O'Melveny to attend the trials and supervise the legal strategies.[4] Somewhat surprised, but accustomed to eccentric demands from wealthy clients, O'Melveny simply listened to the multimillionaire's plan without judgment. Like many of O'Melveny's clients, Doheny was at his office partly because of his own mistakes. But O'Melveny was not one to chastise those who sought his help. Instead, he deftly focused on damage control—how to minimize problems and maximize advantages. After a long, complex discussion, the three men retired to the exclusive California Club where they dined lavishly as Doheny's guests.

On Monday, August 11, O'Melveny met with his law partners, Ernest E. Milliken and Walter K. Tuller, to determine if they were in favor of representing Doheny. In the associated cases under the umbrella of *United States v. Pan American Petroleum and Transport Company*, the government sought to cancel Doheny's naval reserve leases, claiming they were based on fraud. Tuller, with brusque impatience, emphatically warned O'Melveny that representing Doheny could damage the firm's reputation, might destroy his own chance of running for the U.S. Senate, would certainly delay O'Melveny's anticipated retirement, and undoubtedly would deter prominent clients from hiring the firm.

"I would never injure your chances in the political picture," O'Melveny assured him. "And I would never let my political aspirations stand in the way of the best interests of the firm," Tuller retorted.[5] The men ended their discussion without resolution; they sagely decided to sleep on the question and hold another conference the following morning.

O'Melveny fully understood Tuller's misgivings—even the unstated ones. The case seemed almost unwinnable. How could even the most silver-tongued attorney explain the $100,000 in Ned's little black bag? Surely, the transfer looked more like a bribe than a loan. And how would O'Melveny and his associates rebuff the government's conspiracy charges against Doheny? Tuller had good cause for alarm. And Milliken, whose approach to the law was plodding and deliberate, also harbored reservations about accepting the case. His opinion was important; O'Melveny frequently relied on Milliken's keen insight and analytical breadth. He had worked with O'Melveny for two decades, and the men considered themselves trusted friends as well as respected business associates.

By the following morning, tempers had cooled considerably and conversation was more cordial. O'Melveny attempted to allay his partners' fears. He reviewed the key defense points with fervor: Doheny had acted out of patriotism, there was open and competitive bidding for the oil leases, and the $100,000 transaction was merely a loan. Also, he reminded them, this huge case would bring "significant revenue" into the firm's coffers. Together, they came up with case law, strategy, and legal theories to buttress Doheny's case. After a round robin of "what ifs" and a heavy dose of devil's advocacy, Tuller and Milliken acquiesced and consented to representing the already-notorious defendant. Although the partners rightly anticipated that the trial would consume several years of the firm's time and resources, they could not foresee that the Pan American litigation would eventually mushroom into over half a dozen trials—associated legal work would stretch nearly ten years and the government would lay out millions of dollars to prosecute Doheny.

Doheny waited impatiently at Chester Place for their decision. He was relieved when hours later he was telephoned with the news that he had been officially accepted as a client. O'Melveny asked Doheny for an initial retainer of $25,000, which Doheny sent immediately by messenger.[6]

On August 25, Doheny's newly assembled legal team convened at O'Melveny's office. An engaging and energetic Frank Hogan recited the facts he knew about the case. Painstakingly, the team began to assemble evidence, chart chronology, and devise a complex strategy they hoped would save their client from prison. Despite their earlier misapprehensions, Milliken and Tuller were now relatively confident that they could prevail against the government. They agreed that trial-savvy Hogan would present the defense case in Los Angeles Federal District Court in the civil suit and would act as chief defense litigator in the criminal trials. O'Melveny would work behind the scenes, acting as the team's coach and coordinating the overall strategy of the multiple lawsuits.

All realized that the stakes for Doheny were high. Although the Pan American Petroleum and Transport Company had been named as the defendant, Doheny himself was at risk. Defeat could mean the personal loss of tens of millions of dollars. In addition, the specter of the bribery case hung over Doheny's head. To be convicted of bribery could cost him far more than money: it could rob him of his freedom and permanently destroy his good name. The lawyers understood that the two cases were critically interrelated; they had to ensure a victory for Doheny in the Pan American civil trial in order to keep Doheny out of prison in the ensuing criminal trial. They also worried about the powerful influence of the press, which seemed eager to condemn their client before the trials had even begun. How could the lawyers quell the media's seemingly boundless appetite for scandal? How could they divert attention from "Teapot Dome," a catchy name that fell easily from the lips of everyday Americans and inaccurately linked Doheny with the activities of Harry Sinclair?

As the end of the summer approached, O'Melveny and Hogan had Doheny undertake the tedious process of sifting through mounds of correspondence, paperwork, billings, work logs, and so on in a search for documentation to bolster his defense.

In Three Rivers, New Mexico, Albert Fall was also rummaging through files, collecting all relevant letters, telegrams, memoranda, and official papers that could vindicate him. Fall sent Doheny two batches of confidential documents concerning the naval leases, which arrived at Chester Place on August 22 and 29, respectively. Doheny was quite thankful for the shipments: "Your letter . . . contained many very valuable documents," he told Fall, "some of which have covered gaps in the record, and others have explained relations which before were not quite so well understood."[7] When Doheny turned the collection over to Hogan, the attorney was visibly pleased. Calling the material "extremely useful," he had Doheny instruct his secretaries to make additional copies for hand delivery to O'Melveny at his downtown Los Angeles law office.

Doheny and Fall continued corresponding and venting their feelings about the situation in which they found themselves. On September 4, Doheny sent a letter both seeking a metaphor for their plight and presumably chastising Fall, albeit with great indirection, for lying about the loan and creating a now hard-to-remove stain:

> I cannot help thinking . . . that in shooting at these leases in this cowardly way, they are firing toward the glass windows of the Republican mansion; that it would have been much wiser for them to have left these leases alone. . . .
>
> You know that when a garment is stained, the best way to take it out is by immediately applying some solvent for the stain and thus cleanse the garment. You also know if this is not done immediately that it must be allowed to soak in some solvent that does not deteriorate the garment, and that it takes time and effort to accomplish what might have been done easily in the beginning.
>
> In the beginning with us it was impossible, on account of the flood of discoloring testimony, to accomplish anything quickly. Now we must put the situation in soak, and when the time comes obliterate the stain. After Court action we must make a vigorous effort to do so in every way.[8]

THE MAKING OF THE CASE

On Saturday, September 6, the weary legal team accompanied Doheny on a train to Mammoth Lakes, in the Sierra Nevada mountains, some 225 miles north of Los Angeles. There they would enjoy a relaxing fishing trip and continue to plan their strategy in a less stressful environment. "It is the first vacation I have ever taken," Doheny told Fall before he left, "and it is not one hundred percent vacation, as I expect to go over with [O'Melveny] many of the matters concerning our suits and try and get him up to date on the general atmosphere surrounding the situation."[9]

For six days, the men smoked cigars, drank whiskey, played poker, and, in between their diversions, discussed Doheny's predicament. Away from the media's relentless scrutiny, Doheny was more relaxed than he had been in months. Mammoth's beautiful scenery seemed to have a tranquilizing effect upon him. O'Melveny, in contrast, seemed unable to shrug off worries about the trial looming before them. Throughout the trip, to the concern of his travel mates, the attorney was afflicted with severe stomach cramps. Ever the trooper, O'Melveny told his associates he did not wish to return home early; he was sure the discomfort would subside. But privately he feared he was developing bleeding ulcers: "I try to keep [the pain] to myself," O'Melveny wrote in his journal, "but I can't run along this way very much longer."[10]

By the end of the trip, the men's friendship had grown stronger and Doheny had grown more confident of victory. At 5 A.M. on Friday, September 12, he bid farewell to the lawyers and headed back to Los Angeles to attend to an urgent oil matter. O'Melveny and his crew stayed at Mammoth for an additional three days before returning to their office to pore over the Pan American case's voluminous records. O'Melveny personally reviewed all the records of the Senate investigation and subsequent pleadings in order to create his own detailed chronology. He had spent no less than six hours a day on the case, and would continue to do so throughout the trials. Unfortunately his stomach problems worsened; by mid-September, he noted in his journal that the chronic pain was becoming intolerable.

The first formal hearing connected with the Pan American trial took place on September 19, 1924, inside the chambers of Federal District Judge

Paul J. McCormick. O'Melveny and Hogan appeared and were given a trial date of September 29. That evening, while continuing to work on the case in his office, O'Melveny experienced such severe stomach cramps that he phoned his doctor and pleaded for medication. After being examined, O'Melveny was ordered confined to bed and placed on a healing regimen of enemas and hot abdominal presses. For the next two weeks, O'Melveny could only digest meager spoonfuls of cereal and sip whole milk. He slept fitfully and greatly reduced his cigarette and pipe smoking in order to hasten his recovery. Nonetheless, while lying in bed, he continued to work on the Pan American case.

After reviewing thousands of pages of testimony, analyses, and reports on the case, O'Melveny was convinced that Doheny had innocently loaned Fall the $100,000. These actions were foolish, O'Melveny believed, but not criminal. O'Melveny began to focus on his client's mental state at the time of the loan. This, O'Melveny felt, was a critical element in Doheny's defense. As he wrote to Tuller:

> Throughout all his adventuresome life, and particularly under the white light that beats upon the wealthy, not a single blot or stain can be pointed to any act of his, and not one occasion wherein he ever went back upon his word.
>
> A life character such as this becomes fixed. It creates a subconscious self that by habit works along fixed lines. A man is not an upright, honorable, honest, patriotic man for sixty-six years of his life and becomes a traitor in his sixty-seventh year.[11]

By October 9, Henry O'Melveny was able to leave his bed, dress himself, and descend the stairs at his home. Soon, he was back at his office, tackling the stack of paperwork that seemed to mount taller with each passing day.

In one magazine, a rare pro-Doheny argument was published which suggested that Doheny had demonstrated his innocence by sending his own son to deliver the money: "He did not see anything wrong in sending that suitcase full of money to Fall. . . . I'll tell you why. If he had seen anything out of the way about it, he wouldn't have sent his own boy with the money. That boy, [Ned,] is the apple of his eye. Whatever he might do himself, he would rather lose his right hand than see [Ned] do anything that seemed to him questionable."[12] After Frank Hogan read it, he mailed it to O'Melveny.

Ned Doheny, too, was suffering from the stress of the pending federal indictments. Though far less visible a figure than his father, he was also being maligned in the press and gossiped about in public. He was notified that the board of directors of the Methodist Church had voted to compel the University of Southern California to remove him from his position as a university trustee, in case the criminal charges against him proved valid.[13]

Ned tried valiantly to continue his life with as much normalcy as he could. He traveled frequently on business, often taking Hugh Plunkett with him for companionship. Hugh was now employed full-time for Ned as his private secretary. When Ned was home in Los Angeles, he and Lucy maintained a busy social schedule, and he continued to be a doting father to his four children: Lucy, nine; Edward L. III, seven; William, five; and Patrick, almost two years old. Despite the frustrations connected with the legal battle into which he, too, had been drawn, Ned readily accepted his responsibilities as intended heir and future head of the Doheny empire. The line of succession was clear, and even in the face of grave legal threats, Edward continued to groom Ned for his role.

The files, exhibits, correspondence, and miscellaneous materials related to the case had grown so voluminous that more space was needed. Doheny converted his mansion's bowling alley into a temporary law office. A wooden plaque installed over the entrance, inscribed in gold leaf, read "Hogan's Alley." As the story spread through the legal community, it soon became the nickname for Hogan's Washington law office as well.[14]

On October 16, Doheny's team held an important conference at 8 Chester Place.[15] Hogan, Tuller, O'Melveny, and Frederick R. Kellogg, one of Doheny's corporate attorneys from Manhattan, plotted out their trial strategy through the long day, halting only briefly for lunch. The attorneys continued to convene almost daily in "Hogan's Alley," and Doheny set up a shooting gallery near one of the bowling lanes, complete with moving white rabbits and a flock of small ducks. During particularly long planning sessions, Doheny and his attorneys would stop discussion and take aim at the bobbing targets with mechanical pistols. Hogan declared that the exercise was a "great amusement" and kept the legion of staff members "fit and trim and in perfect physical condition."[16]

To combat the increasing number of anti-Doheny editorials, Hogan set up a series of press conferences. The *Washington Post* later published one of Hogan's explanatory speeches in which Hogan described publicly, for the first time, the terms of Doheny's contract with the navy:

> The contracts between the government and the Pan American Petroleum Company required the latter to furnish the government—
> First. A complete naval fuel plant to Hawaii with 4,200,000 barrels of fuel oil, lubricating oil, Diesel engine oil and aircraft gasoline in permanent reserve storage ready for the Navy's use in any national emergency;
> Second. One million barrels of navy fuel oil always in storage at points designated by the Navy on the Pacific Coast of the United States, and 3,000,000 barrels in like storage on the Atlantic coast; this is kept by the Pan American on hand at all times subject to the Navy's call at any time;
> Third. An obligation to sell to the Navy for a period of fifteen years its oil requirements at ten percent below current market prices;
> Fourth. Building and maintenance of a refinery on the Pacific coast and of terminal storage facilities for naval oil there, and the bunkering of naval war vessels at cost.
> These things Mr. Doheny's companies agreed to do. These agreements his companies to date have carried out to the letter. These are things which the present litigation attacks and which our government would be deprived of if that litigation succeeds. The importance to the security of the nation of these things cannot be overestimated and that is why I say that the big issue in the oil cases is—
> "The national defense."[17]

On Sunday, October 19, O'Melveny took a break from the lengthy legal sessions to play a round of golf at Los Angeles' Wilshire Country Club. As an acquaintance shut the door of his automobile, he caught O'Melveny's right hand; one finger was smashed.[18] O'Melveny was rushed to a nearby hospital to have the wound examined and dressed. He returned home, hand throbbing with pain, unused golf clubs in his foyer, to endure a tortured, sleepless night. Doheny's trial would begin in less than seventy-two hours.

THE FIRST TRIAL

Judge McCormick called his Los Angeles court to order on October 21, 1924. He was aware that the case before him (which he would hear without a jury) had attracted worldwide attention. Courtroom seats were at a premium; men queued outside for a chance to see the spectacle. Doheny's friends and foes alike vied for entrance.

Prosecutors Owen Roberts and Atlee Pomerene would represent the people. Indefatigable Frank Hogan would lead Doheny's battery of defense lawyers; he would also be assisted by the brothers Charles Wellborn and Olin Wellborn Jr., as well as by Olin Wellborn III. The Wellborn men were highly regarded and accomplished courtroom lawyers.

The government's complaint was read, calling for the revocation of the Elk Hills oil leases as having been obtained through conspiracy and fraud. Frank Hogan rose to respond. Immaculately groomed, he strode before Judge McCormick and delivered his opening presentation in an eloquent, dramatic tenor voice. Despite a noticeable speech defect that prevented him from pronouncing the letter *r*, Hogan managed to turn his voice into a spell-binding asset. He rarely stumbled. Prior to trial, Hogan prepared meticulously. He was a flamboyant speaker, who could address juries for hours without ever consulting a note. One *Los Angeles Times* reporter wrote that Hogan could outsmart Houdini with his bag of tricks, relying on his incredible memory to escape from any legal straitjacket.[19]

Each day, courtroom wags noted, Hogan would appear in a different expensively tailored suit, drawn from an apparently inexhaustible wardrobe. Though physically slight, he commanded the full attention of everyone in the courtroom. Some press reports claimed the small Irishman "looked like an eagle"; however, others described him as a "cocky little son-of a bitch."[20]

Atlee Pomerene, wearing a wide black bow tie and wire-rimmed glasses that frequently slipped to the edge of his nose, stood to address the court after his noted adversary had concluded his speech. In quick, businesslike fashion, with brow wrinkled and semibald head shining under the intense white lights of the courtroom, Pomerene delivered the first portion of the government's opening statement, then turned the proceedings over to coprosecutor Owen Roberts.

In a deep, splendid voice, the six-foot-two-inch-tall Roberts emphatically outlined the facts of the government's case. At all times Roberts addressed his remarks to the bench, ignoring the engrossed faces in the gallery. Roberts depicted Doheny to Judge McCormick as the unworthy recipient of lucrative Elk Hills oil leases worth an estimated $100 million. He told McCormick that Doheny had received the leases from Secretary Fall through illicit favoritism.

Neither Fall nor Doheny would take the stand in this civil action, and each man, through his lawyer, invoked his Fifth Amendment privilege against self-incrimination, an action taken because of their pending criminal cases. However, it became evident that Roberts and Pomerene intended to quote the testimony given by Secretary Fall and Doheny to the Senate committee investigating the oil leases. Hogan objected vigorously, but Judge McCormick permitted Roberts to read the Senate testimony into evidence. This issue worried Hogan and O'Melveny, but the lawyers recognized that should they lose the case, they might be able to use Judge McCormick's admission of the testimony as a basis for an appeal.

For the next five days, Roberts presented a series of witnesses and evidentiary documents intended to prove that Doheny's leases had been illegally obtained. He introduced evidence that the secretary of the navy lacked legal authority to make such contracts and argued that the transactions defeated the intent of Congress. According to Roberts, Fall had been eager to procure a lucrative lease for Doheny, and that was why he had insisted on wrapping their deal in secrecy. Roberts also attempted to prove that Fall had shown blatant favoritism toward his longtime friend; for, the prosecutor claimed, no other oil company had been given the chance to bid on the valuable leases.

Then it was Hogan's turn to argue in Doheny's defense. He launched a scathing attack on the government's careful construction of the evidence, declaring that, indeed, the navy had full authority to enter into a contract for storage tanks; therefore, any subsequent transaction under its aegis was legal and condoned by presidential authority. Furthermore, Hogan added, it was Navy Secretary Denby, not Interior Secretary Fall, who controlled the leases. Fall had been only a peripheral figure in the transactions.

Hogan then called Admiral Robison, the defense's star witness, to the stand. Robison testified that, yes, Navy Secretary Denby was fully cognizant of all negotiations concerning the leases and Fall was merely acting as agent for the Navy Department, with Denby's approval. Robison additionally testified that the fear of two things had expedited the signing of the leases: first, he and his superiors worried that the navy's valuable oil would be lost through "drainage" to nearby commercial wells, and, second, there was the ominous possibility that were the navy not to immediately secure storage tanks at Pearl Harbor, the United States could conceivably lose a war in the Pacific theater.

Hogan then asked Robison to describe for the court the long conversation he had held with Edward Doheny in December 1921, at Ned Doheny's New York City apartment, during which he begged Doheny to place a bid for the storage tanks. "I talked to him about what war is like," Robison testified, "not in terms of dead men, but in terms of shame, and I told him that it couldn't be done except by the exchange of crude oil, and I appealed to him to help in the accomplishment of the security of this part of the country. I tried to show him that it would not involve any risk to him."[21]

On cross-examination, Roberts forced Robison to admit that Fall had taken a very active, extensive part in the leasehold negotiations. Roberts also attempted to show that Robison, in league with Secretary Fall, had colluded to keep details of the leases secret from Congress and the public. Roberts belittled Robison's explanation that the leases were kept secret for reasons of national security: "Couldn't enemies of the United States easily see twenty or thirty oil tanks rising into the air?" In their book on Teapot Dome, M. R. Werner and John Starr write that "Before Robison left the stand, Roberts had made clear to the judge, and the country, that the Admiral had been virtually a co-conspirator with Fall and Doheny, rather than a trustee for the Navy's valuable reserves."[22]

Edward C. Finney, assistant secretary of the interior, was then called to the stand. He testified that Fall had delegated practically all naval reserve land functions to him. He told the court that Fall was absent from

Washington, D.C., during the contract negotiations and had assigned H. Foster Bain, chief of the Bureau of Mines, and A. W. Ambrose, chief petroleum technologist, to aid Robison in ironing out the contract details.

Because Doheny and Fall had refused to take the stand, Pomerene read into the record testimony by both men to the Senate investigating committee about the $100,000 loan. Pomerene, bolstering the government's argument, asked the court to take special note that Doheny made the "loan" only one day after Secretary Fall had approved the issuing of additional naval reserve land leases to Doheny's company, Pan American. And, unsurprisingly, Pomerene asked Judge McCormick to consider the "unusual features" of the transaction—an extremely large amount of cash transported by satchel across state lines. "If this was a legitimate transaction," Pomerene posed, "can Your Honor conceive why it was done in this way? In exchange for this cash, Mr. Doheny received a note. It was an extraordinary note, and given under extraordinary circumstances."

Depicting his government nemeses as "groggy and on the ropes" in resorting to far-fetched reasoning, Hogan addressed each of Pomerene's accusations. Hogan argued that no fraud had been committed; the government had received substantially more than fair market value for its crude oil. He reiterated that Fall had scrupulously refrained from doing any favors for Doheny after accepting the loan, reminding Judge McCormick that Fall had performed no material function in connection with Doheny's contracts and leases. The charges of fraud against Doheny and Fall, Hogan told the judge, were "preposterous, even infamous. This conspiracy contained in the terrible charges alleged in the bill of complaint, never were heard of, never even thought of, until given birth in the minds of politicians."

Hogan gave a stirring closing argument, completely from memory as was his custom. Then, the following morning, Roberts and Pomerene droned monotonously for hours in their summation in a nonstop attack against Secretary Fall and Edward Doheny.

The trial concluded on its tenth day. Now, Judge McCormick was left to consider his decision. Hogan was pleased with his performance, and his colleagues heartily congratulated him. Things looked bright for Doheny; even the daily press were running stories predicting a defense victory—and crediting Hogan's outstanding performance. O'Melveny, too, was relatively assured that his team would prevail. He wrote to a close friend in New York: "As to the charge of conspiracy there is not a shadow of a doubt but that [it] has been shattered into a thousand fragments and there is nothing left of it; and I confidently expect . . . that the opinion and judgment of the court will completely exonerate Mr. Doheny and show that no fraud was perpetrated or bribe given."[23]

Doheny felt so confident about his anticipated victory that on November 19, he invited his legal team to 8 Chester Place for a pre-celebration lunch. When the men arrived, they were surprised to find that Doheny had also hired a film crew to record moving pictures of the gourmet meal. Awkwardly, the lawyers posed for the cameras, as directed, in front of various rooms, including the office, library, arboretum, and, naturally, "Hogan's Alley." O'Melveny, still nervous about the trial's outcome, excused himself early and, relieved to escape the theatrics, visited another legal client, *Los Angeles Times* publisher Harry Chandler, to discuss an unrelated legal concern.[24]

Weeks passed, but Judge McCormick remained confoundingly mute. Doheny spent the Christmas holidays with his wife, son, and daughter-in-law inside the elaborately decorated Chester Place compound. Days later, he rang in the New Year with a fervent wish that the matter of *United States v. Pan American Petroleum and Transport Company* would soon be far behind him.

AWAITING THE FIRST VERDICT

With no verdict on the horizon, Doheny forced himself to return to his business operations. O'Melveny decided to sail to Europe with his wife, Nette, for a much-deserved respite. Hogan returned to his practice in Washington, D.C., while Tuller and Milliken initiated work on other, lower-profile cases.

Although Doheny remained confident that he would prevail, he was greatly concerned that his image and reputation had been irreparably damaged by the litigation and ensuing publicity. Hoping to orchestrate a change in public opinion, Doheny invited movie mogul Cecil B. DeMille and codefendant Albert Fall to lunch at his Chester Place mansion to discuss the possibility of making a moving picture that would tell "the real story" to American audiences.

Doheny had his staff set out an exquisite lunch in the formal dining room. After some initial pleasantries, Doheny announced what he had in mind. DeMille later wrote in his autobiography that he believed Doheny's idea "would have made one of the most talked-of motion pictures of the decade," but he nonetheless declined the offer, citing conflicting obligations. DeMille realized, but did not tell Doheny, that no studio executive in his right mind would shoot such a controversial film, knowing that it would invite great public attack.[25]

Doheny was bitterly disappointed that DeMille rejected his idea. The oilman had already approached Will H. Hays, a political colleague of Fall's and currently head of the film censorship office, about such a motion picture, without generating interest from him. The intended film, which was to show how Doheny's and Fall's role in the naval oil leases benefited the nation, would have stressed "the long history of intimacy and complete trust between Mr. Doheny and Mr. Fall, as shedding light on the informality of their financial transactions."[26]

In spite of lack of response, Doheny continued to devise public relations strategies to clear his name. He put various writers and newspapermen on his payroll to work alongside his public relations representatives, and he also consulted famous novelists and nonfiction writers about a sweeping account of his life. Doheny hired consultants to guide his public relations efforts, and he was able to maintain close ties with media tycoons such as William Randolph Hearst, Clarence W. Barron (publisher of the *Wall Street Journal*), and B. C. Forbes,[27] despite his legal woes.

Eventually, Doheny sponsored a biography of Albert Fall to be written by Mark B. Thompson, a lawyer in the oil cases who had literary interests. A series of letters among the parties reflected their belief that a popular account of Fall's rise to the highest sector of government following an exciting and colorful life in the frontier would have a tremendously favorable effect on public opinion.[28] Doheny finally funded the book project, paying Fall and Thompson handsomely. The book was written at Fall's ranch during the summer months of 1925. Doheny took an active interest, and drafts of the book were sent back and forth between Las Cruces and Los Angeles. However, by winter, the project was abruptly canceled. The reason remains unknown.

Doheny didn't overlook the visual arts. He commissioned a European painter, Detleff Sammann, to create a mural on the walls of his study at 8 Chester Place. Doheny proposed that the whole work depict the history of the United States—from the arrival of the pilgrims to the discovery of oil, the latter scene showing Doheny and his late partner, Charles Canfield, discovering oil in old Los Angeles in 1892.

Although Sammann began the commission with enthusiasm, one day he suddenly quit. In 1926 the mural was finished by western artist Charles Russell. Russell brought the panorama up to its "discovery of gold" scene from the 1840s.[29] Apparently, the mural had been ill-planned: Russell ran out of wall space, and Doheny's most important scene—his discovery of oil—was much reduced in scale. Doheny came to regard the expensive art commission as a disappointment.

As he awaited Judge McCormick's verdict, Doheny directed his attention to the enviable problem of high yield from his Mexican wells. He needed to improve sales in order to accommodate the ever-increasing production of heavy crude. He was also intent on developing new operations in the United States rather than in Mexico. During this time, he personally scouted the San Francisco Bay Area for new real estate, purchasing a tract of land in Oakland's Clinton Basin, where he would soon build a warehouse, pipelines, corporate offices, twenty new storage tanks, and an 850-foot concrete pier for his fleet of tankers. Doheny also planned more than twenty service stations near San Francisco and additional stations in Oregon and Washington State.[30] The Elk Hills lease was expected to provide the lighter weight oil and gasoline he needed to expand his service station operations.

In keeping with his effort at image building, as well as demonstrating his religious faith and sincere belief in the goals of his church, Doheny continued to make substantial donations to the Roman Catholic Church. In the early 1920s a fund-raising drive had been inaugurated by Bishop John J. Cantwell for a new church to be located at the corner of Adams Boulevard and Figueroa Street, adjacent to the Dohenys' compound at Chester Place. Doheny agreed to finance its construction on condition that the design be based on Santa Prisca, a historic church in Tasco, Mexico, dating from 1748. Boston architect Ralph Adams Cram, known as "America's greatest designer of churches," was asked to draft plans for a structure that would incorporate the Spanish Renaissance features of Santa Prisca.[31]

Santa Prisca, too, had been built by a single patron: José de la Borda, a wealthy silver miner. "So careful was Mr. Doheny to emulate Jose de la Borda," wrote historian Monsignor Francis J. Weber, "that he allowed a statue of his patron saint, at the far left in the base of the reredos, to bear a striking resemblance of himself. A small enough indulgence for the gift of a church!"[32] The exterior of the church was of stucco with Indiana limestone trim, ornament, and statues. Ornamental tile covered a dramatic dome. Inside, the reredos of the main altar was created in the powerful churrigueresque style, with a distinct Marian theme. Cram positioned St. Vincent's so that the axis of the building was at a 45-degree angle with both Adams and Figueroa, ensuring a dramatic view of the structure. The completed church was widely appreciated as one of the most beautiful in the western United States.

The first mass in St. Vincent's Church was offered by Bishop John J. Cantwell in April 1925. The construction of the costly landmark brought Doheny the highest regard of church officials during the middle of what were his worst days of the Teapot Dome–Elk Hills scandal.

After twenty-four years in Mexico, Doheny was growing weary of combating employee unrest, coping with strikes and labor stoppages, and dealing with the continuing political instability. The Mexican government might yet wrest his Mexican holdings away by nationalizing the oil industry. Litigation by stockholders and business associates loomed as additional threats. Doheny considered what changes he might make to his corporate structure that would make his operations more manageable and secure in a future that seemed increasingly uncertain. To this end, Doheny, now approaching sixty-nine years old, gave considerable time and thought to devising a more profitable and stable business to pass on to Ned and the grandchildren.

On April 1, 1925, a date that would be recalled when later events awarded the fool's crown, one of the most sensational deals in oil history was made: Doheny sold a majority of the voting stock of his Pan American Petroleum and Transport Company plus his Mexican Petroleum Company to the Standard Oil Company of Indiana. The merger of Pan American Petroleum and Transport Company (exclusive of its California properties) with Standard Oil of Indiana was the largest oil consolidation in the history of the industry. Together, the two companies boasted assets of $584 million with securities appraised in the open market at $787 million. Operation of Pan American, its Mexico operations, pipelines, refineries, and shipping fleet of thirty-one tankers would be controlled by a newly created Standard Oil holding company to be called the "Pan American Eastern Corporation." Doheny would still retain his California oil properties, which would now be incorporated in his newly created holding company, "Pan American Western Corporation."[33]

Colonel Robert W. Stewart, chairman of the Board of the Standard Oil Company of Indiana, was credited with masterminding the historic transaction and single-handedly transforming his domestic oil company into the industry's world leader by acquiring control of Pan American. On the day the contracts were to be executed, Doheny issued the following statement:

> Interests controlled by my family today consummated the sale of a majority of the voting stock of the Pan American Petroleum and Transport Company. We have not, however, parted with all our interest in that company; on the contrary, we remain owners of a larger number of shares of the company's stock than any other stockholders excepting only Pan American Eastern Petroleum Company, the purchaser in today's transaction.
>
> I have retired from the chairmanship of the Board of the Pan American Petroleum and Transport Company, but remain Chairman of the Board of Directors of its California subsidiary and every stockholder in the Pan American Petroleum and Transport Company will be offered an

opportunity to participate in the Western Company. It is my intention to have a continuing and active part in the management and development of the Pacific coast properties, including the California Naval reserves, which is under a lease to our California subsidiary.[34]

The creation of the new giant oil enterprise changed the world's "oil map" overnight. Paul H. Giddens, author of Standard Oil of Indiana's business biography, observes that the acquisition of an interest in the Pan American Petroleum and Transport Company by Standard Oil was "the most significant event in the oil industry since the dissolution of Standard Oil [Trust] in 1911. By one stroke, it had placed Standard in the front rank as a world oil power and made it a vastly greater factor in the petroleum industry than ever before."[35] Some oil industry analysts praised the consolidation. Others criticized it as a bold attempt to monopolize a very volatile industry. The *New York World* declared that "with men like Stewart and his fellow directors in charge, there can be no peace between the people and the oil industry," asserting that "an industry managed by men who will allow a Cabinet officer to be corrupted, the courts disregarded, and their stockholders ignored, has earned suspicion."[36]

The St. Louis *Post-Dispatch* ran an editorial declaring that Doheny's resignation from Pan American could only benefit the company: "Big business is getting bigger, but if bigger business is to grow and prosper into a ripe old age it will need a quality of leadership that will not stoop to bribery or flee from subpoenas." To which the *New York Commercial* indignantly replied that "there has as yet been no proven evidence of fraud in the oil leases and that there is nothing new in the merger to call for any talk about high-crimes and misdemeanors."[37]

The merger of the two giant oil firms remained the top business story for months. Some analysts pointed out that the numbers in the transaction didn't seem to add up. Doheny's enormous holdings had been valued at more than $155 million in 1924; by 1925 his Mexican Petroleum Company had produced 560 million barrels of oil, making him one of the wealthiest men in America; yet, in April 1925, he sold his considerable empire, except for his California properties, for only $38 million.[38]

Although many of Doheny's acquaintances were shocked at his sudden abandonment of the companies that had consumed his life, others conjectured that he was merely commencing a new, more conservative chapter in his life. Doheny was nearly seventy years old, and his health was declining. He could not predict with certainty what the verdicts would bring in the Teapot Dome–Elk Hills lease litigation, and he shrewdly acted to protect the family's interests. Indeed, Doheny's decision, thought by many to have been rash, would prove surprisingly canny. When the stock market crashed in 1929, and when later the Mexican government expropriated his former holdings, Doheny's earlier move to "cash out" of Mexico saved him from financial ruin.

Doheny intended that Ned eventually would be the chief executive of the new California subsidiary and the other family holdings. As part of this plan, he built a handsome new building at the corner of Tenth (later renamed Olympic Boulevard) and Flower Streets in downtown Los Angeles to house the new operations. Despite the loss he incurred at the time of selling his oil interests, Doheny was able to preserve for Ned and his grandchildren a remarkable financial legacy.

THE VERDICT

On Saturday, May 30, 1925, O'Melveny returned to his London hotel after a pleasant day of sightseeing to be informed by the hotel clerk that an urgent cable had arrived for him. O'Melveny became nervous, intuiting bad news. The cable had been sent by Tuller, alerting O'Melveny that Judge McCormick had ruled against Doheny's Pan American Corporation. O'Melveny sank into a chair, disoriented; then, after catching his breath, he made arrangements to return to the United States immediately.

Judge McCormick ruled against Pan American's defense team on nearly every point. He had declared that the $100,000 paid by Doheny was indeed a bribe—one that had induced Secretary of the Interior Albert B. Fall to award the valuable Elk Hills naval leases improperly and fraudulently to the Pan American Corporation. The judge ordered that the transactions be voided, as they had been consummated through conspiracy and fraud. He spared no words: "This colossal infamy, regardless of whether it was a bribe, gift, or a loan, requires this court in conscience to strike down the deals which are inextricably connected with it, to restore the nation its naval oil reserves."[39] However, McCormick allowed Pan American to receive credit for the oil it had extracted from the reserves and for its drilling and operational expenditures, tank construction expenses, sundry storage facilities charges, and other costs. At least the company was to be reimbursed for the great sums Doheny had spent in constructing the Pearl Harbor storage tanks, drilling at Elk Hills, and supplying oil to the government.

Owen Roberts could not have been more pleased with the court's ruling, and his praise of Judge McCormick's decision was widely quoted in the press. "Today's decision marks a great step forward in the government's case," he claimed. "The importance of the civil cases cannot be overestimated. They involve questions of conservation of the public lands and fundamental principles of government."[40]

Doheny, of course, was shocked and devastated; his legal team was equally stunned, particularly because Harry Sinclair, also charged with conspiracy in a similar civil suit, had recently been vindicated. Contrary to the findings of Judge McCormick, Judge T. Blake Kennedy of Wyoming, presiding in the Sinclair case, found that President Harding had legitimately turned over authority for the naval reserves to the Department of the Interior. Furthermore, he found that Secretary of Navy Edwin Denby had remained legally responsible for making the transactions. The urgency of the military situation justified Fall's failure to seek competitive bids. Ruling that the Mammoth Oil Transaction was authorized by law and that there was no fraud intended or perpetrated against the United States, the judge therefore dismissed the suit.[41]

Sadly for Sinclair, however, Kennedy's liberal ruling was overturned by the U.S. Circuit Court of Appeals on September 28, 1926. In the subsequent ruling, the Sinclair lease of Teapot Dome, found to be fraudulent and "tainted with favoritism, collusion and corruption," was canceled. Three U.S. Court of Appeals judges agreed that "A trail of deceit, falsehood, subterfuge, bad faith, and corruption, at times indistinct but nevertheless discernible, runs through the transaction incident to and surrounding the making of this lease."[42]

But the reversal on appeal lay in the future. In May 1925, the adverse ruling in the Pan American case, side by side with the favorable outcome of Sinclair's case, left the Doheny team shocked and astounded.

Doheny himself continued his media campaign to set the record straight. He granted a seven-hour interview with L. C. Speers, a reporter from the *New York Times*, which was printed in its entirety on the front page of the newspaper on July 1, 1925. A transcript was made by a stenographer who sat with Doheny and Speers in the library of the Chester Place mansion during the interview. Hogan and O'Melveny had been adamantly opposed to the undertaking, but Doheny could not be deterred. He claimed that he needed to give the public "the full truth" about the oil cases and his loan to Albert Fall.

Doheny's most astonishing revelation in the *Times* interview was his proffering of the "missing telegrams" that had been sent between officials of the Navy Department and the Department of the Interior following competitive bidding on the naval lands on April 15, 1922. Doheny told Speers that these telegrams could have helped clear his name; but they had "mysteriously disappeared" from the Interior Department's files after, Doheny alleged, the files had been "ransacked" by persons "in the employ of the Senate Investigating Committee." However, some diligent clerk in the General Accounting Department had fastened copies of the telegrams to the Western Union invoices; thus their content was preserved after all. "Had the committee made these telegrams a part of the oil investigation record," Doheny continued, "it would have been disclosed to the country that Secretary Fall had no part in the making of the contracts which were actually supervised by Assistant Secretary of the Interior Finney, Secretary Denby and Admiral Robison."

The *New York Times* reprinted the full text of the mysteriously lost telegrams. From Washington, D.C., Navy Secretary Denby had telegraphed Secretary Fall in New Mexico and informed him of the results of the sealed bids. Fall had responded by telegram placing the awarding of the contract in the hands of the secretary of the navy.

Hogan was beside himself with worry about possible repercussions from the interview. He feared that Speers would paint Doheny in a terrible light. But fortunately, this was not the case; after the story ran, Doheny was flooded with congratulatory wires from well-wishers who commended him for his brave stand. "Your recital in the Times this morning was masterful, and complete," wrote public relations man Caspar Whitney. "Confutation of mud slingers, in language specific, illuminating and convincing. Friends rejoice in your disregard of lawyers advice not to speak, which thus gives them entire story first time."

A wire sent by Doheny's friend William B. Joyce confirmed Whitney's sentiments: "It was . . . a thrill to read in the Times this morning your wonderful statement. No fair minded man can read it without being impressed with your honesty, your magnanimity and your patriotism. Hearty congratulations and affectionate regards." Oil producer Charles MacFadden agreed: "Accept congratulations from one of your host of friends for masterful statement in New York Times today. The full story thus clearly told for the first time to the general public wins you unanimous acquittal by the patriotic citizens of the nation. Many of your oil producer friends acquainted with the facts have long hoped you would make this statement. You have won your case definitely."[43]

Surprisingly, Albert Fall was not happy about his codefendant's venture into the public spotlight. In fact, he was outraged that Doheny would take such a risk without contacting him first. Fall sent Doheny a series of troubled telegrams warning him about the consequences of overexposure. On July 2, Doheny attempted to relieve Fall's anxiety. His letter reveals how much Doheny yearned to be appreciated by the public, a desire that now surpassed his previous longing for wealth.

> I was very much disturbed by the information contained in your telegrams. . . . I need not assure you that in the interview with Mr. Speers, the representative of the New York Times, had with me, which required more than 4 hours to dictate, and many hours to type, and again many hours to revise, there was nothing said that you or any other friend of mine could wish to have stated differently.
>
> The [positive] comments evidenced by the telegrams, copies of which I send here with as well as an article by Frazer Edwards published in this morning's Los Angeles Examiner, are but a few of the many expressions that I have had from people all over the country, congratulating me upon the straightforwardness and evident truthfulness of the story.

I had hoped that when you saw it, as you would in time, that it could elicit nothing but satisfaction to you and praise from you; consequently my great disturbance at the tenor of your message. I do not know that anything that I, or anybody else, can say will do any good; I merely lend myself to the doing of these things in the same way that I do anything else which promises to produce results. Long, long ago I attained that state of mind which the good old Abbot Mael expressed, when asked how, under the most unfortunate circumstances, he could still smile and seem happy. He said, "It's probably because I expect nothing, and refuse nothing."

I have long ceased to calculate on the benefits to be derived from the convincing of others. I have always placed, and still do place great reliance on the return which nature gives in the way of fruits of efforts and industry. I have come, however, at this late date in my life, to that period when substantial returns which nature has so bounteously given do not supply that which I seem to want most—the good opinion of the public, or in other words, recognition on its part of real effort made to serve. If there is one thing more than another that a man possesses who has followed the life of a prospector, it is hope, and I have not yet given up hope that public opinion may be greatly changed with regard to both you and I, and those who have reviled us because of our efforts to serve the government.[44]

Doheny's media blitzkrieg caused a crack in what had been a united front in presenting their case. Fall began to worry that Doheny was only interested in protecting his own reputation, and would do whatever was necessary . . . even if it meant turning his back on their friendship. O'Melveny, too, was angry at Doheny, but for a very different reason. Ever the worrier, he feared Doheny would misstate his case to reporters and provide fodder for the opposition. In a huff, O'Melveny refused to attend the *New York Times* interview; only Hogan, albeit with misgiving, agreed to be present.

Doheny and O'Melveny did not speak for three months until August 22, 1925, when Edward and Estelle Doheny celebrated their twenty-fifth wedding anniversary. Nearly a hundred guests attended the lavish dinner party at the Chester Place compound, including O'Melveny, who hesitantly shook Doheny's hand, then heartily embraced him. Throughout the evening neither uttered a word about the pending trials.

THE APPEAL

Bolstered by the response from the media and public, Doheny was newly optimistic. He patiently awaited the decision of the Circuit Court of Appeals. Two days before Thanksgiving 1925, in an effort to mend fences with Fall, Doheny wrote to him about their anticipated vindication:

> I have heard some rumors as well as predictions from prominent sources, that the decision will be in our favor. I am not allowing myself, however, to be influenced by anything, except the not-to-be-doubted action which will sooner or later be made public. If the court will read, with unprejudiced minds, the record on appeal, and the brief, I have no doubt what so ever, notwithstanding the false statements made by Roberts, and the slanderous ones made by Pomerene, that the court will arrive at the truth and render a decision accordingly.[45]

Sensing that a rift between the codefendants could hurt both parties, Hogan, too, attempted to encourage Fall to remain optimistic. On December 23, 1925, he wrote to apprise Fall of what he believed would be the government's new strategy against them:

> My idea is, as I know yours is, once we find that we are going to have any trial, to prepare, primarily on facts and secondarily on law, to the very last degree; to leave nothing to chance; to know every fact in all of the cases and as far as humanly possible to consider every point of law involved.
>
> The government's position in support of the bribery indictments is going to involve the invoking of the de facto officer doctrine. Pomerene and Roberts will contend that you, as Secretary of the Interior, were de facto in charge of the conservation and administration of the naval petroleum reserves, and that those general terms included leasing and contracting in respect of the lands and the products therefrom. Just how the Secretary of the Interior could do de facto the function of the office of Secretary of the Navy, at a time when there was a de jure Secretary of the Navy, I have not been able to figure out. But that is their case. . . .
>
> This letter will not reach you until after Christmas; but even if it arrives before Christmas I should hesitate to express the bromide "Wishes of the Season" because I know that until we can look upon our cases as closed you will consider rather hollow talk of being "merry." I

do however send to you and Mrs. Fall very sincere wishes for that which
I know will mean happiness in the New Year, namely, the final and
victorious ending of all this litigation.

    With kind regards,

    Yours very sincerely,

    Frank J. Hogan[46]

Just after New Year's, the Pan American Corporation's legal team and
their entourage traveled from Los Angeles to San Francisco by adjoining
railcars for the court of appeals hearing. During the trip, Hogan attempted
to lift the team's spirits with hopeful predictions. However, the year
opened badly, for on January 4, 1926, the group learned that the appeals
court had affirmed the district court's judgment. Even worse, the court expanded the lower court's ruling to brand Pan American a "trespasser"
who had entered upon the naval lands illegally; as such, it would not be
entitled to any reimbursement of its cash outlays.

Doheny's small consolation from the previous trial had now been lost.
He sat in stunned silence at 8 Chester Place as O'Melveny explained the
ruling by telephone. Both men understood that this negative ruling could
greatly damage the finances of Doheny's remaining corporate concerns
and, more important, jeopardize Doheny's defense in his upcoming criminal bribery trial. "Were it not for my natural fighting spirit," Hogan confided to Fall, "I would almost be ready to confess that I am heartbroken
by this news."[47]

Though O'Melveny was disheartened and infuriated by the court of
appeals ruling, his head remained clear; he suggested to Doheny that
they immediately appeal to the U.S. Supreme Court. Preparing the proper
documents and briefs would require tremendous time and effort, he admitted, but he felt the action was essential. Later that day, when O'Melveny returned home, he retreated to his library; he examined old photographs, and then worked in his garden, seeking solace. "The circuit court
of appeals handed down a decision adverse to us on every proposition.
It's just hell," O'Melveny wrote in his journal that night. He also questioned whether he was now too old to keep practicing law or whether he
just "didn't have it anymore." He ended his entry by reminding himself
that he would soon be retiring altogether.[48]

Across town, O'Melveny's once-confident client was beginning to suffer great anxiety; the magnitude of his predicament was now sinking in. Throughout his life, he had always believed, despite hardships, setbacks, and tricks of fate, that a worthy man only needed to persevere to claim reward. Now, however, an ugly pessimism was overtaking him. He could no longer be sure of anything: his vindication, his future security, or his receipt of timely justice.

Nonetheless, in February 1926 he sent another long, heartening letter to Albert Fall. In the upcoming criminal trial, the two would need to stand together.

> My Dear Mr. Fall,
> My failure to write to you during the past months does not indicate that you have not been in my thoughts many times since we last met. . . .
> I have often wondered whether or not you have been as fortunate in having your time fully taken up with the affairs of the day, with the mental advantage of not having to dwell too often too much upon those particular past and present events which have resulted so unjustly to both of us.
> The public tendency to misconstrue, and, in fact, to attach a viciously false interpretation to everything that we may do, is one of the reasons which has prevented a more frequent and closer exchange of views between us, and developed that reciprocity of feeling which should naturally exist between friends of such long standing, especially when their peace of mind as well as other interests are alike menaced by the pernicious activity of the agents of the government which we have not only endeavored to serve, but have actually served with great sacrifice to ourselves and great benefit to the country.
> I have been waiting for that orderly progress of events which would dissipate the atmosphere of suspicion and aversion which surrounds the scene of activity—the Senate Slander Promulgating Committee—that we might resume, without fear of unfavorable criticism, the friendly intercourse which our mutual feelings would naturally inspire. . . .
> The continuing adverse results of our court hearings have greatly disturbed and mightily shaken that belief which I have always had in our Judiciary, and for whom, notwithstanding the many instances which have come to me [giving me] knowledge of their venality, I have always had the greatest respect.

Doheny told Fall that he had been delving into his family's history and had found similarities to the present situation.

I have lately been reading a book published by a relative of mine who died about 75 years ago. The book is a story of the strife in Ireland from 1830 to 1850, in which the author took part. It goes minutely into the details which transpired during those decades, involving those who were ostensibly seeking to bring about the same results,—i.e. a greater measure of political freedom for Ireland and of liberty of conscience for Catholics of that unfortunate land. . . .

Not only were these men who openly espoused the cause of political freedom, treated as conspirators and traitors by laws adopted by the English Parliament, which designated their most natural and patriotic acts as acts of treason, but the conspiracy against them seemed to be aided by the highest authorities in this world. . . .

It seemed to those men who had sacrificed their personal careers for the cause which they upheld, and the end of all things had come with the breaking up of the Young Ireland Party. But inasmuch as my father was one of those who fled his native soil as a consequence of these political disturbances, as did John Purroy Mitchell's grandfather, and the ancestors of many well-known families in the United States, and as the meeting between my father, who fled from Ireland at 16 years of age, and my mother, who was a school teacher, born at St. John's Newfoundland, occurred after his flight from Ireland, I am forced to the belief that the event of my own existence, and of that of everyone living who is dear to me through ties of sanguinity, was one of the direct results of that historical event which was considered a great disaster by my father and his relatives and friends who took part in the events that led to the debacle of 1848.

All of this makes one wonder what good can possibly come in some way that we cannot at present surmise, out of the slanders which have been worked up against us.

Doheny went on to share with his friend and companion of yesteryears his particular insight into the motivation of divine Providence. He believed that a God who would go to so much trouble in creating an Irish rebellion and a famine as the vehicle to bring forth an Edward Doheny must have something in mind for his creation. After reciting the failure of faith and hope, Doheny commended to Fall the virtue charity—in the Christian canon, a transcending love for God—as their only remaining comfort, asserting that irrespective of the judgment of others, reliance on God's purposes will sustain them in self-vindication.

It looks as though the fates have conspired against us, and that we are being tried in our souls by the passing events, with the intention of destroying, if possible, the last ray of hope which we might have of getting justice. Though faith be largely destroyed, our hope will continue, of course, while life lasts, which means until the curtain is finally rung down upon this situation. The only thing that remains to us and that we do not depend upon the acts of others to sustain us in, is that charity which is the last but greatest of the trio upon which human existence depends.

This is not exactly the kind of a letter that you have a right to expect from me. My letters should express a spirit of pugnacity, but when one thinks of fighting, there must be something to fight. And never did Don Quixote, or other mythical hero of romance, meet more intangible enemies than is public opinion, the desire for political preference, or the lethargy which is indulged in by a tribunal when it approves, without proper consideration and study of the surrounding facts, the hasty judgment formed in a time of excitement or based upon political ambitions.

By the end of the letter, Doheny's fighting spirit has pierced the gloom and he is eager to hold strategy meetings with Fall:

Would it be possible for you and Mrs. Fall to run over and visit us for a short while during this spell of sunny weather. If you find it convenient to come, we can do some things and discuss many situations which it is impossible to endeavor to do by mail. I will try and shake myself loose from some of the affairs that have engaged my attention, and try and make it interesting and pleasant for you while you are here. . . . I am really anxious to get your reaction on the latest decisions which have been handed down and your opinion as to future action concerning our joint interests—

If it will not be too great a hardship or sacrifice of time more valuable for other uses I would like very much to see you in the near future.[49]

Doheny summoned O'Melveny, Hogan, Tuller, and their associates to his Pan American offices in Los Angeles. There, he announced that he indeed would launch a U.S. Supreme Court appeal, but he wished to hire outside counsel to assist. Relieved to be able to share such an onerous legal burden, O'Melveny and the others heartily approved Doheny's decision.

Despite this good news about additional legal help, O'Melveny's health continued to decline under the incessant strain of the numerous Pan American actions still before the courts. One week after meeting with Doheny at his estate, O'Melveny developed a serious case of shingles.

Fortunately, the Doheny family received some good news during these tense times: Frank Hogan was later notified that the U.S. Supreme Court had granted a writ of certiorari for the Pan American cases, agreeing in effect to review Doheny's case. "Great joy to us all. [The] third time will be the charm," O'Melveny happily announced.[50]

But Doheny, twice disappointed, remained guardedly optimistic this time. Pleased that the Supreme Court had not shut its doors to him, but ever aware that he could face another defeat, he girded himself for this next legal battle. O'Melveny's legal team prepared its Supreme Court appeal, filed it on October 4, 1926, then held its collective breath. As they concluded their work, Doheny turned to family plans, hoping the burdensome litigation would soon be over.

Edward and Estelle had their private attorneys draft a grant deed for 12.58 acres of a 400-acre parcel in Beverly Hills known as the Doheny ranch; they intended to sell it to Ned and Lucy for the princely sum of $10. The hilltop acreage, which possessed stunning views of verdant Beverly Hills below and of the Santa Monica Bay to the west, was to be the site of "Greystone," a tremendous estate that would soon be built for Ned's growing family.

At the same time that Edward was bracing himself for word from the U.S. Supreme Court regarding the civil case, his criminal trial for fraud and conspiracy began in November 1926. (The criminal trial on bribery charges would follow in 1930.) Accompanied by Estelle, he left Los Angeles by train for Washington, D.C., to face the charges levied against him and Albert Fall by the U.S. government. O'Melveny would remain in Los Angeles to monitor the events by telephone and wire. Frank Hogan was already awaiting Doheny's arrival in Washington.

Eleven Scared Rich Man

Doheny and his entourage arrived in the nation's capital on Sunday, November 7, 1926. Along with his battery of attorneys and law clerks, he installed himself at the Columbia Building across from Judiciary Square, where the criminal conspiracy trial would take place.

Doheny hired a stenographer's pool for the lawyers, assistants to handle mail and operate a telephone switchboard, a crew of waiters to serve food and refreshments, and a special chef to prepare the group's meals. He also employed a public relations expert who would remain at his side at all times and serve as his spokesperson to the press.

As *United States v. Albert Fall and Edward Doheny* began, media representatives set up camp at the courthouse. They seemed charmed by Frank Hogan's garrulous, likable personality and repeated for their readers one of his first remarks to them: "The ideal client is a rich man who is also scared."[1] Indeed, the journalists were very aware that Doheny perfectly fit Hogan's aphorism: he was anxious—this no one doubted—and he was wealthy enough to afford the reported $1 million in legal fees that Hogan would receive by the end of the decade-long trials.

The government's conspiracy trial against Doheny and Fall officially began on November 22, 1926. Judge Adolph A. Hoehling, a tough but respected jurist, would be presiding. Owen J. Roberts and Atlee Pomerene, the two attorneys who prosecuted the civil trial, would again represent the government. Impanelment of the jury took only three hours.

In a forceful but brief opening statement, Roberts concisely outlined the government's claim that Edward L. Doheny, one of the nation's richest men, had bribed a highly placed federal official in order to illegally secure valuable naval oil reserves. At the end of Roberts's presentation, he yielded the floor to Frank Hogan.

Hogan, in contrast, took two hours to complete his detailed opening statement, assuring the jury that he would refute every item of the government's case and reveal Doheny to be "an honest, patriotic citizen who had responded to the call of the Navy officials to help the government." Again speaking completely from memory, without giving a glance to his notes, Hogan gave names and dates as though reading from a carefully chronicled diary. He recited the contents of letters and telegrams from address to signature before an amazed jury. He recalled intricate details of complex contracts, and then delivered an impressive discourse on oil lands, oil leases, and the oil industry, explaining technical phrases with great facility. No objections were raised by the government during Hogan's opening remarks, and, according to one wire service account, Hogan's brilliance that day simply "eclipsed them all."[2]

Over the next ten days, fifty witnesses were called by both sides. The opening days were slow going, with witnesses called mainly to identify the Senate investigating committee's procedural records and to describe the location and nature of the oil reserves in question. The proceedings grew heated when the prosecutors offered into evidence the testimony given by Doheny and Fall before the Senate committee; once again the defense team vehemently objected, but Judge Hoehling allowed the incriminating testimony that brought to light the transfer of $100,000 from Doheny to Fall.

Dr. George Otis Smith of the U.S. Geological Survey was called to the stand as a government witness to describe the potential of the leases Doheny obtained. He testified that Reserve No. 1 in Elk Hills, California, was estimated to contain 250 million barrels of oil and was "the largest unappropriated tract of oil-bearing land in America."[3] A series of other government witnesses then described Secretary Fall's recent financial history, particularly his sudden unexplained prosperity following the naval reserve transactions in 1922.

One of the trial's tensest moments came when Roberts introduced the $100,000 note into evidence. Graham Youngs, of the New York brokerage firm Blair and Company, told the jury that he had arranged to withdraw $100,000 in cash for Ned Doheny on November 30, 1921. Youngs testified that he personally delivered the currency to Ned, who then placed the money inside a "small brown valise."

The government then called witnesses to describe how it came about that the Elk Hills reserves were to be leased to a private oil company. During a two-day examination, Assistant Secretary of the Interior Finney told the court that officials of the U.S. Navy, U.S. Geological Survey, and Bureau of Mines had determined that portions of the Elk Hills reserve should be leased in order to build protective "off-set wells" on the sites. According to Finney, they also agreed that in the interests of national security, fuel storage facilities were needed at Pearl Harbor, Hawaii, for the navy's use. Finney further testified that Fall had told him that he and Doheny had already calculated the probable cost of constructing the tanks. Fall was not present when construction bids were opened and considered by Interior and Navy Department representatives, but Doheny's bid was unanimously chosen and the contract awarded him. Roberts laboriously read the various oil contracts—including those dated April 25, June 5, and December 11, 1922—to the jury. And then, Roberts and Pomerene rested their case.

After attorney Wilton J. Lambert made a brief opening statement on behalf of Secretary Fall, Frank Hogan set to work to give the jury a picture of a perfectly reasonable explanation of the series of events.

Hogan's first witness was Dr. H. Foster Bain, former director of the Bureau of Mines. Under Hogan's skillful examination, Bain confirmed that

Finney, Admiral Robison, and other key government leaders had been conferring about the threat of drainage from the California reserves as early as 1921. Describing the chronology of the search for a solution, Bain said that in November 1921 Assistant Secretary of the Interior Finney had obtained an opinion from a naval judge advocate general that confirmed the legality of the proposed exchange of crude oil for fuel oil and opened the way to utilizing crude oil from the reserves to swap for fuel oil needed at Hawaii. Bain further testified that he and Finney considered advertising publicly for bids but then decided not to, since this lengthy action was not required by law.

The crowded courtroom stirred noisily when former navy secretary Edwin Denby, who had resigned in the wake of the Senate investigations, took the stand. Denby testified that almost immediately after he had assumed the cabinet office, he began receiving "alarming information" about the drainage of the California reserves, and he asked Secretary Fall to assist him in researching this troublesome dilemma. Together the men submitted their findings to President Harding. Denby told the court that he asked the president to place the reserves under the Department of the Interior's jurisdiction, and Harding complied. Finally, he testified that he met Doheny on December 11, 1921, when Doheny received formal assignment of the Elk Hills lease, but, Denby told the court, he did not discuss the terms of the document with either Doheny or Secretary Fall at that time.

Prosecutor Roberts attempted to destroy Denby's credibility during cross-examination, but the former naval commander held his own. Roberts asked Denby why he had been unable to recall the details of the Elk Hills contract when he testified before the Senate committee in 1924, but suddenly was able to remember them now. Denby responded that at the time of the first hearings, he had just been released from the hospital where he had been treated for a painful illness. Since then, he said, he had recovered, reexamined the records, and was now testifying with a refreshed memory. Roberts then excused Denby from the stand.

In rebuttal to Denby's testimony, Roberts called Joseph A. Carey, one of Denby's executive assistants, to the stand. But Roberts was surprised by Carey's testimony that when the lease was signed December 11, 1922, Doheny specifically asked that a public announcement be made.

Edward Doheny was called to the stand. At Frank Hogan's prompting, Doheny readily proffered autobiographical information, then described his friendship with Albert Fall. He explained to the court that he had previously lent his fleet of tankers to the government during the Great War, as an act of patriotism; years later, at the urging of Admiral Robison, he had built the Pearl Harbor storage tanks at considerable expense as a second act of patriotism. He explained that his tender of $100,000 cash to Albert Fall was a loan that would help Fall pay his back taxes and allow him to buy the adjoining ranch, which had water rights that he needed.

Looking grandfatherly with his pure white hair, rosy cheeks, and soft voice, Doheny seemed forthright and earnest. His appearance was made more poignant by an injury—an infected right arm, which forced him to wear a dark brown sling over his shoulder. As he testified in the witness box, he rested his arm on a silk cushion.

At Hogan's request, Doheny explained to the jury that Fall had asked that his loan be made in cash so that he could most quickly and easily purchase the land adjoining Three Rivers. According to Doheny, such a transaction was "customary in New Mexico," where there was little confidence in the banking system.[4] Then, in a marked divergence from his previous testimony, Doheny stated that in 1925, Fall had given him thirty-three shares of stock in the Three Rivers Cattle and Land Company as security for the $100,000 loan. Doheny said that the shares constituted one-third of the company's capital stock and represented a combined value of $200,000, double the amount of the note.

Doheny then recounted his several conversations with Admiral Robison. Doheny said that Robison told him that he had received secret naval intelligence indicating a potential Japanese threat of attack and that this intelligence called for constructing a huge fuel oil base at Pearl Harbor to strengthen the United States' defenses. Doheny further testified that Robison, calling the situation "critical," urged him to place a bid for constructing the tanks. Though reluctant to undertake such an action, after much consideration he acceded to Robison's request. Doheny said that he felt the terms and conditions of the contracts were "eminently fair" to both parties. He acknowledged, however, that his company's profit could amount to as much as $100 million, "over a lifetime of whoever could live that long."

In the final moments of his direct testimony, Doheny adamantly insisted that he had not bribed Secretary Fall at all. He claimed he had not even talked to Fall from February 1922 until December 1922, when they had met at the Wardman Park Hotel in Washington, D.C. He claimed he had not promised any favors to Fall, or begged him for the Pearl Harbor contract. When Doheny made the $100,000 loan, he said, Fall was not even active in the bid's consideration.

Now it was time for Owen Roberts's cross-examination. A shrewd litigator, he had spent months preparing for this moment. For the next two and a half hours, Roberts sharply interrogated Doheny, hoping to elicit critical testimony from him. Doheny admitted that he had expected huge profits from his "patriotic duty" and that there indeed had been glaring irregularities in his $100,000 "loan arrangement" with Fall. "Why was this deal kept secret?" Roberts asked. "And why was there no record of it in any of Doheny's financial records or bank statements? Why was his own son used as a courier in this clandestine transaction?" After a short pause, Roberts turned to Doheny and asked him directly: "May I ask, if there was any reason why you sent your son with the money, rather than somebody else?"

"Because I would rather trust my son to take money than anybody else," Doheny replied.

"Was it because it was a confidential transaction?" Roberts continued.

"No, not necessarily confidential," Doheny replied. "It was a personal transaction of some importance, and I was to get a note in return for the money. I sent my most trusted agent, whom I was endeavoring to work into every phase of the business of handling the fortune that I expected sometime or other he would handle all of."

"Of course, it would not give him any particular education in handling your fortune to have him take $100,000 to Washington, would it?" Roberts asked.

"Yes, sir," Doheny replied, "even if he had been held up on the way he would have learned something. He would have had something in experience." Laughter rippled through the gallery.

"He would have had a very serious experience if he had been held up, would he not?"

"Yes," Doheny said to the sound of more quiet laughter.

Doheny attempted to answer each of these discomforting questions in a calm, matter-of-fact voice. Then Roberts posed another daunting query: why, he asked, had Doheny carried Fall's note—with the signature torn off—in his wallet, rather than leaving it in a secure place, such as a safety-deposit box? When Doheny did not respond, the prosecutor restated his question. "Is it your habit to carry $100,000 notes around in a wallet?" Roberts asked.

"Well, if I choose to do so," Doheny answered.

Roberts then suggested that there was "something sinister" about Doheny's removal of Fall's signature from the note, but Doheny simply stuck to his already-familiar story: he had loaned an old friend money and it had nothing whatsoever to do with the Elk Hills leases.

After a short pause, Roberts asked Doheny if he had given Fall any other funds beside the $100,000 proffered on November 30, 1921. Doheny surprised the courtroom—as well as his own lawyers—by admitting that shortly before the start of the trial he had advanced his codefendant another $5,000 cash to cover legal expenses. In this case, Doheny said, he had not formalized any loan agreement nor requested collateral, because Fall's word "is as good as his bond to me as long as Senator Fall is alive."

During the considerable length of this cross-examination, Doheny acknowledged that he had "pledged the Fifth" in his civil suit in order not to incriminate himself, on the advice of his attorneys, who warned him not to testify because criminal cases were pending against him.

When Doheny finally was excused from the witness stand, he breathed a long sigh of relief. The worst part of the trial was over; he had proved himself an excellent witness. One journalist later gushed that Doheny "gave an award-winning performance and probably saved himself from jail."[5] Most trial observers believed that despite the government's fierce interrogation of Doheny and despite its parade of witnesses, it had failed to discredit him to any significant degree.

Estelle Doheny then followed her husband to the stand. Her demeanor was, according to one journalist, "smiling, youthful and unembarrassed,"[6] and she was treated by the prosecutors with dignity and respect. She answered every question posed by Roberts precisely, testifying that sometime in 1920 or 1921, her husband had mentioned that he had promised to loan Fall $100,000 so that Fall could purchase a ranch adjoining his property. Doheny told her that, should anything happen to him, she should be sure to take responsibility for the loan. She said that Doheny showed her the promissory note and explained his concern that in the event of his death, his executor might force Fall to pay back the note even if he were still experiencing hardships. After pondering this, Mrs. Doheny recounted, Doheny tore Fall's signature from the note and handed the document to her for safekeeping.

But what had become of the portion of the note that contained the signature? Roberts asked Mrs. Doheny. She replied that she had put it into her safety-deposit box at the Security and Trust Savings Bank in Los Angeles. She had not remembered this when her husband testified at the Senate committee hearings, but later recalled its place of safekeeping. During his redirect, Hogan displayed the torn promissory note to the jury. Then, in a dramatic demonstration, he showed that its tear line perfectly fit with the ripped signature block.

The prosecution waived further cross-examination of Mrs. Doheny.

After a brief recess, Ned Doheny was called to the stand. Like his father, he briefly provided autobiographical information and then stated that Albert Fall had been an intimate friend of his father's for many years. In 1921, Ned recalled, his father had informed him that he intended to loan Fall $100,000 so he could buy a ranch in New Mexico.

Ned testified that sometime in mid-November, Fall telephoned the Dohenys to say that he had completed negotiations for the adjoining Harris ranch property and now needed the money to purchase the acreage. Ned said that his father then asked Ned to call Blair and Company of New York to determine his current balance; as it happened, there was then only $10,000 to $11,000 in that particular account.

When Ned told his father that he himself had more than $100,000 on deposit with Blair, and would gladly draw a check on his own account if his father could later reimburse him, Doheny agreed. He directed his son to obtain the $100,000 in cash and carry it to Fall in Washington, D.C. Ned told the court that accompanied by his longtime friend and secretary, Hugh Plunkett, he left for his apartment in New York City, withdrew the funds from Blair and Company, and then met Fall at his Wardman Park

Hotel apartment and gave him the money. Fall promptly removed the cash from its satchel and counted it on a table.

Fall then wrote a promissory note and handed it to Ned. Ned said he noticed that a rate of interest was not stated, but Fall replied that he had not discussed the matter with Mr. Doheny, and asked that Doheny fill in whatever rate he thought was appropriate. Ned testified that after returning to New York with Plunkett, he delivered the promissory note to his father.

CLOSING ARGUMENTS

The trial continued for three weeks. Fall was never summoned to the stand. Instead, defense counsel built its case chiefly via character witnesses, such as a Catholic bishop, Baptist minister, and several former district attorneys and judges who, under oath, praised Fall and Doheny for their impeccable integrity.

All testimony was concluded on December 11, 1926. The following Monday, Roberts launched his closing arguments and again denounced Fall and Doheny before the jury as "criminal conspirators" who had intended to defraud the U.S. government. Roberts ridiculed the defendants' tangled tales of patriotic leases and compassionate cash loans; he told the jurors that Doheny's "torn signature" fable was preposterous. No, said Roberts, Doheny was not a savior-patriot nor a concerned friend of a downtrodden politician; he was a "calculating and canny" man. One by one, he impeached the character of the defense's other witnesses, branding each one a sycophantic admirer and an easily manipulated toady.

Roberts had not finished his oration when the court adjourned at 5:30 P.M. The following morning, he focused the jury's attention on the inconsistencies between Doheny's testimony before the Senate committee and his testimony at the current trial, and he itemized the many lies allegedly told by Fall under oath about the sources of his income. As the noon hour struck, Roberts concluded by pleading with jurors to ignore the defendants' prominent status and wealth and to instead use common sense in finding them guilty of conspiracy and fraud.

After lunch, Hogan began his energetic, engrossing five-hour summation of the facts and circumstances to support Doheny's innocence. He told the jury that Roberts's summation was "as wholesale and as vicious a vilification as ever polluted the atmosphere of a court of justice." "Do you think," he asked the court, "that a man who left his home at the age of sixteen and followed the trails of the pioneer West, who dug in mother earth for the minerals hidden therein, who with pick and shovel sunk wells that he might bring out the gold and the liquid that today mean safety for worlds, would, even if he himself could, stoop so low as to bribe a Cabinet officer of the United States of America in order that he might swindle and cheat the land that had given him plenty?"

Hogan told the jury that there was nothing sinister in Doheny's actions in making a loan to a longtime friend and giving the note's torn signature to his wife for safekeeping. "Have you ever heard or thought or dreamed of an honorable man, constantly thinking of the possibility of his approaching end that may come at any moment because of advanced years, saying, 'If I die, when I am gone and no possible advantage can come to me, I ask you, partner of my life, you who have shared my sorrows and my joys, you to whom I will leave my worldly goods, I ask you to carry out the friendly loan to my old friend, to keep the pledge and promise which voluntarily I have offered . . .'" Overwhelmed by emotion, Hogan never finished his question. Instead, he plunged into a lengthy character analysis of the multimillionaire, seated at the counsel table.

Hogan told the jury of Ned's war service, saying of the father and son that the "old man offered that young man's life upon the altar of patriotism. He went on ships of war over the turbulent and submarine-infested oceans in his country's service, the only son, the only child. And you are asked to believe that when Edward L. Doheny, near the end of his life, corruptly intended to bribe Albert B. Fall, Secretary in the cabinet of Warren G. Harding, he deliberately and purposely used as an instrument therefore his son, the pride of his youth, the hope of his maturity, the solace of his old age!" He continued, almost shouting, "And yet, unless you believe that, you cannot believe that there was a bribe; you cannot believe that here was a criminal mind and a corrupt heart motivating this thing; you cannot believe in all the labored argument of our opponents."

In his summation, Hogan depicted Doheny as a grossly maligned patriot; he read a letter from the late President Harding, which showed the president's approval of the oil leases in question, and ended by announcing that Doheny's motivation was described in three simple words—"the national security."

Mark Lambert, Fall's attorney, followed Hogan's remarks by offering the jury a concise but well-crafted closing argument in which he admitted that though Fall had lied about his lender's identity, he did so to protect his friend, Doheny, from embarrassment.

When the defense had finished, prosecutors Roberts and Pomerene reviewed the government's charges: the two influential men, Albert Fall and Edward Doheny, had conspired to defraud the United States of its valuable oil leases at Elk Hills; their conduct was criminal and they deserved to be punished.

At two o'clock Wednesday afternoon, December 15, Judge Hoehling issued jury instructions to the panel members, defining for them the term "criminal conspiracy" and admonishing them to consider the case without passion, prejudice, or regard for the wealth or social positions of the defendants. Deliberations then commenced.

All afternoon and evening, Doheny sat in the witness room playing solitaire, while Ned Doheny and several newspapermen played bridge. Fall and his family awaited the verdict in a courtroom down the hall, and prosecutor Roberts puffed on a pipe in a vacant district attorney's office. Of all the major players in the case, only Frank Hogan now milled about the court hallways, offering interviews to the press and admitting to one journalist, "That man Roberts is the toughest proposition I ever went up against in my thirty years of practice."[7]

Soon all were given word that the jury had retired for the night.

THE VERDICT

The following afternoon, after a total of nineteen hours of deliberation, the twelve men who were to decide Doheny's fate returned with a verdict. As the jury resumed its place in the box, the courtroom grew tense; every seat in the room was now filled. Lawyers waited apprehensively and reporters sat at the edge of their chairs, ready to rush to the telephones.

"Will the defendants please rise," Justice Hoehling ordered.

Doheny was the first on his feet. Fall, with some difficulty, rose next, and assumed a military posture. Both men stoically faced the jury box. The foreman was asked the verdict first on Doheny, then Fall.

"Do you find Edward L. Doheny guilty or not guilty?"

"Not guilty!" Alphonso E. Parker, the foreman, quickly answered. The silence of the courtroom had been palpable, but now a solitary scream pierced the air. It had come from Alexina, Fall's oldest daughter, who was now trying to suppress her joy.

Doheny's pale face grew flushed. He tried to speak to his nearby counsel, but wept instead. Leaning over to Fall, he whispered something inaudible.

"Do you find Albert B. Fall guilty or not guilty?" asked the clerk.

"Not guilty," answered the foreman. A surge of cheers and enthusiasm filled the room. Justice Hoehling frantically pounded his gavel to restore order, but he might as well have tried to calm the roar of Niagara Falls. Pandemonium had broken loose, and the defendants and their supporters were on their feet, embracing and weeping with joy. Nearby, the two defense teams jubilantly patted each other on the back, and reporters attempted to wade through the crowd to interview the acquitted men.

Waiting in her nearby hotel suite, Mrs. Doheny was elated when she heard the news. "My prayers have been answered," she cried.

It was later revealed that at 10:00 P.M. the previous night, the jury had deadlocked six for conviction, and six for acquittal. But by the following morning, nine had decided to acquit. Finally, after much debating, the last three holdouts changed their verdicts to make the judgment unanimous. Some jurors later admitted that they had been moved by Hogan's colorful tales of the "frontier friendship" between Doheny and Fall, and by the two men's ages and ailing health. Later, Doheny would express great gratitude for the jury's decision.

"Boys, I am mighty glad," were the first words Doheny said to waiting newspapermen as he left the courtroom. "It's what I deserved and what I expected, but if the verdict had been different I could have stood it." A

more formal press release, issued later that afternoon by Doheny's public relations manager on his behalf, read: "I am gratified by the result. The
ordeal has been a terrible one. After a lifetime of honorable effort I have
seen my principal work, which was to make a good name to hand on to
my son and my grandchildren, almost destroyed. I hope that the American people, whose belief in trial by jury amount almost to a religion, will
accept the verdict of this typically American jury."[8]

Although the defendants and their legal teams were elated, many
throughout the nation, including Democratic party leaders, politicians,
editorial writers, and plain folks, were justifiably confused and appalled.
How could a civil court determine that the Teapot Dome and Elk Hills
leases were fraudulent, and later a Washington criminal court find the alleged conspirators innocent?

Senator Thomas J. Heflin of Alabama echoed the thoughts of most citizens when he bellowed on the floor of the Senate: "A rich man cannot be
convicted under this administration. If a man has money he has the pass-
port to freedom."

THE OIL BARON RETURNS HOME

Despite the disgruntlement of those who had hoped to see Doheny and
Fall in stripes, an ebullient crowd of nearly 6,000 well-wishers came to
Los Angeles' Santa Fe Station to greet Edward Doheny on his return
home. The *Los Angeles Evening Express* reported that the crowd was second in size only to that which had come to greet humorist Will Rogers on
his own triumphant return to the city: "Men and women—business leaders, priests, stenographers from the great Pan American Company offices, clerks, intimate friends of the family and a throng of just curious,
held Doheny at the steps of his car, 'Willow Bank,' for 20 minutes. A parade of hundreds passed in a line hastily formed by police, all seeking to
shake the oil magnate's hand, with scores of women and girls kissing him
and Mrs. Doheny, who stood beside him." There were tears in Doheny's
eyes when he said: "I am deeply touched at the splendid reception given
me by such a representative committee of my friends in Los Angeles."[9]

Although Doheny said he wished nothing more than to go into seclusion for a much-needed rest, he remained in the public eye, staging a series of high-profile appearances at various fetes, including an "Appreciation Banquet" held in his honor at the Biltmore Hotel on January 10, 1927. Over four hundred prominent citizens, including the mayor of Los Angeles, the mayor of San Francisco, Hollywood movie stars, top businessmen and financiers, and high-ranking officials of the Catholic Church, honored Doheny at the dinner. The occasion assumed a semi-official air when the invitations were posted bearing the historic seal of the City of Los Angeles.

Frank Hogan, the banquet's featured speaker, declared that Doheny's Washington, D.C., victory was won after "every fact and document concerning the assailed transactions had been placed before the court and jury." Hogan again called Doheny one of "our greatest patriots."[10] The room exploded into a thundering standing ovation. Ned, dressed in black tie and seated next to his father at the head table, leaped to his feet, clapping and cheering. Unfortunately, Albert Fall, returning to his Three Rivers Ranch in New Mexico, did not receive a similar reception. He faced still other criminal conspiracy charges with Harry Sinclair and found himself ostracized by many of his peers. Stressed by the intolerably long trial, Fall became ill with pneumonia.

GIVE THEM EVERYTHING

It was a happier Christmas inside the Doheny household in 1926, thanks to the December acquittal. Doheny had even embarked on a massive architectural undertaking, the grand Beverly Hills estate that would soon be called "Greystone," a gift to Ned and Lucy. Groundbreaking for the stunning multimillion-dollar home began by year's end.

Of all the lavish gifts Edward Doheny gave his beloved son, the fifty-five room baronial castle was, by far, the most extraordinary, considered to be the most luxurious private residence south of William Randolph Hearst's spectacular estate at San Simeon, California. The huge (over 46,000 square feet), magnificent structure rose high above Sunset Boulevard, sited on a promontory of Doheny's 400-acre Beverly Hills ranch. Its grounds would include an enormous stable (close to 16,000 square feet), dozens of riding trails, a two-bedroom gatehouse, formal gardens, terraces, a sixty-foot swimming pool, several greenhouses, badminton and tennis courts, and a waterfall that cascaded down an eighty-foot-high hillside before filling an artificial lake gloriously landscaped with white water lilies. The estate's interior was equally awe-inspiring: it contained seven Georgian fireplaces, a thirty-seat motion picture theater, a two-lane bowling alley, a recreation room and gymnasium, a walk-in fur and jewelry vault, a temperature-controlled wine cellar, and a billiard room with a hidden bar that, in this Prohibition era, retracted into the wall at the push of a button.

Doheny selected Gordon B. Kaufmann, one of the West's most sought-after residential architects, to design Greystone after holding a "design competition" between Kaufmann and Wallace Neff, another leading architect. Kaufmann had already designed some of the Southwest's most talked-about buildings, including the *Los Angeles Times* headquarters in downtown Los Angeles, the Athenaeum at the California Institute of Technology in Pasadena, and the Arrowhead Springs Hotel in San Bernardino.[11] Neff, who was known as the "architect to the stars" and had designed homes for Mary Pickford and Charlie Chaplin, submitted a rendering of his proposed design—an ornate, European "Versailles-inspired" mansion—to Doheny, which the oilman flatly rejected, preferring instead Kaufmann's ponderous English Tudor.[12] The choice of English Tudor conformed to the then-prevailing architectural taste in stately homes.[13]

Construction of Greystone began on February 15, 1927; Kaufmann supervised all work. The ambitious project served as a convenient, much-needed diversion for father and son, who now attempted to take their minds off the continuing repercussions of the oil lease scandal. And as an architectural critic has observed, "An estate like Greystone also would offer a secluded residence for their family which was enduring the relentless nationwide publicity and the extended trials of the Teapot Dome Scandal."[14] At Doheny's urging, Kaufmann spared no expense. Landscape architect Paul G. Thiene, who had created the stunning gardens at the nearby estate of Ben Meyer, president of Union Bank, installed the largest sprinkler system in the world beneath Greystone's lawns. When the landscaper was asked by his sizable crew exactly what Mr. Doheny wanted in the way of gardens to please his son and daughter-in-law, Thiene purportedly replied, "Give them everything."[15] The hillside behind the mansion was gently terraced with a series of Italian Renaissance–inspired "garden rooms" containing formal rose gardens and cypress alleys linked by a series of winding paths. Each garden walkway was made of Vermont slate. The garden room walls were crafted from Indiana limestone, which matched the estate's facade. Ornamental garden metalwork and sculpture were shipped from England. Carved stone figures populated the grounds.

On the broad sloping hillside leading to Greystone, Thiene planted an immense grass lawn, similar to those that blanketed the grounds of English country estates in a far wetter climate. Ten gardeners would be required to maintain these lawns. Greystone's three-foot-thick gray Indiana limestone walls gave the mansion its name. Its steeply pitched roof, framed with steel-reinforced concrete, was covered with solid Welsh slate. Many windows of the home featured an inspiring east-to-west panoramic view from downtown Los Angeles to the Santa Monica Bay.

Ned appointed his secretary, Hugh Plunkett, to oversee the construction work. Hugh worked closely with the Greystone contractors and landscapers from 1926 to 1928 and consulted with Ned about the project's financial details. Because he proved himself a consistently trustworthy and conscientious employee, Hugh was entrusted to sign many of the Doheny checks for the construction costs, some of which totaled hundreds of thousands of dollars. Ned's friendship with Hugh deepened as the two men, by necessity, spent most of their waking hours immersed in the completion of the complex construction project. Lucy, Ned's wife, was extremely relieved to turn over the difficult task of supervising workmen to Hugh, who pleased the Dohenys by keeping the crews on schedule.

Under Lucy's direction and Hugh's close watch, the Cheesewright Studios of Pasadena provided the sumptuous interior decoration and lavish furnishings. As the work progressed, Ned and his family wandered spellbound through Greystone's rooms. The master suite was decorated in soft ivory tones, with two separate bedrooms, his and her dressing rooms, two bathrooms, and a shared sitting room. On the upper floor near the master suite was a combination trophy room/library that contained Ned's collection of various firearms, including antique guns, hunting rifles, and smaller, more modern revolvers. The children's rooms were located in the east and north wings of the mansion. They had been painted in bright, cheerful colors. Also in the west wing was a separate kitchen for the youngsters and their nannies.

Beverly Hills residents came to regard Greystone as a self-contained principality.[16] The estate had its own gatekeepers, watchmen, mechanics, house staff, field crews, and even its own fire station. A neo-Gothic garage, which housed ten of Ned and Lucy's cars,[17] featured its own gas pumps, lifts, and machine shop. Among the staff were cooks, housemaids, a kitchen maid, laundresses, a maintenance worker, a painter, ten gardeners, four chauffeurs, and two operators who ran Ned's two telephone switchboards. The main service wing for the staff included a butler's pantry, kitchen, flower room, servants' dining room, maids' sitting room, and maids' sleeping rooms, plus a service stairway to the second floor, where a second service wing contained a sewing room, linen room, four more maid's rooms, and a gift room where Lucy Doheny could wrap fabulous presents for her family, friends, and staff at Christmas time.[18]

Construction of Greystone got under way early in the year, before the family knew that the torturous legal battles were to take an ugly turn.

Twelve The Last Appeal

On February 28, 1927, the United States Supreme Court rendered its decision on Doheny's appeal of the civil judgment against his Pan American Corporation. Despite the strong argument made by O'Melveny and Hogan, the Court unanimously confirmed the lower court's ruling and found the naval leases at Elk Hills illegal.

The transactions, wrote the justices, were "tainted with corruption" and, therefore, were null and void. Now Pan American would absolutely receive no credit for the money and labor it had expended to build the Pearl Harbor storage tanks. In setting aside the Elk Hills oil leases, the Court issued a vitriolic opinion against Doheny and Fall. Writing for the majority, Justice Butler declared that "The facts and circumstances disclosed by the record show clearly that the interest and influence of Fall as well as his official action were corruptly secured by Doheny . . . and that the consummation of the transaction was brought about by means of collusion and corrupt conspiracy between him and Doheny."[1]

The ruling had potentially ruinous implications for Doheny. Pan American had expended more than $8 million in the construction of the Pearl Harbor storage tanks, another $2.3 million in shipment costs, and nearly $1.3 million in drilling and production expenses at the naval reserve. Now, all of these expenditures were a total loss.[2] In addition, Doheny would be forced to repay the government millions of dollars in restitution for oil already removed from Elk Hills. As news of the Supreme Court's ruling hit the press, Pan American's stock prices began to plummet; shareholders were disposing of their holdings as quickly as they could. After conferring with his financial consultants, Doheny was forced to conclude that he would have to liquidate a portion of his fixed assets, corporate holdings, and stock to remain solvent.

Greystone was a significant financial drain, but construction plans went forward nevertheless. Greystone would not only be Doheny's greatest material gift to Ned, it would also serve as a symbol of his love for his son. Ned had served his father well through these trying years—as a confidant, loyal family member, and a key board member of the Pan American Company. Throughout Doheny's stressful legal struggles, Ned remained at his side, offering constant assistance and encouragement, and, when needed, assuming responsibility for corporate matters when Doheny was preoccupied with the litigation. Doheny had not forgotten how Ned withstood government investigation and weathered an indictment for bribery all because of his father's relationship with Albert Fall.

SINCLAIR'S LEGAL TROUBLES

The criminal trial for conspiracy against Harry Sinclair and Albert Fall began on October 17, 1927, in the District Supreme Court with Judge Frederick J. Siddons presiding. New Mexico attorney Mark Lambert represented Fall; Martin W. Littleton, a former congressman and highly respected lawyer from New York, represented Harry Sinclair. The government was again represented by Owen Roberts and Atlee Pomerene.

The trial proceeded for two tedious weeks without any unusual developments. A jury of ten men and two women had been selected, opening statements had been made, and the government proceeded quickly with its case. But just as the prosecution was nearing the end of its presentation, the trial was suddenly halted by a sensational announcement.

Roberts asked Judge Siddons to declare a mistrial because the government had discovered a plot by Sinclair to tamper with the jury. Roberts told Judge Siddons that Sinclair had secretly contacted William J. Burns, former Bureau of Investigation chief under President Harding, to ask him to order detectives from his well-known detective agency to shadow jurors. Apparently, Sinclair had hoped to find a "makable juror" who could be bribed to deadlock the jury. Through intelligence received from the Burns detectives, Sinclair selected juror Edward J. Kidwell, a leather goods worker who reportedly had a drinking problem.

However, one of the detectives hired by Sinclair, William J. McMullin, began to grow nervous about his involvement in Kidwell's surveillance. McMullin contacted government prosecutors, confessed everything, and then became, in effect, a double agent, feigning continued loyalty to Sinclair and Burns while reporting their covert activities to the prosecutors. When Sinclair, through intermediaries, offered Kidwell $25,000 to hang the jury, the government had evidence to present to Judge Siddons, who immediately declared a mistrial and discharged the jury. Fall, who was to have been tried alongside Sinclair, returned to his ranch in New Mexico, ill and exhausted. Newspapers fed daily details of Sinclair's purported jury tampering to their readers.

In an action that surprised no one, a Washington grand jury indicted Harry F. Sinclair, William J. Burns, and several of Burns's detectives for "jury shadowing." The men stood trial on December 5, 1927, and, three months later, despite protests by Burns that he was "innocent as a child unborn," Siddons found the men guilty. Burns was sentenced to only fifteen days in jail; Sinclair was given a six-month prison sentence but was released on $5,000 bail, pending his appeal.

Prosecutors then pressed for a retrial of the conspiracy charges remaining against Fall and Sinclair. Fall's attorneys pleaded for a lengthy delay because of Fall's poor health. Several continuances were granted to Fall after court-appointed physicians determined that he was seriously ill. On March

23, Roberts decided to wait no longer to try Sinclair and announced that the government intended to proceed against the oilman alone. The court then entered an order of severance, and the fortunate former secretary of the interior escaped trial for conspiracy in his transactions with Harry Sinclair.[3]

Sinclair's criminal trial resumed on April 10, 1928. Roberts and Pomerene were determined to obtain his conviction. To make certain they achieved this goal, the prosecutors subpoenaed Ned Doheny to appear in Washington and testify about the $100,000 in cash that he had delivered to Fall in the little black bag. The purpose of Ned's testimony was simple—to confirm that Fall reaped large financial returns from not only Sinclair but also Edward Doheny, the two men who were granted the naval oil reserve leases.

Outraged to learn of Ned's subpoena, Doheny contacted O'Melveny and Hogan. Hogan, who happened to be in Washington at the time, appeared before Judge Jennings Bailey on April 14 to represent the Doheny interests. He argued that Ned could not be compelled to testify because his Fifth Amendment constitutional rights protected him against testifying against himself. His own bribery trial was only months away.

Then, in a move that stunned all connected with the case, Roberts offered Hogan a deal: the government would drop its bribery indictment against Ned, if Ned would agree to testify in the Sinclair case. However, the charges against Doheny Sr. would remain intact.[4] Pleased, but very surprised, Hogan told the court that the Dohenys had "no objection" to this agreement.

Of course, now Ned and his father faced new concerns; any statement made by Ned Doheny on the stand in the Sinclair trial could be used against Edward Doheny in his upcoming bribery trial. Hogan advised Ned to take the stand anyway, to tell the truth, and to remember that Hogan would be by his side every step of the way.[5]

As the government case against Sinclair for criminal conspiracy began, the evidence that Roberts and Pomerene presented was substantially that submitted in the previous civil trial against Sinclair's Mammoth Oil Company. In this case, however, Fall's son-in-law, Mahlon T. Everhart, testified for the first time as a prosecution witness. He had been excused from testifying in the earlier trial, having invoked his Fifth Amendment rights. But in December 1927, President Coolidge signed a new bill (pushed through Congress by Senator Walsh) that reduced the statute of limitations from six to three years for the offenses with which Everhart could have been charged. Since Everhart was no longer subject to indictment, he could not use the Fifth Amendment to escape testifying.

Now legally compelled to take the stand, Everhart reluctantly told jurors how he had traveled to Washington, D.C., at his father-in-law's request in May 1922 and arranged on Fall's behalf the sale to Sinclair of a one-third interest in the Three Rivers Land and Cattle Company. Everhart met Sinclair at Fall's apartment at the Wardman Park Hotel, and Sinclair handed him a package containing $198,000 in Liberty Bonds. A later, second packet of bonds would bring the total to $233,000, to complete the purported sale. Everhart also testified that Fall had issued three certificates of stock. The certificates did not name Sinclair but were issued to a dummy director and to Everhart as trustee. Fall had told Everhart that Everhart was acting as "trustee for Sinclair."

Everhart told the court that he had the certificates in his possession when he received the funds from Sinclair. He stated that he believed the land and property of the Three Rivers Land and Cattle Company was worth $700,000; therefore, a 33 1/3 percent interest would total approximately $233,000 (the amount in Liberty Bonds paid to Fall). When Everhart returned to Three Rivers, New Mexico, he gave the package containing Sinclair's $233,000 in Liberty Bonds to Fall. Fall removed $2,500 worth of bonds, then had Everhart deposit the remainder at the First National Bank of Pueblo, Colorado. Later, Fall used $140,500 of the Liberty Bonds to repay company loans, and placed the rest in a safety-deposit box. In December 1922, Sinclair visited Three Rivers and paid Fall an additional $10,000. This sum, and a second payment of $25,000, Everhart said, were intended for "ranch expenses."

Everhart's testimony was the first evidentiary proof that Fall had received money, not only from Doheny but from Sinclair as well. Newspapers across the country predicted that the former secretary's downfall was imminent, following his son-in-law's unfortunate admissions. Everhart's explosive new information created a strong case for prosecutors, much stronger than the one they had previously presented against Fall and Doheny in the trial of 1926 in which both men were acquitted.

In late April, Ned Doheny took the stand and testified about the events of November 30, 1921, when he and Hugh Plunkett had taken their own satchel of cash to Secretary Fall. Courtroom spectators commented that young Doheny seemed sincere and earnest in his testimony.

Spectators had hoped to see Sinclair take the stand in his own defense, but the oilman demurred. His defense attorney, Martin Littleton, ably argued that Sinclair only gave the Liberty Bonds and cash to Fall to complete a perfectly legitimate business transaction, securing a one-third interest in the 700,000-plus-acre Three Rivers Ranch. Furthermore, he emphasized, Sinclair's financial dealings with Fall had been totally unrelated to the oil lease that Sinclair received and did not influence Fall's official conduct. Littleton stressed to the jury that Sinclair had bid for the naval reserve leases only after he was pressured by government officials who were concerned about drainage, and that, like Doheny, he acted out of patriotic concern. Sinclair had dealt with the government at arm's length in all the negotiations, Littleton argued, and while over time Mammoth Oil's profits might be substantial from the leases, the company's operations at Teapot Dome were highly beneficial to the government.

Roberts passionately disputed Littleton's version of the Fall-Sinclair transaction. Sinclair offered a bribe, plain and simple, he insisted, in exchange for lucrative naval reserve oil leases, and young Doheny's testimony was further proof of Fall's systematic conspiracy and fraud against the government.

After closing arguments at the ten-day trial, the judge gave the jury members their instructions. He admonished them to take careful note of the difference between *bribery*, for which Sinclair was not charged, and the crime of *conspiracy*, with which he was charged; conspiracy had to be proven absolutely and not merely deduced from a preponderance of the evidence.

After deliberating only two hours, on April 21, 1928, the jury returned to the courtroom and declared Sinclair "not guilty." The government lawyers were dumbfounded when they heard the verdict. The courtroom crowd was silent, but later in the halls there was much to be heard about "millionaires." Oilman Harry Ford Sinclair, jubilant, left the courthouse surrounded by well-wishers and reporters.

Several jurors spoke to newsmen after the verdict's announcement to explain their reasoning. One juror said that if a man like Sinclair wanted to enter a conspiracy, he would not have merely tendered a "trifling" $200,000; and if Fall were selling Teapot Dome, he could have easily received more than $250,000 for it.[6]

After the trial, Littleton told reporters, "Let persecution cease." On the floor of the U.S. Senate, an angry Senator Edward Nye declared, "This is emphatic evidence that you can't convict a million dollars in the U.S. under the order that now prevails. The Supreme Court had got the number of this whole gang, and in the minds of the American people, Sinclair stands convicted."

Meanwhile, in Los Angeles, Edward Doheny was delighted when he learned of Sinclair's acquittal in a case in which the defense was far weaker than his own. Ned Doheny returned home to his family from the trial in Washington a very relieved young man.

Sinclair's legal troubles, however, were far from over. He still awaited the final conclusion of his two Supreme Court appeals: one for the contempt of Senate conviction and the other for jury tampering. Sinclair would remain free of prison for only a year.

While Ned had been away in Washington, Hugh Plunkett and Lucy Doheny had continued to oversee Greystone's construction. The family had hoped to move soon, but completion of the great estate was taking longer than anticipated.

By summer, Hugh was working long days and most evenings, rarely returning home to his wife. He and Harriett Marian Hall had been married eleven years. For some time there had been rumors that the Plunketts were experiencing marital difficulties, and Hugh's sustained absences only made matters worse. Finally, in August 1927, the couple formally separated. Hugh moved to the Stanford Apartments on Cochran Avenue, a short distance from Greystone, sharing an apartment with bachelor George Riley. Marian Hall Plunkett filed for divorce; in October 1928, her petition was granted on the grounds of desertion.[7]

With his marriage dissolved, and the stress of Greystone's construction adding to that caused by his fears about the pending criminal trial in which he would have to testify, Hugh began to show signs of severe emotional strain. Ned did whatever he could to reassure his assistant and friend, but he worried that Hugh's supervisory duties were too much for him.

Greystone was completed in September 1928 at a total cost of $3.1 million (roughly $27 million in 1996 dollars). Architectural critics proclaimed the estate a success. It was the grandest and most expensive "dream palace" in Los Angeles.[8] Certainly, it had surpassed the highest expectations of Ned and Lucy; they were so pleased by Kaufmann's architectural creation that they made him a gift of a racy new black Cord automobile.[9]

Just prior to Thanksgiving 1928, Ned, Lucy, and their five children—Lucy, thirteen; Edward III, eleven; William, nine; Patrick, five; and Timothy, two—moved into the mansion at 501 Doheny Road. The young couple entertained lavishly in the days before Christmas in Greystone's grand two-story living room. Musicians played holiday songs in an orchestra gallery above the ballroom floor as over one hundred guests danced to the festive music. In the corner of the room, a thirty-foot Christmas tree blazed with lights and hundreds of beautifully wrapped presents were piled at its base.

The holiday season was an especially welcome respite, as the new year portended stress and pressure for everyone at Greystone, with the approaching criminal trial. Because the government had dropped its indictment against Ned, there was an increased probability that both Ned and Hugh would be compelled to testify at Edward Doheny's trial for bribery.

Ned, who spoke frequently with his father, was concerned but not overly frightened by this proposition, but Hugh was terrified by the prospect. He worried that he would be arrested and jailed for his participation in the delivery of the black bag. Agonizing over growing publicity about the case, he sought to stay out of the spotlight at all costs. On Christmas Eve, he completely collapsed and suffered what the Dohenys'

physician termed a "nervous breakdown." Dr. Ernest Clyde Fishbaugh
ordered Hugh to remain under the care of a private nurse and stay housebound in the guest room at Greystone for a complete rest.[10]

Edward Doheny spent much of the holiday season at home at the Chester
Place compound, nervously helping his attorneys prepare for Albert Fall's
bribery trial. He knew all too well that the outcome for Fall could very
well affect his own future.

After the 1924 indictments were handed down charging Doheny, Sinclair, and Fall with conspiracy to commit fraud and bribery of a government official, the respective legal teams had jockeyed for the best defense
positions. The resultant sequence was that Doheny and Fall would be
tried on one set of conspiracy charges, Fall and Sinclair in a separate trial
on another. Defense motions and judicial rulings channeled the bribery
charges into individual trials for each man. By the end of 1928, Doheny
and Fall had successfully weathered the 1926 criminal trial for conspiracy,
even though earlier the Pan American Corporation had been found
guilty of fraud in the civil suit and the Elk Hill leases ordered canceled.
In the trial charging Fall and Sinclair with conspiracy, Fall was severed
from the case due to illness and Sinclair was acquitted. Ahead of them
were the bribery trials: one for each man.

In spite of the acquittals on conspiracy charges, Doheny and Fall could
not rest comfortably as the trials approached. Their attorneys had told
them that bribery was a more difficult charge to defend, and they were
warned that much of the bribery case against Fall would hinge on the testimony of Ned and Hugh Plunkett, who had delivered the $100,000.
Events were closing in on the family. No longer able to take the Fifth
Amendment, Ned could be forced to testify under oath against his father.
Everyone understood that Doheny's freedom and reputation now rested
largely in his son's hands. Hugh Plunkett also was made aware that his
performance on the stand could alter the future of the Doheny family. Although Ned was granted immunity as a condition of his testimony in the
Sinclair trial, Hugh did not have such protection and was panic stricken.

In anticipation of more legal troubles, and to protect his heirs' fortunes, Doheny began methodically in 1928 to sell additional portions of what remained of his once-impressive oil empire. He sold Pan American Western to the Richfield Oil Company of California for $7.5 million. And later, he offered 40,000 acres of oil lands in Ventura, Kern, Santa Barbara, Monterey, Los Angeles, Orange, and King Counties to Blythe, Witter, and Company and to J. and W. Seligman and Company for $25 million.

Coupled with the prior 1925 sale of his Mexican oil properties, Doheny's liquidations netted him a total of $100 million in cash, stock, and bonds.[11] Although analysts at the time branded the series of sales astute, considering the legal entanglements that Doheny still faced, shareholders of the liquidated companies were infuriated by Doheny's actions. They filed a series of costly civil suits against him, arguing that he had breached his fiduciary duties. The suits would linger for several more years and cost Doheny additional millions in judgments, settlements, and attorneys' fees, but he remained resolute that he had acted judiciously.

To further protect Ned's financial interests, and to secure a substantial inheritance for his grandchildren, Doheny divided his personal holdings. He transferred one-third of his estate to Estelle, one-third to Ned, and retained one-third for himself. Then, he placed 50 percent of his own share in a trust for his five grandchildren called the "Los Nietos Trust" (*los nietos* means "grandchildren" in Spanish). Because of these financial rearrangements, only Doheny's share (totaling one-sixth of the original estate, or roughly $12,500,000) would be subject to federal inheritance taxes.[12]

Doheny prayed that the worst of his troubles had passed, and hoped that 1929 would bring better fortune to his family. But should an adverse fate rule against him in the upcoming trial, he took satisfaction in knowing he had preserved a strong financial future for Ned and the children, come what may. Sadly, Doheny was about to face a tragedy not in his power to prevent, alter, or undo.

part three La Calavera del Final

Thirteen Night of Terror

On the evening of Saturday, February 16, 1929, at 9:30 P.M., a dark blue Dodge Sport Cabriolet stopped before the massive iron gates at Greystone. The Doheny guard in the main gatehouse at Doheny Road, John E. Morris, recognized the driver as Hugh Plunkett and nodded "hello." Morris then opened the gates and permitted Hugh to drive inside, as he had hundreds of times before.

Hugh drove the car into Greystone's circular driveway and parked near the garage. He opened the door to one of the garages, stepped inside, and walked toward an interior closet where he kept some fishing equipment and firearms. Greystone guard Edward McCarthy, who had been stationed at the home's rear gate, heard noise and came forward to investigate. McCarthy recognized Hugh, and the two men spoke briefly as Hugh rummaged through the closet. McCarthy then watched Hugh walk toward the front door of Greystone, use his own key, and enter the mansion. His arrival was also heard by Joe Maurice, the children's riding master, who was in his living quarters over the multicar garage.

Hugh then ascended the black-and-white marble staircase that led to the second-floor family quarters. He surprised Ned and Lucy in their master suite as they were talking, dressed in bedclothes. Hugh was dressed in a pin-striped suit and tie.

Ned stood to greet his friend, who appeared nervous and upset. Ned then led Hugh downstairs to the guest room where they could talk privately. Still dressed in his pajamas, silk bathrobe, and slippers, Ned offered to pour Hugh a drink. The two men spoke for some time, drinking and smoking cigarettes. Hugh grew increasingly upset, the men began to argue, and at some point Ned went to the telephone to call Dr. Ernest Clyde Fishbaugh, who had treated Hugh during his nervous breakdown at Christmas.

Dr. Fishbaugh, who was attending a play at the Hollywood Playhouse across town, was called to the theater's office to take an urgent telephone call from his maid at home. The maid told Fishbaugh to go to Greystone at once. Fishbaugh's chauffeur immediately drove the doctor to the Doheny residence and returned to the theater to wait for Mrs. Fishbaugh, who was still watching the performance.

Fishbaugh arrived at Greystone at about 11:00 P.M. and was admitted by night watchman John E. Morris. At about the same time, Lucy heard a loud noise from the guest room that she thought sounded like an overturned piece of furniture. As the doctor walked down the main entrance hall, he was met by Lucy, who seemed very agitated. She told Fishbaugh that Hugh was acting very disturbed, and quickly led the doctor to the guest room where Ned and Hugh remained inside. As Dr. Fishbaugh approached the door, Hugh suddenly rushed toward him, and shouted at him to leave. Over the doctor's protests, Hugh slammed the door shut. Fishbaugh retreated with Lucy.

Immediately, a gunshot was heard, then another. The doctor left Lucy in the main hall and ran to the guest suite hallway where, to his horror, he saw Hugh lying face down on the floor in front of the doorway leading to the guest room, blood oozing from his skull. Peering further into the guest room, Dr. Fishbaugh could see Ned Doheny also lying on the floor, near the foot of the bed. Next to the body was an overturned armchair. Ned was still breathing, and as Fishbaugh checked his wrist, he found a faint pulse. Ned was bleeding from both sides of his head, and blood was trickling from his mouth.

In a futile effort to save Ned's life, the doctor turned Ned on his side and tried to clear his breathing passages. Morris, the watchman, who had heard the two gunshots, ran into the guest suite from the west hall doorway and saw Hugh lying on the floor, dead. Fishbaugh then turned to Morris and told him that Ned, too, had been shot.

At Dr. Fishbaugh's urging, Morris led Lucy Doheny, who was now hysterical, from the room and into her master bedroom. Sobbing uncontrollably, she picked up the telephone and called her sister, Kate, and brother-in-law, Anson Lisk. She told them of the night of terror and begged them to come to her aid. Within minutes, Lisk was at the Doheny home.

The next few hours inside the Greystone mansion were utter confusion and chaos, and the events have remained subject to debate for some sixty-eight years.[1]

Edward Doheny Sr. was asleep in his bedroom at Chester Place when he received an urgent telephone call from Anson Lisk, just after midnight on February 17, informing him that Ned had been killed. Dressing quickly, he hurried by car to Greystone, speeding down the dark streets of the city across town to the mansion in Beverly Hills.

A security guard met Doheny at the front gate and escorted the shaken man inside. Doheny descended the marble staircase to the guest room to view the body of his son. Wordlessly, he knelt beside the corpse and grasped Ned's hand, gently caressing it.

"My boy," the white-haired man sobbed. After excruciating minutes, Doheny rose and went to his daughter-in-law's bedchamber, where she was lying on her bed, grief-stricken and in shock. Doheny, also sobbing, crumpled to the floor and wept aloud. A member of the household staff discreetly shut the door so that the father and daughter-in-law could be alone.

Leslie T. White, a young detective for the Los Angeles District Attorney's office, was one of the first investigators to arrive. Lisk had placed a frantic call to the Beverly Hills Police Department, and Chief of Police Charles

Blair had immediately turned the case over to homicide detectives at the Los Angeles police force; they dispatched White to the scene.[2]

It was approximately 2:00 A.M. when White arrived at Greystone and was escorted to the guest bedroom, where the bodies of the two men remained. White's superior, Lucien Wheeler, chief investigator for the Los Angeles District Attorney's office, was already there, inspecting the crime scene. Ned Doheny's body, still clad in nightclothes and silk dressing gown, was face up, beside an overturned chair near the foot of a pair of twin beds. Bullet holes were observed in both his left and right temples, indicating that a single bullet had entered and then exited his skull. Nearby, the body of Hugh Plunkett lay outstretched, face down across the threshold of the bedroom, his head resting on his right arm, which lay over a .45 Colt Bisley revolver. A single bullet hole was visible on the right side of his head. Ned was lying on his back, blood covering his face and forehead. His right arm was extended and lying palm-down on the floor, a highball glass on its side nearby; his left arm was bent at the elbow across his midsection.

White found the bullet that had passed through Ned's head embedded in the wall, six feet from the floor, a few inches from the door jam. He also found two discharged cartridges near Plunkett's body. Slowly, carefully, White made note of other important details of the crime scene. One tumbler glass had been knocked from a table near a bottle of Johnny Walker whisky. A half-burned cigarette lay near Plunkett's fingers. An unlit cigarette was on the floor near Ned Doheny.

White touched the Colt revolver; it was very warm. He then carefully wrapped the gun inside his pocket handkerchief so as not to destroy any fingerprints. Next, he photographed the bodies and collected various pieces of evidence, including the opened bottle of whisky, the cigarettes, and several glasses.

From his notes, White recounted his reconstruction of the events:

> There were no eyewitnesses to the actual shooting, but all other witnesses belonged either to the family or to the household staff, with the exception of a prominent "society" physician. A sufficient lapse of time had passed between the actual shooting and the arrival of the authorities to allow the witnesses to recover their emotional equilibrium.

The testimony dovetailed with remarkable accuracy. Briefly it went something like this: that Plunkett had gone berserk; that on hearing the shots, witnesses had run towards the hallway which led to Doheny's bedroom, only to be met at the door by Plunkett. They retreated when he threatened to kill them. Plunkett then slammed the door and a moment later they heard the shot which presumably ended his life. When the witnesses went in and found the bodies, they retreated without disturbing anything.[3]

A thorough investigator, White found some of the witnesses' testimony perplexing. On Sunday, February 17, he traveled to the morgue to have a closer look at the bodies. There, he discovered powder burns surrounding the bullet hole in Ned Doheny's temple, proving that the murder weapon had been held less than three inches from Ned's head at the moment it had been fired. But White had found no such markings on Plunkett's head, causing him to question which man held the gun to his own head.

The trajectory evidence showed that Ned was shot while sitting in the armchair; the chair then toppled, and Ned fell on his back. If Plunkett fired the shot, he would have shot from waist level at an awkward upward angle.

There were several other issues that disturbed White. Although he fired the Bisley several times, it did not become as hot as it had been when he first recovered it from under Plunkett's body. Had someone deliberately warmed the weapon to mislead investigators? Even more puzzling, there were no fingerprints at all on the gun. The weapon should have borne some prints or smudges. Although guns kept stored are often heavily oiled and would therefore resist fingerprints, it was possible that this gun had been wiped clean. White spent the rest of the evening developing the crime scene photographs, dusting the latent fingerprints on the bottle of whisky he had recovered, and conducting further tests on the revolver that had allegedly been used by Plunkett in the murder/suicide.

When White confronted Dr. Fishbaugh with the seemingly contradictory evidence, Dr. Fishbaugh reiterated his story: he had rushed into the bedroom within seconds after the shooting, and found Ned dead. Fishbaugh remained emphatic that the body had not been moved. But the detective then presented Fishbaugh with a startling observation: although Ned's body had been found face up, the blood on his face congealed in a pattern from his ears across his face. This could only have occurred, White told Fishbaugh, if Ned had fallen face down when shot. His body had to have been repositioned.

After a moment's hesitation, Dr. Fishbaugh confessed that Ned had lived for approximately twenty minutes after the shooting, contrary to the story he had originally told investigators. In reality, Dr. Fishbaugh claimed, he had actually picked up Ned's body, tried to revive him, and when that failed replaced him on the floor.[4]

Still, White was troubled. Many statements given by the witnesses seemed rehearsed and artificial. On Monday morning, February 18, White telephoned Wheeler and enumerated his concerns. Wheeler told White to take his findings straight to District Attorney Buron Fitts.

As White recalled later, he said to the district attorney, "Mr. Fitts, I don't believe Hugh Plunkett killed Doheny and then committed suicide —at least it could not have happened in the manner described by witnesses. The physical facts, and the testimony of witnesses do not jibe. I understand, too, that some people believe that the Doheny family are too influential to tamper with."

"There isn't a man in the United States big enough to stop me from conducting a criminal investigation," Fitts replied.

"Despite testimony to the contrary," White said, "I can prove by fingerprints on both the glasses and the liquor bottle that Plunkett and Doheny were drinking together just prior to the shooting. . . . When I examined Plunkett lying on the floor . . . he had a half-burned cigarette held in his left hand in such a way that it would have been impossible for him to have opened the door and threatened witnesses as they so testified. He had the gun in his right [hand] by their story."[5]

Detective Lieutenant W. W. White and Sergeant B. E. McGhee questioned Dr. Fishbaugh at the scene at about 1:25 A.M. on February 17. Fishbaugh explained he had been Ned's doctor for seven or eight years. According to the report the officers filed with Beverly Hills Chief of Police Charles

Blair, Fishbaugh said he had come to Greystone earlier on the day of the shootings, at about 5:00 P.M., to see Ned Doheny. Ned told the doctor he was "feeling splendidly" but remarked that "Plunkett is the man who needs [your] attention."

Dr. Fishbaugh told the officers that he had occasionally attended to Plunkett's needs during the previous two years and that starting sometime in 1927, Plunkett received treatment for infected and abscessed teeth. After each one was pulled, Fishbaugh said, Plunkett suffered a "severe nervous reaction . . . from a few minutes to a few hours after the extractions" that consisted of twitching muscles and "lack of self-control." These attacks were relieved by sedatives, and generally Plunkett was able to return to work the following day.[6]

Fishbaugh told officers that at some point around Christmas, Plunkett had developed a red and swollen pimple or abscess over his left eyebrow, was running a fever, and complained of a "terrific headache." The infection cleared, but Plunkett remained extremely nervous and exhibited severe "twitching spells." He told Fishbaugh that during the previous six months, he had been unable to sleep more than one to three hours a night, and then only by taking five to ten doses of such sedatives as Dial or Veronal. Fishbaugh recommended bed rest. Plunkett remained at the Doheny residence for a week or so, under the care of a nurse. He stayed in the downstairs guest bedroom suite at the west end of the residence. Following the illness, Hugh continued to be nervous and unable to sleep. He complained of pain in the back of his head. Ned and Lucy Doheny had urged Hugh to go to a hospital or take a vacation—advice he had consistently refused, Fishbaugh said.

In answer to the officer's questions, Fishbaugh reported that Hugh had been extremely nervous for several days before the shooting. Hugh appeared more nervous than usual the afternoon of February 16, and for about a half hour, Fishbaugh discussed his condition with him in the presence of Ned and Lucy Doheny. Again, Hugh was urged to go to a hospital or to have a nurse take care of him at his own apartment. Hugh resisted any suggestion that he stay at Greystone under medical supervision. In the midst of the conversation, Hugh got up and walked out of the room without saying good-bye. He left in his own car.

The statements of Lucy Doheny to Lieutenants White and McGhee seemed to corroborate the doctor's version of the events. Lucy stated that after dinner she and Ned, concerned about Hugh, had gone to his apartment to try and persuade him to go to the hospital, or "do something to get straightened out." Hugh refused, and Ned and Lucy then went to a theater to see a moving picture. She could not remember what time they arrived home, or at what time Hugh came to Greystone.

On Monday, February 18, 1929, less than thirty-six hours after the fatal shooting, Lucien Wheeler declared the Edward L. Doheny Jr. murder case closed. A roomful of reporters gathered with eager anticipation to hear the chief investigator announce that the district attorney's office had concluded "beyond all doubt" that Hugh Plunkett shot Ned Doheny in an insane frenzy, and then had taken his own life.

He issued the following statement:

> The autopsy performed by Chief Autopsy Surgeon A. F. Wagner on the head of Plunkett clearly shows that the case was one of murder and suicide. The autopsy shows that Plunkett placed the heavy revolver muzzle against the right side of his head a little above the ear.
>
> This was proven by the residue of powder that was found with the brain of Plunkett. This was further proven by the jagged fourway fracture of the skull. The skull had been fractured by the explosion and the bullet had passed through the brain, causing the instant death of Plunkett.[7]

Wheeler explained that he hoped this early announcement would quell the wild rumors that a robber or other villain had concealed himself in Ned's room and had murdered Ned Doheny, then slain Hugh Plunkett. He also hoped to stop the spread of another rumor—that Hugh might have quarreled with Ned in a possible attempt at blackmail—for which there was no evidence. Wheeler insisted that all of the medical and physical evidence, as well as the witnesses' accounts, substantiated the conclusion that Hugh Plunkett had suffered a nervous breakdown, went violently insane, murdered his employer, and then killed himself.

THE FUNERAL OF EDWARD L. DOHENY JR.

Ned's body was first brought to the Beverly Hills morgue and then later transported to the Bresee Brothers Mortuary in Los Angeles. Funeral services were held the following Tuesday, February 19, at St. Vincent's Church, which Doheny had built. The requiem mass was celebrated by Los Angeles Bishop John Joseph Cantwell, a close friend of the Dohenys for twenty years.

The honorary pallbearers were men on whom Edward Doheny Sr. had depended for business and emotional support throughout the years: Pan American manager Herbert G. Wylie, educator and neighbor Rufus B. Von Kleinsmid, Mexican geologist Ezequiel Ordóñez, and attorneys Frank J. Hogan, Henry O'Melveny, and Olin Wellborn III.

The church was filled with friends of the Dohenys who had come to pay their last respects to Ned and offer condolences to his widow, stepmother, and father. The pews were filled to capacity; standees numbered four deep and lined the aisles from the rear of the church to the altar.

The sanctuary was filled with members of the clergy and priests from various orders. There were also three red-clad monsignors. Bishop Cantwell presided over the services from beneath a purple canopy. He concluded the rites in front of the casket, blessing it with holy water and incense.

Father O'Mallet, pastor of St. Vincent's, delivered the eulogy. The thought of saying good-bye, O'Mallet said, was difficult enough when it is to little ones just starting out in life or to those who have seen three score and ten, "but to have to say good-by to one in the full flush of manhood, to have to stand at the grave of one in the full bloom of life—this, in sober truth is bitter death!" Father O'Mallet said of Ned that "He left life with all that it held forth to him. A man of keen mind, fine judgment, a practical business capacity to carry on the achievements of a successful sire. And then a bitter death says, 'NO!'"[8]

By 10:00 A.M., when the hearse arrived at St. Vincent's front doors, a great crowd, unable to get into the building, had gathered at the church's steps. Dozens of police officers attempted to control the crowd to ensure that the bier containing the slain scion's body could be safely placed inside the hearse. A church bell began to toll, and whispers ran through the crowd that the family was leaving. The grieving father had to be supported by friends as he left the church. As the bell continued to peal, the pallbearers, preceded by Reverend John Martinez, with an altar boy bearing the processional cross and accompanied by two acolytes in black cassock and white surplice, carried the casket from the church. Behind the pallbearers were members of Ned's family. Lucy wore a black veil that completely obscured her face and extended past her waist. She clung to her daughter, sobbing bitterly as the two descended the church steps.

After church services concluded, Ned's body was taken by hearse to Forest Lawn Memorial Park in Glendale, California. His final resting place was to be the Temple of Santa Sabina. The Italian marble monument was reputed to have once contained the remains of Santa Sabina, a martyr of the second century. Shortly after Ned's sudden death, Dr. Herbert Eaton, founder of the memorial park, suggested that the historic altar he had recently acquired be utilized as a memorial for the Doheny family. It was purchased by Doheny, and, in accordance with his wishes, the marble sarcophagus was unmarked.[9]

From all over the country and around the world, messages of condolence came to the famous father who had lost his only son, but these did little to assuage the tycoon's bitter grief. Gilmore Millen, writing for the *Los Angeles Examiner,* expressed the feelings of thousands whose hearts went out to Doheny:

A tired old man walked slowly and hesitantly behind his son's casket today, bent beneath grief that had darkened the evening of his life.

Of course that is not unusual—other tired men have walked and will walk, behind the caskets of their sons. . . . But this old man was the magnet that drew the gaze of thousand of eyes as he walked in sorrow. He was a man who had built one of the world's colossal fortunes and had depended on his son to carry forward the work he was relinquishing.

So when Edward L. Doheny followed the bronze casket of his son down the aisle of St. Vincent's Church this morning, as an organ intoned a funeral march of Chopin, a sense of high tragedy came over all in the church, and all the thousands that stood outside, on curbing on each side of West Adams and Figueroa Streets, and the steps that led to the entrance of the building.

And there was sorrow for the old man, deep felt and perhaps as great as that many felt for his son.

No one could attend that funeral without feeling the irony that had come into the life of Edward L. Doheny—the struggle in oil that led to his great fortune and the terrific blow that had come to him when he was ready to rest and let his son continue his work.[10]

THE FUNERAL OF THEODORE HUGH PLUNKETT

Funeral services for Hugh Plunkett were held at 11 A.M. on Wednesday, February 20, 1929, at the White Company Mortuary located on West Washington Boulevard, in a modest Los Angeles suburb. Several hundred persons attended. Great wreaths of flowers had been sent to the White Funeral parlor by Lucy, and a large-sized truck had to be employed to transport the floral arrangements sent to Plunkett's resting site. After a hearse delivered Plunkett's body to Forest Lawn Memorial Park, Plunkett was laid to rest on Sunrise Slope, beside a graceful olive tree, barely thirty feet from the magnificent mausoleum where Ned had been entombed the day before.

Two of Lucy's brothers, J. Clark Smith and C. Warren Smith, acted as pallbearers; the gesture was thought by observers to show that the Doheny family believed Hugh had not been accountable for his insane actions.[11]

The Rev. George Davidson of St. John's Episcopal Church conducted both the funeral and burial services. Mrs. Charles Plunkett, Hugh's mother, leaned heavily on her husband's arm, sobbing. Marian Hall Plunkett, who had received her divorce decree only a few months earlier, stood apart from the family, accompanied by two male friends.

Isabelle Plunkett, the younger sister of the dead man, fainted as his coffin was lowered into the ground. A moment later, Plunkett's brother, Robert, also collapsed. Both mourners were revived and comforted by friends, then quietly taken away.

"I do not think disease, gunshot or accident is the cause of death," said Reverend Davidson.

They are but the incident. The great cause is in the mind of God. The incident is but the time when it is best. The cause we may not know.

This was but the method by which his soul was to be dispatched into eternal life. It is difficult for us to understand why. Perhaps we shall never know.

May God have mercy.[12]

Then the mourners filed away. The gravestone simply read, "T. Hugh Plunkett 1896–1929."

In the days following the death, there was scarcely a man or woman in Los Angeles who did not have a theory on the killing. Newspapers throughout the nation pandered to speculation: "Bullet-Torn Bodies Found in Oil Man's Home," read the front-page headline of the *Los Angeles Examiner* on Monday, February 18. "Black Shadow of Tragedy" and "Palace of Grief" were some of the hundreds of banners heading columns about the gruesome murder and suicide.[13]

Acquaintances who had known Plunkett eagerly stepped forward to talk about the alleged killer and his "nervous condition." Most stories that featured these interviews lent credibility to the family's version of events—Hugh had suffered a complete mental breakdown and shot Ned in a moment of insane rage. In a lengthy interview to reporters at the *Los Angeles Times*, Dr. Fishbaugh gave a detailed account of his own speculations about Plunkett's mental degeneration:

> He was nervous, very nervous and irritable. And he was stubborn, too. Mr. Doheny always treated him with the utmost consideration. They were more than just servant and master. They were close friends, men of the same years with many interests in common.
>
> He was rather secretive. He never would say what worried him.
>
> He spoke little of his personal affairs, but his nerves were at the trigger's edge. . . .
>
> Along about Christmas, he broke down completely and showed definite evidence of derangement. But he rallied. His condition seemed to be improving. He had been cared for at Mr. Doheny's home during his illness, about three weeks.

Ned was worried. He really felt a high regard [for] Plunkett. Ned and Lucy tried to reason with Plunkett who appeared very upset. The couple were trying to persuade him to drop everything and go to a sanitarium for a rest.

Plunkett was acting strangely. He seemed angry when a sanitarium was suggested. Ned and Lucy pleaded with him to let up for a while. They warned him and they humored him, but he wouldn't budge. I also tried to get him to listen, but it was a waste of effort.[14]

There were those who did not accept the theory that Hugh Plunkett had acted in a fit of insanity. They pointed out that evidence at the crime scene conflicted with witnesses' accounts and that the stories of members of the Doheny household staff seemed rehearsed: they believed that the explanation given by the family and servants to detectives was a cover-up. Curiously, some staffers had said that the two men had not been drinking, yet both men's fingerprints were found on the glasses and whisky bottle. However, this was the Prohibition era, and loyal servants habitually denied the presence of alcohol. It had already been revealed that Fishbaugh had lied about several aspects of the murder scene: he had concealed from the police that Ned had lived for some time and that he had moved Ned's body.

Even more confusing, there were no fingerprints or smudges on the murder weapon. And the gun was warm when it was first touched by Leslie T. White, leading the detective to suspect that it had been heated in the kitchen oven or by some other means in order to mislead investigators about the time of the murder. The lit cigarette in Hugh's left hand was highly suspicious, too. Was it likely that Plunkett had fired a gun in a heat of rage while puffing on a cigarette? Could he have opened a door, as Fishbaugh claimed, with a gun in one hand and a lit cigarette in the other? And the positioning of the bodies was equally disturbing—based on bullet trajectories, some investigators hypothesized that Hugh shot Ned when the two had been seated several feet apart. This, too, conflicted with the family's testimony.

Moreover, despite many witnesses' claims that Hugh was unstable, other acquaintances indicated he was an easygoing man, not at all on the verge of a mental breakdown. George Riley, Hugh's roommate, recalled that on the days just prior to the murders, Hugh appeared fine and only "slightly nervous." "He was a wonderful man and would not intention-ally harm anyone," Riley added. "I have roomed with him for a long time. He did not fear any man, and was never a man to start an argument or fight. For a long time now his nerves have been shattered. He has been ill, but I think it was his tremendous responsibilities that caused him to break as he did."

Riley expressed complete shock that Hugh could have committed the murder and then killed himself: "He seemed to have the Doheny interests so much at heart he would lie awake thinking of them. I cannot imagine him doing harm to anyone or anything."[15]

But the Doheny family and their closest associates believed that mounting stress had driven Hugh Plunkett into an out-of-control rage. According to George W. Johnson, business secretary for Edward Sr., and Mrs. George Johnson, who was Lucy's personal secretary, Hugh became noticeably "nervous" as Greystone neared completion and the trial dates approached. The family felt that the pressure on Hugh was another part of the unjust curse visited on the family in the course of the never-ending, unfounded charges regarding the oil leases.

"Plunkett had become morose," Mrs. Johnson said later. "The one thing that appeared to be constantly on his mind was the upcoming crim-inal trial. He enjoyed all the confidences of the whole family. He often signed checks for Mr. Doheny totaling hundreds of thousands of dollars. He attended to most of the details of the new home and actually paid most of the contractor's bills with checks which he made out in Mr. Do-heny's name."[16]

Ned had urged Hugh to "take a long rest" and enter a nearby sanitar-ium. Ned was naturally nervous about what harm Hugh could do in his testimony at the upcoming trial, especially in his volatile state. There is strong evidence to suggest that at first, Hugh had decided to go along with Ned's urging and voluntarily commit himself to Camarillo State Mental Hospital, thereby dodging the government's subpoena to force him to testify in Doheny's bribery trial and enabling him to recover his mental balance.

On February 2, 1929, two weeks before the murder, Hugh had visited the B. H. Dyas Company Dry Goods store in Hollywood, where he had purchased twelve pairs of socks, twelve pairs of men's drawers, and twelve pairs of undershirts in addition to an array of other personal items that he would need at such a facility, indicating that he did plan to enter the sanitarium. He also had his car serviced and purchased new spark plugs—not the act of a man bent on suicide.[17] He told his roommate that he would soon be taking an "extended vacation."

Other factors may have also led to Hugh's precarious mental state. According to the *Los Angeles Evening Herald*, he may have been addicted to "habit-forming" drugs, especially Veronal, a highly narcotic over-the-counter barbiturate that was used to induce sleep. Hugh also was reportedly a heavy user of Dial, another barbiturate.[18] The consumption of the drugs undoubtedly contributed to Hugh's clouded thinking. He evidently was unsure of what to do and, after purchasing clothing for a sanitarium stay, changed his mind about committing himself.

Thus it is quite possible that the argument Ned and Hugh had the night of the murder concerned Hugh's refusal to follow the family's plan for him. By this account, when Hugh told Ned he would not commit himself, Ned grew angry and the two men argued bitterly. It would have seemed to Hugh that his future options—shaped by the Dohenys' troubles—had become nightmarish. Hugh feared that he would not be free to leave the sanitarium at will. He also realized that were he to testify at the upcoming trial, he himself could very well be deemed an accomplice to bribery and sent to jail.

In those few moments on the night of February 16, 1929, Hugh and Ned, two friends of fifteen years, struggled over these issues. Both were tired and under great strain. Both wanted freedom from further legal harassment. But their difference in status placed them worlds apart—Ned had the legal support, political influence, and financial resources of the Doheny family to save him; Hugh, of modest circumstances, suddenly felt himself alone, unaided, and facing confinement of some kind: a sanitarium or a prison. Behind the closed doors of the guest room, this conflict escalated and for both men ended tragically in death.

Although for the past six decades Hugh Plunkett has remained identified as the crazed killer of Ned Doheny, some writers have laid the tragedy at the feet of Edward Doheny himself. Dan La Botz is harsh in his condemnation:

> So who killed Ned Doheny and Plunkett that night? We will never know for sure. But we do know that Edward L. Doheny Sr. was responsible. Not only in the sense that Doheny had created the whole environment in which Ned grew up—the mansions and private schools, the inherited fortune—but in the more particular sense that he had used his son and his son's friend to carry out the dirty business of bribery and deceit. . . .
>
> Today, years later, it seems clear that Ned Doheny and Hugh Plunkett were victims of Doheny's ambition. No matter whose hand did the deed, it was Doheny's character that killed them, his egotism, his hubris. Through years of public virtue and private vice Doheny had pursued property, oil above all, in a career that left many victims strewn in its path, of whom his son and his son's friend were merely the last.

La Botz sees Doheny's life as driven by ruthless ambition: "It was a life of a man whose almost sole and constant object had been the extraction of minerals from the ground and the effort of turning those minerals into money, and who had shown time and time again that he was prepared to go to any lengths and to do virtually anything in order to carry out the alchemy that turned base minerals into wealth and power."[19] He finds Doheny to be a Midas whose golden touch led to his own son's death.

Weeks after Doheny buried his son at the Forest Lawn Memorial Park, he contacted managers at the Evergreen Cemetery in East Los Angeles, where he had buried Carrie Doheny, Ned's mother, who had died in 1900, and Eileen Doheny, the daughter who had died at age seven in 1892. He asked that the remains of his first wife and daughter be exhumed and their caskets moved to Forest Lawn, where they would be placed adjacent to Ned's sarcophagus within the marble mausoleum of Santa Sabina. It was the first time Doheny had publicly acknowledged Carrie Louella Wilkins in over twenty-eight years.

Only a few months later, a still-grieving Doheny would follow news accounts in dread as the U.S. Supreme Court on April 8, 1929, affirmed

Harry Sinclair's contempt conviction for refusing to testify before the Senate Committee on Public Lands and Surveys. The court also upheld his criminal contempt conviction for jury tampering. Weeks earlier, John D. Rockefeller Jr. had been successful in rallying the stockholders of the Standard Oil Company of Indiana to oust company chairman Col. Robert W. Stewart because of his involvement with Sinclair in the Continental trading scandal.[20] Doheny painfully observed the newspaper photographs showing Sinclair, in handcuffs, being led to a federal prison near Washington, D.C.

Described as the "richest man who ever met such a fate," Sinclair continued to protest his innocence, telling reporters that he had been "railroaded to jail in violation of common sense and common fairness."[21] Within months, Albert Fall and Edward Doheny would be back in Washington to face their own federal charges.

Fourteen A Broken and Changed Man

Edward L. Doheny was a shattered man. Estelle, herself wracked with grief, tried valiantly to comfort her husband. He neglected all business matters and would not receive any of the many visitors who came to pay their respects.

Only Henry O'Melveny managed to persuade Doheny to let him visit during this lonely time. The lawyer made numerous trips to Chester Place over the next few months, sometimes showing up unannounced, and would sit for hours with the ailing oilman, just to keep him company. O'Melveny described Doheny to intimates as "a broken and changed man" who no longer cared about world affairs, or his own fate. O'Melveny was greatly troubled about Doheny's deteriorating mental state, and he wondered whether the aging multimillionaire would hold up in the forthcoming final courtroom battle.

Estelle realized that, more than anything, Doheny needed to be moved from Los Angeles and its oppressive memories. Several months after Ned's death, she hired architect Wallace Neff to build a ranch-style home for the couple in Santa Paula, a scenic area in Ventura County. Years before, Doheny had purchased 142 acres of land there, intending to drill for oil at the site. Although oil was never discovered there, Doheny had chosen not to develop the land. Instead, he kept it as a pristine place for himself and his wife to visit. The property was located on North Ojai Road amid the region's plush chaparral with a commanding view of the nearby Topa Topa Mountains.[1]

Estelle told Neff that she needed to have the entire project—design, blueprints, and construction—completed within six weeks. Neff was extremely hesitant to make such a guarantee, but finally, after much frantic planning, he relented. Hundreds of workers were hired to complete the job; they labored forty-two days and nights. Miraculously, they finished the job ahead of schedule.

Noteworthy examples of Neff's work included handsome, functional residences in the adobe style. The 9,000-square-foot, five-bedroom, seven-bath Santa Paula home that he built for Estelle and Edward Doheny was an Iberian-influenced ranch house constructed with two-foot-thick adobe brick walls, framed with massive wooden beams and columns. There was an interior garden with a seventy-eight-foot-long galleria and a fountain; the adjoining rooms featured cozy fireplaces. In addition to the main residence there was a manager's house, guest house, gatehouse, horse stables, citrus orchards, an aviary, a nine-hole golf course, three large pools, and a small lake stocked with trout. A handsome stone-and-wrought-iron entry gate had the words "Ferndale Ranch" on its grillwork.

The ranch grounds were landscaped with a lush array of trees and plants: California oaks, Japanese maples, redwood trees, palm trees, and an assortment of rare bamboo. At Estelle's urging, Neff had also built a private thirty-two-seat chapel on the grounds and constructed a stone grotto displaying a statue of Our Lady of Guadalupe, the Virgin of Mexico. When Estelle and Edward stayed at the Ferndale Ranch, they attended mass at the chapel each morning and prayed for Ned. After much time had passed, Estelle would take great delight in the Ferndale site, even affectionately referring to it as the "Enchanted Ranch."

Doheny remained in seclusion at the Ferndale Ranch for nearly three months during the summer of 1929. As the summer ended, he learned that Albert Fall would be prosecuted first; a trial date of October 7 had been set. Doheny's own case would begin in March 1930. "We here are endeavoring to carry on," Doheny wrote to Fall prior to his trial, "with fortitude which is most difficult to have. The legacy of the five little grandchildren who now so completely occupy our hearts and thoughts [comforts us]. The affection and the thoughtfulness of our friends have contributed so much to aiding us in our effort."[2]

Fall's trial date drew near, and on September 27, 1929, a deeply depressed Edward Doheny boarded the Los Angeles Limited for Washington, D.C. A collection of newsmen and photographers had gathered at the railway station to watch him depart.

"My friend will be on trial back there and I am going to testify in the case—that's about all there is to it," Doheny said quietly, his former bravado noticeably absent. Some reporters later commented that the oilman looked old and feeble.

"Do you expect the fireworks to be brief?" one reporter asked.

"There won't be any fireworks," Doheny replied. "Mr. Fall has been waiting for this for five years and we might as well get it over with. Most people seem to think they know more about the situation than I do."[3]

Doheny had insisted that Frank Hogan take charge of Fall's defense and present his case to the jury; Doheny had agreed to pay all the legal fees and expenses incurred. Wilton J. Lambert of New Mexico would serve as co-counsel in the matter. His fees were paid by Doheny as well.

In the case *United States v. Albert B. Fall,* the prosecution again charged Fall with accepting a bribe while acting as an officer of the United States government. Owen Roberts cited Section 117 of the United States Criminal Code, which defined the crime of bribery as being committed by an individual who may "ask, accept or receive any money . . . with intent to have his decision . . . which may at any time be pending before him in his official capacity . . . influenced thereby."[4] Whether the accused's subsequent actions were desirable or undesirable, beneficial or harmful, was of no legal significance. Unfortunately for the defense, this charge was nar-

rower, and technically easier for the government to prove, than the conspiracy and fraud charges that Fall and Doheny had defeated in 1926.
Hogan and O'Melveny knew they would have to mount the finest legal
defense work in their careers to keep their two clients out of prison.[5]

Sixty-seven-year-old Fall had become so debilitated by the five-year
strain of the two previous trials and incessant front-page publicity that he
was now a gaunt shadow of his former self—so weak that he was no
longer able to walk unaided. On October 7, 1929, he entered the courtroom led by his doctor and a nurse and seemed pale, confused, and very
exhausted. His hair was now snow-white and his face lined and emaci-
ated. The doctor escorted Fall to a large green leather chair that had been
placed near the defense table. Fall supported himself with pillows and
kept a blue automobile robe thrown over his knees.

In many ways, the proceedings evoked an eerie sense of déjà vu for
Fall, Doheny, and their defense team, because the same prosecutors,
Roberts and Pomerene, were again offering their fervent opening remarks
to the same judge who had presided in the 1926 trial. While not legally obligated to do so, Doheny decided to attend his friend's trial every day in
order to show moral support.

Hogan used his same dramatic opening remarks from three years
prior: Doheny had been a great patriot who attempted to serve his country by constructing storage facilities at Pearl Harbor; Fall had not been involved in negotiating Doheny's lease; the $100,000 transaction had been
a loan between friends. Once again, Hogan traced for the jury the frontier
friendship of Doheny and Fall. Then Edward Doheny, and later Estelle
Doheny, took the stand and recounted the now-infamous tale of their
loan to Fall, and both explained why Fall's signature had been innocently
separated from the note.[6]

Hogan made a point of gesturing frequently to Fall, who lethargically
watched the proceedings from the large, heavily pillowed green chair.
Hogan implied that his end was imminent, beseeching the jury to vindicate Fall "before he passes into the Great Beyond." Indeed, at one point
Fall collapsed to the floor and had to be rushed to the hospital on a
stretcher. Three different doctors later testified that Fall had suffered a
lung hemorrhage, was near death, and, in their opinion, was in no condition to appear again in court.

Attorneys for both sides were debating postponement of the trial in order to allow Fall to recover when the courtroom door flew open and the defendant, wan and haggard, stumbled inside clutching a cane. All eyes were fixed on him. He looked like a crazed Davy Crockett, wearing an old fur overcoat, western-style hat, and cowboy boots. Fall angrily waved his cane in the air, and was quickly assisted to his special leather chair by his doctor, nurse, and daughter. After Fall's dramatic entrance, the defense lawyers hovered over Fall as though he were about to die, and Hogan used every opportunity in his pleadings to mention Fall's "imminent demise" to the startled jury.

When prosecutor Roberts took his turn before the jury, he had no words of sympathy for Fall. Still aggravated about losing the fraud and conspiracy case to Hogan in 1926, Roberts was dedicated to sending Albert Fall to prison—ailing or not—for his misdeeds. Roberts sneeringly described Fall's sudden prosperity in January 1922, when he received money from then-unknown sources that enabled him to purchase an adjoining ranch in Three Rivers, New Mexico, and pay thousands of dollars in back taxes.

Roberts attempted to introduce evidence about Fall's financial transactions with convicted briber Harry Sinclair, but Hogan leaped to his feet and objected. Only Fall's interactions with Doheny, Hogan told Judge Hitz, were relevant for this trial. But Roberts argued that Fall's acceptance of $200,000 in Liberty Bonds from Sinclair for a similar lease transaction showed Fall to be capable of criminal intent in such matters. Roberts reasoned that the parallel of Fall's dealings with Doheny and Sinclair was particularly significant because Fall had lied before the Senate investigating committee, claiming that he had never received a single dollar from Doheny, Sinclair, or their oil companies, directly or indirectly. In the first major blow to Fall's defense, Hitz overruled Hogan's objection.

Fall's case was further jeopardized when his son-in-law, M. T. Everhart, took the stand. Just as he had testified in Sinclair's conspiracy trial, he recounted how he had exchanged Sinclair's Liberty Bonds for shares of ranch stock. Hogan heroically attempted to depict the transactions as legitimate, but his efforts were useless. The lasting impression to court spectators was that Sinclair's money had ended up in Fall's welcoming hands not for real estate equity but to favorably influence an upcoming government transaction.

At his lawyers' urging, Albert Fall decided not to testify on his own behalf.

On October 22, prosecutor Atlee Pomerene delivered a powerful closing summation, prompting one reporter to label his work a "complete, dispassionate and devastating summary of the evidence." Following Pomerene, Hogan offered what seemed, in comparison, to be a gentle plea: the former secretary of the interior deserved fair consideration. He had been a faithful civil servant who was now at the mercy of fate for no proven wrongdoing. Throughout Hogan's closing summation, he referred numerous times to Fall as a "tragic figure . . . shattered and broken . . . an old man tottering on the brink of the grave." But in an omission noticed by all, Hogan never once made reference to Fall's dealings with Harry Sinclair.

Hogan's lyrical summary brought tears to the eyes of spectators . . . and of one female juror.

Afterward, Roberts tersely concluded the government's case: "It is simple," he told the jurors. "There are four things of a controlling nature for you to remember. One is that Doheny wanted the lease of the Elk Hills. The second is, Fall wanted money. The third is, Doheny got the lease, and the fourth is, Fall got the money."

After both sides rested their cases, Judge Hitz cautioned the jurors not to be swayed by sentimental stories about Doheny and Fall in the days of their youth. He reminded them to consider only whether Albert Fall had accepted a bribe. In a devastating blow to the defense, Hitz also told the jury that in evaluating whether Fall had possessed criminal intent in his dealings with Doheny, they could properly consider the Fall-Sinclair relationship.

All day Thursday, October 24, 1929, the jury of eight men and four women deliberated. Then, nearly eight years after Ned Doheny had delivered cash in a black satchel to Albert Fall, the jury returned to the courtroom and rendered a verdict of "guilty" against Fall. However, they then requested leniency.

Frank Hogan, accustomed to victory, was stunned. One spectator reported he was "bug-eyed" and his visage became "pale to the point of ashiness." It took Hogan several moments to regain his composure. Fall, who had been forced to stand up to hear the verdict, collapsed into his chair and looked tearfully back at his wife and daughter, who sat weeping in the rows behind him.

Attorney Mark Thompson, who had close connections with the Fall family, fell to the floor unconscious. Then the entire courtroom broke into pandemonium as Fall's doctor and nurse began to administer to the stricken young man. Fearing the lawyer had suffered a heart attack, the doctor administered a heart stimulant to Thompson and was able to revive him. Throughout the chaos, Doheny, who was seated at the far end of the counsel table, remained stiff and ashen.

Hogan immediately moved for a new trial on grounds that the court had erred in its instructions to the jury, but Hitz rejected his plea. Within days, Fall was sentenced to serve one year in jail and ordered to pay a fine of $100,000. Indeed, this sentence was lenient; the maximum penalty that Fall could have received was three years in prison and a $300,000 fine. Hitz explained to the former secretary that he had given him a light punishment because of his age, physical condition, and the jury's appeal for mercy. It was a sobering moment in U.S. history to have a cabinet member convicted of a felony and sentenced to prison.

Fall was released on $5,000 bail pending appeal of his conviction. He quickly returned to his ranch at Three Rivers. Unbeknownst to the general public, a few months earlier, on May 6, 1929, Doheny had secretly purchased Fall's sprawling ranch for $168,250 at a foreclosure auction. He then leased it back to his old friend for only $1 per month. Doheny repeatedly assured Fall that so long as the two of them remained alive, Fall would never want for anything. And thanks to Doheny's benevolent action, Fall was able to return to Three Rivers to put his personal effects in order, as he awaited incarceration. When somehow reporters learned of Doheny's purchase of the ranch, they published reports of the land deal together with additional speculations about corruption and collusion.

Making matters worse, Emma Fall continued to insist that she and her husband were living on income from an "unexpected family inheritance," and not from any gift from Edward Doheny. To her credit, though, Emma remained steadfastly loyal to her convicted husband. She even went so far as to pose for Fox Movietone News cameras and plead to the American public on her husband's behalf. The film clip was run in cinemas throughout the country; before the main full-length feature, a gray-haired Emma Fall told audiences that nine jurors had been for acquittal on the second ballot but were badgered until there was only one holding firm. "The twelfth and last man who came over to the eleven for conviction, three days later came to me in tears begging forgiveness. He had not slept, had walked the floor since his terrible mistake, praying God to forgive his terrible weakness."[7]

Sadly for the Falls, this issue of improper juror conduct gave them only momentary hope of overturning Fall's guilty verdict and obtaining a mistrial. Attorney Wilton J. Lambert began to investigate the matter and, after interviewing several jurors, was able to piece together the story. One juror, Daniel Weisbach, may have been coerced into rendering a guilty verdict against Fall. When the jury first retired to consider its verdict, a count showed that seven recommended acquittal, and five believed he was guilty. But after much discussion that evening, several jurors changed their votes. By the second morning of deliberation, on Friday, October 25, the jury stood eleven to one for conviction, with Weisbach as the only holdout. Lambert's investigation indicated that Weisbach may have been harassed by one or more of the jury members and may have been told that he would keep being badgered for days if he did not change his vote. Weisbach was said to be suffering from a cold at the time, and the lack of heat in the Metropolitan Hotel where the jury was sequestered was exacerbating his condition. In addition, Weisbach's wife was nine months' pregnant and expected to go into labor any day. Lambert believed that Weisbach had become so worn down by his ailing health and ostracism by other jurors that he changed his vote to guilty.

Lambert drew up an affidavit that stated these points and submitted it to Weisbach for signing. But for reasons not known today, Weisbach refused to sign the document; hence, Fall's hopes for a new trial were dashed.[8] When newsmen caught up with Weisbach in Washington, D.C., the former juror took a very different, even combative, position. He accused Emma Fall of lying, saying that he had not asked for her "forgiveness" and had never said that his fellow jurors—in particular the jury foreman, Thomas Norris—had "forced" the verdict. Weisbach's adamant refutation left Fall little recourse to avoid prison.

THE AFTERMATH

On October 26, one day after Fall's conviction, Hogan met the press on the courthouse steps and issued a 3,000-word statement on Fall's behalf. While again insisting that he was completely innocent in this matter, Fall admitted through Hogan that he had made an "unspeakable blunder" in stating to the Senate committee that Ned McLean, and not Doheny, had loaned him the $100,000: "My borrowing the money may have been unethical. I certainly did not realize it at the time, and my employing a falsehood to prevent a volcano of political abuse from pouring upon the administration that had honored me deserves condemnation; but neither one or the other justifies the charge that I was disloyal or dishonest as Secretary of the Interior and as a member of President Harding's cabinet."[9] This prepared statement, however, did not convince the press and public. More than one commentator wrote that Fall's postconviction confession actually made him look "more foolish and more guilty."[10]

Despite Hogan's attempts to bolster Doheny's confidence, both men knew the odds for Doheny's acquittal had been drastically reduced. In Los Angeles, local media supported Fall's conviction, which caused additional worry to Doheny's chief counsel. Henry O'Melveny now feared that the growing adverse pretrial publicity could further jeopardize his client, already an underdog in the upcoming proceedings.

Doheny, O'Melveny, and Hogan quietly cursed Fall's bad luck. Because of the jury's verdict, Doheny would now have to face trial for bribing a man who was already convicted of accepting that very bribe.

Fifteen The Final Trial

In March 1930, the date of Doheny's long-dreaded trial for bribery finally arrived. Ironically, his case would be tried in the same courtroom where, five months earlier, Albert Fall had been found guilty of receiving the bribe Doheny now had to deny giving.

Frank Hogan explained to Doheny that he would attempt to prevent the new jury from hearing testimony about Fall's financial dealings with Harry Sinclair. The case, Hogan warned, was likely to pivot on his success or failure in this critical matter, since the prosecution would try to establish a pattern of payments going to Fall.

Most newspaper coverage of the anticipated trial was pointedly critical of Doheny. Only a few maverick editorialists attempted to evoke sympathy for the beleaguered oilman. One such writer, at the *Atlantic City Republican*, declared that Fall's conviction on bribery charges was based on the "manufactured propaganda of his enemies"; he called the criminal charges against Doheny an "unholy attack" and "the worst example of political tyranny and treachery ever exhibited in this country."[1] And Will Rogers, in his popular nationally syndicated newspaper column, claimed that Doheny had received a bum rap. He reminded the public of the recent release from prison of gangster Al Capone: "Capone goes free to take up his useful life's work, and on the same front page, Doheny, who developed a great industry and has given high wages to thousands for years, is called a menace to society."[2]

Rogers's cynical case for Doheny's innocence was balanced by the compassion of a journalist from New York who simply argued that the seventy-three-year-old grandfather had already paid for his indiscretions: "Lamentable though his conduct has been, he has suffered enough. His reputation is gone, his personal pride and self-respect. The friend who accepted his money and betrayed his country still faces the prospect of years in prison. Doheny's own life . . . has tumbled down about him[;] . . . any capacity for harm has been removed."[3]

But the general consensus throughout the country was that Doheny should be found guilty as charged. The fact that Fall had already been convicted of bribery for the same transaction fortified the public's belief. The nation watched with grave curiosity as the familiar figures in the previous oil cases assembled at this final trial: Atlee Pomerene and Owen Roberts were in charge of the government's case as special prosecutors, and Frank Hogan was chief counsel for the defense. Again, Judge William Hitz would preside.

Jury selection was quick. During voir dire, each juror chosen stated that he had not yet formed an opinion about Doheny's guilt or innocence. Most said that they had paid little attention to the media stories about the oil scandals. One journalist expressed amazement that twelve such persons could have been found in the world, let alone the United States.

The newly impaneled jurors would struggle with many daunting questions about the instigation of the oil leases: Had a cabinet member lied to the president of the United States? Had the government's executive branch inappropriately taken legislative action that allowed it to receive oil royalties in exchange for construction work? Had a rear admiral inveigled his chief-in-command to approve a defense contract that would prove detrimental to U.S. security? And, most important for Doheny, had his $100,000 payment to U.S. Secretary of the Interior Fall been a bribe or a friendly loan? At first, many of the jurors seemed awed by Doheny's presence; the aging multimillionaire had achieved an impressive notoriety in the press, newsreel documentaries, and radio broadcasts. But as the complex case wore on and the disputed matters of the case were presented, they settled into the job at hand.

Although the attorneys' opening statements were virtual repetitions of their initial arguments in the six previous related trials, the speeches seemed unparalleled in their passion and vitriol. Hogan fervently spoke of tragic heroes, loyal friendships, and devoted patriotism while Roberts spun dark tales of bribery, cunning, lies, and greed. Then, once again, Roberts read Doheny's now-famous testimony before the Senate Committee on Public Lands and Surveys in which he admitted that he had loaned Fall $100,000 at about the same time he had secured valuable leases of naval reserve land. Once again, Estelle Doheny repeated her familiar testimony for the new set of jurors to explain why Fall's IOU lacked a signature.

After Roberts had finished calling witnesses, Hogan summoned Edward Doheny to the stand, though he knew that permitting any defendant to testify on his own behalf was an incredibly risky undertaking. In fact, in Fall's own recent case, Hogan had urged the secretary not to take the stand, because he believed that Fall would appear unsympathetic. But today, Hogan was convinced that Doheny would present a likable persona to the jury and could withstand Roberts's potentially blistering cross-examination. This proved to be Hogan's defining trial strategy; and as the trial moved forward, he must have experienced many a sleepless night wondering whether he had made the right decision.

Hogan led Doheny through his life story and encouraged him to describe his enduring frontier friendship with cabinet Secretary Fall. Doheny obliged, portraying himself as a modest, though extremely successful Horatio Alger figure who also was a loyal friend. Doheny mentioned that in the 1880s, he had fallen down a mine shaft in New Mexico and had broken both legs. Thus incapacitated, he could not work, but his good friend Albert Fall offered to lend him law books so he could study law as he recovered. The story seemed genuine and the jury was fascinated by it. However, no evidence has ever been produced that could corroborate this story. In fact, contrary to one of the myths Doheny liked to relate about his past, he never practiced law or was admitted to any state bar.[4]

Next, Hogan had Doheny review his career as an oilman. Doheny told the jury how he had discovered oil in Los Angeles and had gone on to develop the colossal Tampico fields in Mexico. At Hogan's prompting, he explained to the jurors how he had come to control the valuable Elk Hills leases at the naval reserve in California, holdings that were expected to earn him $100 million. Doheny had told these autobiographical anecdotes many times before, but this time he carefully elaborated on each one's important details. He answered each question posed by Hogan slowly and deliberately. Only once during Doheny's examination did his composure fail him. Hogan asked Doheny about Ned Doheny's service in the U.S. Navy, and Doheny winced at the mention of his deceased son's name. When Hogan pressed Doheny about what Admiral Robison had said about his son, Doheny's face grew flushed; he swallowed hard, and tears welled in his eyes.

"I find it pretty difficult to answer that," Doheny whispered quietly. Noticing his client's distress, Hogan requested a five-minute recess. Doheny was excused, and he paced quietly in the corridor until the session resumed. Hogan's questions had served their purpose by eliciting emotion from his defendant and provoking sympathy from the jury.

When Doheny returned to the stand, Hogan closely questioned him about the oil leases. To spectators, Doheny's answers seemed truthful and his manner earnest. By all accounts, the jury appeared transfixed by his testimony.

Next, to bolster Doheny's testimony, Hogan called a number of supporting witnesses to the stand. Because Ned Doheny, one of the key witnesses to the alleged bribe, was now dead, Hogan resorted to an unorthodox tactic to introduce the missing testimony. Taking a seat in the witness box, Hogan assumed the role of Ned, reciting from memory his statements given in the previous trial. Hogan's associate, Joseph J. Cotter, read the corresponding interrogatories to him.

Prosecutor Roberts's outraged objections were immediately overruled by Judge Hitz. Hogan's melodramatic reenactment of Ned's testimony about the day he delivered the money to Secretary Fall at his father's behest moved Edward Doheny and Estelle Doheny to tears, and courtroom spectators to melancholy silence.

During the trial's last two days, the multimillionaire was forced to sit quietly and listen to Roberts condemn him as a greedy investor who paid a $100,000 bribe to Albert Fall in order to coax him to award the Pan American Petroleum and Transport Company a lucrative naval reserve lease. Roberts hoped to show the jury that Doheny had offered to build the storage tanks in Hawaii at cost because he had anticipated huge profits from the valuable leases at Elk Hills. Roberts also intended to prove beyond a reasonable doubt that the $100,000 Doheny gave to Fall was a bribe. Why else had the money been proffered in cash, Roberts asked the jurors, except to ensure that there would be no record of the transaction?

Doheny then heard his own attorney, Frank Hogan, praise him as a patriotic man agreeing to bid on the Pearl Harbor job out of a sense of civic duty. Hogan argued that if the jury concluded the $100,000 was a loan, then they also had to acknowledge Doheny had no intention to bribe his friend. In an impassioned three-hour summation, Hogan urged the jury to acquit. With his blue-gray eyes flashing, Hogan pointed to the somber oilman. "Do you believe that man is a crook? If he's a crook, convict him. But can you believe that he had fallen so low that he selected his own son . . . as the instrument of his bribery?"

Tears welled in Hogan's own eyes as he whispered in a choked voice, "Ned Doheny says to you from the grave that which in life he said from this very witness stand"—that there was no criminal intent. "This indictment charges that young Doheny was a briber. Can you believe that?" Once again Hogan was asking a jury to take a reasonable view of the facts. "Can you believe that a man who a few years before had offered his only son to his country had fallen so low that he took him, the expected solace of his old age and made him an instrument of his bribery? It isn't human to believe it!"

The government was entitled to have the final say in its closing argument. Roberts simply but firmly insisted that Doheny was a "briber and manipulator, bent on making a huge profit from the government's coffers." Eschewing dramatics, he recapitulated matter-of-factly the evidence against Doheny that, he claimed, showed "beyond any doubt" that Doheny had given Fall the money to unduly influence him into awarding Doheny the valuable Elk Hills leases.

"When this money was passed," Roberts told the jury, "the man who passed it felt in his heart of hearts, and knew, that it would have an influence on a public official. The criminal in this case strikes at the very heart of government. Nobody can deny and nobody has denied, that Mr. Doheny's company was after those leases," Roberts slowly stated. "And nobody can deny there was an advance of $100,000 to Fall."[5]

Then there was silence. The room was cold. Spectators huddled in their overcoats; many of the women present drew their fur pieces and wraps closely about them. Edward Doheny wiped off his spectacles with a crisp linen handkerchief while Estelle Doheny, dressed in black and wearing small pearl earrings and a pearl necklace, remained seated behind her husband, her eyes riveted on the lawyers and the judge.

When all was said and done, the verdict rested upon the jury's deciding two key issues: Why had Doheny sent money to Fall in cash under suspicious circumstances? And had Fall actually sought a loan from Doheny for personal needs?

THE FINAL VERDICT

On Saturday, March 22, shortly after 11 A.M., both sides rested and the case was officially concluded. Before dismissing the jurors for deliberation, Judge Hitz surprised all in the courtroom by offering instructions that were distinctly favorable to Doheny—and oddly in contrast to the ones he had recently given during Albert Fall's trial. Hitz told the jurors that they could conceivably find one party in the $100,000 transaction (Fall) guilty of bribery, but not the other (Doheny). Because the law considers intent, it was possible for one party to receive money and perceive it as a bribe, even when the other party had not intended the transaction to be a bribe. As Hitz concluded his brief speech, Hogan smiled broadly. Then the jurors filed out of the room.

During the jury's extremely brief deliberations, the courtroom atmosphere remained tense. Reporters stood ready to report the decisive verdict; Doheny and his entourage remained silently seated. Although most spectators expected a quick verdict, few were willing to speculate on what that verdict would be. Less than sixty minutes later, word arrived that the jury had reached its decision. Members of the press crowded into the courtroom, ready to file their news stories. At the Petroleum Securities Building at Tenth and Flower Streets in downtown Los Angeles, Doheny's corporate headquarters, all work stopped as the rumor spread that the verdict was due.

The twelve jurors filed back into the courtroom and assumed their seats. The foreman, at Judge Hitz's request, stepped forward to pronounce the transformative words: "not guilty." Hearing this, Doheny looked up, with an incredulous, almost dazed look on his face. Behind him, spectators burst into applause and cheers but were quickly subdued by the bailiffs. Then, as all watched, the old man began to cry. Tears rushed down his face as he was embraced first by Hogan, then by his wife. He collapsed into her arms and for several minutes continued to weep and shake as he clung to her.

Countless well-wishers pressed forward to congratulate the finally vindicated Doheny. When he recovered sufficiently, he politely moved through the jubilant throng and thanked each jury member for his verdict. "Thank you, and God bless you," he and Estelle repeated over and over as they warmly clasped the jurors' hands. Some of the jurors wept as they bid good luck to the exhausted but much relieved couple.

Finally, for all, the ordeal was over.

In a final show of professional panache, Doheny remained at the courthouse to answer newsmen's questions and pose for photographs and sound pictures. "Of course, I am happy," he repeated several times. "I am only sorry that the same verdict could not have gone to my friend, Mr. Fall, who deserved it as much as I do."

Meanwhile, back at Doheny's Tenth Street headquarters, joyous employees passed along the good news. Hundreds of congratulatory telephone calls poured into the Pan American switchboards from all parts of the United States. Doheny himself telephoned his office from Washington,

D.C., to express his great relief and happiness at being "freed after only one ballot." He told his workers that at his wife's insistence, he would rest in Washington for a few days, then briefly visit New York City before returning to Los Angeles.[6]

In Three Rivers, Albert Fall angrily ruminated over the incongruity of the two trial rulings. Although he bravely told reporters that "truth and innocence have finally triumphed," and said he was pleased that his friend Doheny had been acquitted, he remained puzzled at his own misfortune. "The evidence was identical," Fall told reporters. Fall's wife, Emma, echoed her husband's sentiments, terming Doheny's acquittal a "splendid vindication that surely will call to the attention of the entire world the terrible injustice that has been done to Mr. Fall and his family."[7] One newspaper account captured the general public confusion by quoting Fall's thirteen-year-old granddaughter, Emmadair, as gravely asking her mother the question on everyone's mind: "But Mother, if Mr. Doheny is not guilty of giving a bribe, how can grandfather be guilty of accepting one?"[8]

When Doheny returned to Los Angeles by train on March 30, 1930, a crowd of about 500 well-wishers, including judges, naval officers, clergymen, and Pan American Petroleum and Transport Company employees, gathered to greet him. Despite the spirited homecoming and the triumphant jury verdict, Doheny felt he was enjoying a Pyrrhic victory. Over the past six years, as lawsuits mounted against him, he had seen a large portion of his oil empire go to the Standard Oil Company of Indiana; his only son, the focus of his plans and dreams, had been murdered; and his reputation as a respected, powerful business magnate would remain forever tarnished despite his final court triumph. When vindication in the oil trials at last came, he was unable to rejoice; he was an old man, broken in health and spirit and bereft of heir.

After several weeks back in the city, Edward took Estelle, Lucy, and several of his grandchildren on an extended summer cruise aboard their 279-foot ocean yacht, the *Casiana*. It was a temporary release from his troubles; on his return, he had an additional legal hurdle to overcome. Angry stockholders of Doheny's Pan American had recently filed a civil suit against him for corporate mismanagement and sought $16 million in damages. The trial was scheduled for April 29, 1930.

"We will fight that out together," Estelle Doheny told reporters, "and then we will get some rest."

THE DOHENY-FALL PARADOX

Certainly, the contradictory verdicts of the two trials of defendants Doheny and Fall became the talk of legal historians and political pundits for years. A legal anomaly had found one guilty and one not.

Many months after Doheny's trial, when the jurors who had acquitted him were interviewed, they admitted that they had been greatly swayed by the appearance of the stooped, aging tycoon who clearly was mourning the loss of his son. Nine of the jurors, in fact, stated that they had wanted to acquit Doheny from the very outset of the trial. Two had leaned toward convicting him, and one had remained undecided. Some of the jurors sympathetic to Doheny also admitted that they had been offended by Roberts's calculating, unemotional attacks upon Doheny. They felt Roberts had oversimplified a very complicated transaction between two old friends. Because of this, several of the jurors became determined to vote against the prosecutor.

"Doheny is a millionaire," one juror told reporters. "Why shouldn't he loan [Fall] the money? Whatever happened in connection with the loan was their own business."[9] Another juror, expressing the opinion of many of his peers, said that the government simply had not proved its case adequately. It had not offered any direct evidence that the $100,000 given by Doheny to Fall was consideration for the valuable leases.

But the jury's surprising verdict was blasted by most editorialists across the nation, and headlines repeatedly asked the same question: "When is a $100,000 bribe not a bribe?"[10] In its story on the trial, *Time* magazine attempted to answer this question with hair-splitting care by explaining to its readers that the $100,000 loan Doheny gave Fall was a "legitimate loan," but that the $100,000 Fall took from Doheny was a "corrupt bribe." The magazine pronounced the historic verdict as justified: "Bribery, like adultery, is a peculiar crime in fact if not in law. Injury is done to a third party. And culpability between partners is not always equal before the law. . . . A bribe-taking official is more punishable, because he has betrayed a public trust, than the bribe-giver, who is under no specific oath of honesty."[11]

Doheny never hesitated to express his gratitude to Hogan and the other lawyers who helped acquit him. The day after the conclusion of his trial, he sent a Rolls Royce down to Frank Hogan's Washington, D.C., home on Sheridan Circle, and a Lincoln convertible tied in red ribbon to the Kalorama Circle residence of John W. Guider, a Hogan associate who had worked tirelessly on the case behind the scenes.

Doheny then requested that his defense team reassemble at Hogan's Washington office to celebrate their final victory. With his attorneys surrounding him, Doheny offered words of thanks, attributing his acquittal to their diligence, brilliance, and unceasing optimism. Then, to the astonishment of the assembled group, Doheny began to hand out envelopes to the lawyers and their secretaries. Nubby Jones, an attorney at the gathering, found a $10,000 bill in his envelope; he told Doheny that at that moment, he was richer than ever before in his life.[12]

Later, it was reported that Doheny gave Hogan a "bonus" check for $1 million as appreciation for his inspired defense work. Hogan consistently refused to confirm the amount of this largesse, however, citing ethical considerations. Hogan also maintained that he and Doheny had never discussed fees, agreeing that "much would depend on the jury verdicts."

Doheny's legal victory brought professional benefits to the fifty-three-year-old Hogan as well. In April 1930, *Time* magazine called him America's most envied attorney and "the federal government's No. 1 legal antagonist." He was now rich and very famous—the best-known trial lawyer in the country. Wealthy clients were now routinely seeking him out: "There is a lawyer named Frank Hogan," wrote one reporter for the *Brooklyn Eagle*, "whose health every oil man inquires about before he faces the judge and jury. He is a very interesting man, rather slight of build but a giant in legal intellect and advice. The captains of the oil industry think he is one of the greatest men they ever knew."[13]

Doheny continued his close ties to officials of the Catholic Church, and although he had been acquitted of the criminal charges, critics still argued that he used his religious philanthropies to court public favor. Dan La Botz describes Doheny's relationship with the church as a "religious shield" for a "wealthy communicant in his hour of need." In his highly critical analysis, he writes that "Doheny and [Bishop] Cantwell each needed the other. Doheny's oil fueled Cantwell's ambitions, and Cantwell was in a position to offer Doheny social status and prestige that were also important business assets. . . . The Catholic Church provided a vehicle for Doheny's social aspirations and a cover for his political problems."[14]

Bishop Francis Clement Kelley was a source of strength to Doheny during the lengthy and arduous trials. One of Kelley's admirable qualities was "his capacity to uphold some of the mavericks of his generation," and Kelley's biographer noted of his loyalty that "it is one thing to befriend talented artists and businessmen and quite another to remain faithful to those who have fallen from grace."[15]

Doheny's release from infamy after his acquittal, his financing of the magnificent St. Vincent's Church, and his many philanthropies ensured his continued prominence in Roman Catholic life. Through Bishop Cantwell's efforts, on February 11, 1931, Doheny was made a Knight of the Equestrian Order of the Holy Sepulchre by Pope Pius XI, an honor he had long coveted. Undoubtedly the oilman was deeply thankful that divine Providence had brought an end to his ten-year legal ordeal.

Doheny remained very close to Frank Hogan, even after the final trial. In one of many gestures of gratitude, Doheny lent Frank and his wife, Mamie, the *Casiana* yacht—complete with captain and crew—for a month-long voyage to Hawaii.

The bond between the two men was growing stronger and would last for the remainder of their lives. Hogan would continue to serve as Doheny's in-house counsel, advising family members and representing Doheny's corporate concerns. He would spend at least four months annually in Los Angeles, working at Doheny's Petroleum Securities Building on Tenth Street, where Doheny had set up an office for him.

Years after the civil and criminal proceedings had ended, at a small dinner party at the Hogans' home in Washington, D.C., on the occasion of Mamie Hogan's fifty-first birthday, Doheny asked permission to speak after dinner. Rising to his feet, Doheny described the affection that had developed between him and the Hogan family. He then told of a ritual that he followed of giving Estelle $1,000 for every year of her age on her birthday. Asking permission to repeat that tradition with Mamie, Doheny handed Hogan's astounded wife an envelope with $51,000 inside.[16] It was undoubtedly her most memorable birthday party.

Mamie grew close to Estelle. And Frank introduced Estelle to the hobby of rare book collecting, which, until her death in 1958, became an enduring avocation for her. During the next ten years, Estelle was able to amass one of the finest rare book and manuscript collections in the world.

On April 6, 1931, the Court of Appeals of the District of Columbia rejected Albert Fall's request for a new trial, finding no error in the lower court's jury instructions.[17] In a last-minute effort, Fall, supported by the New Mexico state legislature, launched an impassioned appeal to the governor of New Mexico, which failed. In June, Fall was denied review of his case by the U.S. Supreme Court. After President Herbert Hoover turned down Fall's request for an executive pardon, Fall's legal remedies were exhausted.

Despite this, however, Frank Hogan would not abandon his client. He petitioned the Department of Justice on Fall's behalf, citing Fall's "chronic respiratory ailments" as conditions that should preclude him from serving jail time. Eventually, Hogan managed to get Fall assigned to the Santa Fe State Prison instead of the harsher, more austere federal penitentiary in El Paso—a small victory for Fall, at least.

Accompanied by his daughter Jouett and his eldest granddaughter, Martha, Albert Bacon Fall left his residence on Arizona Street in El Paso at 6:45 on the evening of July 18, 1931, in an ambulance, making a final visit as a free man to his ranch at Three Rivers. There, he rested until July 20, when he was loaded by stretcher into another ambulance and escorted to the state prison. Inside the jailhouse walls, the once-celebrated secretary of the interior became Convict No. 6991.

During his one-year incarceration, Fall battled chronic tuberculosis and spent many days in the prison hospital receiving treatment. Later, he filed a "pauper's oath" through his attorney and was able to get his $100,000 civil fine expunged. The case of *United States v. Albert B. Fall* cost him a total of seven years of his life, sapped the last of his strength, and claimed the remainder of his money. When Fall began his prison sentence, he had no way of raising the money necessary to pay off Doheny's loan, let alone pay his court-ordered fine.[18] Hundreds of letters were written to the parole board on his behalf, urging that Fall be released on humanitarian grounds because of ailing health. Drs. J. H. Gambrell, Felix P. Miller, and R. B. Homan sent repeated telegrams to the board and the Department of Justice: "In our judgment [continued] imprisonment will result in untimely death. Badly broken in health as he is he will be unable to withstand a threatened pleurisy and active bronchitis."[19]

Later that year, Dr. James Safford went to see Fall in prison, examined him, and reconfirmed to authorities that Fall's physical condition was so precarious that he feared the prisoner would not live more than a year. Safford's diagnosis detailed illnesses that included severe arteriosclerosis, myocarditis, arthritis, tuberculosis, and pleurisy. In addition to medical problems, the former secretary was predictably suffering bouts of severe depression. Confinement to a prison cell was proving debilitating for the formerly active man, who had little to do during the days other than pen long, rambling letters to his friends and family members.

In the winter of 1931, Fall received yet another bitter blow, this time from an unexpected direction: the wife of his former codefendant and oldest friend. On November 20, Estelle Doheny wrote to Fall's wife, Emma, demanding that the Falls vacate their Three Rivers Ranch in New Mexico. In a carefully worded letter, Estelle made it clear that the Doheny corporations now were the legal owners of the property, and they intended to dispose of the ranch in a sale. This meant that Emma and her family immediately had to remove themselves and their possessions from the premises they had occupied for thirty-five years.

Oddly, after telling Emma, whose husband was incarcerated and penniless, that the Fall family was about to be homeless as well, Estelle requested pity from the Falls for her own husband's plight: "My husband has not written a letter since your husband's trial. He is absolutely a different man. The result of the trial, coming so closely after Ned's tragic death has completely crushed him. He has lost interest in everything, and I can almost say in everybody." Urging Emma to face the painful reality that she had lost her beloved ranch, Estelle requested that the Fall family move out as soon as they could. Then she rather insensitively concluded:

> I know how tired you must be with all your work and with the sorrow of your husband's confinement and ill health. We feel very badly, more so each day, that human life can be regarded so lightly. I have just read a very interesting book, "The Strange Career of Mr. Hoover." It makes one wonder about life in a more serious way.
>
> My husband looks well but he is not. He is a little weaker the last few days and I know he doesn't speak ten words in the entire day, he doesn't seem a bit like his former self, but we are grateful that he is as well as he is. I take him for a ride in a wheelchair about an hour a day when it is nice and warm. Otherwise, with about an hour at the office in the morning, and after lunch until about three o'clock on our porch, the rest of the time is spent in the house. He retires between seven-thirty and eight. He joins me [in] prayerful good wishes to you, your husband, and your family.
> Affectionately,
> Estelle Doheny[20]

Upon receiving the letter, Emma Fall collapsed, her world shattered. Estelle Doheny's actions were inexplicable; it is not known whether she acted at Edward's behest or simply wrote independently, thinking she needed to protect her husband's financial interests. The result was the same, whatever the reason: the letter ended a time-tested, five-decade friendship between two battle-scarred men.

Estelle Doheny, after spending her youthful years in loneliness while Edward was building his empire, now found the years they had expected to spend together in comfort and luxury were instead filled with misery. Estelle had reason to hold the Falls responsible—it was her husband's impetuous loan to Albert and Albert's foolish lies and illegal acts with Sinclair that, she felt, had pulled Edward into a maelstrom of misfortune. Estelle must have found it galling when during the years of the trials she could not express the anger she felt about what Albert had done to them; they were forced to unite with Fall, like it or not, and work on his behalf.

Perhaps the stoic veneer she maintained through six years of tortuous court hearings later caused Estelle to lash out against the former cabinet secretary in deep-seated rage.

On Friday, February 18, 1932, three years after the murder of her husband, Lucy Smith Doheny married Leigh M. Battson, a San Francisco investment banker associated with S. W. Strauss and Company, in a quiet ceremony inside the living room at Greystone. The marriage was performed by the Rev. Robert Freeman, pastor of Pasadena's First Presbyterian Church. Edward and Estelle warmly supported Lucy's new marriage. They had attended the small wedding along with their three youngest grandchildren; the two oldest, Dickie Dell and Laurence, were already attending school in the East.

Lucy wore a simple wedding gown of fine beige lace and one piece of jewelry—a jade and diamond baguette pin, given to her by the groom. The couple departed shortly after a wedding breakfast, refusing to reveal their destination. Following the wedding, they enjoyed a pleasant European sojourn before returning to California.

After serving nine months and nineteen days of his sentence, Albert Fall was released from prison on May 9, 1932. He was met by his family and quietly escorted to his El Paso home. After a short rest at the Arizona Street house, Fall was taken to Three Rivers, where he and Emma remained in seclusion on the ranch that Estelle Doheny had ordered them to leave. On "good" days, when Albert was able, he would leave his bed and walk unsteadily to the front porch, where he would sit in a rocker and watch his dogs play in the yard. Occasionally, a reporter would call on the former secretary and ask for a quote. One journalist boldly asked him what he believed the public would think of him in later years. Fall reflected for a moment, head propped up against the pillows of his rocker, white mustache tickling the stub of his ever-present cigar. "Some of my friends believe I will be completely vindicated," he said. "They believe the world will see that I did what I thought was best for the country. Others insist that I will go down in history in an unfavorable light. The unfortunate thing is that my health broke and I could not do my own fighting. If I could have, perhaps the result could have been different."[21]

Edward Doheny, too, was in poor health, greatly weakened from the strain of the tragic death of his son in February 1929 and by the years of litigation. As his health worsened and mental acuity diminished, Estelle stepped in quietly to assume many of his social and business responsibilities. She was a masterful executive in her own right. Except for her dealings with the Fall family, which were weighted with unspoken accusations attributing the Doheny travails to Albert Fall, her business decisions were forthright and sound. She undoubtedly preserved for the Doheny family assets that would otherwise have been lost.

Estelle and Edward discussed plans for a memorial for Ned, a permanent remembrance that would bring to life Edward's dashed hope to hand to an heir, to a new generation, the rewards and responsibilities he took so seriously. At Estelle's urging, Doheny offered a $1 million endowment and $1 million construction grant for the "Edward L. Doheny Jr. Memorial Library," which would be built at the University of Southern California campus in Los Angeles. The lead architect for the facility was Ralph Adams Cram of Cram and Ferguson, who had previously designed St. Vincent's Church at Figueroa Street and Adams Boulevard, which the Dohenys had financed in 1924. Samuel E. Lunden served as the project's resident architect, and P. J. Walker, who had helped build Greystone, was the library building's general contractor. The four-level Italian Romanesque–style building would be constructed in the form of an abbreviated "H" with walls of Roman brick and Cordova cream-colored limestone trim. The entryway featured a monumental marble staircase that led to a soaring hall illuminated by stained-glass windows. The 168,150-square-foot library would house an impressive collection of nearly half a million books. The new library was called the crown jewel of the university.[22]

By this time, Doheny was confined to his bed and required constant medical attention. Estelle insisted on taking Doheny to the Ferndale Ranch whenever he was well enough to travel. She continued to believe that the beautiful wooded setting had curative powers. Certainly, it would bolster

Edward and Estelle Doheny's home, 8 Chester Place, Los Angeles, ca. 1910.
Courtesy of the AALA.

The aviary at 8 Chester Place. Doheny had the 90-foot-tall plant conservatory built
as a "palm house" and filled it with exotic plants, including 10,000 orchids (cycads),
palms, and trees imported from Mexico. Courtesy of the AALA.

Inside the aviary at 8 Chester Place. The swimming pool was large enough for a gondola and a canoe. Courtesy of the AALA.

The Pompeian Room. The room was the center of Estelle's formal dinner parties, sometimes given for over one hundred guests. Doheny petitioned the Italian government to permit a Russian-born artist, Eugene Murmann, to reproduce furniture found in the Museum of Rome. Courtesy of the AALA.

The custom-made Steinway piano was given by Edward Doheny to his wife for her thirtieth birthday, August 2, 1905. Under the gilt-wood lid was a painting of Estelle at the entrance of Chester Place. Courtesy of the AALA.

Estelle Doheny's bedroom suite at 8 Chester Place. Courtesy of the AALA.

The library at 8 Chester Place. Courtesy of the AALA.

The sitting room at 8 Chester Place. Courtesy
of the AALA.

The exterior and interior of Ned Doheny's New York City apartment at 15 East 84th Street, ca. 1924. A pivotal conversation that took place in front of the fireplace figured in the testimony at the Senate hearings and the subsequent criminal trials. Courtesy of Department of Special Collections, University of Southern California Libraries.

"Hogan's Alley," located in the basement of 8 Chester Place. Originally designed as a bowling alley, it served as legal headquarters during the lengthy oil scandal trials. Courtesy of Department of Special Collections, University of Southern California Libraries.

Teapot Rock at Teapot Dome, Wyoming, site of the oil reserves, prior to the windstorm on November 8, 1927, that blew off the famous spout. Photo courtesy of Nicholas A. Curry.

Albert Bacon Fall, Doheny's friend from the New Mexico Territory mining camps, who became U.S. secretary of the interior. Both men were indicted for bribery and conspiracy to defraud the U.S. government in 1924. Courtesy of Emadair Chase Jones.

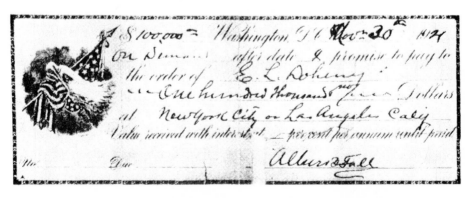

Albert Fall's IOU to Edward Doheny, dated 1921. The note was the subject of ten years of fierce conflict in the oil scandal trials. Courtesy Emadair Chase Jones.

Edward and Estelle Doheny during a quiet moment at Chester Place in 1930.
Courtesy of the AALA.

Greystone Mansion was given to Edward Doheny Jr. (Ned) by his father. The fortified, gated compound failed to save the Doheny family from a devastating tragedy. Courtesy of Department of Special Collections, University of Southern California Libraries.

Edward and Estelle Doheny with Laura and William Smith (their daughter-in-law's parents) and grandchildren during happy times for the family in the 1920s. Courtesy of the AALA.

The Doheny family at the cornerstone-laying ceremony for the Edward L. Doheny Jr. Memorial Library at the University of Southern California in 1930. The children of the slain Edward Doheny Jr. stand with their mother, Lucy Doheny, and their grandparents, Estelle and Edward Doheny. Courtesy of Department of Special Collections, University of Southern California Libraries.

The Edward L. Doheny Jr. Memorial Library at the University of Southern California in Los Angeles, 1932. Courtesy of Department of Special Collections, University of Southern California Libraries.

Harry Ford Sinclair, ca. 1927–28. The oilman
was convicted of wrongdoing during the Teapot Dome trials. Courtesy of Department of
Special Collections, University of Southern
California Libraries.

Ned McLean, ca. 1930. This prominent figure
in Washington, D.C., political and financial
circles was drawn into the oil lease scandal.
Courtesy of Department of Special Collections,
University of Southern California Libraries.

Attorney Frank Hogan with Edward and Estelle Doheny on the courthouse steps following Doheny's triumphant acquittal on bribery charges in 1930. Doheny's hand is clasped by a well-wisher offering congratulations. Courtesy of Hogan & Hartson, L.L.P.

Edward L. Doheny Memorial Library at St. John's Seminary in Camarillo, California, 1940. The building was designed by architect Wallace Neff. Courtesy of the AALA.

Estelle Doheny with building contractor J. A. McNeil, architect Wallace Neff, and the Very Reverend William B. Barr on December 2, 1939, at the groundbreaking of the Edward L. Doheny Memorial Library at St. John's Seminary in Camarillo, California. Courtesy of the AALA.

Estelle Doheny and her personal secretary, Lucille Miller, examining the Gutenberg Bible, a part of Estelle's book collection. After her husband's death, Estelle became a capable executive, managing vast sums and pursuing her philanthropic interests. Courtesy of the AALA.

Edward Doheny in 1932. Acquitted of bribery charges, he was broken in spirit after the loss of his son. Courtesy of the AALA.

her husband's mood and maybe even stabilize his declining health. There, he could rest, read, or watch the babbling Santa Paula Creek splash into a series of three inviting pools. Estelle had stocked the uppermost pool with trout so that Doheny could fish from his wheelchair, if he wished.

By January 1933, Edward Doheny and Estelle were back at the Chester Place compound. The couple read with disbelief newspaper accounts of President Roosevelt's selection of a new attorney general. The appointee was Thomas J. Walsh, the senator who had grilled Doheny with a vengeance during the Teapot Dome–Elk Hills investigations. Walsh had demonstrated his qualifications for the post in large measure through his pursuit of Doheny and Sinclair over the naval oil reserves. He was seen by Roosevelt as "anticorruption" and "anti–big business," a perfect choice for his new presidential cabinet.

But on March 2, 1933, only six weeks after being chosen, the seventy-three-year-old lawyer suffered a fatal heart attack. Five days earlier, he had married Nieves Perez Chaumont de Truffin, a prominent Havana divorcee; he and his bride were traveling by train to Washington, D.C., to attend the inaugural ceremonies and his own confirmation hearings when he suddenly dropped dead.

Eight days later, on March 10, 1933, a tremendous earthquake rumbled through Los Angeles as Edward and Estelle were eating dinner in their formal dining room at Chester Place. Books and artwork crashed to the floors as the Dohenys, along with their household staff, scrambled to safety. When the trembling stopped, Edward and Estelle surveyed the damage. Although the estate's exterior and foundation were intact, much of the interior furnishings and precious collectibles had been badly damaged.

The earthquake, which occurred at 5:30 P.M., centered in Long Beach, twenty miles south of Los Angeles. It was one of the largest quakes in Los Angeles' history, registering 6.5 on the Richter scale. Hundreds of buildings were destroyed, 3,000 people were injured, and 127 died. Property damage was estimated at over $30 million.

Estelle was so frightened by the event that she summoned the family chauffeur and told him that she and Mr. Doheny wished to leave immediately for the Ferndale Ranch. Estelle ordered the staff to load up several cars with prized family possessions. Fearing another earthquake, she soon had the caravan speeding north toward Ferndale in Ventura County.

Fortunately, however, no large-scale aftershocks occurred, and the Dohenys were able to return to their Chester Place mansion and initiate repairs. Edward already had been infirm and in poor spirits prior to the quake; for the remaining last two years of his life, he would become increasingly disoriented, bedridden, and completely dependent upon Estelle.

As Doheny's health worsened, Estelle spent an increasing amount of time caring for his daily needs and tending to her rare book collection. Estelle began to acquire rare books as her interests grew and she became a more knowledgeable collector. Her book collection eventually included English and American first editions, rare Bibles, illuminated manuscripts, incunabula (books printed before 1501), valuable books with paintings decorating the page edges, and autographed manuscripts (including all fifty-six signers of America's Declaration of Independence). Her interests extended to nineteenth-century European and American paintings, Currier and Ives prints, European and American paperweights, antique lace, fans, porcelain, jade, sculpture, tapestries, antique furniture, and a significant collection of Western Americana.

By 1935 news of Doheny's eviction proceedings against the Falls had made national headlines. A process server had presented Emma Fall with official eviction papers in July, but she and her husband decided to bring the matter to court. Fall himself told a reporter from the *El Paso Herald Post:* "I won't move! I've written Mrs. Doheny that I will not give up possession of this place until there has been a complete settlement between Mr. Doheny and me." He continued, "The order to move came from Mrs.

Doheny, who is really running the company. It was a curt letter. Doheny has been in ill health and I don't know whether he knew about the letter [she] sent me. He and I are still friends."

Emma Fall, who was supporting her family by operating a Mexican restaurant in El Paso, added that they intended to hire "the best lawyer in New Mexico" to file a countersuit to save their home. "I'm going to file a lawsuit myself," she declared. "I know I've got the right to do it, and I'm not going to wait for somebody to move us out."[23]

Hoping to sway the Dohenys through public embarrassment, the Falls continued to grant interviews to the press and even allowed reporters to reprint their eviction notices. By this time, however, the Dohenys had ceased all personal communication with the Falls and had referred all further discussion of the matter to a Pan American executive, Robert Sands. On August 12, 1935, he wrote:

> My dear Mr. Fall,
> We are disposing of the Tres Ritos [sic] Ranch at Three Rivers, N.M., and as the purchaser desires immediate possession I am writing to ask you and Mrs. Fall to please arrange to remove your personal belongings from and vacate the premises at your earliest convenience. In any case we wish to have this accomplished by August 15 as the new owner takes possession on that date.
> Mr. and Mrs. Doheny join me in kindest regards and best wishes for your speedy and complete recovery.
> Sincerely yours,
> R. M. Sands Vice-President[24]

On the appointed day, Fall obdurately remained locked behind the doors of the Three Rivers ranch house. He announced to assembled reporters, "I am going to fight eviction and I am confident I can retain my home."[25] Although unable to reach his former friend through urgent telephone calls and plaintive letters and telegrams, Fall remained convinced that he would be permitted to stay in his home—if only Doheny would talk to him.

Long ago, Doheny had declared, "Fall will never want for anything,"[26] but now Doheny was seriously ill, and it was unlikely that he was fully aware of the hardships that had befallen his friend. To his death, Albert Fall maintained the belief that his old friend was too ill to have known about his eviction. He vainly awaited a last-minute reprieve until a local sheriff arrived and ordered him to leave. Fall and Doheny would never speak to one another again, for within weeks, Edward Doheny would be dead.

On September 8, 1935, Estelle urgently called Edward's physicians to the Chester Place compound. After examining him, the doctors quietly told Estelle that there was no more that they could do. Estelle summoned Lucy and the five grandchildren to Edward's bedside. With his family in attendance, Edward Doheny passed away at 8:00 P.M. He was seventy-nine years old.[27]

Two days later, an elaborate funeral was held for Doheny at St. Vincent's Church. Several thousand mourners came to pay tribute to the oilman.

Two bishops, many monsignors, and fifty priests attended. Bishops John J. Cantwell of the Archdiocese of Los Angeles and Francis C. Kelley of the Diocese of Tulsa, Oklahoma, conducted the service. As a choir of priests sang softly, Estelle and her two older grandsons—Edward L. III, eighteen, and William Henry, sixteen—followed the casket to the church's altar. Behind them followed the other grandchildren: Lucy Estelle ("Dickie Dell"), twenty; Patrick Anson, twelve; and Timothy Michael, nine.

Bishop Cantwell intoned the prayers of the mass for Edward Doheny:

Eternal rest grant unto him, O Lord;
And let perpetual light shine upon him.

The bishop eulogized Doheny as a good and generous man. Doheny's life and work were praised and no hint of fault was noted. There was a passing mention that on one occasion, Edward Doheny's trait of excessive generosity had brought him sorrow, but there was no revelation of mistakes he regretted, of forgiveness sought or amends undertaken. One who was hearing of Doheny for the first time would have learned only that Doheny's life was an exemplary one and that he was held in the highest esteem by thousands. "He does not go empty-handed into eternity, he prepared for the greatest journey man can take; he prepared by his faith and his good works. He died as he lived with a prayer on his lips. May perpetual light shine upon him!"[28]

When the ceremony ended, friends who had been important in Doheny's life—Herbert G. Wylie, R. M. Sands, C. Warren Smith, Frank J. Hogan, Olin Wellborn Jr., Olin Wellborn III, and Anson Lisk—carried his casket back up the church aisle to a waiting hearse. Estelle did not weep en route to Calvary Cemetery. There, the final services were conducted by Bishop Cantwell in the sunswept forecourt of the Doheny mausoleum.

The inscription on the bronze placard beneath which Edward Doheny would be interred read simply:

Edward Laurence Doheny
Aug 10 1856–Sept 8 1935

The stained-glass window within the family alcove bore the following inscription:

O Mary Conçeived Without Sin
Pray for Us Who Have Recourse to Thee

Hours later, Estelle returned home to Chester Place. It was there in the mansion's basement, with the help of her sister, Daysie, that she assembled and burned Edward Doheny's papers, destroying much of the existing written record of his life.

After a proper number of days had passed, Estelle Doheny, along with the family's battery of personal attorneys, turned themselves to the matter of Doheny's will. For a man of such immense wealth and intricate corporate holdings, Edward Doheny left a surprisingly simple will.[29]

Dated August 22, 1932, the will was only two pages in length. It named Estelle as executor, as well as two longtime friends of Doheny's—Olin Wellborn III, his family lawyer, and Robert M. Sands, an executive at Pan American—as co-executors. Doheny had bequeathed his entire estate to

Estelle. In life, he had already provided for his daughter-in-law, Lucy, and his five grandchildren through the generous Los Nietos Trust he had created in 1928 and through a new corporation, the Los Nietos Producing and Refining Company, that he had organized in 1934 to generate revenue for his young descendants.

Doheny's entire estate at this time was appraised at only slightly over $9 million, which shocked many who had followed his long and illustrious career. But the bulk of his assets had been distributed to his heirs years before, and Pan American stock had become greatly devalued during the Depression. Doheny's decision to bequeath his holdings prior to his death was a wise one; in 1934, President Franklin D. Roosevelt initiated a rigorous inheritance tax that would have cost Doheny's heirs hundreds of thousands of dollars in estate taxes.

He had also wisely chosen executor Robert Sands to assume the weighty responsibility of overseeing Pan American's enterprises. As Estelle Doheny took the position of president and chairman of the company, Sands took control of the day-to-day operations of the multimillion-dollar oil concern.

By divesting his Pan American Corporation's Mexican holdings, much to the surprise of his contemporaries, Doheny also evaded another long-dreaded disaster: true to his predictions, the Mexican government in 1938 began to nationalize its oil industry. At that time, President Lazaro Cardenas announced a "Six-Year Plan" to appropriate all foreign-owned and -operated oil company holdings and merge them into one national concern, the Pemex Corporation. Cardenas also detailed his intentions to redistribute the 45 million acres of foreign-held Mexican land to local farmers. Doheny's Mexican oil fields (at the time in the nervous hands of Standard Oil Company of New Jersey, which had purchased them from Standard Oil of Indiana in 1932) soon became part of Cardenas's new oil empire.

THE YEARS AFTER

During the final decades of her life Estelle Doheny grew closer to Father William Ward, the soft-spoken pastor of St. Vincent's, who had also served as her private chaplain at Chester Place. Now he became her spiritual advisor and a close confidant, and assisted her in administering her philanthropic programs. In June 1939, in recognition of her philanthropy, Mrs. Doheny was awarded the distinction of "Countess" by Pope Pius XII, a rare title that could only be conferred by the pope.[30]

Following her conversion to Catholicism in 1918, she had endeavored to become the model Catholic, demonstrating compassion, high-mindedness, responsibility for others, and devotion to God. She was a remarkable philanthropist. Effecting the wishes of her wealthy husband and more, she greatly expanded the couple's original plan, with unprecedented largesse. Yet she could be a difficult taskmaster. Even Lucy Doheny was said to have tread lightly in her presence. Estelle Doheny was respected as the Doheny matriarch, and was called by the family "Ma D," but she was feared as well. The complex personality of the woman devoted to her faith and her family included a shrewd and tough business mind, attuned to protecting her vital interests.

In 1939, at the suggestion of Bishop John J. Cantwell, Estelle Doheny offered to build a library as her contribution to the new St. John's Seminary in Camarillo. The building would house the library for the students, and the second floor would be used to house her collection of rare books and objets d'art. It was named the Edward Laurence Doheny Memorial Library in tribute to her husband. The facility was located in Ventura County, a two-hour drive sixty miles northwest of Los Angeles. She again hired Wallace Neff to design the monumental library in the architect's distinctive Spanish colonial style. The two-story building, 110 feet in length, faced south from a sunny hilltop; its ornate entrance was flanked on both sides by a roof-high loggia of graceful columns. Over the entrance was positioned a Celtic cross. Beneath the cross in four quadrants were the coat of arms of His Holiness Pope Pius XII, the coat of arms of Archbishop Cantwell, Mrs. Doheny's coat of arms as papal countess, and a star to represent her name, Estelle.

One room of the library was known as the Treasure Room, where bookcases with doors of bronze grillwork lined the four walls. The Western Room contained the collections of Californiana and the paintings of William R. Leigh, Frederick Remington, H. W. Hansen, and the Sammann-Russell murals.

Estelle Doheny's most remarkable achievement as a book collector was the purchase of one of the forty-eight extant Gutenberg Bibles (the Dyson-Amherst-Perrins paper copy). She also gathered seventy-seven of the titles listed in the *Zamarano 80*, designating the most important volumes of Western Americana.[31] Experts consider the collection to have been one of the most respected rare book libraries in the United States and Doheny herself the foremost woman collector of her era.[32]

In August 1944, on her sixty-ninth birthday, while engaged in prayer at her third-floor chapel at Chester Place, Estelle Doheny suffered an ocular hemorrhage that left her completely blind in her left eye and partially blind in her right eye. Estelle had reached a turning point in her life. She directed much of her activities toward conserving the sight that remained to her. What seemed at the time a grievous affliction proved to be the opening of a new path. During her efforts to learn all she could about the disease of glaucoma, Estelle became convinced of the need for further research. Two years later, with the assistance of attorney Olin Wellborn III, she created a foundation with the intended purpose "to further the conservation, improvement, and restoration of human eyesight"; it set up both a research laboratory and an eye bank at St. Vincent's Hospital in Los Angeles. Over the next several decades, the Estelle Doheny Eye Foundation would be recognized as one of the world's finest ophthalmologic facilities.[33]

Despite the hardship of her worsening eyesight, Estelle worked daily in her office, managing business details and attending to her book collection. She continued to be "Ma D" to the family and to her favorites among her longtime staff.

FINAL BOWS

Frank Hogan had a lengthy list of illustrious clients and cases after his long association with Doheny: successfully defending Andrew Mellon against charges of tax fraud, representing the Hearst newspaper empire in a series of precedent-setting libel cases, and continuing his clashes with Congress, as he defended clients and businesses that had the misfortune to be investigated by its committees.

Hogan died at his home at Sheridan Circle of Parkinson's disease on May 14, 1944, at age sixty-seven.[34] For the previous six years, his activities and visits to the law office had been increasingly limited by the crippling effects of the disease.

The roots of the firm that Hogan founded were strong. Not only did it survive his death, but it built on the strengths inherited from its magnetic founder to become one of Washington's most respected legal establishments. Hogan's law firm has grown into a major international practice (known today as Hogan & Hartson, L.L.P.) that employs over 400 lawyers. Great lawyers have come and gone, but few have left such a living monument in the legal arena. "I love court work," Hogan once said. "It requires all the faculties a man has to give."[35]

Owen J. Roberts, Hogan's opponent for over ten years who had called Edward Doheny "the instigator of corruption in the highest circles of American government," died at the age of eighty in Philadelphia on May 17, 1955. He had been appointed justice of the U.S. Supreme Court by President Herbert Hoover in 1930, thanks to his prosecutorial work during the Teapot Dome trials. Atlee Pomerene, the U.S. senator from Ohio and Robert's special coprosecutor, had died of bronchopneumonia eighteen years earlier on November 12, 1937. He was seventy-three.

Though no one would have guessed that the frail Albert Fall could cling to life far longer than his more robust friend Edward Doheny, he managed to remain in fair health for twelve years after his incarceration. At age eight-three, he died in his sleep at El Paso's Hotel Dieu Hospital on November 30, 1944, two years after his wife Emma had passed away. According to his granddaughter Jouett Fall, during the last years of his life he had lived solely on his Spanish-American War veteran's pension of $32 a month.

Emma Fall, from the day of her impetuous marriage to the handsome Albert Fall, had been his loyal supporter and an unbroken thread of strength and courage in the fabric of their tumultuous life. Columnist Dorothy Thompson found occasion to call Emma Morgan Fall "the most courageous woman in America."[36]

Oilman Harry Sinclair died a very rich man at the age of eighty in Pasadena, California, on November 10, 1956. Sinclair is interred in the main mausoleum at the Catholic Calvary Cemetery, in East Los Angeles, just fifty feet away from Edward Doheny.

In 1954 Lucy Doheny Battson, Ned's widow, sold the 400-acre Doheny ranch in Beverly Hills, which she had received from Estelle Doheny in 1945. She sold the property, except for the Greystone mansion and surrounding grounds, to Paul Trousdale, who subsequently developed the Trousdale Estates, a tract of expensive homes. In 1955 the Battsons gave up Greystone as well, selling the estate to Chicago industrialist Henry Crown.

The same year that she sold the Doheny ranch, Lucy Battson started building a 27,000-plus-square-foot mansion on a ten-acre estate called the Knoll at 1130 Schuyler Road. At over 46,000 square feet, the Greystone mansion was simply too large for herself and Leigh Battson, she told her children. As befitted the woman for whom Greystone was built, the Knoll was one of the grandest estates to be created in Los Angeles after World War II. Today, Greystone is considered a historic treasure, and the U.S. Department of the Interior recognized its architectural and historical importance by placing the property on the National Register of Historic Places. It is now owned by the City of Beverly Hills.

Lucy died at the age of one hundred in 1993. Many items in her collection of art, antiques, and jewelry were sold in an auction conducted by Butterfield's in 1995.

In 1949 Estelle Doheny, though nearly blind and housebound, was still ably conducting business matters. She decided to sell Doheny's last remaining domestic oil operations and her share of the Los Nietos Producing and Refining Company to Union Oil Company of California (now known as UNOCAL). In a chatty letter to Monsignor William Doheny, whom she called "Cousin Billy," she mentions that the grandchildren's trust will shortly follow her lead and sell at a handsome figure:

> Since my last letter, the Los Nietos Producing Company, which belonged to the grandchildren, has been negotiating with the same company that purchased my interests in the oil properties, and the sale of the one-

fourth interest owned by the grandchildren will be definitely settled on Wednesday the 26th.

They settled for $22 million cash and 600,000 shares of Union Oil Co. stock. Union Oil is a very old company and one of the first ever organized in the state of California.

I have an exceptionally neat tailor-made dress on today and [my secretary] Miss Miller says if I feel as well as I look today, all your prayers are answered. But she doesn't realize that I asked the Blessed Mother to teach me to grow old gracefully and the prose and thanksgiving should go to her.[37]

On receiving the proceeds from these sales, Mrs. Doheny decided to establish a foundation in her name. She established and funded the Carrie Estelle Doheny Foundation on June 17, 1949; its assets by 1995 would total over $110 million.[38] The foundation supports the advancement of education, medicine, religion, and the health and welfare of children and the needy. It is one of the most substantial charitable endeavors ever created in the history of Los Angeles. She also established an impressive array of other philanthropic projects, including the construction of a chapel and two buildings for the Los Angeles orphanage today known as Maryvale and the commissioning of the Estelle Doheny Hospital and Pavilion at St. Vincent's Medical Center. In 1954 Estelle Doheny was named the "Woman of the Year" by the *Los Angeles Times*.

At this time, she was suffering the debilitating effects of arteriosclerotic heart disease. Sensing that her own demise was nearing, she wrote to a favorite priest at St. Vincent's Church:

Dear Father Flavin:
I have been thinking of the Masses to be offered for me after my death. We will never know how many have been offered for my husband that have not come to our notice, and many have been offered here which have not been recorded.
. . . [I]t will take a very long time to settle my estate. I am enclosing a check for $2500. Will you please open an account for Masses to be said for the repose of my soul the day after I pass away?
Ma Dee[39]

In keeping with her attention to detail, Estelle's will (in marked contrast to her husband's brief will) would be found to be thirty-nine pages long, with detailed instructions for the dispersal of an estate valued at over $37 million.[40] Her Schedule E listed 158 separate cash bequests: 33 to institutions and 125 to relatives, friends, and employees. She bequeathed her furs and jewelry to her sister Daysie, but stipulated that Lucy receive her pearl necklace with diamond clasp. Each employee at 8 Chester Place was remembered, and those who had worked for her for more than twenty years received $6,500. The Chester Place compound was willed to the Catholic Church. It became the Doheny campus of Mount St. Mary's College, a small liberal arts college based in Brentwood, California, in 1962. The mansion at 8 Chester Place, where so many of Estelle Doheny's grand dinner parties had taken place, was converted into a faculty residence, and the lavish Pompeian Room is used today for formal college functions and fund-raisers.

Estelle's cherished book collection did not remain intact. In 1985 officials of the church determined that the sale of the collection could allow them to establish a new teaching endowment at St. John's Seminary. Estelle Doheny's valuable holdings were sold at seven auctions from 1987 until 1989.[41] Sale proceeds were nearly $38 million. A Japanese publishing firm purchased the Gutenberg Bible for over $5 million—more than seventy-five times what Estelle had paid in 1950. Many criticized the church's actions. Jake Zeitlin, one of America's foremost book collectors, has described the auction as representing the loss of a "great cultural resource."[42]

The young woman with the enticing timbre to her voice who bewitched an oil millionaire grew into her role as a supportive wife and companion. She confronted with courage the enigmatic fate that befell her husband and imbued her life with dedication and purpose through significant endeavors of her own that would long survive her. Estelle succumbed to heart disease on October 30, 1958. She was eighty-three years old.[43] She died in a private room at St. Vincent's Hospital and, in accordance with her wishes, was interred with her husband at the Doheny mausoleum at Calvary Cemetery.

Epilogue
La Calavera del Futuro

Edward Doheny never joined the ranks of other U.S. financial and industrial giants—Rockefeller, Vanderbilt, Carnegie, Morgan, Frick, Astor, Getty, Huntington—whose contributions to U.S. economic growth and industrial prominence are recounted. If school history texts mention Doheny at all, it is in a brief paragraph about the oil lease scandal of the 1920s.

By omitting Doheny, historians fail to recognize his role in the ascendance of the United States as a world power. His foresight and drive, his great belief in oil as the fuel for progress and industrial development, and his willingness to risk his personal fortune to find and market oil played a crucial part in the economic growth of the nation in the twentieth century, though it is a contribution not generally acknowledged. Doheny firmly believed that hard work will result in capitalist success and spoke with pride of his contribution to the industrial wealth of the nation. He equated fortune building with public service and praised peers who, like himself, had the courage to risk all in their quest for great financial reward.

In the popular mind, Doheny's name is connected with the Teapot Dome scandal and the bribery of a government official, even though he was not involved in the Teapot Dome lease (that was Harry Sinclair—Doheny's leases were at Elk Hills and Buena Vista, California) and even though a jury declared him not guilty of bribery. In spite of his acquittal, his image remains tarnished. The public when it disagrees with a jury's finding can take justice in their own hands by refusing to restore good name and reputation to a defendant. In a measure, this was Doheny's paradoxical fate.

It may be, as I have suggested, that a more balanced picture of Doheny is warranted: that history has done him an injustice by dismissing his achievements and depicting him as motivated only by greed. At the same time, there is merit in the verdict issued by the jury of public opinion that Doheny fell short of the standards expected for greatness.

There were still divergent views about Doheny at his death. His funeral brought mourners who were civic leaders—important figures in the business world, in government, and in the Catholic Church—to a service that lauded Doheny with the highest praise. It is to be expected that a man would be spoken of well at his funeral; but the prestigious people attending also held him in high esteem and believed that he had been wrongly accused in the oil scandal and was the victim of a political and philosophical struggle over natural resources.

There were many contradictions in Edward Doheny's life; the opposing views of his culpability in the matter of the oil leases provide only one example. His story seems to juxtapose two antithetical worldviews: on the one hand, there is the Mexican folk tradition of the *calavera,* the skull or skeleton, representing omniscient, unpredictable, and often malevolent fate; on the other hand, the more northern outlook is characterized by optimism, ambition, and a drive to control events.

Writers have accused Doheny of great misdeeds in Mexico, and he has been transformed in fact and fiction into the archetypal evil Yankee imperialist. Exposés have described him riding roughshod over a simple and naive people, plundering natural resources, and bribing government officials and judges. He has been accused of maintaining a private army, overthrowing Mexican governments, and ordering the assassination of a Mexican president. More recent scholarship, however, argues that Doheny and the other oilmen in Mexico lacked such power. Their political machinations and armed guards were directed at protecting their own oil investments. What they could be accused of was a failure to understand and respect the social heritage of Mexico. The economic miracle that President Díaz hoped to achieve by opening the doors to foreign capital stalled as immense oil profits left the country without making a commensurate contribution to the country's social welfare. Continuing hardship provoked opposition to Díaz and resistance to modernization and progress. Furthermore, as oil dollars rolled in, the displacement of the traditional social order contributed to the unrest that brought on the overthrow of successive governments; no conspiracy on the part of foreign oil barons was needed.

Mexicans had long practice in using ridicule as a means of resisting authoritarian rule, and with their deep-rooted regard for the marvelous and fantastic they saw artist Guadalupe Posada's *calaveras* as expressing their frustration and their suspicion of foreign innovations. The artist staged his famous skeletons in compositions ridiculing and damning Díaz and the headlong rush to modernize. "Progress" came to be viewed as the uninvited and disruptive guest—the skeleton at the feast. But the idea that progress was not necessarily desirable was not a notion that Edward Doheny could accept. Moving what he saw as civilization forward—bringing fuel, energy, transportation, capital, and economic expansion to Mexico—was to him a noble endeavor. Steeped in the can-do spirit of the United States, he came to Mexico full of confidence, certain that he was bringing what Mexico needed, that he would be welcomed, and that he would make a fortune.

As Edward Doheny arrived, Mexico was defining itself, shaking off colonialism, considering what social and economic structures would best serve its needs, picking and choosing from the philosophical, political, and economic theories of Europe and the United States. Mexican artists and writers were turning from the European academy and searching for that which was uniquely expressive of Mexico.

There was a strong component of authoritarianism and paternalism in Mexican tradition. The customs of indigenous peoples, the policies of colonial administrations, and the Catholic Church were fundamental parts of that culture. Successive constitutions reserved natural resources to the state in lieu of private ownership so the government could fulfill traditional obligations to the populace. Abandoning Mexico's long-standing customs and substituting free enterprise could not be accomplished in one swift sweep, no matter how desirous Porfirio Díaz might be to modernize Mexico and to expand the economy, and no matter how eager Edward Doheny and other industrialists might be to help him do so.

There was much about the Mexican psyche that puzzled Doheny, though it is surprising that he was not more instinctively attuned to the Mexican representations of fate. The workings of luck figured often in his own life as prospector, oilman, and capitalist. Doheny, however, felt that it was not luck but merit that brought success. He worked hard and with determination, always with great self-confidence and the belief that good things were in store for him.

When events turned bleak in the course of the conspiracy and bribery trials and public opinion damned him on all sides, he wrote Albert Fall to urge him not to give up. He confided that he was sure divine Providence had an important use for him; and it was that sense of mission, of being anointed, that motivated many of his decisions after he became wealthy. He believed that he had vision that others lacked. Woodrow Wilson did not see the dangers that he did, and so it was up to him to attempt to protect national security and the industrial strength of the nation. To that end he welcomed a conservative president in office in the 1920 elections and looked forward to a business-friendly administration.

When the naval reserve oil leases came under question in 1923, Doheny attributed his part in the affair to patriotism. Though this might not at first seem a credible defense to a charge of fraud and bribery, Doheny's record of concern for the national security, his fears born of Wilson's inaction, and his consciousness of his place in the industrial power structure led him to feel that certain decisions for the good of the country must be made by him. When Admiral Robison confided to him the navy's concern that the United States would be defeated in a war with Japan for want of oil storage at Hawaii, Doheny recognized immediately his duty to provide oil tanks and fill them. The importance of such planning meshed with his own concern for national readiness and addressed the future threat of Asian strength, perceived at the time in starkly racist terms. And as for his being compensated, the navy was awash with oil in underground reserves and he was confident a suitable arrangement could be devised.

The one snag, as it appeared to Doheny, was that conservationists, with no experience of the big picture and of the need for exploiting resources for the economic strength of the nation, were protesting the development of federal lands. These gadflies had the ear of powerful Democrats and were lobbying to stop construction of dams, halt lumbering in national forests, limit grazing on federal lands, and, worst of all, prevent drilling at the oil sites reserved for the navy. Fortunately, the Harding administration now had a secretary of the interior, Albert Fall, who was an enthusiastic advocate for development, and the new secretary of the navy (unlike his predecessor) was receptive to leasing the reserves.

Doheny and Fall had known each other since their prospecting days in Kingston, New Mexico, and although Doheny may have felt the garrulous Fall had his shortcomings, he was glad to see him appointed secretary of the interior. It seemed to Doheny that the country needed men like Fall in office to hold the conservationists in check. If public service was straining Fall financially, Doheny saw nothing wrong with assisting him with a loan. As he had said to the congressional investigating committee, he would be happy to welcome Fall to his employment when Fall left office. (Certainly there were those who believed Doheny would have made the loan to Fall had there been no oil leases involved. To his wife's exasperation, he was known to be generous to the oldtime miners who approached him for help.)

There was still the troubling question, however, of why the money was delivered in cash by so special a courier. Perhaps the transaction was a bribe, or perhaps it wasn't a bribe but the parties feared its being so construed. Or perhaps Doheny's sending his beloved son to deliver the funds to his friend was evidence of the innocence of the gesture. Or perhaps (as the jury found) the act was a bribe in Fall's mind and a compassionate loan in the mind of Edward Doheny.

It is ironic that Doheny, so incapable of grasping the concept of a seignorial system in Mexico and accepting the responsibilities of El Patrón, took on that attitude in regard to his own country's citizens. Acting on his belief that he knew what was best for the country, he subverted the democratic process and the tradition of representative government. In the election of 1920, Doheny like others of his corporate peers was convinced that the national welfare urgently required the presence of men in government devoted to economic expansion and concerned about national security—indeed, that the country would be better off in the hands of businessmen. Doheny perceived it as his responsibility to make decisions for the citizenry. He had been confident that he could impose his will on nature, on Mexican presidents, on the U.S. electorate, and on history itself. It may well be that it was self-importance and patronizing arrogance rather than greed that led to Doheny's downfall.

Edward Doheny may have rejected the Mexican attitude toward fate, but the events of his life proved to be a dark mixture of fortune and oil that led inexorably to tragedy. Whatever Doheny's misdeeds, the murder of his only son and the discrediting of a lifetime of achievement was an exorbitant penalty. Doheny defended his actions to the end of his life, and his family and associates believed that he was innocent of wrongdoing. There is no report of self-blame, or quest for atonement. Bishop Cantwell at the funeral service said that Doheny found repose in his last years and that his Catholic faith was a comfort to him. It is left to others to ponder Doheny's motivations and puzzle out the truth about his actions.

Doheny's story—his individualism and drive coupled with the opportunities afforded by his era both to build and disrupt—comes to us now as a cautionary tale. Developing countries and those revising their economic system look to the U.S. model with anxiety, both eager to follow it and fearful of creating their own Dohenys. His most significant legacy, the modern petroleum industry, is also surrounded by controversy. It has not been the unqualified blessing that Doheny envisioned. As the world faces widespread pollution and international tensions over oil, planners of the postmodern era are more skeptical about the benefits of progress and economic expansion. New generations can evaluate Doheny's contribution and assess his petroleum legacy. We are all Doheny's heirs.

Notes

PROLOGUE

1. *New York Times*, September 9, 1935, p. 1.

2. John J. Cantwell, *Sermon of His Excellency, Most Reverend John J. Cantwell, D.D., at Requiem Mass for Mr. Edward Laurence Doheny, St. Vincent's Church, Sept. 11, 1935* (San Francisco: printed for Estelle Doheny by John Henry Nash, 1935), p. 3. Courtesy of Nicholas A. Curry.

3. Francis C. Kelley, *Tribute by His Excellency, Most Reverend Francis C. Kelley to Mr. Edward Laurence Doheny* (San Francisco: printed for Estelle Doheny by John Henry Nash, 1935), p. 5. Courtesy of Nicholas A. Curry.

CHAPTER I. THE YOUNG PROSPECTOR DOHENY

1. Bertie Forbes, *Men Who Are Making the West* (New York: Forbes Publishing, 1923), p. 107.

2. John L. Doheny was born in either 1849 or 1850, Thomas Doheny was born

in 1854, Ellen ("Ella") was born in 1860, and James Doheny was born in 1863. It is believed that two more children were stillborn; their names and dates of birth are unknown. Extract from 1870 census, p. 10, line 34, June 2, 1870, Fond du Lac, Wis., 4th Ward; also 1860 census, p. 123, line 3, June 25, 1860, Fond du Lac, Wis., 4th Ward. Courtesy of Nicholas A. Curry.

3. *Fond du Lac Commonwealth*, July 6, 1872.

4. *Brigham & Co.'s City Directory, Fond du Lac, Wisconsin, 1857–58* (Fond du Lac: Union Book, 1858), p. 37; *Fond du Lac County Gazetteer* (Fond du Lac: Commonwealth Power Press, 1868), p. 71; *Holland's Fond du Lac City Directory* (Chicago: Western Publishing, 1872), p. 104.

5. The early details from Doheny's life are compiled from Edward Doheny, "How I Made My Millions," *Los Angeles Record*, March 29, 1924, p. 3, and April 1, 1924, p. 4 (in Frank J. Hogan scrapbooks, vol. 2; courtesy of Hogan & Hartson, Washington, D.C.); *The Great Register of Los Angeles County* (Los Angeles: Evening Express, 1892), p. 47; *Who's Who on the Pacific Coast*, ed. Franklin Harper (Los Angeles: Harper Publishing, 1913), p. 163; *Who's Who in the Pacific Southwest* (Los Angeles: Times-Mirror Printing and Binding House, 1913), p. 119; John Steven McGroarty, *Los Angeles: From the Mountains to the Sea* (Chicago: American Historical Society, 1921), 2:10–12; *History of Los Angeles County*, ed. John Steven McGroarty (Chicago: American Historical Society, 1923), 1:59, 437–38; *California of the South*, ed. John Steven McGroarty, vol. 4 (Chicago: S. J. Clarke, 1933), pp. 431–35; *Biographical Dictionary of American Business Leaders*, ed. John N. Ingjam (Westport, Conn.: Greenwood Press, 1948), 1:282–84; *Who's Who in America*, ed. Albert Nelson Marquis (Chicago: A. N. Marquis, 1926), 14:607; *The National Cyclopedia of American Biography* (New York: James T. White, 1930), A:490–500; *Dictionary of American Biography*, ed. Harris E. Starr (New York: Scribner, 1935), 21:254. Also Marco R. Newmark, "Edward L. Doheny," *Historical Society of Southern California Quarterly* 37 (1955): 76–78; Forbes, *Men Who Are Making the West*, pp. 107–19; Ward Ritchie, *The Dohenys of Los Angeles* (Los Angeles: Dawson's Book Shop, 1974); Patrick Doheny, interview with the author, November 15 and December 19, 1996.

6. Grant County, Mining Locations, 3:245–46, Grant County Courthouse, Silver City, New Mexico. See also Martin Ansell, "Such Is Luck: The Mining Career of Edward L. Doheny in Mexico, 1880–1891," *New Mexico Historical Review* 70 (1995): 49.

7. Fritz L. Hoffman, "Edward L. Doheny and the Beginnings of Petroleum Development in Mexico," *Mid-America*, April 1942, p. 95.

8. Grant County, Mining Record of Deeds, 8:399, 10:682; see also Ansell, "Such Is Luck," p. 49.

9. Ansell, "Such Is Luck," p. 50.

10. Caspar Whitney, *Charles Adelbert Canfield* (New York: privately printed, 1930), p. 69. The following descriptions draw on Whitney's account.

11. Quoted in ibid., p. 77.

12. Ibid., p. 68.

13. *Kingston Weekly Shaft*, January 4, 1890. See also Ansell, "Such Is Luck," p. 50. Carrie Louella E. Wilkins was born between the years 1862 and 1864 either in an unknown city in Arizona; in Osawatomie, Kansas; or somewhere in the state of New York. The records conflict regarding her date and place of birth, as well as her ethnicity. Some have speculated that she was a Native American, but no one has produced substantive evidence supporting this claim.

14. Grant County, Marriage Register, 1872–1899, Grant County Courthouse, Silver City, New Mexico. Their residence was indicated in the 1885 New Mexico Territorial Census.

15. *Kingston Weekly Shaft*, November 2, 1889. See also Ansell, "Such Is Luck," p. 57.

16. Quoted in James A. McKenna, *Black Range Tales* (New York: Wilson-Erickson, 1936), p. 116.

17. Whitney, *Canfield*, p. 71.

18. David H. Stratton, introduction to *The Memoirs of Albert Bacon Fall*, ed. Stratton, Southwestern Studies, vol. 4, no. 3 (El Paso: Texas Western Press, 1966), p. 7.

19. Gordon R. Owen, *Two Alberts: Fountain and Fall* (Las Cruces, N.M.: Yucca Tree Press, 1996), p. 239.

20. Ibid., p. 236.

21. Quoted in Martha Fall Bethune, *Race with the Wind: The Personal Life of Albert B. Fall* (El Paso: Complete Print, 1989), pp. 15–16.

22. Ansell, "Such Is Luck," p. 52.

23. Whitney, *Canfield*, pp. 84–86.

24. Ibid., p. 98.

25. *Kingston Weekly Shaft*, December 7, 1889. See also Ansell, "Such Is Luck," p. 56.

26. See *Silver City Enterprise*, ca. 1889–91.

27. *Silver City Enterprise*, February 14, 1890. See also Ansell, "Such Is Luck," p. 59.

28. *Southwest Sentinel*, October 28, 1890.

29. *Silver City Enterprise*, January 23, 1891.

30. Whitney, *Canfield*, p. 101.

31. Ibid., pp. 102, 104.

32. Ibid., p. 107.

CHAPTER 2. HER COLDEST WELCOME

1. Oil had been obtained from surface pools for thousands of years, but underground petroleum was not used until 1859 when the first oil well was drilled

by Edwin L. Drake near Titusville, Pennsylvania. Drake's innovation, plus the invention in the late 1800s of the internal combustion engine, initiated an oil boom that was the beginning of the modern oil industry.

2. Quoted in Bertie Forbes, *Men Who Are Making the West* (New York: Forbes Publishing, 1923), p. 108.

3. Eileen died of heart disease stemming from rheumatism and of a lung infection. Certificate of Death, filed December 15, 1892, County of Los Angeles, Registrar-Recorder, County Clerk's Office.

4. Quoted in Forbes, *Men Who Are Making the West*, p. 110.

5. This and the following description of the incident relies on Helen J. Lundwall, *Pioneering in Territorial Silver City: H. B. Ailman's Recollections of Silver City and the Southwest, 1871–1892* (Albuquerque: University of New Mexico Press, 1983), pp. 103–7, as well as the recollections of Doheny as quoted in the *Los Angeles Times* (ca. 1930; clipping in the Frank J. Hogan scrapbooks, vol. 26; courtesy of Hogan & Hartson, Washington, D.C.). His remarks were made at a ceremony commemorating the thirty-eighth anniversary of the first well drilled in the southland. Charles O. Canfield, son of Charles A. Canfield, was also in attendance.

6. Quoted in Caspar Whitney, *Charles Adelbert Canfield* (New York: privately printed, 1930), p. 151.

7. Lundwall, *Ailman's Recollections*, p. 106.

8. Quoted in Forbes, *Men Who Are Making the West*, p. 111.

9. Carey McWilliams, *Southern California Country: An Island on the Land* (New York: Duell, Sloan, & Pearce, 1946), p. 130.

10. Keith L. Bryant Jr., *History of the Atchison, Topeka, and Santa Fe Railway* (New York: Macmillan, 1974), pp. 362–65. See also Dan La Botz, *Edward L. Doheny: Petroleum, Power, and Politics in the United States and Mexico* (New York: Praeger, 1991), p. 14.

11. La Botz, *Doheny*, p. 14.

12. Whitney, *Canfield*, p. 115.

13. Quoted in ibid., p. 58.

14. *San Francisco Evening Post*, May 30, 1899; cited in Whitney, *Canfield*, p. 125.

15. Whitney, *Canfield*, p. 130.

16. Bryant, *History of the A.T. & S.F.*, pp. 362–63. See also La Botz, *Doheny*, p. 14.

17. Edward L. Doheny to W. G. Nevins, general manager, A.T. & S.F., memorandum, October 24, 1901, Estelle Doheny Collection, Archive of the Archdiocese of Los Angeles, Mission Hills, California, box 1.

CHAPTER 3. RIVERS OF BLACK GOLD

1. In 1876, a Boston ship captain drilled several wells near the Tuxpan River and built a crude refinery, but his efforts ended in disaster and he committed suicide. Later, a British syndicate failed as well.

2. Pan American Petroleum and Transport Company, *Mexican Petroleum* (New York: Pan American Petroleum and Transport Company, 1922), p. 17.

3. Jonathan C. Brown, *Oil and Revolution in Mexico* (Berkeley: University of California Press, 1993), p. 27.

4. Pan American Petroleum, *Mexican Petroleum*, p. 20.

5. Jonathan C. Brown notes the importance of Mexico's social heritage as a factor in managing economic growth: "As a force for change, economic growth posed a serious challenge to a society that had not been accustomed to dividing property strictly according to economic criteria" (*Oil and Revolution*, p. 3).

6. Testimony of Edward L. Doheny, U.S. Congress, Senate Committee on Foreign Relations, *Investigation of Mexican Affairs*, 66th Cong., 1st sess., 1920, 1:212, 218–19, 225; cited in Brown, *Oil and Revolution*, p. 29. Doheny's attorney, Martinez del Rio, also managed to secure for Doheny additional perquisites, including the valuable right to import machinery duty-free for ten years.

7. Díaz was highly suspicious of Rockefeller's business operations, and he wanted Standard Oil to play no role in the future of Mexico's oil industry. Journalist Ida Tarbell would publish her powerful condemnation of Rockefeller in a twenty-four-month series of articles in *McClure's Magazine* beginning in November 1902.

8. Both of Doheny's wives, Carrie Louella Wilkins and Carrie Estelle Betzold, shared the same given name. For obvious reasons, Doheny preferred to call Carrie Betzold "Estelle" and she soon began to refer to herself by that name. After the couple were wed, however, she would occasionally sign her letters "Carrie" when she was angry at Doheny.

9. The City Directory of Marshalltown, Iowa, in 1882 lists John E. Betzold's occupation as a carpenter on the Central Iowa Railroad (a.k.a. Iowa Central Railroad). In 1885 he is listed as a railroad car upholsterer; in 1889, a railroad car inspector. Other biographical sources have stated that Betzold worked as an undertaker, but no evidence supports the claim. See *Tipton and Heald's New City Directory, Marshalltown, Iowa, 1882–3* (Marshalltown: Reflector Steam Printing House, 1882), p. 21; *1884*, p. 27; *1888–9*, p. 26. See also *Mail Carriers' City Directory, Marshalltown, Iowa, 1890* (Marshalltown: Statesman Steam Printing House, 1890), p. 13; *Los Angeles City Directory and Gazetteer of Southern California* (Los Angeles: Geo. W. Maxwell, 1892), p. 130, and subsequent editions: 1893, p. 147; 1894, p. 232; 1895, p. 242; 1896, p. 263.

10. *Maxwell's Los Angeles City Directory and Gazetteer of Southern California* (Los Angeles: Los Angeles Directory Co., 1896), p. 263; see also the 1897 edition, p. 130.

11. Certificate of Marriage, Carrie Estelle Betzold and Edward Laurence Doheny, August 22, 1900, Territory of New Mexico, County of Bernalillo, filed August 25, 1900. Courtesy of Nicholas A. Curry.

12. The Dohenys were wed in Albuquerque, New Mexico Territory, but railroad historian Donald N. Duke has identified the location of the wedding party

photograph as the Las Vegas, Nevada, railyards of the San Pedro to Los Angeles to Salt Lake Railroad (a precursor of the Union Pacific). One newspaper account states that the wedding took place aboard a railcar owned by A. P. Maginnis.

Estelle did not convert to Catholicism until October 1918 at St. Patrick's Cathedral in New York City.

13. Certificate of Death, Carrie Doheny, Register of Deaths, City of Los Angeles, filed September 28, 1900; Return of a Death Index, Albert Brown Mortuary, Oakland, California. Courtesy of Nicholas A. Curry. See also *Husted's Oakland, Alameda, and Berkeley Directory* (Oakland: F. M. Husted, 1901), p. 142.

14. *Oakland Enquirer*, September 27, 1900, p. 2; *San Francisco Chronicle*, October 6, 1900, p.12.

15. *Los Angeles Times*, September 28, 1900, p. 3; *Los Angeles Herald*, September 28, 1900, p. 4; *Los Angeles Evening Express*, September 28, 1900, p. 3; *Oakland Enquirer*, September 27, 1900, p. 2.

16. The April 1906 San Francisco earthquake destroyed many of the region's vital records, including the Dohenys' divorce records.

17. Estelle Doheny to Edward L. Doheny, letter, ca. 1900, Estelle Doheny Collection, Archive of the Archdiocese of Los Angeles, Mission Hills, California (AALA), box 1.

18. Estelle Doheny to Edward L. Doheny, letter, ca. 1900, AALA, box 1.

19. Brown, *Oil and Revolution*, p. 29.

20. Doheny quoted in Pan American Petroleum, *Mexican Petroleum*, p. 33.

21. Reports indicate that Doheny sold or pawned his wife's jewels in the trying days between 1901 and 1904; see Fritz Hoffman's interview with Frank R. Seaver, September 11, 1941, in Hoffman, "Edward L. Doheny and the Beginnings of Petroleum Development in Mexico," *Mid-America*, April 1942, p. 103.

In "Report on Kern Co. Field to W. G. Nevins of Atchison, Topeka, and Santa Fe" (memorandum, ca. 1901, AALA, box 1), Doheny proposed that the rail carrier purchase his 1,537 oil-rich acres with their attendant oil derricks and machinery in addition to 40,000 barrels of oil in storage, valuable water rights, and pending service contracts for a total cost of $1.8 million. See also Hoffman, "Doheny," p. 101.

22. The cities named soon became "the best paved cities in the world," Doheny boasted; see Hoffman, "Doheny," p. 102.

23. Fairchild and Gilmore to Edward L. Doheny, letter, ca. 1901, AALA, box 1.

24. Estelle Doheny to Edward L. Doheny, letter, August 12, 1901, AALA, box 1.

25. Lucille V. Miller, "Edward and Estelle Doheny," *Ventura County Historical Quarterly* 6, no. 1 (1960): 6.

26. Estelle Doheny to Edward L. Doheny, letter, ca. 1901, AALA, box 1.

27. Estelle Doheny to Edward L. Doheny, letter, November 28, 1901, AALA, box 1.

28. Estelle Doheny to Edward L. Doheny, letter, November 29, 1901, AALA, box 1.

29. Edward L. Doheny to Estelle Doheny, telegram, December 1, 1901, and Estelle to Edward, letter, December 7, 1901; both in AALA, box 1.

CHAPTER 4. SPOONY VISITS

1. Edward L. Doheny Jr. (Ned) to Edward L. Doheny Sr., letter, May 14, 1902, Estelle Doheny Collection, Archive of the Archdiocese of Los Angeles, Mission Hills, California (AALA), box 1.

2. Estelle Doheny to Edward L. Doheny, letter, May 17, 1902, AALA, box 1.

3. Estelle Doheny to Edward L. Doheny, letter, August 23, 1902, AALA, box 1.

4. Estelle Doheny to Susan Betzold and Daysie May Anderson, letter, ca. 1902, AALA, box 1.

5. Estelle Doheny to Edward L. Doheny, letter, October 14, 1902, AALA, box 1.

6. Estelle Doheny to Edward L. Doheny, letter, October 28, 1902, AALA, box 1.

7. Together, Doheny and Canfield had invested nearly $3 million in Mexico by 1902; see Dan La Botz, *Edward L. Doheny: Petroleum, Power, and Politics in the United States and Mexico* (New York: Praeger, 1991), p. 30.

8. Quoted in Pan American Petroleum and Transport Company, *Mexican Petroleum* (New York: Pan American Petroleum and Transport Company, 1922), p. 28.

9. Quoted in Fritz L. Hoffman, "Edward L. Doheny and the Beginnings of Petroleum Development in Mexico," *Mid-America*, April 1942, p. 103.

10. Ibid., p. 106.

11. Ezequiel Ordóñez, "El Petróleo en México: Bosquejo Historico," *Revista Mexicana de Ingeniería y Arquetectura* 10, no. 3 (1932): 155–57; quoted in Hoffman, "Doheny," p. 134.

12. Jonathan C. Brown, *Oil and Revolution in Mexico* (Berkeley: University of California Press, 1993), p. 30.

13. Ibid., p. 32.

14. Ibid., p. 36.

15. Ibid., p. 37.

16. Estelle Doheny to Edward L. Doheny, letter, ca. 1905, AALA, box 1.

17. Estelle Doheny to Edward L. Doheny, letter, November 1, 1905, AALA, box 1.

18. Estelle Doheny to Edward L. Doheny, letter, ca. 1905, AALA, box 1.

CHAPTER 5. THE GOLDEN LANE

1. *Los Angeles Times*, January 28, 1906, p. 1.

2. See Alfred Cohn and Joe Chisholm, *"Take the Witness!"* (New York: New

Home Library, 1957), pp. 136–37; *Los Angeles Herald,* January 28, 1906, p. 1; *Los Angeles Times,* January 28, 1906, p. 1.

3. Margaret Leslie Davis, "Prosecuting a Socialite's Killer," *San Francisco Daily Journal,* November 29, 1996, p. 1. See also Cohn and Chisholm, *"Take the Witness!"* pp. 138–40.

4. Morris Buck, Certificate of Death, filed December 7, 1907, County of Marin, San Rafael, California. Courtesy of Nicholas A. Curry. See also *San Francisco Chronicle,* December 7, 1907, p. 2.

5. Rockwell D. Hunt, *California and Californians* (New York: Lewis Publishing, 1926), p. 466.

6. Norman Bridge, *The Marching Years* (New York: Duffield, 1920), p. 217.

7. Ibid., p. 209.

8. Doheny loved his frijoles so much that Estelle instructed Louise, their cook in Los Angeles, to prepare them for each of his noon meals served at Chester Place.

9. Pan American Petroleum and Transport Company, *Mexican Petroleum* (New York: Pan American Petroleum and Transport Company, 1922), p. 29.

10. Edward L. Doheny to Estelle Doheny, letter, December 29, 1906, Estelle Doheny Collection, Archive of the Archdiocese of Los Angeles, Mission Hills, California (AALA), box 1.

11. Jonathan C. Brown, *Oil and Revolution in Mexico* (Berkeley: University of California Press, 1993), pp. 40, 39.

12. Quoted in ibid., p. 39.

13. Dan La Botz, *Edward L. Doheny: Petroleum, Power, and Politics in the United States and Mexico* (New York: Praeger, 1991), p. 32; Gene Z. Hanrahan, *The Bad Yankee–El Peligro Yankee: American Entrepreneurs and Financiers in Mexico* (Chapel Hill, N.C.: Documentary Publications, 1985), 1:7–8.

14. Hanrahan, *The Bad Yankee,* 1:7–8.

15. Brown, *Oil and Revolution in Mexico,* pp. 40, 39.

16. Ruth Sheldon Knowles, *The Greatest Gamblers: The Epic of American Oil Exploration,* 2d ed. (Norman: University of Oklahoma Press, 1978), p. 101.

17. "El Eduardo," like "Toots," was a pet name of Estelle's for Doheny. Edward L. Doheny to Estelle Doheny, letter, May 1, 1910, AALA, box 1.

18. On Trees and Benedum, see *The National Cyclopedia of American Biography* (New York: James T. White, 1945), 32:217; *Who Was Who in America* (Chicago: Marquis Who's Who, 1943–), 2:538; *New York Times,* May 20, 1943, p. 21, and July 31, 1959, p. 23. South Penn was John D. Rockefeller's first entry into the petroleum business as an oil producer, rather than a refiner and marketer. The company later became known as the Pennzoil Corporation.

According to Ruth Sheldon Knowles, the term *wildcat* describes a well drilled in an area where oil has not previously been found; the oil explorer who drills this well is a *wildcatter.* No one is sure where the terms originated. One story claims that in the early days, those working in the hills described themselves as drilling "out among the wildcats." Before the discovery of oil in Pennsylvania by Edwin L. Drake, "the term was used in connection with unsound banking ventures, land booms, and stock schemes. Its usage in the oil business may have begun with these implications of recklessness and risk, but in oil terminology the words never developed questionable or disreputable connotations" (Knowles, *Greatest Gamblers*, p. 101).

19. Pan American Petroleum, *Mexican Petroleum*, p. 31.

20. Quoted in Knowles, *Greatest Gamblers*, p. 103.

21. Sam T. Mallison, *The Great Wildcatter* (Charleston, W.Va.: Education Foundation of West Virginia, 1953), pp. 33–37.

22. Though Posada came to be recognized as a significant Mexican artist, his works at the time were dismissed as political broadsides and black humor. Official art was dominated by standards of the French academy, with its neoclassical emphasis on the beauty of the human body—Posada defied the influence of imported art with his skeletons. Though *calaveras* literally means "skulls," the word came to designate more generally the skeleton figures in Posada's work.

23. Brown, *Oil and Revolution in Mexico*, p. 101.

24. Knowles, *Greatest Gamblers*, p. 103.

25. In *Standard Oil Co. of New Jersey v. United States*, 221 U.S. 1 (1911), the U.S. Supreme Court ordered the dissolution of the Standard Oil Company, ruling that it was in violation of the Sherman Antitrust Act, which prohibited contracts, combinations, or conspiracies "in the restraint of trade or commerce." Under the authority of that act, the federal government initiated suits against the Standard Oil Company and American Tobacco Company.

26. Daniel Yergin, *The Prize: The Epic Quest for Oil, Money, and Power* (New York: Simon & Schuster, 1992), p. 110.

27. Ibid.

28. Pan American Petroleum, *Mexican Petroleum*, p. 35.

29. Yergin, *The Prize*, p. 112.

30. Brown, *Oil and Revolution in Mexico*, p. 54.

CHAPTER 6. POWERED BY OIL

1. Gene Z. Hanrahan, *The Bad Yankee–El Peligro Yankee: American Entrepreneurs and Financiers in Mexico* (Chapel Hill, N.C.: Documentary Publications, 1985), 1:9.

2. Jonathan C. Brown, *Oil and Revolution in Mexico* (Berkeley: University of California Press, 1993), pp. 130–31.

3. Estelle Doheny to Susan Betzold, letter, April 14, 1912, Estelle Doheny Collection, Archive of the Archdiocese of Los Angeles, Mission Hills, California (AALA), box 1.

4. Estelle Doheny to Susan Betzold, letter, April 15, 1912, AALA, box 1.

5. Doheny was a member of the board of directors of Hearst's *Los Angeles Herald.*

6. *Herald Examiner,* April 14, 1962, sec. B, p. 1. Courtesy of the Doheny family.

7. Estelle Doheny to Susan Betzold, letter, April 24, 1912, AALA, box 1.

8. Estelle Doheny to Susan Betzold, letter, ca. 1912, AALA, box 1.

9. Estelle Doheny to Susan Betzold, letter, ca. 1912, AALA, box 1.

10. Estelle Doheny to Susan Betzold and Daysie May Anderson, letter, May 12, 1912, AALA, box 1.

11. Ibid.

12. Estelle Doheny to Daysie May Anderson, letter, May 19, 1912, AALA, box 1.

13. Estelle Doheny to Susan Betzold, letter, May 13, 1912, AALA, box 1.

14. Estelle Doheny to Daysie May Anderson, letter, May 19, 1912, AALA, box 1.

15. Estelle Doheny to Susan Betzold, letter, June 1, 1912, AALA, box 1.

16. Estelle Doheny to Daysie May Anderson and John Crampton Anderson, letter, June 1, 1912, AALA, box 1.

17. Estelle Doheny to Daysie May Anderson, letter, June 12, 1912, AALA, box 1.

18. Estelle Doheny to Susan Betzold and Daysie May Anderson, letter, July 5, 1912, AALA, box 1.

19. Walter W. Jennings, *A Dozen Captains of American Industry* (New York: Vantage Press, 1954), p. 217.

20. Estelle Doheny to Susan Betzold and Daysie May Anderson, letter, July 5, 1912, AALA, box 1.

21. Estelle Doheny to Susan Betzold and Daysie May Anderson, letter, July 5, 1912, AALA, box 1.

22. Estelle Doheny to unknown addressee in care of Daysie May Anderson, letter, August 2, 1912, AALA, box 1.

23. Lucille V. Miller, "Edward and Estelle Doheny," *Ventura County Historical Society Quarterly* 6, no. 1 (1960): 5–6.

24. Estelle Doheny to Edward Doheny, note, ca. 1912–13, AALA, box 1.

25. Ray Stannard Baker, *Woodrow Wilson, Life and Letters,* vol. 4, *President, 1913–1914* (New York: Doubleday, Doran, 1931), p. 247. See also Dan La Botz, *Edward L. Doheny: Petroleum, Power, and Politics in the United States and Mexico* (New York: Praeger, 1991), p. 48.

26. Daniel Yergin, *The Prize: The Epic Quest for Oil, Money, and Power* (New York: Simon & Schuster, 1992), p. 168.

27. Winston S. Churchill, *The World Crisis* (New York: Scribner, 1928), 1:130–36.

28. Yergin, *The Prize,* p. 12.

29. Death Certificate of Charles Adelbert Canfield, filed August 18, 1913, Los Angeles, vol. 89, no. 4313. (The cause of death was listed as angina.)

30. *Los Angeles Times,* August 16, 1919, p. 8.

31. Caspar Whitney, *Charles Adelbert Canfield* (New York: privately printed, 1930), p. 202.

32. *Los Angeles Daily Tribune,* August 16, 1913, p. 7.

33. *Los Angeles Times,* August 16, 1913, p. 8. In addition to his work for MPC, Canfield served as a board member of the American Oilfields Company, California Petroleum Company, Bankers' Oil Company, the Mexican Paving Company, the Mexican National Gas Company, and the Valley Sugar Company. He was director of the Citizen's National Banks of both Los Angeles and Redlands and was director of the Security Savings and Trust of San Diego. He held large blocks of stock in the Rodeo Land and Water Company and was the principal stockholder of the Pacific Wharf Company. He held controlling interests in ten small oil ventures and had accrued substantial stock holdings in the Del Mar Hotel Company. Canfield also owned several thousand acres of land in the San Luis Rey Valley and the San Joaquin Valley, as well as hundreds of acres near the Imperial Valley.

34. Memorial tribute to Charles Canfield, in AALA, box 1.

35. Quoted in La Botz, *Doheny,* p. 50.

CHAPTER 7. MILLIONS MADE KNOWING HOW

1. Wedding journal of Lucy Marceline Smith. Courtesy of the Doheny family.

2. *Los Angeles Evening Herald,* June 10, 1914, p. 16. Details of the wedding are taken from this article and from the wedding journal.

3. Plunkett's father, Charles Albert, was born on July 30, 1867, in Ottawa, Canada, or in Michigan (the records conflict). He worked as a housepainter. Clara Isabel ("Belle") Orchard, Plunkett's mother, was born in Iowa on November 2, 1867, and was a homemaker. The couple had three sons and one daughter. Theodore, their second son, was born in Illinois on March 28, 1895. In Los Angeles the Plunkett family first lived on West 47th Street, and later at 555 East Florence Avenue. Family group record, compiled by Nicholas A. Curry, 1994.

4. U.S. State Department, "Internal Affairs of Mexico," file M274–32, National Archives. See also Dan La Botz, *Edward L. Doheny: Petroleum, Power, and Politics in the United States and Mexico* (New York: Praeger, 1991), p. 52.

5. William Jennings Bryan to Special Agent Silliman, telegram, April 1915; U.S. State Department, "Internal Affairs of Mexico."

6. Edward L. Doheny to Ned Doheny, letter, April 2, 1915, p. 1. Courtesy of the Doheny family. Hereafter, this letter is cited parenthetically in the text.

7. Porfirio Díaz to Edward L. Doheny, letter, undated, Estelle Doheny Collection, Archive of the Archdiocese of Los Angeles, Mission Hills, California (AALA), box 1.

8. Quoted in Pan American Petroleum and Transport Company, *Mexican Petroleum* (New York: Pan American Petroleum and Transport Company, 1922), p. 96.

9. Ibid., p. 98.

10. Ibid., p. 100. This calculation did not take into consideration the large quantities of oil that were carried by winds in form of spray, two miles away.

11. Ibid., p. 108.

12. Quoted in ibid., p. 96.

13. Pershing's attack lasted from March 16, 1916, to February 6, 1917.

14. Quoted in W. A. Swanberg, *Citizen Hearst: A Biography of William Randolph Hearst* (New York: Scribner, 1961), pp. 352–53. See also La Botz, *Doheny*, p. 55.

15. Bernard Baruch, *Baruch: My Own Story* (New York: Henry Holt, 1957), 1:213. See also La Botz, *Doheny*, p. 74.

16. Caspar Whitney, *What's the Matter with Mexico?* (New York: Macmillan, 1916), p. 145.

17. Clarence N. Barron, *They Told Barron: Conversations and Revelations of an American Pepys in Wall Street* (New York: Harper & Brothers, 1930), p. 302.

18. State Department, "Internal Affairs of Mexico." See also La Botz, *Doheny*, pp. 52, 59–60.

19. Friedrich Katz, *The Secret War in Mexico: Europe, the United States, and the Mexican Revolution* (Chicago: University of Chicago, 1981), p. 500. See also La Botz, *Doheny*, p. 60.

20. State Department, "Internal Affairs of Mexico." See also La Botz, *Doheny*, p. 63.

21. La Botz, *Doheny*, p. 65.

22. M. R. Werner and John Starr, *Teapot Dome* (New York: Viking Press, 1959), p. 42. See also testimony of Admiral John K. Robison to the Senate Committee on Public Lands and Surveys, *Leases upon Naval Oil Reserves: Hearings before the Committee on Public Lands and Surveys*, 68th Cong., 1st sess., October 22, 1923–May 14, 1924, and during the subsequent legal actions taken by the United States against Pan American Petroleum.

23. Frank Simpson Jr. to Mr. and Mrs. Frank Simpson Sr., letter, May 31, 1917. Courtesy of Norman Marshall, Esq.

24. Record of Officers, U.S. Navy, National Personnel Records, statement of service of Edward L. Doheny Jr., Records Center (Military Records), GSA, 9700 Page Blvd., St. Louis, Mo.

25. *Pan American Record*, January 1918, p. 5. See also La Botz, *Doheny*, p. 72.

26. *Gulf Coast Oil News*, August 25, 1917, p. 22.

27. *Gulf Coast Oil News*, May 26, 1917, p. 19. See also La Botz, *Doheny*, p. 72.

28. *Pan American Record*, November 1917, p. 5.

29. Katz, *Secret War in Mexico*, p. 312. See also La Botz, *Doheny*, p. 75.

30. *New York Times,* March 7, 1937, p. 1.

31. E. Digby Baltzell, *The Protestant Establishment: Aristocracy and Caste in America* (New York: Random House, 1964), p. 74.

32. Francis J. Weber, *Southern California's First Family: The Dohenys of Los Angeles* (Fullerton, Calif.: Lorson's Books and Prints, 1993), p. 8.

33. La Botz, *Doheny,* p. 78.

34. The ranch was located on the western slopes of Sierra Blanca, a few miles north of Tularosa and a hundred miles north of El Paso. Fall's obsession with the verdant ranchland would eventually help bring about his downfall.

35. Fall had served in both houses of New Mexico's territorial legislature; he had been appointed an associate justice of the New Mexico Supreme Court in 1893 by Democratic President Grover Cleveland. Later he briefly served as territorial general. In 1910 Fall was selected as a delegate to the convention that produced New Mexico's state constitution, and in 1912 he was elected U.S. senator from New Mexico. See David H. Stratton, "New Mexico Machiavellian? The Story of Albert Bacon Fall," *Montana, the Magazine of Western History* 7 (October 1957): 2–14, which cites the label "political boss"; C. L. Sonnichsen, *Tularosa: Last of the Frontier West* (1960; reprint, Albuquerque: University of New Mexico Press, 1980), pp. 68–78, 259–65.

36. Katz, *Secret War in Mexico,* p. 578.

37. Carleton Beals, *Glass Houses: Ten Years of Free-Lancing* (Philadelphia: J. B. Lippincott, 1938), p. 72. See also La Botz, *Doheny,* p. 80.

CHAPTER 8. PERFECTLY LEGAL

1. Francis X. Busch, *Enemies of the State* (New York: Bobbs-Merrill, 1962), p. 93.

2. Quoted in ibid.

3. Hughes resigned as associate justice of the U.S. Supreme Court to make an unsuccessful bid for the presidency in 1916. After serving as secretary of state from 1921 to 1925, he returned to the Court as chief justice (1930–41).

4. M. R. Werner and John Starr, *Teapot Dome* (New York: Viking Press, 1959), pp. 28–29.

5. Edward L. Doheny to Albert B. Fall, telegram, March 6, 1921, Albert B. Fall Papers, Manuscript Collection 8, Rio Grande Historical Collections, University Library, New Mexico State University, Las Cruces (RGHC).

6. Quoted in Werner and Starr, *Teapot Dome,* p. 29.

7. According to historians M. R. Werner and John Starr, Edward Doheny was at one point considered for the nomination for vice president of the United States (*Teapot Dome,* p. 26).

8. Edward L. Doheny to Albert B. Fall, letter, ca. 1921, RGHC.

9. Frederick Lewis Allen, *Only Yesterday* (New York: Harper, 1959), p. 164.

10. Daniel Yergin, *The Prize: The Epic Quest for Oil, Money, and Power* (New York: Simon & Schuster, 1992), p. 209.

11. Ibid., p. 218.

12. President William Howard Taft had first set aside public lands for the navy's use with the Withdrawal Act of 1909 and the Picket Act of 1910. Later, in 1912, he set aside federal naval oil reserves at Elk Hills and Buena Vista, California. On April 30, 1915, the Wilson administration created Naval Reserve No. 3 at Teapot Dome. The naval reserves not only conserved petroleum for use by the navy but were intended to insulate the government from rapid price changes.

13. Quoted in Burl Noggle, *Teapot Dome: Oil and Politics in the 1920's* (New York: Norton, 1962), p. 17.

14. Quoted in Werner and Starr, *Teapot Dome*, p. 41.

15. C. L. Sonnichsen, *Tularosa: Last of the Frontier West* (1960; reprint, Albuquerque: University of New Mexico Press, 1980), p. 266; see also Geoffrey Perrett, *America in the Twenties* (New York: Simon & Schuster, 1982), p. 139; Gordon R. Owen, *Two Alberts: Fountain and Fall* (Las Cruces, N.M.: Yucca Tree Press, 1996), p. 422.

16. The June 4, 1920, act was a provision in the naval appropriation bill that directed the secretary of the navy to take possession of all naval reserve lands on which there were no pending claims or applications for permits under the general leasing law and "to conserve, develop, use and operate the same in his discretion, directly or by contract, lease or otherwise and use, store, exchange or sell the oil and gas products thereof, and those from all royalty oil farmlands in the naval reserves for the benefit of the United States." According to Werner and Starr (*Teapot Dome*, p. 46), news of the Executive Order was buried in the inside pages of a few newspapers and the text was not published in full. The *Washington Evening Star* had a seven-line story about it on the second page, which was seen by Senator Robert La Follette and Harry A. Slattery.

17. "Fall's Own Story of the Oil Leasing Scandal," *Los Angeles Times*, July 19, 1931, p. 1. This was the fifth of fifteen articles written in collaboration with Magner White and syndicated in newspapers throughout the United States in which Fall told the story of his experiences in Washington.

18. Quoted in Werner and Starr, *Teapot Dome*, pp. 46–47. See also Owen, *Two Alberts*, p. 422.

19. Noggle, *Teapot Dome*, p. 16.

20. Ibid., p. 19. Albert Fall did serve in the Spanish-American War, but he was never dispatched to Cuba.

21. Ibid.

22. Estelle Doheny to Albert B. Fall, letter, June 12, 1921, RGHC.

23. The Dohenys to Albert B. Fall, telegram, July 26, 1921, RGHC.

24. "Doheny Tells His Story of Oil Leases; Breaks Silence Despite His Counsel Insisting That Public Hear Truth," *New York Times*, July 1, 1925, p. 14.

25. Albert B. Fall to James Weeks, letter, November 10, 1921, RGHC.

26. Edward L. Doheny to Albert B. Fall, letter, November 22, 1921, RGHC.

27. Albert B. Fall to Edward L. Doheny, note, November 23, 1921, RGHC.

28. *New York Times*, July 1, 1925, p. 14.

29. Pinchot mentioned Fall's dislike of the Forest Service in a speech at the American Society of Newspaper editors, reported in the *New York Times*, April 25, 1924, p. 4. See also Noggle, *Teapot Dome*, p. 25.

30. David H. Stratton, introduction to *The Memoirs of Albert Bacon Fall*, ed. Stratton, Southwestern Studies, vol. 4, no. 3 (El Paso, Tex.: Texas Western Press, 1966), p. 7.

31. Ibid.

32. Quoted in Noggle, *Teapot Dome*, p. 26.

33. *New York Times*, March 7, 1922, p. 2. See also Noggle, *Teapot Dome*, p. 28.

34. Noggle, *Teapot Dome*, p. 29.

CHAPTER 9. THE $100,000 BAGATELLE

1. This account of events is taken from the testimony of Edward L. Doheny, Senate Committee on Public Lands and Surveys, *Leases upon Naval Oil Reserves: Hearings before the Committee on Public Lands and Surveys*, 68th Cong., 1st sess., January 24, 1924, 2:1771–75, 1778–79, 1795–97, 1800, as well as his testimony in the associated cases of *United States v. Pan American, United States v. Fall and Doheny*, and *United States v. Doheny* (1924–30). Much of the voluminous trial record can be found in the Albert Bacon Fall Papers, Center for Southwest Research, Archive 131, boxes 1–3, 12–16, University of New Mexico, Albuquerque. See also clippings and notes from the Frank J. Hogan scrapbooks; courtesy of Hogan & Hartson, Washington, D.C.

2. The list of the partial annual production of Doheny's Mexican wells in 1921 demonstrates the enormous profits he was enjoying: Cerro Azul No. 3, 30,000 barrels; Cerro Azul No. 7, 75,000; Tierra Blanca No. 1, 75,000; Cerro Azul No. 9, 100,000; Cerro Azul No. 8, 100,000; Cerro Azul No. 11, 100,000; Cerro Viejo No. 3, 40,000; Cerro Azul No. 12, 25,000; Cerro Azul No. 10, 25,000; Cerro Azul No. 15, 75,000; Cerro Azul No. 16, 25,000; Cerro Azul No. 14, 20,000. Pan American Petroleum and Transport Company, *Mexican Petroleum* (New York: Pan American Petroleum and Transport Company, 1922), pp. 57, 107; see also Fritz L. Hoffman, "Edward L. Doheny and the Beginnings of Petroleum Development in Mexico," *Mid-America*, April 1942, p. 107.

3. Doheny oil storage and distribution stations were located in Portland, Maine; Boston and Fall River, Massachusetts; Providence, Rhode Island; the

ports of Carteret and Passaic, New Jersey; Baltimore, Maryland; Norfolk, Virginia; Jacksonville and Tampa, Florida; New Orleans and Franklin, Louisiana; Galveston, Texas; Cristobal in the Canal Zone; Para, Pernambuco, Bahia, Rio de Janeiro, and Santos, Brazil; Montevideo, Uruguay; Buenos Aires, Argentina; and Southampton, Liverpool, Avonmouth, South Shields, and Glasgow, Great Britain.

4. This conversation, and the following account, was as told by Doheny in an interview with the *New York Times* (July 1, 1925, p. 1) and in his testimony under oath during subsequent criminal and civil trials.

5. Stoddard warned, "Thus the colored world, long restive under white political domination, is being welded by the most fundamental of instincts, the instinct of self-preservation, into a common solidarity of feeling against the dominant white man." And Grant declared bluntly, "Democratic ideals among an homogeneous population of Nordic blood, as in England or America, is one thing, but it is quite another for the white man to share his blood with, or trust his ideals to, brown, yellow, black or red men. This is suicide pure and simple, and the first victim of this amazing folly will be the white man himself." Lothrop Stoddard, *The Rising Tide of Color against White World-Supremacy* (New York: Scribner, 1920), p. 9; Madison Grant, introduction to *The Rising Tide of Color*, p. xxxii.

6. The ubiquity in the 1920s of the topic of racial peril is clear from F. Scott Fitzgerald's mocking reference in *The Great Gatsby*, as a wealthy host holds forth on the decline of civilization and recommends to his guests "'The Rise of the Colored Empires' by this man Goddard" (*The Great Gatsby* [New York: Scribner, 1925], p. 13).

7. On February 28, 1922, Sinclair created the Mammoth Oil Company of Delaware for the express purpose of executing the lease agreement for Teapot Dome.

8. H. Foster Bain to Secretary Finney, memorandum, April 17, 1922, Rio Grande Historical Collections, University Library, New Mexico State University, Las Cruces (RGHC). At the request of the government, Doheny had already engaged in a small leasehold at Elk Hills during the previous year.

9. According to Doheny's defense attorney Frank Hogan, this telegraphic correspondence disappeared mysteriously during the subsequent investigation of the Senate Committee on Public Lands and Survey in late 1923 and early 1924. The telegrams resurfaced only when Hogan traced copies to the office of the controller general of the United States in the Treasury Department, where they were found attached to the bills of the Western Union Telegraph Company rendered to the government for their transmittal. They were printed in their entirety in *New York Times*, July 1, 1925, p. 15.

10. A second Pearl Harbor contract was executed on December 11, 1922; its provisions concerned, among other services, storage of 270 million barrels of

oil, including lubricating oils, diesel oils, and aviation gasoline for naval airplanes.

11. Francis X. Busch, *Enemies of the State* (New York: Bobbs-Merrill, 1962), p. 101.

12. Ibid., p. 96.

13. *Congressional Record*, 67th Cong., 2d sess., April 12, 1922, 5567–68.

14. Department of Interior memorandum, April 19, 1922, RGHC.

15. President Harding, Letter of Transmittal, June 7, 1922, to Senate Committee on Public Lands and Surveys, *Lease upon Naval Oil Reserves*, 67th Cong., 2d sess., 1922.

16. Quoted in Noggle, *Teapot Dome*, p. 39.

17. Quoted in David H. Stratton, "Behind Teapot Dome: Some Personal Insights," *Business History Review* 31 (1957): 389. See also Burl Noggle, *Teapot Dome: Oil and Politics in the 1920's* (New York: Norton, 1962), p. 53.

18. Quoted in Noggle, *Teapot Dome*, p. 56.

19. William Allen White, *Masks in a Pageant* (New York: Macmillan, 1928), p. 425. See also Noggle, *Teapot Dome*, p. 56.

20. William Allen White, *The Autobiography of William Allen White* (New York: Macmillan, 1946), pp. 623–24. See also Noggle, *Teapot Dome*, p. 58.

21. Busch, *Enemies of the State*, p. 97.

22. Noggle, *Teapot Dome*, p. 20, n. 13.

23. The account given here and following, unless otherwise specified, is taken from the committee record: Senate Committee on Public Lands and Surveys, *Leases upon Naval Oil Reserves: Hearings before the Committee on Public Lands and Surveys*, 68th Cong., 1st sess., October 24, 1923–May 14, 1924.

24. In fact, as described above, Sinclair sent various livestock worth $1,400. Fall paid Sinclair $1,100 for the stock and Sinclair paid the $800 for freight charges from New Jersey to New Mexico.

25. Albert B. Fall and Magner White, "Fall's Own Story of the Oil Leasing Scandal," *Los Angeles Times*, July 19, 1931, pt. 1, p. 1. See also "Fall Gives Background of Oil Reserve Leases," *Los Angeles Times*, July 20, 1931, pt. 1, p. 4.

26. William Hard, "Oil Speaks," *Nation*, February 6, 1924; from Hogan scrapbooks, vol. 3.

27. Quoted in M. R. Werner and John Starr, *Teapot Dome* (New York: Viking Press, 1959), p. 145.

28. Doheny's various oil companies had removed some 100,000 barrels of oil daily from Mexico. In combination with non-Mexico derived oil, these production values for 1923 totaled 40 million barrels of oil.

29. Pan American Petroleum and Transport Company, *1923 Annual Report*. Courtesy of the Doheny family.

30. *New York Times*, February 17, 1924, sec. 2, p. 1.

31. *New York Times*, July 1, 1925, p. 1.

CHAPTER 10. GAPS IN THE RECORD

1. "Sinister Shadows behind the Oil Scandal," *Literary Digest*, March 1, 1924, p. 44.

2. Henry O'Melveny, diary, August 6, 1924, Papers of Henry O'Melveny, Huntington Library, San Marino, California.

3. William W. Clary, *History of the Law Firm of O'Melveny and Meyers: 1885–1965* (Pasadena: Castle Press, 1966), 1:351.

4. O'Melveny diary, August 7, 1924.

5. O'Melveny diary, August 11, 1924.

6. O'Melveny diary, August 28, 1924.

7. Edward L. Doheny to Albert B. Fall, letter, September 4, 1924, Albert B. Fall Papers, Manuscript Collection 8, Rio Grande Historical Collections, University Library, New Mexico State University, Las Cruces (RGHC).

8. Ibid.

9. Ibid.

10. O'Melveny diary, September 9, 1924.

11. Quoted in Clary, *O'Melveny and Meyers*, 1:351.

12. "Sinister Shadows behind the Oil Scandal," p. 44.

13. *New York Times*, September 29, 1924, p. 1.

14. Lester Cohen, *Frank Hogan Remembered* (Washington, D.C.: Hogan & Hartson, 1985), p. 6. Courtesy of Hogan & Hartson, Washington, D.C.

15. O'Melveny diary, October 16, 1942.

16. *Los Angeles Examiner*, October 27, 1924; in Frank J. Hogan scrapbooks, clippings, ca. 1924, vol. 5. Courtesy of Hogan & Hartson, Washington, D.C.

17. Albert W. Fox, "Presenting the Truth about the Oil Cases," *Washington Post Magazine*, May 10, 1925, p. 1; in Hogan scrapbooks, clippings, ca. 1925, vol. 8.

18. O'Melveny diary, October 19, 1924.

19. Cohen, *Frank Hogan Remembered*, p. 15.

20. Hogan scrapbooks, clippings, ca. 1924, vol. 5.

21. Much of the trial is summarized in the appellate record (1924–27): see *United States v. Pan Am. Petroleum Co.*, 6 F.2d 43 (S.D. Cal. 1925); *aff'd in part, rev'd in part, and remanded, Pan Am. Petroleum Co. v. United States*, 9 F.2d 761 (9th Cir. 1926); *cert. granted, Pan Am. Petroleum & Transp. Co. v. United States*, 170 U.S. 640 (U.S. Cal. 1926), *aff'd Pan Am. Petroleum & Transp. Co. v. United States*, 273 U.S. 465 (U.S. Cal. 1927). The testimony that follows, unless otherwise indicated, is from the trial record of *United States v. Pan Am. Petroleum & Transp. Co.*, 6 F.2d 43 (D.C. Cal. 1925), Hogan scrapbooks, ca. 1924, vols. 5–8. See also Albert Bacon Fall Papers, Center for Southwest Research, Archive 131, boxes 3, 12, 13, 14, 15, University of New Mexico, Albuquerque; Hogan scrapbooks, ca. 1924, vol. 5.

22. M. R. Werner and John Starr, *Teapot Dome* (New York: Viking Press, 1959), p. 198.

23. Henry O'Melveny to Samuel F. Pyror (director of Shell Union Oil Corporation), letter, November 8, 1923, papers of Henry O'Melveny.

24. O'Melveny diary, November 19, 1923.

25. Cecil DeMille, *The Autobiography of Cecil B. DeMille* (Englewood Cliffs, N.J.: Prentice-Hall, 1959), pp. 318–20.

26. David H. Stratton, introduction to *The Memoirs of Albert Bacon Fall*, ed. Stratton, Southwestern Studies vol. 4, no. 3 (El Paso: Texas Western Press, 1966), p. 9.

27. In one undated letter from B. C. Forbes to Doheny, Forbes expresses thanks for Doheny's loan of $10,000, which enabled him to launch his successful magazine enterprise. Estelle Doheny Collection, Archive of the Archdiocese of Los Angeles, Mission Hills, California, box 2.

28. Albert Fall, Edward Doheny, and Mark Thompson, letters, ca. 1924, RGHC.

29. Ruth Powell and Chuck Powell, *Chester Place*, Historical Society of Southern California and Southern California Chapter of the American Institute of Architects (Los Angeles: R. & C. Powell, 1964), p. 13.

30. "Doheny Oil Interests Enter San Francisco," *San Francisco Chronicle*, December 4, 1924, p. 1.

31. Francis J. Weber, *Southern California's First Family: The Dohenys of Los Angeles* (Fullerton, Calif.: Lorson's Books and Prints, 1993), p. 111.

32. Among the twelve apostles of the reredos of the main altar was Saint Edward, who closely resembled Doheny; ibid., p. 105.

33. The amount of money Doheny received in the sale was not made public; but, based on prices quoted in the open market, Doheny's 501,000 shares of voting stock were valued at approximately $38 million. However, Doheny told reporters at the *New York Times* that his own personal financial interest from the transaction would total nearly $50 million in cash (*New York Times*, March 11, 1925; April 2, 1925; from Hogan scrapbooks, ca. 1925, vol. 8).

34. *New York Times*, April 2, 1925, p. 1; *Washington Post*, April 2, 1925, p. 1. See also "From Jobbership to Integration," *National Petroleum News*, August 25, 1954, pp. 31–34. Following Doheny's announcement, a new directorate for Pan American Petroleum was created. Frederick H. Rickett (formerly president of Dixie Oil Company) was appointed chairman of the board; Herbert G. Wylie remained company president.

35. Paul H. Giddens, *Standard Oil Company (Indiana): Oil Pioneer of the Middle West* (New York: Appleton-Century-Crofts, 1955), p. 244.

36. As quoted in *Literary Digest*, April 25, 1925; Hogan scrapbooks, ca. 1925, vol. 8.

37. Ibid.

38. Fritz L. Hoffman, "Edward L. Doheny and the Beginnings of Petroleum Development in Mexico," *Mid-America*, April 1942, p. 107; *Chicago Journal of Commerce*, April 2, 1925; *Oil and Gas Journal*, April 2, 1925, p. 23, and April 9, 1925, p. 142.

39. *United States v. Pan Am. Petroleum & Trans. Co.*, 6 F.2d 43, 62 (S.D. Cal. 1925).

40. *Washington Post*, May 10, 1925; from Hogan scrapbooks, ca. 1925, vol. 8.

41. *United States v. Mammoth Oil Co.*, 5 F.2d 330, 354 (D.Wyo. 1925).

42. *United States v. Mammoth Oil Co.*, 14 F.2d 705, 733 (8th Cir. 1926).

43. Doheny sent copies of these telegrams to Fall; see Edward L. Doheny to Albert Fall, letter, July 2, 1925, RGHC.

44. Ibid.

45. Edward L. Doheny to Albert Fall, letter, November 24, 1925, RGHC.

46. Frank Hogan to Albert Fall, letter, December 23, 1925, RGHC.

47. Frank Hogan to Albert Fall, letter, January 4, 1926, RGHC.

48. O'Melveny diary, January 4, 1926.

49. Edward L. Doheny to Albert Fall, letter, February 17, 1926, RGHC.

50. O'Melveny diary, March 22, 1926.

CHAPTER 11. SCARED RICH MAN

1. Lester Cohen, *Frank Hogan Remembered* (Washington, D.C.: Hogan & Hartson, 1985), p. 41.

2. Unless otherwise indicated, testimony is taken from the trial of *United States v. Fall and Doheny* (D.C. 1926). Much of the trial transcript can be found in the Albert Bacon Fall Papers, Center for Southwest Research, Archive 131, boxes 12–15, University of New Mexico, Albuquerque. See also Frank J. Hogan scrapbooks, ca. 1926, vols. 19 and 20; courtesy of Hogan & Hartson, Washington, D.C.

3. Francis X. Busch, *Enemies of the State* (New York: Bobbs-Merrill, 1962), p. 124.

4. Doheny's statement was essentially true; the federal reserve system of banking protections that now safeguard depositors' savings had not yet been implemented, and a series of bank failures in the region and increasing lack of confidence in the New Mexico territorial banking system had prompted many businessmen to trade only in cash.

5. Unidentified clipping, Hogan scrapbooks, ca. 1926, vol. 19.

6. Busch, *Enemies of the State*, p. 141.

7. M. R. Werner and John Starr, *Teapot Dome* (New York: Viking Press, 1959), p. 221.

8. Unidentified clippings, Hogan scrapbooks, ca. 1926, vol. 23; *Washington Post*, December 22, 1926, p. 1.

9. *Los Angeles Evening Express*, December 21, 1926, p. 1.

10. Speech of Frank Hogan, "Appreciation Banquet" given by the Breakfast Club in honor of Edward L. Doheny, January 10, 1927, Biltmore Hotel, Los Angeles; Hogan scrapbooks, ca. 1927, vol. 23. See also *Evening Herald*, January 11, 1927; *Los Angeles Examiner*, January 11, 1927.

11. Henry Withey and Elsie Rathburn Withey, *Biographical Dictionary of American Architects* (Los Angeles: Hennessey & Ingalis, 1970), p. 322.

12. Wallace Neff Jr., interview with author, October 17, 1996, Newport Beach, Calif. See also Charles Lockwood, *Dream Palaces: Hollywood at Home* (New York: Viking Press, 1981), p. 218.

13. Lockwood, *Dream Palaces*, p. 14.

14. Ibid., p. 11.

15. Charles Lockwood and Peter V. Persic, "Greystone Historical Report," submitted to the City Council of Beverly Hills, August 30, 1984. Courtesy of Mr. Lockwood. According to Lockwood, Thiene's principal designer was Emile Kuehl, who spent the "better part of three and one half years" on the project. Kuehl was given a free hand in designing the lavish gardens and "the sky was the limit."

16. The Greystone mansion was reportedly the model for the Sternwood mansion in Raymond Chandler's *The Big Sleep* and was also said to make an appearance in *Farewell, My Lovely:* "The house itself was not so much. It was smaller than Buckingham Palace, rather gray for California, and probably had fewer windows than the Chrysler building" (quoted in Elizabeth Ward and Alain Silver, eds., *Raymond Chandler's Los Angeles* [Woodstock, N.Y.: Overlook Press, 1987], pp. 1–3). See also "Literary L.A.," *San Diego Magazine*, January 1979, p. 90.

17. When the young couple moved into Greystone, Ned owned a Packard sedan, a Dodge sport sedan, a Ford coupe, a Graham truck, a Lincoln touring car, and a brand-new 1929 Packard limousine. He also owned a Buick, a Zephyr, and two Cadillacs. Probate File of Edward Laurence Doheny Jr., Los Angeles Superior Court Archives, March 22, 1929, File No. 101995.

18. Timothy Doheny described the house to Charles Lockwood; see Lockwood and Persic, "Greystone Historical Report."

CHAPTER 12. THE LAST APPEAL

1. *United States v. Pan Am. Petroleum & Trans. Co.*, 273 U.S. 456, 497–98 (1927).

2. William W. Clary, *History of the Law Firm of O'Melveny and Meyers: 1885–1965* (Pasadena, Calif.: Castle Press, 1966), 1:354.

3. See clippings in Frank J. Hogan scrapbooks, ca. 1927–29, vols. 27–29. Courtesy of Hogan & Hartson, Washington, D.C.

4. The legal term to describe the quashing of the indictments is "nolle processing," which is defined by *Black's Law Dictionary* (5th ed. 1979) as a "formal entry on the record by the prosecuting officer by which he declares that he will not prosecute the case further" (s.v.).

5. Hogan scrapbooks, ca. 1927–28, vols. 14–16.

6. *Time*, April 30, 1928; in Hogan scrapbooks, vol. 29.

7. Marian Plunkett was granted a divorce by Los Angeles Municipal Judge Walter Guerin in October 1928 on grounds of desertion; they had no children. Divorce file of Theodore Hugh Plunkett, Los Angeles Superior Court Archives, File No. D68049.

8. Charles Lockwood, *Dream Palaces: Hollywood at Home* (New York: Viking Press, 1981), p. 215. The calculation was made by Aaron Yelowitz, professor of economics, UCLA; see Anna Marie Stolley, "Haunted House," *Los Angeles Times*, November 17, 1995, Westside weekly supplement, p. 13.

9. Charles Lockwood and Peter V. Persic, "Greystone Historical Report," submitted to the City Council of Beverly Hills, August 30, 1984. Courtesy of Mr. Lockwood.

10. Hogan scrapbooks, ca. 1929, vol. 34.

11. *New York Times*, November 13, 1928, p. 40.

12. *Los Angeles Times*, September 9, 1931, p. 1.

CHAPTER 13. NIGHT OF TERROR

1. The reconstruction of the events of that day, and of the months preceding it, is based on Beverly Hills Police Department Homicide File, Case No. 599, obtained through the California Public Records Act; Leslie T. White, *Me, Detective* (New York: Harcourt, 1936), pp. 106–14; and the scrapbooks and diary of Frank J. Hogan and Henry O'Melveny. See Henry O'Melveny, diary, Papers of Henry O'Melveny, Huntington Library, San Marino, California; Frank J. Hogan scrapbooks, ca. 1929, vol. 34 (courtesy of Hogan & Hartson, Washington, D.C.). See also Certificate of Death, Edward L. Doheny Jr., County of Los Angeles, filed March 11, 1929; Probate File, Edward L. Doheny Jr., File No. 101995, County of Los Angeles, filed March 21, 1929.

2. The homicide of Edward Doheny Jr. was said to be the first murder in the new city of Beverly Hills, and officials from the Los Angeles police force and the district attorney's office were asked to handle the sensitive case.

3. White, *Me, Detective*, pp. 109–10.

4. Ibid., p. 113.

5. Ibid., p. 112.

6. Plunkett's probate file (Los Angeles Superior Court Archives, File No. 102684, County of Los Angeles, filed April 24, 1929) contains various unpaid bills to doctors as well as dentists, and the dates of his appointments coincide with those given in Fishbaugh's statement to police.

7. "No Inquest on Doheny," *Los Angeles Times*, February 18, 1929, pt. 1, p. 1; Hogan scrapbooks, vol. 34; Coroner's Report, Edward L. Doheny Jr., Los Angeles

County, February 18, 1929, CC #29-285 (obtained under California Public Records Act). See also Certificate of Death, Theodore Hugh Plunkett, County of Los Angeles, filed February 21, 1929.

8. *Los Angeles Times*, February 20, 1929, pt. 2, p. 1.

9. Francis J. Weber, *Southern California's First Family: The Dohenys of Los Angeles* (Fullerton, Calif.: Lorson's Books and Prints, 1993), p. 106.

10. *Los Angeles Examiner*, February 20, 1929; in Hogan scrapbooks, ca. 1929, vol. 34.

11. *Los Angeles Times*, February 20, 1929, pt. 1, p. 22, and February 21, 1929, pt. 2, p. 1.

12. *Los Angeles Times*, February 21, 1929, pt. 2, p. 3.

13. Hogan scrapbooks, ca. 1929, vol. 34.

14. Ibid.

15. *Los Angeles Times*, February 18, 1929, p. 1.

16. Hogan scrapbooks, ca. 1929, vol. 34.

17. Probate file of Theodore Hugh Plunkett.

18. Newspaper articles ca. February 1929; in Hogan scrapbook, vol. 34. Veronal was highly addictive and freely available for sale over the counter at any pharmacy. It was known by police for its widespread use among addicts hooked on morphine, cocaine, and heroin when they were unable to obtain those drugs.

19. Dan La Botz, *Edward L. Doheny: Petroleum, Power, and Politics in the United States and Mexico* (New York: Praeger, 1991), p. 173.

20. The five individuals involved were Harry F. Sinclair, Col. Robert W. Stewart, Henry M. Blackmer, James E. O'Neil, and Toronto-based attorney H. M. Osler, who reportedly collectively defrauded their own respective companies and stockholders in a scheme to enrich themselves in a multimillion-dollar oil scam.

21. Hogan scrapbooks, ca. 1929, vol. 36.

CHAPTER 14. A BROKEN AND CHANGED MAN

1. The site was also believed to be an ancient burial ground, and UCLA archaeologists who unearthed an ancient cemetery in 1976 believed that the region was once the home of the lost Chumash village of Mupu. See Nikki Batalis, "Enchanted Ranch: Behind the Gate Was Another World," *Vista Magazine* (Ventura County Star-Free Press), December 14, 1986, p. 19.

2. Edward L. Doheny to Albert B. Fall, letter, May 28, 1929, Albert B. Fall Papers, Manuscript Collection 8, Rio Grande Historical Collections, University Library, New Mexico State University, Las Cruces (RGHC).

3. *Los Angeles Times*, September 27, 1929, pt. 2, p. 9.

4. Gravamen of offense of bribery is acceptance by an officer of the United States of a bribe to influence official conduct; Cr. Code §117 (18 U.S.C.A. §207).

5. Francis X. Busch, *Enemies of the State* (New York: Bobbs-Merrill, 1962), p. 163.

6. Testimony is taken from the trial transcripts of *United States v. Fall*, in Albert Bacon Fall Papers, Center for Southwest Research, Archive 131, boxes 12–13, University of New Mexico, Albuquerque. Much of the trial record is summarized in the appellate record: *Fall v. United States*, 49 F.2d 506 (D.C. Cir. 1931), *cert. denied*, 283 U.S. 867 (1931).

7. *Time*, November 5, 1929, p. 12.

8. Unsigned affidavit drafted by Wilton J. Lambert, November 1929, mailed on November 5, 1929, to Mrs. Albert B. Fall. The envelope also contained a draft of an affidavit to be signed by Mrs. Fall that read in part, "The twelfth and last [juror] to come over to the eleven for conviction came to me in tears three days later, a most pathetic picture of remorse, begging forgiveness. He had not slept, had walked the floor since his awful mistake, praying for God to forgive his weakness. We are going to use every honorable means within our power to remove from a clean name valued by us more than all the gold in the world the stain that has gone on the record" (Fall papers, RGHC). The issue of juror misconduct was also the subject of various letters between Fall, Lambert, and Hogan; see Fall papers, Center for Southwest Research, Archive 131, boxes 12–14.

9. Press release, ca. 1929, in Fall papers, Center for Southwest Research, Archive 131, box 12.

10. Frank J. Hogan scrapbooks, vol. 36. Courtesy of Hogan & Hartson, Washington, D.C.

CHAPTER 15. THE FINAL TRIAL

1. *Atlantic City Republican*, April 6, 1930, p. 1.

2. *New York Times*, March 19, 1930, p. 1.

3. Unidentified editorial, Frank J. Hogan scrapbooks, unnumbered volume titled "Biographies, Speeches, Magazines," ca. 1930. Courtesy of Hogan & Hartson, Washington, D.C.

4. Martin Ansell, "Such Is Luck: The Mining Career of Edward L. Doheny in Mexico, 1880–1891," *New Mexico Historical Review* 70 (1995): 58. Ansell writes that there is no evidence to substantiate the story that Doheny studied law after falling down a mine shaft and breaking both legs: "If the local press did anything well, they scrupulously reported mining accidents. . . . If a well-known miner like Doheny would have had an accident serious enough to break both his legs it would have been newsworthy, but there was no mention of it in either the Kingston or Hillsboro papers" (p. 56).

5. The trial testimony is from the court record of *United States v. Doheny*, District Supreme Court, 1930, from Albert Bacon Fall Papers, Center for Southwest Research, Archive 131, boxes 14–15, University of New Mexico, Albuquerque. See also Hogan scrapbooks, "Biographies, Speeches, Magazines."

6. "Fight Won by Doheny," *Los Angeles Times*, March 23, 1930, pt. 1, p. 2.

7. *Los Angeles Times*, March 23, 1930, pt. 1, p. 2.

8. *Chicago Tribune*, March 23, 1930, p. 1.

9. Unidentified clipping, ca. 1930, in Hogan scrapbooks, "Biographies, Speeches, Magazines."

10. *Literary Digest*, April 5, 1930; in ibid.

11. *Time*, March 31, 1930; in Hogan scrapbooks, "Biographies, Speeches, Magazines."

12. Lester Cohen, *Frank Hogan Remembered* (Washington, D.C.: Hogan & Hartson, 1985), p. 49; John Billings Jr., "How Hogan Earns Million Fee," from unidentified magazine; "Fee of $1,000,000 Reported Paid by Doheny to F. J. Hogan as Chief Counsel in Oil Case," *New York Times*, undated; in Hogan scrapbooks, vol. 29.

13. Undated clippings in Hogan scrapbooks, vol. 29.

14. Dan La Botz, *Edward L. Doheny: Petroleum, Power, and Politics in the United States and Mexico* (New York: Praeger, 1991), pp. 115, 185.

15. Quoted in Francis J. Weber, *Southern California's First Family: The Dohenys of Los Angeles* (Fullerton, Calif.: Lorson's Books and Prints, 1993), p. 8.

16. Cohen, *Frank Hogan Remembered*, p. 49.

17. See *Fall v. United States*, 49 F.2d 506 (D.C.Cir. 1931); Certiorari denied by *Fall v. U.S.*, 283 U.S. 867. Also "Fall's Final Plea Is Rejected by Supreme Court," *New York Times*, June 2, 1931, p. 1.

18. Gordon R. Owen, *Two Alberts: Fountain and Fall* (Las Cruces, N.M.: Yucca Tree Press, 1996), p. 458.

19. Application of Hon. Albert B. Fall for parole, November 4, 1931, Albert B. Fall Papers, Manuscript Collection 8, Rio Grande Historical Collections, University Library, New Mexico State University, Las Cruces (RGHC).

20. Estelle Doheny to Emma Fall, letter, November 20, 1931, RGHC.

21. *El Paso Herald Post*, August 15, 1935, p. 1.

22. As told to the author by Victoria Steele, head, Special Collections, Edward L. Doheny, Jr. Memoral Library, University of Southern California, Los Angeles, February 14, 1996. See also Charlotte M. Brown, "Edward L. Doheny, Jr. Memoral Library," *Library Journal*, November 1, 1932, p. 896.

23. *El Paso Herald Post*, August 15, 1935, p. 1.

24. R. M. Sands to Albert B. Fall, letter, August 12, 1935, RGHC.

25. Unidentified clipping, "Fall and Family Stay at Ranch Defy Eviction," August 14, 1935, RGHC.

26. Owen, *Two Alberts*, p. 458.

27. Edward Laurence Doheny, Certificate of Death, County of Los Angeles, Registrar/Recorder, filed September 10, 1935. Courtesy of Nicholas A. Curry.

28. John J. Cantwell, *Sermon of His Excellency, Most Reverend John J. Cantwell, D.D., at Requiem Mass for Mr. Edward Laurence Doheny, St. Vincent's Church, Sept. 11, 1935* (San Francisco: printed for Estelle Doheny by John Henry Nash, 1935), p. 4.

29. Last Will and Testament of E. L. Doheny, August 22, 1932. Courtesy of Nicholas A. Curry.

30. "Dilecta in Christo Filia," Pius PP. XII, Carrie Estelle Betzold Doheny, June 29, 1939, Estelle Doheny Collection, Archive of the Archdiocese of Los Angeles, Mission Hills, California (AALA).

31. The Huntington Library possesses seventy-nine of the eighty, while the Henry Clifford Collection of Pasadena, California, and the Beinecke Rare Book and Manuscript Library at Yale University in New Haven, Connecticut, boast the only two complete collections. Estelle Doheny's copy of the Gutenberg Bible, purchased in October 1950 for just over $70,000, contained the Old Testament only.

32. Robert O. Schad, curator of rare books, Henry E. Huntington Library and Art Gallery, "The Estelle Doheny Collection," in *Addresses at a Meeting of the Zamorano Club, May 16, 1950* (Los Angeles: Ward Ritchie Press, 1950), pp. 7–27. See also Robert O. Schad, *The Estelle Doheny Collection* (New York: Duschnes, Cranford, 1950); Francis J. Weber, *The Estelle Doheny Collection of Californiana* (Mission Hills, Calif.: Archival Center for the Archdiocese of Los Angeles, 1987).

33. Stephen J. Ryan and J. S. Webb, *Envisioning Tomorrow: The Estelle Doheny Legacy* (Los Angeles: Estelle Doheny Eye Foundation, 1987), pp. 31–33.

34. Certificate of Death, Frank Joseph Hogan, District of Columbia Health Department, Bureau of Vital Statistics, filed May 17, 1944. Frank Hogan's wife, Mary Adair ("Mamie"), died in 1949. They are both buried at Mt. Olivet Cemetery in Washington, D.C.

35. Cohen, *Frank Hogan Remembered*, p. v.

36. Quoted in Owen, *Two Alberts*, p. 458.

37. Estelle Doheny to Monsignor William Doheny, letter, ca. 1949, AALA, box 2.

38. *The Carrie Estelle Doheny Foundation Annual Report, December 31, 1995*, p. 9.

39. Estelle Doheny to Father Flavin, letter, undated, AALA, box 2.

40. Last Will and Testament of Carrie Estelle Doheny, dated January 22, 1951, Probate File, Los Angeles County Archives, 925:377.

41. The Estelle Doheny Collection was sold by the fine art auctioneers Christie, Manson, and Woods International, in a series of seven sales (six of books and manuscripts, one of works of art) in New York, London, and Camarillo.

42. Quoted in "Scholars, Historians Grumble Over Sale of Doheny Collection," *Los Angeles Times*, March 7, 1987, pt. 2, p. 5; see also Bevis Hiller, "Art for Sale," *Los Angeles Times Magazine*, October 11, 1987, p. 30.

43. Carrie Estelle Doheny, Certificate of Death, County of Los Angeles, Registrar/Recorder, filed November 1, 1958. Courtesy of Nicholas A. Curry.

Bibliography

INTERVIEWS

Patrick Anson Doheny, November 15 and December 19, 1996; March 13 and 23, July 10, April 22, and August 27, 1997; Beverly Hills, California

Patricia Elizabeth Halbriter Doheny, November 15, 1996, and March 13, 1997, Beverly Hills, California

Kathleen Clark ("Kacey") Doheny McCoy, November 8, 1996, Beverly Hills, California

Lucy Estelle ("Dicky Dell") Doheny, March 13, 1997, Beverly Hills, California

Timothy Michael Doheny, August 27, 1997, Beverly Hills, California

William Henry Doheny, August 27, 1997, Beverly Hills, California

Rudy Cole, president of Greystone Foundation and member of the City of Beverly Hills Recreation and Parks Commission, January 23, 1996, Beverly Hills, California

Nicholas A. Curry, historian, December 11, 1995; February 10 and 28, March 8, July 14, September 19, 25, 27, and 30, 1996; January 10, 1997; February 13, April 23, July 14, and November 19, 1997; January 8–9, 1998; Los Angeles and Pasadena, California

Austin Doherty, director, Information Resource Center, Hogan & Hartson,
    L.L.P., December 13 and 16–18, 1996, Washington, D.C.
Donald N. Duke, railroad historian and publisher, April 23, 1997, Los Angeles
Rita Faulders, former curator of the Estelle Doheny Collection of Rare Books
    and Manuscripts, St. John's Seminary, Camarillo, January 24, 1997; July 15,
    November 19 and 25, 1997; Camarillo, California
Austin Hoover, director, Rio Grande Historical Collection, University Library,
    New Mexico State University, Las Cruces, September 2–10, 1996, Las Cruces
John Luder, deputy district attorney, Los Angeles County, December 23, 1996;
    July 10, August 4–6 and 13, 1997; Los Angeles
Wallace Neff Jr., author and son of architect Wallace Neff, October 17, 1996,
    Newport Beach, California
Frank Q. Newton Jr., photographic historian, April 23, 1997, Los Angeles
Bob Glen Odle, managing partner, Hogan & Hartson, L.L.P., December 13, 1996,
    Washington, D.C.
Joe Ryan, Los Angeles City Historical Society, September 24, 1996, Los Angeles
Victoria Steele, head, Special Collections, Edward L. Doheny, Jr. Library,
    University of Southern California, January 29, February 9, 14, and 28, 1996;
    June 10, 1997; Los Angeles
Monsignor Francis J. Weber, Archdiocese of Los Angeles, Mission Hills,
    California, October 14, November 11, 19–22, 18–22, and 27–29, December 11
    and 30, 1996; February 6–8, 1997; San Fernando, California
Les Zoeller, detective, City of Beverly Hills Police Department, August 13, 1997,
    Beverly Hills, California

ARCHIVAL MATERIAL

ARCO Corporation Archives, Los Angeles
Ralph Arnold Collection, Huntington Library, San Marino, California
Catholic University of America Archives, Washington, D.C.
Robert Glass Cleland Research Collection, Huntington Library, San Marino,
    California
E. L. Doheny Research Fund Papers, Occidental College Library, Eagle Rock,
    California
Edward L. Doheny, Jr. Memorial Library, Archives, University of Southern
    California; Los Angeles
Estelle Doheny Collection, Archive of the Archdiocese of Los Angeles, Mission
    Hills, California (AALA)
Albert B. Fall Collection, Huntington Library, San Marino, California
Albert B. Fall Papers, Manuscript Collection 8, Rio Grande Historical

Collections, University Library, New Mexico State University, Las Cruces (RGHC)
Albert Bacon Fall Papers, Center for Southwest Research, Archive 131, Zimmerman Library, University of New Mexico at Albuquerque
Fond du Lac County Historical Society, Fond du Lac, Wisconsin
Papers of Warren Gamaliel Harding, Ohio Historical Society Collection, Columbus, Ohio
Papers of Dr. John Randolph Haynes, Special Collections, University Research Library, University of California at Los Angeles
Frank J. Hogan scrapbooks, courtesy of Hogan & Hartson, L.L.P., Washington, D.C.
West Kern County Historical Collection, Taft, California
National Archives, Laguna Niguel, California
National Archives, Washington, D.C.
Papers of Henry W. O'Melveny, Huntington Library, San Marino, California
U.S. Navy, Archives, Washington, D.C.
University of Southern California, Archives, Los Angeles, California
Ventura County Historical Society, Ventura, California
Papers of Thomas James Walsh, Library of Congress, Washington, D.C.

PUBLISHED SOURCES

Adams, H. Austin. *The Man John D. Spreckels*. San Diego: Frye & Smith, 1924.
Allen, Frederick Lewis. *Only Yesterday*. New York: Harder, 1959.
Ansell, Martin. "Such Is Luck: The Mining Career of Edward L. Doheny in Mexico, 1880–1891." *New Mexico Historical Review* 70 (1995): 47–65.
Baker, Ray Stannard. *Woodrow Wilson, Life and Letters*. Vol. 4, *President, 1913–1914*. New York: Doubleday, Doran, 1931.
Baltzell, E. Digby. *The Protestant Establishment: Aristocracy and Caste in America*. New York: Random House, 1964.
Barron, Clarence W. *The Mexican Problem*. New York: Houghton Mifflin, 1917.
———. *They Told Barron: Conversations and Revelations of an American Pepys in Wall Street*. New York: Harper & Brothers, 1930.
Baruch, Bernard. *Baruch: My Own Story*. Vol. 1. New York: Henry Holt, 1957.
Beals, Carleton. *Black River*. Philadelphia: J. B. Lippincott, 1934.
———. *Glass Houses: Ten Years of Free-Lancing*. Philadelphia: J. B. Lippincott, 1938.
Beebe, Lucius. *Mansion on Wheels*. Berkeley, Calif.: Howell-North, 1959.
Bethune, Martha Fall. *Race with the Wind: The Personal Life of Albert B. Fall*. El Paso: Complete Print, 1989.

Birmingham, Stephen. *California Rich*. New York: Simon & Schuster, 1980.

Blakey, G. Robert. "Bribes (Book Review)." *Notre Dame Law Review* 60 (1985): 1255–61.

Boyle, Louis Lawrence. "Reforming Civil Service Reform: Should the Federal Government Continue to Regulate State and Local Government Employees?" *Journal of Law and Politics* 7 (1991): 243–91.

Bridge, Norman. *The Marching Years*. New York: Duffield, 1920.

Brigham & Co.'s City Directory, Fond du Lac, Wisconsin, 1857–58. Fond du Lac: Union Book, 1858.

Brown, Charlotte M. "Edward L. Doheny, Jr. Memorial Library." *Library Journal*, November 1, 1932, pp. 894–900.

Brown, Jonathan C. *Oil and Revolution in Mexico*. Berkeley: University of California Press, 1993.

Bryant, Keith L., Jr. *History of the Atchison, Topeka, and Santa Fe Railway*. New York: Macmillan, 1974.

Busch, Francis X. *Enemies of the State*. New York: Bobbs-Merrill, 1962.

Campbell-Mohn, Cecilia, Barry Breen, and J. William Futrell, eds. *Environmental Law Institute: Integrating Natural Resources and Pollution Abatement Law from Resources to Recovery*. St. Paul, Minn.: West Publishing, 1993.

Cantwell, John J. *Sermon of His Excellency, Most Reverend John J. Cantwell, D.D., at Requiem Mass for Mr. Edward Laurence Doheny, St. Vincent's Church, Sept. 11, 1935*. San Francisco: printed for Estelle Doheny by John Henry Nash, 1935.

Caughey, John, and LaRee Caughey. *Los Angeles: Biography of a City*. Berkeley: University of California Press, 1993.

Churchill, Winston S. *The World Crisis*. Vol. 1. New York: Scribner, 1928.

Clary, William W. *History of the Law Firm of O'Melveny and Meyers: 1885–1965*. 2 vols. Pasadena, Calif.: Castle Press, 1966.

Coggins, George Cameron, and Doris K. Nagel. "'Nothing Beside Remains': The Legal Legacy of James G. Watt's Tenure as Secretary of the Interior on Federal Land Law and Policy." *Boston College Environmental Affairs Law Review* 17 (1990): 473–545.

Cohen, Lester. *Frank Hogan Remembered*. Washington, D.C.: Hogan & Hartson, L.L.P., 1985.

Cohn, Alfred, and Joe Chisholm. *"Take the Witness!"* New York: New Home Library, 1957.

Davis, Margaret Leslie. *Bullocks Wilshire*. Los Angeles: Balcony Press, 1996.

———. *Rivers in the Desert: William Mulholland and the Inventing of Los Angeles*. New York: HarperCollins, 1993.

Davis, Mike. *City of Quartz: Excavating the Future in Los Angeles*. New York: Vintage Books, 1990.

DeLong, Sidney W. "Blackmailers, Bribe Takers, and the Second Paradox." *University of Pennsylvania Law Review* 141 (1993): 1663–93.

DeMille, Cecil. *The Autobiography of Cecil B. DeMille*. Englewood Cliffs, N.J.: Prentice-Hall, 1959.

Development of the Edward Laurence and Carrie Estelle Doheny Seminary Foundation. Los Angeles: Archdiocese of Los Angeles, 1987.

Doheny, Edward L. "History and Future of the Oil Industry in Mexico." In *Mexican Petroleum*, by Pan American Petroleum and Transport Company, pp. 13–48. New York: Pan American Petroleum and Transport Company, 1922.

"Edward Laurence and Carrie Estelle Doheny Seminary Foundation" (press release). Archbishop Roger Mahony, Archdiocese of Los Angeles. March 2, 1987.

The Estelle Doheny Collection of the Edward Laurence Doheny Memorial Library. Camarillo, Calif.: St. John's Seminary.

Fall, Albert B. *The Memoirs of Albert Bacon Fall*, edited by David H. Stratton. Southwestern Studies vol. 4, no. 3. El Paso: Texas Western Press, 1966.

Fanning, Leonard M. *Foreign Oil and the Free World*. New York: McGraw-Hill, 1954.

"Ferndale." *Victoriana* 6, no. 2 (1984): 4–5.

Fitzgerald, F. Scott. *The Great Gatsby*. New York: Scribner, 1925.

Fond du Lac County Gazetteer. Fond du Lac, Wis.: Commonwealth Power Press, 1868.

Forbes, Bertie. *Men Who Are Making the West*. New York: Forbes Publishing, 1923.

Franks, Kenny A., and Paul F. Lambert. *Early California Oil: A Photographic History, 1865–1940*. College Station: Texas A & M University Press, 1985.

Gebhard, David, and Robert Winter. *Los Angeles: An Architectural Guide*. Salt Lake City: Gibbs Smith, 1994.

Giddens, Paul H. *Standard Oil Company (Indiana): Oil Pioneer of the Middle West*. New York: Appleton-Century-Crofts, 1955.

Hagland, Charles G. "The Naval Reserve Leases." *Georgetown Law Journal* 20 (1932): 293–328.

Hall, Calvin S., and Gardner Lindzey. *Theories of Personality*. New York: John Wiley & Sons, 1970.

Hancock, Ralph. *Fabulous Boulevard*. New York: Funk & Wagnalls, 1949.

Hanrahan, Gene Z. *The Bad Yankee–El Peligro Yankee: American Entrepreneurs and Financiers in Mexico*. 2 vols. Chapel Hill, N.C.: Documentary Publications, 1985.

Hariman, Robert, ed. *Popular Trials: Rhetoric, Mass Media, and the Law*. Tuscaloosa: University of Alabama Press, 1990.

Hoffman, Fritz L. "Edward L. Doheny and the Beginnings of Petroleum Development in Mexico." *Mid-America*, April 1942, pp. 94–108.

Holland's Fond du Lac City Directory. Chicago: Western Publishing, 1872.

Hunt, Rockwell D. *California and Californians*. New York: Lewis Publishing, 1926.

Jennings, Walter W. *A Dozen Captains of American Industry*. New York: Vantage Press, 1954.

Johnson, Thomas H. *The Oxford Companion to American History*. New York: Oxford University Press, 1966.

Kaplan, Sam Hall. *L.A., Lost and Found: An Architectural History of Los Angeles*. New York: Crown, 1987.

Katz, Friedrich. *The Secret War in Mexico: Europe, the United States, and the Mexican Revolution*. Chicago: University of Chicago, 1981.

Kelley, Francis C. *Tribute by His Excellency, Most Reverend Francis C. Kelley to Mr. Edward Laurence Doheny*. San Francisco: printed for Estelle Doheny by John Henry Nash, 1935.

Knappman, Edward W., ed. *Great American Trials*. Detroit: Visible Ink, 1994.

Knowles, Ruth Sheldon. *The Greatest Gamblers: The Epic of American Oil Exploration*. 2d ed. Norman: University of Oklahoma Press, 1978.

La Botz, Dan. *Edward L. Doheny: Petroleum, Power, and Politics in the United States and Mexico*. New York: Praeger, 1991.

Lockwood, Charles. *Dream Palaces: Hollywood at Home*. New York: Viking Press, 1981.

Lockwood, Charles, and Peter V. Persic. "Greystone Historical Report." Submitted to the City Council of Beverly Hills, California, August 30, 1984.

Lowenstein, Daniel Hayes. "For God, for Country, or for Me?" *California Law Review* 74 (1986): 1479–512.

Lundwall, Helen J. *Pioneering in Territorial Silver City: H. B. Ailman's Recollections of Silver City and the Southwest, 1871–1892*. Albuquerque: University of New Mexico Press, 1983.

Lyman, Robert Hunt, ed. *World Almanac and Book of Facts for 1930*. New York: New York World, 1930.

Mallison, Sam T. *The Great Wildcatter*. Charleston, W.Va.: Education Foundation of West Virginia, 1953.

McKenna, James A. *Black Range Tales*. New York: Wilson-Erickson, 1936.

McPhee, John. *Assembling California*. New York: Farrar, Straus, & Giroux, 1993.

McGroarty, John Steven. *Los Angeles: From the Mountains to the Sea*. Vol. 2. Chicago: American Historical Society, 1921.

———, ed. *California of the South*. Vol. 4, *Biographical*. Chicago: S. J. Clarke, 1933.

———, ed. *History of Los Angeles County*. Vol. 1. Chicago: American Historical Society, 1923.

McWilliams, Carey. *Southern California Country: An Island on the Land.* New York: Duell, Sloan, & Pearce, 1946.

Menendez, Gabriel Antonio. *Doheny el cruel: Episodios de la sangrienta lucha por el pétroleo Mexicano.* Mexico: Bolsa Mexicana del Libro, 1958.

Miller, John, ed. *Los Angeles Stories: Great Writers of the City.* San Francisco: Chronicle Books, 1991.

Miller, Lucille V. "Edward and Estelle Doheny." *Ventura County Historical Society Quarterly* 6, no. 1 (1960): 3–20.

———. "In Memoriam: Mrs. Edward L. Doheny." *California Historical Society Quarterly* 38 (1959): 278–79.

Moyers, Bill. *A World of Ideas II: Public Opinions from Private Citizens.* New York: Doubleday, 1990.

Murray, Robert K. *The Harding Era: Warren G. Harding and His Administration.* Minneapolis: University of Minnesota Press, 1969.

Newmark, Marco R. "Edward L. Doheny." *Historical Society of Southern California Quarterly* 37 (1955): 76–78.

Newmark, Maurice H., and Marco R. Newmark, eds. *Sixty Years in Southern California: 1853–1913.* Los Angeles: Dawson's Book Shop, 1984.

Noggle, Burl. *Teapot Dome: Oil and Politics in the 1920's.* New York: Norton, 1962.

Noonan, John T., Jr. *Bribes.* New York: Macmillan, 1984.

Norton, John. *Teapot Dome.* Baton Rouge: Louisiana State University Press, 1962.

O'Keefe, Constance, and Peter Safirstein. "Fallen Angels, Separation of Powers, and the Saturday Night Massacre: An Examination of the Practical, Constitutional, and Political Tensions in the Special Prosecutor Provisions of the Ethics in Government Act." *Brooklyn Law Review* 49 (1982): 113–47.

Ordóñez, Ezequiel. "El Petróleo en México: Bosquejo Historico." *Revista Mexicana de Ingeniería y Arquetectura* 10, nos. 3 and 4 (1932): 154–61, 187–230.

Owen, Gordon R. *Two Alberts: Fountain and Fall.* Las Cruces, N.M.: Yucca Tree Press, 1996.

Pan American Petroleum and Transport Company. *Mexican Petroleum.* New York: Pan American Petroleum and Transport Company, 1922.

Perret, Geoffrey. *America in the Twenties.* New York: Simon & Schuster, 1982.

———. *Old Soldiers Never Die: The Life of Douglas MacArthur.* New York: Random House, 1996.

Powell, Ruth, and Chuck Powell. *Chester Place.* Historical Society of Southern California and Southern California Chapter of the American Institute of Architects. Los Angeles: R. & C. Powell, 1964.

Price, Paxton P. *Pioneers of the Mesilla Valley.* Las Cruces, N.M.: Yucca Tree Press, 1995.

Ragland, Reginald W. *A History of the Naval Petroleum Reserve and of the Present*

National Policy Respecting Them. Bakersfield, Calif.: Kern County Free Library, 1944.

Ritchie, Ward. *The Dohenys of Los Angeles*. Los Angeles: Dawson's Book Shop, 1974.

Robinson, W. W. *Lawyers of Los Angeles*. Los Angeles: Los Angeles Bar Association, 1959.

Ryan, Stephen J., and J. S. Webb. *Envisioning Tomorrow: The Estelle Doheny Legacy*. Los Angeles: Estelle Doheny Eye Foundation, 1987.

Schad, Robert O. "The Estelle Doheny Collection." In *Addresses at a Meeting of the Zamorano Club, May 16, 1950*, pp. 7–27. Los Angeles: Ward Ritchie Press, 1950.

———. *The Estelle Doheny Collection*. New York: Duschnes, Cranford, 1950.

Schlesinger, Arthur M., Jr., and Roger Burns. *Congress Investigates: A Documented History, 1792–1974*. New York: R. R. Bowker, 1975.

Seldes, George. *Freedom of the Press*. Garden City, N.Y.: Garden City Publishing, 1937.

Shade, Christine E. "Venerable Doheny." *University of Southern California Chronicle*, August 29, 1994, p. 16.

Sinclair, Upton. *Oil!* New York: Albert & Charles Boni, 1927.

Sonnichsen, C. L. *Tularosa: Last of the Frontier West*. 1960. Reprint, Albuquerque: University of New Mexico Press, 1980.

Starr, Kevin. *Inventing the Dream: California through the Progressive Era*. New York: Oxford University Press, 1985.

———. *Material Dreams: Southern California through the 1920's*. New York: Oxford University Press, 1990.

Stoddard, Lothrop. *The Rising Tide of Color against White World-Supremacy*, introduction by Madison Grant. New York: Scribner, 1920.

Stratton, David H. "Albert B. Fall and the Teapot Dome Affair." Ph.D. diss., University of Colorado, 1955.

———. "Behind Teapot Dome: Some Personal Insights." *Business History Review* 31 (1957): 385–402.

———. Introduction to *The Memoirs of Albert Bacon Fall*, ed. Stratton, pp. 3–11. Southwestern Studies, vol. 4, no. 3. El Paso: Texas Western Press, 1966.

———. "New Mexico Machiavellian? The Story of Albert Bacon Fall." *Montana—The Magazine of Western History* 7 (October 1957): 2–14.

Sullivan, Mark. *Our Times: The Twenties*. New York: Scribner, 1935.

Swanberg, W. A. *Citizen Hearst: A Biography of William Randolph Hearst*. New York: Scribner, 1961.

Tarlock, Dan. "The Quiet Crisis Revisited." *Arizona Law Review* 34 (1992): 293–309.

Theroux, Peter. *Translating L.A.: A Tour of the Rainbow City*. New York: Norton, 1994.

Trani, Eugene P., and David L. Wilson. *The Presidency of Warren G. Harding.* Lawrence: Regents Press of Kansas, 1977.

Tygiel, Jules. *The Great Los Angeles Swindle: Oil, Stocks, and Scandal during the Roaring Twenties.* New York: Oxford University Press, 1994.

Ward, Elizabeth, and Alain Silver, eds. *Raymond Chandler's Los Angeles.* Woodstock, N.Y.: Overlook Press, 1987.

Weber, Francis J. *The Estelle Doheny Collection of Californiana.* Mission Hills, Calif.: Archival Center for the Archdiocese of Los Angeles, 1987.

———. *Golden State Catholicism.* [Los Angeles: Archdiocese of Los Angeles], 1990.

———. *John Joseph Cantwell His Excellency of Los Angeles.* Hong Kong: Cathay Press, 1971.

———. *Southern California's First Family: The Dohenys of Los Angeles.* Fullerton, Calif.: Lorson's Books and Prints, 1993.

———. "A Tour through the Estelle Doheny Collection." *Evangelist* 29 (1957): 8–9, 23–26.

Weisner, Herman. *The Politics of Justice: A. B. Fall and Teapot Dome: A New Perspective.* Albuquerque: Herman B. Weisner, 1988.

Welty, Earl M., and Frank J. Taylor. *The Black Bonanza.* New York: McGraw-Hill, 1958.

Werner, M. R., and John Starr. *Teapot Dome.* New York: Viking Press, 1959.

White, Leslie T. *Me, Detective.* New York: Harcourt, 1936.

White, William Allen. *The Autobiography of William Allen White.* New York: Macmillan, 1946.

———. *Masks in a Pageant.* New York: Macmillan, 1928.

Whitney, Caspar. *Charles Adelbert Canfield.* New York: privately printed, 1930.

———. *What's the Matter with Mexico?* New York: Macmillan, 1916.

Wilson, Jane. *Gibson, Dunn, and Crutcher, Lawyers: An Early History.* Los Angeles: Gibson, Dunn, & Crutcher, 1990.

Yergin, Daniel. *The Prize: The Epic Quest for Oil, Money, and Power.* New York: Simon & Schuster, 1992.

Index

Note: In subentries, "Doheny" by itself refers to Edward Laurence Doheny. Names of government departments begin with "U.S."

Adriatic, 101–2
Ailman, H. B., 23–24, 25, 26, 27–28
Allen, Frederick Lewis, 129
Ambrose, Arthur W., 147–48, 181
American Association for the Recognition of the Irish Republic, 87
Amoco. *See* Standard Oil of Indiana
Anderson, Daysie May (Estelle Doheny's sister), 3–4, 85, 89–90, 275, 282
Anderson, J. Crampton, 89–90
Ansell, Martin, 312n.4
Appreciation Banquet for Doheny (1927, Los Angeles), 212
ARCO, 77
art, Mexican, 75–76, 297n.22
Article 27 (Mexican Constitution), 112–13, 119–20, 121–22
asphalt, 45–46
Associated Oil Company, 146, 147, 148

Association of Producers of Petroleum (Mexico), 121–22
A.T. & S.F. (Atchison, Topeka, and Santa Fe Railway), 30, 31–33, 78, 294n.21
Atlantic City Republican, 255–56
automobiles, rise of, 78, 128–29

Bailey, Jennings, 219
Bain, H. Foster, 146–48, 164, 181, 201–2
banking system in New Mexico, 203, 308n.4
Barber, Martin, 18
Barlow, W. Jarvis, 99
Barnes, George W., 107
Barron, Clarence W., 183
Baruch, Bernard, 110
Battson, Leigh M., 269
Battson, Lucy. *See* Doheny, Lucy Marceline Smith
Beals, Carleton, 120–21

Beinecke Rare Book and Manuscript Library (Yale University), 314n.31
Benedum, Mike, 73, 74, 76–77
Bertolini's Palace (Naples), 85–86
Beta Theta Pi (University of Southern California), 99
Betzold, Carrie Estelle. *See* Doheny, Estelle Betzold
Betzold, John E. (Estelle Doheny's father), 40, 293n.9
Betzold, Susan (Estelle Doheny's mother), 84–85
Beverly Hills, 310n.2
Big Sleep,The (Chandler), 309n.16
Blackmer, Henry M., 311n.20
Blair, Charles, 231–32
Blair and Company (New York City), 140
Borda, José de la, 185
Boston Telegram Newspaper, 111
Branch, Hillary, 119
brea, 22–23
bribery: charges against Ned Doheny, 168, 176, 219. *See also* civil trial of Doheny; criminal trial of Doheny for bribery; criminal trial of Fall for bribery
Bridge, Norman: on Harding, 128; on MPC's board of directors, 142; as pallbearer for Canfield, 93; sells 10 Chester Place to Ned Doheny, 114–15; visits Huasteca region, 65–66
Britain, 92, 95
British Petroleum (BP), 77
Brooklyn Eagle, 264
Brophy, Mariah, 13, 14, 18
Brown, Edward, 91
Brown, Jonathan C., 57, 69, 293n.5
Bryan, William Jennings, 101
Buck, Morris, 62–63
Buck, William, 63
Buckley, William F., Sr., 96
Buena Vista oil reserves (California), 149
Burns, William J., 218
Butler, Justice, 216–17
Butterfield & Butterfield & Dunnings Fine Art Auctioneers and Appraisers (Los Angeles), 280

calaveras (skeleton figures), 75–76, 285, 297n.22
California: oil strikes in, 26–28, 31. *See also* specific cities
California Furniture Company, 89
Canada, William, 100
Canfield, Charles Adelbert: appearance of, 11–12; attends wedding of Edward and Estelle Doheny, 41; buys/races horses, 19; Coalinga Oil Company formed/run by, 30–33; Comstock Mine success, 17; death of, 93, 298n.29; friendship with Doheny, 30, 93–94; health of, 17; Kingston mining activities of, 11, 12, 16–17; loses fortune, 19–20; oil interests in Mexico, 35–37, 39 (*see also* MPC); oil interests in Southern California, 29–33; oil interests in Westlake Park, 23–24, 25, 27–28; partnership with Doheny, 12, 20, 25–33; personality/character of, 11, 12, 94; Petroleum Development Company formed/run by, 33; reacts to wife's murder, 62–64; real estate success in California, 19; returns to Mexico, 72; wealth of, 94, 299n.33
Canfield, Charles Orville (C. A. Canfield's son), 12, 292n.5
Canfield, Chloe Phoebe Wescott (C. A. Canfield's wife), 11, 12, 17, 19, 30, 62–64
Canfield, Daisy (C. A. Canfield's daughter), 62
Canfield, Florence (C. A. Canfield's daughter), 11, 63
Canfield, Lee (C. A. Canfield's son), 30
Cannon, Sam, 23, 25, 27–28
Cantania (tanker), 115
Cantwell, Bishop John Joseph, 277; eulogizes Doheny, 2, 274–75, 288; friendship with Doheny, 118, 265; holds requiem mass for Ned Doheny, 237; and St. Vincent's Church, 185
Capone, Al, 256
Carden, Sir Lionel, 94–95
Cardenas, Lazaro, 276
Carey, Joseph A., 202
Carnahan, George H., 119
Carranza, Venustiano: assassination of, 121; introduces new Mexican Constitution, 112–13; invades Texas, 110; and Joint High Commission, 116–17; and Obregon, 121; United States supports, 95, 96, 104, 109, 112; U.S. industrialists oppose, 109, 110; and U.S. oil companies, 100–101
Carriboa, Frederico, 92
Carrie Estelle Doheny Foundation, 281
cars, rise of, 78, 128–29
Casasus, Joaquin D., 68
Casiana (yacht), 262, 265
Casiano Hacienda (Huasteca region, Mexico), 67
Casiano-Tampico pipeline (Mexico), 71, 72, 74

Casiano wells (Huasteca region, Mexico), 72–76
Catholic Church, 75, 285–86; inherits Chester Place, 282; sale of Estelle Doheny's book collection, 282, 314n.41
Cerro Azul wells (Mexico), 105–8, 141, 300n.10, 303n.2
Cerro de la Pez (San Luis Potosi, Mexico), 36, 43, 57–58
Cerro Viejo well (Mexico), 57, 303n.2
Chandler, Harry, 182
Chandler, Raymond: *The Big Sleep*, 309n.16; *Farewell, My Lovely*, 309n.16
Chanslor, Joseph A. ("Joe"), 30, 31, 32, 37, 93
Chaplin, Charlie, 213
chapopotes (ponds of brown pitch), 35–36, 56
Charles E. Harwood (tanker), 79, 115
Chaumont de Truffin, Nieves Perez, 271
Cheesewright Studios (Pasadena), 214
Chester Place (Los Angeles): Doheny confers with lawyers at, 176–77; Doheny's purchase of, 46; earthquake damages, 271; Estelle Doheny's dislike for, 46–47, 48; fame of, 47–48; refurbishing of, 47, 49, 85, 88–89, 184; willed to Catholic Church, 282
Chevron. *See* Standard Oil of California
Chicago Tribune, 138
Chihuahua (Mexico), 45, 294n.22
Christian Science Monitor, 138
Churchill, Mr. (night watchman), 53
Churchill, Winston, 92, 104
Científicos (supporters of Díaz), 38
Cincinnati Enquirer, 158
City Council (Los Angeles), 93
civil trial of Doheny, xvi, 178–98; appeal to Circuit Court, 193–95; appeal to Supreme Court, 197–98, 216–17; defense team at, 178, 179–80, 181–82; and Denby's role in oil leases, 180; Doheny/defense team react to appeals ruling, 194–95; Doheny/ defense team react to verdict, 189, 190; Doheny refuses to testify, 179, 181; and Doheny's loan to Fall, 181; Doheny's self-assurance during, xiii–xiv; Fall refuses to testify, 181; and Fall's role in oil leases, 179–81; Finney testifies, 180–81; leases cancelled as obtained by fraud, 188–89, 224; McCormick considers his decision, 181, 182; and national security, 180, 286; prosecutors at, 178–79, 181, 193; Robison testifies, 180; Senate testimony as evidence at, 179, 181
Clark, J. Ross, 99
Clayton, Powell, 37

Cleveland, Grover, 301n.35
Clinton Basin (Oakland, California), 184
Coahuila (Mexico), 95
coal, 22–23, 58, 116
Coalinga Oil Company (California), 30–33
Coalinga oil wells (California), 30, 31
Columbus (New Mexico), 109
Comstock Mine (near Kingston, New Mexico), 17
Conger, Rev. John C., 99
Conoco (*formerly* Continental Oil), 77
conservationists, oil, 130–31, 137–39, 287
Consolidated, 138
conspiracy. *See* criminal trial of Doheny and Fall for fraud/conspiracy; criminal trial of Sinclair and Fall for conspiracy
Constitution, Mexican (1917). *See* Article 27
Constitutionalists (Mexico), 95–96, 100, 101, 113
Constitution of 1857 Revolutionary Army, 113
Continental Oil (*later named* Conoco), 77
Continental trading scandal, 245, 311n.20
Conventionists (Mexico), 100
Coolidge, Calvin, 152, 163, 166, 167, 220
corruption. *See* civil trial of Doheny; criminal trial of Doheny and Fall for fraud/ conspiracy; criminal trial of Doheny for bribery; criminal trial of Fall for bribery; criminal trial of Sinclair and Fall for conspiracy; Senate investigation into oil lease scandal
Cotter, Joseph J., 144, 148, 258
Cowdray, Lord. *See* Pearson, Weetman
Cox, James, 126
Cram, Ralph Adams, 185, 270
Creel, George, 162
criminal trial of Doheny and Fall for fraud/ conspiracy, 198–99; Bain testifies, 201–2; Carey testifies, 202; character witnesses called, 207; Denby testifies, 202; Doheny and Fall acquitted, 210–11, 224; and Doheny's loan to Fall, 200, 201, 203, 204–7; Doheny testifies, 203–5; Estelle Doheny testifies, 205–6; and Finney's role in oil reserve leases, 201–2; Finney testifies, 201; and Harding's role in oil reserve leases, 202; Hoehling presides over, 200, 209; Hogan defends Doheny, 200, 201–2, 208–9; jury selection for, 200; Lambert defends Fall, 201, 209; media coverage of, 199–200; Ned Doheny testifies, 206–7; reactions to verdict, 210–11; Roberts and Pomerene prosecute, 200, 201, 204, 207;

criminal trial of Doheny and Fall (*continued*)
and Robison's role in oil reserve leases,
201–2, 203; Senate testimony as evidence
at, 200; Smith testifies, 201; Youngs
testifies, 201
criminal trial of Doheny for bribery, 198, 224;
Doheny acquitted, 261; Doheny rewards
lawyers, 264; Doheny testifies, 257–58;
Doheny thanks jurors, 261; Estelle Doheny
testifies, 257; and Fall's dealings with Sinclair, 255; Hitz's instructions favor Doheny,
260; Hogan defends Doheny, 255, 257,
258–59; jurors' explanations of verdict,
263; jury selection for, 256; newspaper
coverage of, 255–56, 263–64; reactions to
verdict, 261–64; Roberts and Pomerene
prosecute, 255, 256, 257, 259–60, 263;
Senate testimony as evidence at, 257
criminal trial of Fall for bribery, 198; Doheny
helps attorneys prepare for, 224; Doheny
testifies, 249; Estelle Doheny testifies, 249;
evidence about transactions with Sinclair,
250–51; Fall convicted/sentenced, 251,
252; Fall's health, 249–50; Hogan defends
Fall, 248, 249–50, 251–52; juror misconduct
in, 253–54, 312n.8; jury requests leniency,
251, 252; reactions to verdict, 251–52;
requests for pardon/retrials denied, 266;
Roberts and Pomerene prosecute, 248, 249,
250, 251
criminal trial of Sinclair and Fall for conspiracy, 217–22; Everhart testifies, 220–
21; Hogan represents Ned Doheny, 219;
Lambert defends Fall, 217; Littleton
defends Sinclair, 217, 221; Ned Doheny
subpoenaed, 219; Ned Doheny testifies,
221; Roberts accuses Sinclair of jury
tampering, 218; Roberts drops bribery
charge against Ned Doheny, 219; Roberts
and Pomerene prosecute, 217, 219–20, 221;
severance order is entered for Fall, 219,
224; Siddons declares a mistrial, 218;
Siddons presides over, 217, 221; Sinclair
acquitted, 221–22, 224
Crown, Henry, 280
Cuban Platt Amendment (1901), 117
Cuchillo del Pulque (Mexico), 57
Curry, Nicholas A., xvii

Daniels, Josephus, 130–31
Daugherty, Harry Micajah, 126, 127, 131, 151,
163
Davidson, Rev. George, 239–40
Dawson, Claude, 111–12

DeMille, Cecil B., 182–83
Denby, Edwin, 137; approves Pan American
deal, 148; assigns oil-reserve responsibilities to Bureau of Engineering, 134;
opens oil lease bids, 147; resigns, 163;
testifies at Senate hearing, 155, 164–65;
and transfer of oil-reserve authority to
Department of Interior, 131–32, 189; and
trial of Doheny, 180
Destrehan (Louisiana), 109
Dial (drug), 243
Díaz, Felipe, 90
Díaz, Porfirio, 285; career/presidency of,
35, 37–39, 54–55; and Doheny, 84; and
Doheny's oil operations, 39, 57, 68, 74, 79,
104–5; labor unrest under, 75, 78; ousted
from power, 80–81; and Standard Oil, 39,
293n.7
Dockweiler, Isidore, 99
Doheny, Carrie Estelle Betzold. See Doheny,
Estelle Betzold
Doheny, Carrie Louella Wilkins (Doheny's
first wife), 12–13, 14: appearance/person-
ality of, 13; birth of, 291n.13; death of, 41–
42; declining marriage of, 13, 18, 21, 28–29;
divorces husband, 33, 42, 294n.16; gives
birth to Eileen, 13; gives birth to Ned, 29;
grieves for Eileen, 24–25; health/drinking
of, 13, 18–19, 25, 28–29; remains of moved
to Forest Lawn, 244; singing of, 12, 13, 18
Doheny, Edward Laurence: angry that Fall
lied about loan, 158; appearance of, 9, 22,
161, 165–66, 203; army created by, 111–12;
birth of, 8; bribery/conspiracy charges
against, 68–69, 166–68, 172 (see also civil
trial of Doheny; criminal trial of Doheny
for bribery; Hogan, Frank J.; O'Melveny,
Henry W.); broken-leg story of, 257–58,
312n.4; buys estate in Los Angeles, 46–48;
buys Three Rivers Ranch, 252; Catholic
Church supported by, 118, 184–85, 264–65;
celebrates twenty-fifth wedding anniversary, 192; character/reputation of, 175,
208, 284; childhood of, 8–9; church built
by, 184–85, 307n.32; corresponds with Fall
about bribery charges/lawsuits, 173; criticized for activities in Mexico, 284–85; criticized in the press, 169, 172, 244; death
of, 274; estate of, size of, 276; fails to understand Mexican culture, 76, 285, 286;
Fall gives gifts to, 136–37; Fall's biography
sponsored by, 183–84; on Fall's bribery
trial, 248; Fall sends naval reserves documents to, 173; frijoles enjoyed by, 66,

296n.8; frontier attitude of, 138; funds Edward L. Doheny Jr. Memorial Library, 270; funeral of, 1–3, 274, 284, 288; gambling of, 14; generosity/patriotism of, 2–3, 115; gives Estelle piano, 59; grieves for Chloe Canfield, 63–64; grieves for son, 238–39; health of, 188, 246, 270–71, 272; horse trading of, 9; intervention in/invasion of Mexico sought by, 87, 119–21; involvement in Mexican politics, 54–58, 68–69, 79; on Ireland, 86–87, 195–96; Kingston prospecting of, 8, 10–11, 16–17; law study claimed by, 257–58, 312n.4; lawyers'/publicists' romanticizing of, 7–8; liquidates assets to protect heirs' fortunes, 225, 276; in Los Angeles, 21–22; made Knight of Order of Holy Sepulchre, 265; marriages of (see Doheny, Carrie Louella Wilkins; Doheny, Estelle Betzold); moves remains of first wife and daughter to Forest Lawn, 244; at Ned's death, 231; nicknamed El Eduardo, 73, 296n.17; oil deals with railroads, 30, 31–33; oil interests in Los Angeles, 22–27; oil interests in Mexico, 34–37, 39, 293n.6 (see also MPC); oil interests in Southern California, 29–33, 45; pawns/reclaims Estelle's jewelry, 45, 46, 294n.21; pays attorneys for Fall, 248; personality of, 11, 12, 40, 56, 165, 288; politicians on payroll of, 162–63; promises support to Fall, 252; provides for Lucy and grandchildren, 225, 276; public opinion, tries to influence, 110–12, 118–19, 183, 190, 191–92; railroad car of, 40–41; religious views of, 196–97; returns home after acquittal, 211–12; Robison discusses naval defense plans with, 142–45; role in making United States a world power, 283; at Santa Paula home, 247–48, 311n.1; sells voting stock of Pan American, 186–87, 307n.33; in Silver City, 18; South Dakota prospecting of, 9; stockholder lawsuits against, 167, 225, 262; takes family on cruise, 262; as teetotaler, 49; telegrams that vindicate himself and Fall, 190–92, 308n.43; vacations at Mammoth Lakes with attorneys, 174; visits Europe, 81–88, 101–4; wealth of, 80, 97, 108, 142, 166; will of, 275–76. See also MPC; Pan American Petroleum and Transport Company

Doheny, Edward Laurence, Jr. See Doheny, Ned

Doheny, Edward Laurence, III ("Larry"; Ned and Lucy Doheny's son), 115, 176, 223, 269, 274

Doheny, Eileen (Doheny's daughter), 14, 21, 42; birth of, 13; death/funeral of, 22, 24, 292n.3; health of, 22; remains of moved to Forest Lawn, 244

Doheny, Eleanor Elizabeth Quigley (Doheny's mother), 8, 9

Doheny, Ellen ("Ella"; Doheny's sister), 290n.2

Doheny, Estelle Betzold (Doheny's second wife), xv, 56; anger at Fall, 268–69; attends husband's funeral, 2, 270, 274, 275; attends Unknown Soldier ceremony, 136; birth/background of, 39–40; blindness of, 278, 280; book collection of, 266, 272, 277–78, 282, 314n.31, 314n.41; builds chapel and buildings for Maryvale orphanage, 281; builds Edward L. Doheny Memorial Library, 277; builds Estelle Doheny Hospital and Pavilion, 281; builds Santa Paula home, 247; burns husband's papers, 3–4, 275; Catholicism of, 117–18, 277, 281, 294n.12; celebrates twenty-fifth wedding anniversary, 192; collects Western Americana, 278; comforts husband, 246, 247; death/burial of, 282; dislikes 8 Chester Place estate, 46–47 (see also Chester Place); evicts Falls from Three Rivers, 267–68, 272–74; and Fall, 133–34; founds Carrie Estelle Doheny Foundation, 281; founds Estelle Doheny Eye Foundation, 278; grieves for Chloe Canfield, 63–64; health of, 281; on husband's acquittal, 210; inherits husband's estate, 275–76; loneliness/frustration of, 48–49, 50–51, 53–54, 59–60, 89; made "countess" by Pope Pius XII, 277; meets future husband, 39; meets husband in Albuquerque, 52–53; on MPC's board of directors, 141; musical talents of, 53; orders flight from 1933 earthquake, 272; personality of, 39, 40, 277; relationship with mother, 84–85; relationship with sister, 89–90; relationship with stepson, 42–43, 47, 51–52, 53, 59; sells remaining oil assets, 280; social/business duties of, 47, 49, 270, 276, 280; testifies in husband's criminal trial, 205–6; use of name "Carrie," 293n.8; visits Europe, 81–88, 101–4; and Ward, 276–77; wedding of, 40–41, 293–94n.12; will of, 281–82; Woman of the Year, 281; and Wylies, 87

Doheny, James (Doheny's brother), 290n.2

Doheny, John L. (Doheny's brother), 289n.2

Doheny, Lucy Estelle ("Dickie Dell"; Ned and Lucy Doheny's daughter), 269; birth of, 104; at father's funeral, 238; at grandfather's funeral, 274; moves into Greystone, 223; relationship with father, 176; relationship with grandparents, 115

Doheny, Lucy Marceline Smith (Ned Doheny's wife), 235–36, 239, 282; builds the Knoll, 280; death of, 280; marriage to Leigh Battson, 269; marriage to Ned, 97–100; moves into Greystone, 223; at Ned's death, 230–31; at Ned's funeral, 238; oversees interior decoration of Greystone, 214, 222; relationship with Estelle Doheny, 277; social schedule of, 176; visits Europe, 82, 83, 84, 85, 87; visits Mexico, 97–98

Doheny, Ned (Doheny's son), 49, 224; appearance of, 60, 81, 97; attends appreciation banquet for father, 212; attends father and stepmother's wedding, 41; birth of, 29; bribery charges against, 168, 176; buys 10 Chester Place, 114–15; cars owned by, 309n.17; delivers father's loan to Fall, 139–41, 160, 161, 175–76, 201; education of, 53, 88, 113; funeral of, 236–39; gifts from father, 212–13, 217; lobbies against Article 27, 122; marriage to Lucy, 97–100; memorial library, 270; moves into Greystone, 223; on MPC's board of directors, 141, 142; murder of, xiv, 230–31, 231–36, 240–45, 310n.2; musical talents of, 53; naval career of, 113–15, 134; personality of, 60; public opinion against, 176; relationship with father, 52, 59, 60, 66–67, 72–73, 217; relationship with stepmother, 42–43, 47, 51–52, 53, 59–60; testifies in father's criminal trial, 206–7; visits Europe, 81–88; and Wylies, 87

Doheny, Patrick A. (Doheny's father), 8, 9

Doheny, Patrick (Ned and Lucy Doheny's son), 176, 223, 274

Doheny, Thomas (Doheny's brother), 289–90n.2

Doheny, Timothy M. (Ned and Lucy Doheny's son), 223, 274

Doheny, William (Doheny's uncle), 8

Doheny, William Henry (Ned and Lucy Doheny's son), 176, 223, 274

Doheny, Monsignor William, 280

Doheny Research Foundation, 118–19

Donovan, William H. ("Wild Bill"), 170

Douglas, Walter, 119

Drake, Edwin L., 291–92n.1, 297n.18

Durango (Mexico), 45, 294n.22

Dyas (B. H.) Company Dry Goods (Hollywood), 242–43

Eagle Oil Transport Company (Mexico), 78–79

earthquake of 1933 (Los Angeles), 271–72

Eaton, Herbert, 238

Ebano Station and El Ebano Well (Mexico), 43–46, 50, 55–56, 101

Edward L. Doheny Jr. Memorial Library (University of Southern California, Los Angeles), 270

Edward L. Doheny Jr. (tanker), 79, 115

Edward Laurence Doheny Memorial Library (St. John's Seminary, Camarillo, California), 277

Edwards, E. A., 32

Edwards, Frazer, 191

8 Chester Place (Los Angeles). *See* Chester Place

Eileen Emma, 102

Eisen, Theodore, 46

Elk Hills oil lease scandal: Doheny proposes film about, 183; missing telegrams, 190, 304n.9; prosecutors investigate, 166–67. *See also* civil trial of Doheny; Senate investigation into oil lease scandal

Elk Hills oil reserves (Kern County, California): conservationists on, 130–31; Fall given authority over, 131–32; and leasing of land, 130–31, 302n.16; navy's use of, 130, 302n.12; Pan American drilling leases to, 136, 148, 149, 150, 153, 304n.8. *See also* Elk Hills oil lease scandal

Episcopal Church, 176

Estelle Doheny Collection, 282, 314n.41

Estelle Doheny Eye Foundation (St. Vincent's Hospital, Los Angeles), 278

Estelle Doheny Hospital and Pavilion (St. Vincent's Medical Center, Los Angeles), 281

Everhart, Mahlon T. (A. B. Fall's son-in-law), 146, 220–21, 250

Exxon. *See* Standard Oil of New Jersey

Fairchild and Gilmore (New York City), 45–46

Faja de Oro (Golden Lane; Mexico), 71

Falaba, 102

Fall, Albert B., 147, 182–83; appearance/personality of, 14; authority over oil reserves, 131, 302n.17; biography of, 183–84; bribery/conspiracy charges against, xiv, 166–68 (*see also* civil trial of Doheny; criminal trial of Fall for bribery; criminal trial of Sinclair and Fall for conspiracy); builds fortune, 120; calls for Senate hearing about Mexico, 120–21; childhood of, 15; vs. conservationists, 137–39, 150–51, 287; corresponds with Doheny about bribery charges/lawsuits, 173; death of, 279; Doheny and Hogan encourage him about appeal, 193, 195–97, 286; Doheny buys Three Rivers Ranch in foreclosure, 252; Doheny promises support to, 252; Doheny receives naval lease documents from, 173; on Doheny's acquittal, 262; Doheny sends $100,000 to, 3, 139–41, 146, 159–62, 175–76, 201, 287; Doheny's friendship with, 14–15, 127–28, 133–34, 136–37, 159, 268, 273–74; on Doheny's *New York Times* interview, 191–92; early mining activities of, 10; early work of, 15; eviction from Three Rivers, 267, 272–74; explores exchange of crude oil for fuel oil storage, 135–36; financial straits of, 146, 153, 267, 287; Finney suggests he accept Pan American deal, 148; and Forest Service, 137, 139, 303n.29; frontier attitude of, 137–38; and Harding, 138–39, 150, 151; health of, 15, 212, 218, 249–50, 266–67, 270; on his reputation, 269–70; issues postconviction public statement, 254; letters and telegrams on behalf of, 267; meets with Sinclair about Teapot Dome reserves, 145; ostracized following conspiracy trial, 212; political authority in New Mexico, 120, 301n.35; in prison, 266–67; on publication of lost telegrams, 191; released from prison, 269; resigns from cabinet post, 151; returns to Three Rivers, 269; as secretary of the interior, 127; seeks to contact Doheny, 273; serves in Spanish-American War, 133, 302n.20; Sinclair gives Liberty Bonds/money to, 151, 220; Sinclair gives livestock to, 145–46, 157, 305n.24; Sinclair receives Teapot Dome drilling rights from, 149–50; Sinclair visits at Three Rivers, 145–46, 153, 155, 157; suggests Denby approach Congress about oil-bidding problems, 147; and Three Rivers, 120, 145, 266, 301n.34; vindicated in civil suit, 189. *See also* Senate investigation into oil lease scandal

Fall, Alexina (A. B. Fall's daughter), 16, 134, 210

Fall, Emmadair (A. B. Fall's granddaughter), 134, 262

Fall, Emma Garland Morgan (A. B. Fall's wife), 127; courage/strength of, 279; death of, 279; and Dohenys, 134; eviction from Three Rivers, 267–68, 272, 273; on injustice to husband, 262; marriage to A. B. Fall, 15–16; and Weisbach, 254

Fall, Jack (A. B. Fall's son), 16

Fall, Jouett (A. B. Fall's daughter), 266, 279

Fall, Martha (A. B. Fall's granddaughter), 266

Fall, William Ware Robertson (A. B. Fall's father), 15

Farewell, My Lovely (Chandler), 309n.16

Federated Press, 138

Ferndale Ranch (Ventura County, California), 247, 270–71, 311n.1

Finney, Edward C., 131–32, 148, 180–81, 201

Fishbaugh, Ernest Clyde, 224, 230–31, 233–35, 240–41, 310n.6

Fitts, Buron, 234

Fitzgerald, F. Scott: *The Great Gatsby,* 304n.6

Flavin, Father, 281

Fletcher, Admiral, 96

Folies-Bergère (Paris), 84

Fond du Lac (Wisconsin), 8

Forbes, B. C. ("Bertie"), 7, 8, 183, 307n.27

Foster, Charles, 62–63

Fox Movietone News, 253

fraud. *See* criminal trial of Doheny and Fall for fraud/conspiracy

Freeman, Rev. Robert, 269

Friendship estate (Washington, D.C.), 158

Funston, General, 96

Gambrell, J. H., 267

Garrison, Lindley M., 96, 162

Germany, 102

Giddens, Paul H., 187

Glass, Bishop Joseph, 118

glaucoma research, 278

Glen Springs (Texas), 110

Gonzalez, Pablo, 95

Goodman, W. A., 29

Grand Canal (Mexico City), 71

Grant, Madison, 144, 304n.5

Great Canfield Bonanza, 17

Great Gatsby, The (Fitzgerald), 304n.6

Great Mexican Oil Boom, 76. *See also* MPC

Great War. *See* World War I

Greene, William, 112

Greene, William C., 120, 146

Greene Cananea Copper Company (Mexico), 91

Gregory, Thomas W., 162

Grey, Lord, 103–4

Greystone estate (Beverly Hills), 198, 212–15, 217, 222–23, 280, 309nn.15–17
Griffin, Admiral, 132
Guadalajara, 45, 294n.22
Guerin, Walter, 310n.7
Guider, John W., 264
Gulf Oil Company, 76–77, 128
Gulf Refining Company (United States), 78
Gutenberg Bible, 278, 282, 314n.31

Hacienda de Chapacao (Mexico), 43
Hacienda del Tulillo (Mexico), 43
Hale, William Bayard, 95
Hall, Harriet Marion. See Plunkett, Harriet Marion
Hanrahan, Gene Z., 68
Hansen, H. W., 277
Hard, William, 161
Harding, Warren G.: cabinet of, 127, 131; death of, 152; Doheny meets/supports, 127–28; and Fall, 138–39, 150, 151; gives authority for naval reserves to Department of Interior, 133, 189; presidential campaign of, 125–26, 127; supported by oil companies, 121; visits Alaska, 151–52
Harris, N. W., 146
Harris Ranch (Three Rivers, New Mexico), 157
Hays, Will H., 127, 183
Hearst, William Randolph, 82, 83, 109–10, 183, 212
Heflin, Thomas J., 211
Henry Clifford Collection (Pasadena), 314n.31
Herbert G. Wylie (tanker), 79, 115
Hitz, William, 250, 251, 252, 256, 259, 260
Hoehling, Adolph A., 200, 209
Hogan, Frank J.: appearance of, 170, 178; attends appreciation banquet for Doheny, 212; attends Doheny's New York Times interview, 192; career/reputation of, 170, 178; clashes with Congress, 278; death/burial of, 279, 314n.34; defends Doheny, 170, 172, 173, 176, 254, 255, 256, 257; defends Fall, 248, 266; defends Hearst newspapers, 278; defends Mellon, 278; describes Doheny's contract with navy, 177; as Doheny's in-house counsel, 265; fame resulting from Doheny defense, 264; friendship with Doheny, xvi, 174, 265–66; on ideal client, 199–200; law firm's growth, 279; legal fees of, 200; as pallbearer for Doheny, 275; as pallbearer for Ned Doheny, 237; plans defense strategy at Chester

Place, 176–77; returns to Washington practice, 182; on Supreme Court appeal, 197, 198; on telegrams about Pan American deal, 304n.9; vacations at Mammoth Lakes with Doheny, 174; writes to Fall about appeal, 193–94. See also under civil trial of Doheny and Fall; criminal trial of Doheny and Fall for fraud/conspiracy; criminal trial of Doheny for bribery; criminal trial of Fall for bribery
Hogan, Mary Adair ("Mamie"; Frank Hogan's wife), 265–66, 314n.34
Hogan & Hartson, L.L.P (Washington, D.C.), 279
Hogan's Alley, 176
Homan, R. B., 267
Hoover, Herbert, 152, 266, 279
Huasteca (Mexico), 61–62, 65–66, 69
Huasteca Petroleum Company, 67, 95, 101, 111–12, 116
Huasteco Home Defense Movement, 113
Huerta, Victoriano, 90–92, 94–95, 96, 100
Hughes, Charles Evans, 127, 301n.3
Hunt, Sumner, 46
Huntington, 113–14
Huntington, Collis P., 113–14
Huntington Library (California), 314n.31

Instituto Geologico (Mexico), 55–56, 68
internal combustion engine, 292n.1
Ireland, 86–87, 195–96
Irish Catholic immigrants, 8
Iron King mine (Kingston, New Mexico), 10

J. and W. Seligman and Company, 225
J. G. White Engineering Company, 146, 147
J. Oswald Boyd (tanker), 79
Jennings, Walter W., 87
Jersey Standard. See Standard Oil of New Jersey
Johnson, George W., 242
Johnson, Mrs. George, 242
Johnson, Rev. Joseph H., 93
Joint High Commission, 116–17
Jones, Emadair Chase (A. B. Fall's granddaughter), xiv
Jones, Nubby, 264
Jones, Senator, 154
Joyce, William B., 191
Juárez, Benito, 37

Katz, Friedrich, 112
Kaufmann, Gordon B., 213, 223
Kearns, R. C., 37

Kelley, Bishop Francis C., 2, 118, 265, 274
Kellogg, Frank B., 86
Kellogg, Frederick R., 119, 176
Kelly, C. F., 119
Kendrick, John B., 149–50
Kenna, E. D., 37
Kennedy, T. Blake, 189
Kern County (California), 30, 33, 45, 46, 54. See also Elk Hills oil reserves
Kidwell, Edward J., 218
Kingston (New Mexico), 8, 10, 13, 17
Knoll (Beverly Hills), 280
Knowles, Ruth Sheldon, 296n.18
Kruttschnitt, Julius, 91
Kuehl, Emile, 309n.15

La Botz, Dan, 68, 244, 265
Ladd, Senator, 154
La Follette, Robert, 131, 150, 163, 302n.16
Lambert, Wilton J., 201, 209, 217, 248, 253
Lamont, Thomas W., 119
land titles, 69
Lane, Franklin K., 117, 162
Lansing, Robert, 111, 120, 121
La Pez (San Luis Potosi, Mexico), 36, 43, 56–57
Leigh, William R., 277
Lenroot, Senator, 154, 162
Lerdo de Tejada, 37
letters between Doheny and Estelle, xv
letters between Doheny and Fall, xiv–xv
Letts, Arthur, 40
Liberal Party (Mexico), 80, 81
Liberty Bonds/Liberty Loan drives, 115
Limantour, José Yves, 55
Lind, John, 91–92
Lindsley, William, 15
Lisk, Anson, 99, 231–32, 275
Lisk, Laura Ann, 99
Lisk, Mrs. Anson, 99
Literary Digest, 169
Little, Charles, 140
Littleton, Martin W., 217, 221, 222
Lodge, Henry Cabot, 96, 127
Los Angeles, 19, 26–28, 271–72
Los Angeles Evening Express, 211
Los Angeles Evening Herald, 243
Los Angeles Examiner, 191, 240
Los Angeles Herald, 83
Los Angeles Times, 93–94, 178, 213, 240–41, 281
Los Bocas well (Mexico), 70, 71–72
Los Nietos Producing and Refining Company, 276, 280–81

Los Nietos Trust, 225, 276, 280–81
Louise (cook), 47, 52, 53, 54, 59, 296n.8
Lunden, Samuel E., 270

M. D. Thatcher Estates Company (Pueblo, Colorado), 146
MacFadden, Charles, 191
Madero, Francisco I., 80, 90
Mael, Abbot, 192
Magee, Carl C., 153, 157
Maginnis, A. P., 35, 47
Maier, Edward, Sr., 99
Majón, Ricardo Florés, 80
Maltman, J. S., 64
Mammoth Lakes (Sierra Nevada), 174
Mammoth Oil Company (Delaware), 149–50, 153, 166–67, 169, 189, 304n.7. See also Sinclair, Harry F.
Martinez, Rev. John, 238
Martinez del Rio, Pablo, 37, 293n.6
Maryvale orphanage (Los Angeles), 281
Mata Redonda (Mexico), 67
Maurice, Joe, 230
McAdoo, William G., 162–63
McCarthy, Edward, 229–30
McClure's Magazine, 293n.7
McCormick, Paul J., 174–75, 178, 179, 181, 182
McGhee, B. E., 234, 235–36
McLean, Edward B. ("Ned"), 157–58
McLean, John R., 158
McMullin, William J., 218
media. See newspapers
Mellon, Andrew W., 127, 128, 278
Mexican Central Railway, 34–35, 43, 45, 58. See also National Railways
Mexican Constitution (1917). See Article 27
Mexican Gulf Oil Company, 121
Mexican Natural Gas Company, 78
Mexican Petroleum Company. See MPC
Mexican Revolution, 96, 100, 119
Mexican Supreme Court, 122
Mexico: authoritarianism/paternalism in, 285–86; halts oil drilling by U.S. companies, 121; labor shortages in, 35; labor unrest in, 75, 78, 185, 285; land titles in, 69; nationalizes oil industry, 276; oil in, 34–37, 39, 43–46, 55–57, 61, 292n.1 (see also specific oil companies); oil tax hike in, 67–68; Porfiriato period, 38; socioeconomic order in, 38, 54–55, 293n.5. See also Carranza, Venustiano; Díaz, Porfirio
Mexico City, 45, 294n.22
Meyer, Ben, 213–14

Mike (Ned Doheny's pet monkey), 47, 52
Millen, Gilmore, 238–39
Miller, Felix P., 267
Miller, Lucille V. (Estelle Doheny's secretary), 281
Milliken, Ernest E., 170–71, 172, 182
Ministry of Development (Mexico), 67
Miss M. (Ned Doheny's nanny), 47, 53
Mobil Corporation (New York), 146
Moelia (Mexico), 45, 294n.22
Moffat, Mrs. J., 40
Moffitt, Johnny, 13
Monterrey (Mexico), 95
Morgan, Emma Garland. See Fall, Emma Garland Morgan
Morgan, Jack (E. Fall's uncle), 15
Morgan, Simpson H. (E. Fall's father), 15
Morris, John E., 229, 230, 231
Mount Chief Mine (Kingston, New Mexico), 11, 16
Mount St. Mary's College (Brentwood, California), 282
MPC (Mexican Petroleum Company, California), 54–58, 64, 121, 295n.7; board of directors of, 141–42; buys Liberty Bonds, 115; Casiano-Tampico pipeline, 71, 72, 74; Casiano wells, 72–76; Cerro Azul wells, 105–8, 141, 300n.10, 303n.2; Díaz sells his shares of, 104–5; Ebano interests, 43–46, 50, 55–56, 101; growth/size of, 78, 141–42; Huasteca interests (see Huasteca Petroleum Company); during Madero regime, 80–81; seizure by Mexico threatened, 95–96, 100–101, 110, 112–13; and Standard Oil, 76–78; tanker ships purchased, 79; value of, 187; workers/working conditions, 70
Mupu (a Chumash village; Santa Paula, California), 311n.1
Murmann, Eugene, 89

National Association for the Protection of American Rights in Mexico (NAPAR), 119
National Railways (Mexico), 78, 81, 91. See also Mexican Central Railway
natural resources, development of, 137–38. See also conservationists
Naval Petroleum Reserves, 129–30, 149. See also Elk Hills oil reserves; Teapot Dome oil reserves
Neff, Wallace, 213, 247, 277
Nevada, 116
Nevins, W. G., 37
Newhall (California), 27
New Mexico, 203, 301n.35, 308n.4

newspapers: Fall attacked in, 138; influenced by Doheny, 110–12; on murder of Ned Doheny, 240. See also specific newspapers
New York Commercial, 187
New York Journal, 110
New York Times, 127, 165–66, 190–91
New York Tribune, 138
New York World, 187
Nicholas, Malcolm E., 111
nolle processing, 309n.4
Norman Bridge (tanker), 79, 115
Norris, Thomas, 254
Nuevo Leon (Mexico), 95
Nye, Edward, 222

Obregon, Alvaro, 121
oil: in California, 23–28, 30, 31; industry's growth, 78, 128–29; Mexican, 34–37, 39, 55–57, 61, 292n.1, 305n.28 (see also MPC); production of, 291–92n.1; railroads fueled by, 30–33; use in World War I, 92, 103, 113, 115–16; wildcat wells, 296–97n.18. See also oil reserves
Oil Cabinet, 127, 131. See also Harding, Warren G.
oil lease scandal. See Senate investigation into oil lease scandal
oil reserves, 129–39; Denby assigns navy's responsibility to Bureau of Engineering, 134; exchange of crude oil for storage of fuel oil, 135–36, 137; Fall's control of, 131–33; Naval Petroleum Reserves, 129–30 (see also Elk Hills oil reserves; Teapot Dome oil reserves)
O.K. Stables (Los Angeles), 19
Old George (chauffeur), 82, 84, 85, 88
Old Reliable mine (Lake Valley, New Mexico), 11
O'Mallet, Father, 237
O'Melveny, Henry W.: defends Doheny, 170–73, 174–76, 254; defends Fall, 249; on Doheny's New York Times interview, 192; friendship with Doheny, xvi, 174, 192, 246; health of, 174–75, 177, 198; as pallbearer for Ned Doheny, 237; plans defense strategy at Chester Place, 176–77; reacts to verdict against Doheny, 188; on Supreme Court appeal, 197, 198; vacations at Mammoth Lakes with Doheny, 174; visits Europe, 182. See also under civil trial of Doheny
O'Melveny, Nette, 182
O'Neil, James E., 311n.20
Ophir gold mine (San Diego), 19, 20

Orchard, Clara Isabel ("Belle"), 299n.3
Ordóñez, Ezequiel, 55–57, 237
Osler, H. M., 311n.20
Owen, Gordon, 15

Pacific Gold and Silver Extracting Company, 20
Pacific Oil Company (San Francisco), 135
Pan American Eastern Corporation, 186
Pan American Petroleum and Transport Company (Delaware), 108–9, 115, 116, 128; Bain invites bid on Pearl Harbor oil project, 146; civil suit against, 168–69, 172, 174–75 (see also civil trial of Doheny); distributes and stores oil, 142, 303–4n.3; Doheny's Annual Report, 164–65; drilling leases to Elk Hills, 136, 148, 149, 150, 153, 304n.8; earnings of, 163–64; government tries to cancel naval reserve leases, 171; merges with Standard Oil of Indiana, 186–87, 276, 307n.34; Pearl Harbor oil project, 135–36, 137, 147–49, 167, 304–5n.10; prosecutors investigate, 166–67; stockholder lawsuits against Doheny, 167, 262; stock prices drop following Supreme Court ruling, 217. See also Pan American Eastern Corporation
Pan American Western Corporation, 186–87, 225
Panuco-Boston Oil Company, 121
Parker, Alphonso E., 210
Pearl Harbor: fuel oil storage at, 135, 137, 286–87; oil companies bid on naval project at, 146–49, 304–5nn.8–10 (see also Pan American Petroleum and Transport Company); strategic location of, 142–44
Pearson, Annie Cass, 79
Pearson, Weetman (Lord Cowdray), 71–72, 78–79, 91, 92, 95, 112
Pelaez, Manuel ("General"), 111–12, 113
Pemex Corporation (Mexico), 276
Pennzoil Corporation. See South Penn Oil Company
Pershing, John J. ("Black Jack"), 109, 110, 300n.13
Petroleum Development Company, 33
Phelps-Dodge Company, 91
Phi Nu Delta (University of Southern California), 99
Phoenix mine (Lake Valley, New Mexico), 11
Picket Act (1910), 302n.12
Pickford, Mary, 213
Pierce, Henry Clay, 55, 58
Pinchot, Gifford, 131, 133, 303n.29;

investigates Fall, 154; opposes Fall, 137, 138; urges Senate investigation of Fall, 150
Pittsburgh, 36
Pittsburgh and Des Moines Steel Company, 146, 147
Pius XI, Pope, 265
Pius XII, Pope, 277
"Plow with Petroleum," 119
Plunkett, Charles Albert (Hugh Plunkett's father), 299n.3
Plunkett, Harriet Marion (Hugh Plunkett's wife), 139, 223, 239, 310n.7
Plunkett, Hugh. See Plunkett, Theodore Hugh
Plunkett, Isabelle (Hugh Plunkett's sister), 239
Plunkett, Mrs. Charles (Hugh Plunkett's mother), 239
Plunkett, Robert (Hugh Plunkett's brother), 239
Plunkett, Theodore Hugh, 99, 115, 229, 299n.3; accompanies Ned Doheny to Washington with loan money, 139, 141, 161; anxiety over his upcoming testimony, 224–25; divorce from Harriet, 223, 310n.7; drug use by, 243; friendship with Ned Doheny, 214, 223, 241, 243; funeral of, 239–40; murder of Ned Doheny, xiv, 230–31; as Ned Doheny's secretary, 176; nervous condition of, 223–24, 235–36, 240–42, 310n.6; oversees construction of Greystone, 214, 222–23, 242; suicide of, 230–31; urged to enter sanitarium, 242–43
Pomerene, Atlee: appearance of, 178; death of, 279; investigates oil lease scandals, 166–67; prosecutes Doheny, 178, 256 (see also under civil trial of Doheny; criminal trial of Doheny for bribery; criminal trial of Fall and Sinclair, 217, 249 (see also under criminal trial of Fall for bribery; criminal trial of Sinclair and Fall for conspiracy)
Porfiriato, 38
Posada, José Guadalupe, 75–76, 285, 297n.22
Posey, Oliver P., 46
Post-Dispatch (St. Louis), 187
Potrero del Llano No. 4 (Mexico), 78
press. See newspapers
prospectors, in Kingston, 8, 14, 17
publicists/journalists manipulated by Doheny, 110–12
Puebla (Mexico), 45, 294n.22
Puente (California), 27
Pulitzer, Joseph, 83

Queen Elizabeth, 116
Quidero, Charlie, 9

Quigley, Eleanor Elizabeth. *See* Doheny, Eleanor Elizabeth Quigley

racism, 144, 304nn.5–6
railroads, 30–33, 41. *See also specific companies*
Remington, Frederick, 277
Republican National Convention (1920), 125, 126
Requa, Mark L., 117
Revolutionary War (Mexico), 96, 100, 119
Richfield Oil Company (California), 225
Rickett, Frederick H., 307n.34
Riley, George, 241–42
Rising Tide of Color, The (Stoddard), 144, 304n.5
Ritz Hotel (London), 102–3
Roberts, Owen: appearance of, 179; appointed to U.S. Supreme Court, 279; death of, 279; investigates oil lease scandals, 166–67; praises McCormick, 189; prosecutes Doheny, 256 (*see also under* civil trial of Doheny; criminal trial of Doheny for bribery; criminal trial of Fall for bribery); prosecutes Doheny and Fall, 178 (*see also under* criminal trial of Doheny and Fall for fraud/conspiracy); prosecutes Fall and Sinclair, 217 (*see also under* criminal trial of Sinclair and Fall for conspiracy)
Robinson, Albert A., 34
Robison, John Keeler: discusses naval defense plans with Doheny, 142–45; meets Doheny, 114, 134–35; and oil lease bids, 147, 148; on oil storage at Pearl Harbor, 137, 286; testimony at Doheny's trial, 180
Rockefeller, John D., 39, 293n.7, 296n.18
Rockefeller, John D., Jr., 245
Rogers, Will, 211, 256
Roosevelt, Archibald, 153–54, 157
Roosevelt, Franklin D., 126, 271, 276
Roosevelt, Theodore, Jr., 127, 132, 133
Rosenheim, Alfred F., 88
Royal Navy (United Kingdom), 92
rurales (Mexican rural police), 55
Russell, Charles, 184, 277

Safford, James, 267
Saldivar, Manuel, 66
Salomon Company (New York City and Paris), 79, 81, 84
Sammann, Detleff, 184, 277
Sands, Robert M., 273, 275, 276
San Francisco earthquake (1906), 294n.16
San Luis Potosi (Mexico), 68

San Pedro (Mexico), 95
Santa Paula. *See* Ferndale Ranch
Santa Prisca (Tasco, Mexico), 185
Santa Sabina, 238
Scott, Hugh L., 110
Seaver, Frank R., 142
Senate investigation into oil lease scandal, xvi, 154–67; attendees at, 154; Denby testifies, 155; Doheny reports on, 164–65; Doheny's testimony, 156, 158–62; expert witnesses, 155–56; Fall's testimony, 154–55, 157–58, 160; McLean testifies, 158; press coverage of, 156; Sinclair testifies, 155, 156, 163; Slattery urges investigation of Fall, 150–51; testimony/evidence against Fall, 153–54, 156–57; Walsh chairs investigating committee, 152–55, 156, 158–59, 160, 163
Sherman Antitrust Act, 297n.25
Siddons, Frederick J., 217
Silent, Charles, 46
Silver City (New Mexico), 18
Simpson, Frank, Jr., 114
Sinclair, Harry F., 127, 128; attacked in press, 169; bribery/conspiracy charges against, xiii–xiv, 166–68, 189–90 (*see also* criminal trial of Sinclair and Fall for conspiracy); contempt conviction of, 244–45; and Continental trading scandal, 245, 311n.20; death of, 280; Fall entertains, 145; Fall receives Liberty Bonds/money from, 151, 220; Fall receives livestock from, 145–46, 157, 305n.24; indicted/convicted for jury tampering, 218, 245; prison sentence of, 245; pursues leasing rights to Teapot Dome oil reserves, 145, 304n.7. *See also* Mammoth Oil Company; Sinclair Oil Company
Sinclair Oil Company, 128, 145
Six-Year Plan (Mexico), 276
skeleton figures, in Mexican folk art, 75–76, 285, 297n.22
Slattery, Harry A., 131, 302n.16; on conserving oil fields for national defense, 130, 132–33; investigates/opposes Fall, 137, 138, 150–51, 154
Slauson, James, 99
Smith, C. Warren (Lucy Doheny's brother), 99, 239, 275
Smith, George Otis, 201
Smith, J. Clark (Lucy Doheny's brother), 99, 239
Smith, Laura (Lucy Doheny's mother), 98, 99

Smith, Lucy Marceline. *See* Doheny, Lucy Marceline Smith
Smith, William Henry (Lucy Doheny's father), 82, 98
Smoot, Senator, 154
Sohio (*formerly* Standard Oil of Ohio), 77
Southern Pacific Company (San Francisco), 91
South Penn Oil Company (*later named* Pennzoil Corporation; Pennsylvania), 73, 296n.18
Speers, L. C., 190, 191
Speyer, James, 91
Speyer and Company (New York City), 91
St. John's Seminary (Camarillo, California), 277, 282
St. Vincent's Church (Los Angeles), 184–85, 237, 265, 270, 307n.32
St. Vincent's Hospital (Los Angeles), 278, 282
Standard Oil Company, 39, 121, 293n.7; and Carranza, 100; dissolved by U.S. Supreme Court, 77, 78, 297n.25; and Madero, 90; and MPC, 76–78
Standard Oil of California (*later named* Chevron), 77, 128, 146, 147, 148
Standard Oil of Indiana (*later named* Amoco), 77, 128, 186–87, 245, 262, 276. *See also* Pan American Eastern Corporation
Standard Oil of New Jersey (*later named* Exxon), 77–78, 128, 276
Standard Oil of New York (*later named* Mobil), 77, 128
Standard Oil of Ohio (*later named* Sohio), 77
Starr, John, 180, 302n.16
Stevens, Guy, 119
Stewart, Robert W., 127, 128, 186, 245, 311n.20
Stoddard, Lothrop: *The Rising Tide of Color*, 144, 304n.5
Stratton, David H., 137–38
Swain, Chester O., 119

Taft, William Howard, 302n.12
Tamaulipas (Mexico), 68, 95, 96
Tamiahua Petroleum, 67. *See also* Huasteca Petroleum Company
Tampico (Mexico), 34–36, 43–46, 95–96, 113, 116, 294n.22
Tarbell, Ida, 293n.7
Teapot Dome oil lease scandal, 166–67. *See also* Senate investigation into oil lease scandal
Teapot Dome oil reserves (Natrona County, Wyoming): conservationists on, 130–31;

Fall and Sinclair meet to discuss, 145; Fall given authority over, 131–32; and leasing of land, 130–31, 302n.16; Mammoth Oil's drilling rights to, 149–50, 153; navy's use of, 130, 302n.12; Sinclair pursues leasing rights to, 145, 304n.7
Tehuantepec National Railroad (Mexico), 71
Temple of Santa Sabina (Forest Lawn Memorial Park, Glendale, California), 238, 244
Texas Oil Company, 122, 128
Thatcher (M. D.) Estates Company (Pueblo, Colorado), 146
Thiene, Paul G., 213–14, 309n.15
think tanks, 118–19
Thompson, Dorothy, 279
Thompson, Mark B., 183, 252
Three Rivers Cattle and Land Company, 146, 220
Three Rivers Ranch (Three Rivers, New Mexico), 301n.34; Doheny's purchase of, 252; Falls' eviction from, 267, 272–74; Falls reside at, 120; Sinclair visits Fall at, 145, 153, 157
Tiffany, Louis Comfort, 88
Time, 263, 264
Titanic, 83
titles to land, 69
Torreon (Mexico), 95
Trees, Joseph C., 73, 74, 76
Tres Rios Cattle and Land Company (Three Rivers, New Mexico), 146, 203, 220
trials. *See* civil trial of Doheny and Fall; criminal trial of Doheny and Fall for fraud/ conspiracy; criminal trial of Doheny for bribery; criminal trial of Fall for bribery; criminal trial of Sinclair and Fall for conspiracy
Trousdale, Paul, 280
Trousdale Estates (Beverly Hills), 280
Tuller, Walter K., 170–71, 172, 176, 182, 188, 197
Tuxpan people (Mexico), 65–66, 70
Tuxpan Petroleum, 67. *See also* Huasteca Petroleum Company

Union Oil Company (UNOCAL; California), 146, 280, 281
United Kingdom, 92, 95
United States: blockades port of Veracruz, 96, 100; dependence on Mexican oil, 95; intervenes in Mexican Revolutionary War,

United States (*continued*)
100; on Mexican nationalization of oil
concerns, 100–101, 110; opposes Huerta,
91–92, 95; supports Carranza, 95, 96, 104,
109, 112
United States v. Albert B. Fall. See criminal
trial of Fall for bribery
United States v. Albert Fall and Edward Doheny.
See criminal trial of Doheny and Fall for
fraud/conspiracy
United States v. Pan American Petroleum and
Transport Company, 171; *see also* civil trial
of Doheny
University of Southern California, 176
Unknown Soldier ceremony (November 11,
1921), 136
UNOCAL. *See* Union Oil Company
Ureta, Jésus, 100–101
U.S. Bureau of Engineering, 114, 134
U.S. Bureau of Mines, 156
U.S. Department of Justice, 166
U.S. Department of the Interior: announces
Teapot Dome and Elk Hills drilling con-
tracts, 150; and Forest Service, 137, 139;
naval oil reserves controlled by, 131–33,
155; places Greystone on National Re-
gister of Historic Places, 280; tries to block
investigation, 166
U.S. Forest Service, 137, 139, 303n.29
U.S. Geological Survey Department, 9
U.S. National Guard, 110
U.S. National Park Service, 138
U.S. Navy, 113, 114, 142–44, 166. *See also* Elk
Hills oil reserves; Pearl Harbor; Teapot
Dome oil reserves
U.S. Secret Service, 166
U.S. Senate, 120–21. *See also* Senate investiga-
tion into oil lease scandal
U.S. Senate Committee on Public Lands
and Survey, 150, 304n.9. *See also* Senate
investigation into oil lease scandal
U.S. State Department, 101, 112, 113
U.S. Supreme Court, Standard Oil dissolved
by, 77, 78, 297n.25
U.S. Treasury Department, 304n.9

Veracruz (Mexico), 68, 76, 96, 100, 113
Veronal (drug), 243, 311n.18
Villa, Francisco ("Pancho"), 95, 100, 109
Virreyes, Juan, 55
Von Kleinsmid, Rufus B., 237

Wade, K. H., 32
Wagner, A. F., 236

Wahlberg, G. D., 154, 157
Wakiva, The (yacht), 96
Walker, Harold, 84, 119, 141–42
Walker, P. J., 270
Walsh, Evalyn, 158
Walsh, Thomas J., 152–55, 156, 158–59, 160,
163, 271
War College, 110
Ward, Father William, 276–77
Washington Evening Star, 302n.16
Washington Post, 158, 177
Waters-Pierce Company, 55, 78
Watriss, Frederick, 119
Weber, Francis J., 185
Weeks, James W., 136
Weil, Thomas, 38
Weisbach, Daniel, 253–54
Wellborn, Charles, 178
Wellborn, Olin, Jr., 178, 275
Wellborn, Olin, Sr., 33, 99
Wellborn, Olin, III, 178, 237, 275, 278
Werner, M. R., 180, 302n.16
Wescott, Chloe Phoebe. *See* Canfield, Chloe
Phoebe Wescott
Western Americana collection, 278, 314n.31
Western Union Telegraph Company, 304n.9
Westlake Park oil well (Los Angeles), 22–27
"What Popular Writers Are Saying about
Mexico," 119
What's the Matter with Mexico? (Whitney), 111
Wheeler, Benjamin Ide, 119
Wheeler, Lucien, 232, 234, 236
White, Leslie T., 231–33, 241
White, Magner, 302n.17
White, W. W., 234, 235–36
White, William Allen, 151–52
Whitney, Caspar, 191; *What's the Matter with*
Mexico? 111
wildcatters, 73, 296–97n.18
Wilkins, Carrie Louella. *See* Doheny, Carrie
Louella Wilkins
William Salomon and Company. *See*
Salomon Company
Wilson, Woodrow, 91–92, 95, 96, 100, 113,
286; businessmen's dissatisfaction with,
125; creates Teapot Dome oil reserve,
302n.12; criticized by Fall, 120; establishes
Joint High Commission with Carranza,
116–17; orders Mexican invasions, 109,
110, 300n.13; recognizes Carranza's
authority, 104, 109; and Senate hearings
about Mexico, 120–21
Withdrawal Act (1909), 302n.12
Woodbine, Alonzo H., 114

World War I, 92, 101, 103, 113, 115–16

Wylie, Herbert G., 56, 67, 86; attends
    Canfield's funeral, 93; attends Ned and
    Lucy Doheny's wedding, 99; background
    of, 64; builds Casiano-Tampico pipeline,
    71, 72, 74; at Cerro Azul well, 106; and
    Dohenys, 64, 87; on MPC's board of
    directors, 141–42; as pallbearer for
    Doheny, 274, 275; as pallbearer for Ned
    Doheny, 237; as president of Pan
    American, 307n.34; promoted general
    manager of MPC, 64; supervises Mexican
    workers at MPC, 44–45; visits Huasteca
    region, 65–66

Yergin, Daniel, 78, 92, 129

Young Men's Christian Association (YMCA),
    115

Youngs, Graham, 140, 201

Zapata, Emiliano, 100

Zeitlin, Jake, 282

Indexer: Carol Roberts
Compositor: Integrated Composition Systems
Text: 10/14 Palatino
Display: Snell Roundhand Script and Bauer Bodoni